Volume Two

THE REEF AQUARIUM

A Comprehensive Guide to the Identification and
Care of Tropical Marine Invertebrates
by J. Charles Delbeek and Julian Sprung

Book Design by Daniel N. Ramirez

Published by Ricordea Publishing
Miami Gardens, FL 33169 USA

"Imagine a live coral reef in your living room! It sounds fantastic, but it can actually be done; and as more people experiment with it so much more will be learned about it that someday it may be a commonplace thing."

Robert P. L. Straughan, 1969
The Salt-Water Aquarium in the Home

The Reef Aquarium Volume Two: A Comprehensive Guide to the
Identification and Care of Tropical Marine Invertebrates
by J. Charles Delbeek and Julian Sprung

First Printing: 1997
20 19 18 17 16 15 14 13 12 11 10 9

Published and distributed by
Two Little Fishies, Inc.
d.b.a. Ricordea Publishing
1007 Park Centre Blvd.
Miami Gardens, FL 33169 USA

Printed and bound by Artes Graficas, Toledo S. A.
Design and production by Daniel N. Ramirez
Cover photo: Composite image created by Elliot Sprung and Julian
Sprung with photographs by Julian Sprung and J. Charels Delbeek.
Page ii photo: Ricardo Miozzo's aquarium. Photographer: Alvaro Povoa.
Page ii photo: Ricardo Miozzo's aquarium. Photographer: Alvaro Povoa.

ISBN 978-1-883693-13-8
ISBN 1-883693-13-6

Delbeek, J. Charles, 1958 and Julian Sprung, 1966 - The Reef Aquarium

Table of Contents

This book is dedicated to our parents:
Jan Carel and Ruby Delbeek
and
Doris and Stewart Sprung
for their many years of encouragement, love and support.

Foreword

One of the most attractive icons of the marine aquarium hobby is a pair of bright orange clownfish peering out from between the tentacles of a violet or green hued sea anemone. This relationship has fascinated naturalists, divers, scientists, and aquarists, the latter group having the ability to observe it at home. However, some of the anemones that host clownfish do not adapt well to captivity unless a specific range of requirements are met, and aquarists have been unable to find good information about the anemones' specific needs.

The book, *Anemonefishes and Their Host Sea Anemones* by Daphne G. Fautin and Gerald R. Allen provides an excellent guide to the identification of those anemone species that typically form symbiotic relationships with clownfish, and describes the type of habitat where the anemones come from. With that information one has the foundation for discovering the proper ways to maintain these anemones. However, the book falls short on the subject of anemone husbandry in captivity. This should be no surprise since Dr. Fautin opposes the collection of host anemones for aquaria. In general, we agree with her.

Recently there have been a number of articles published in the aquarium literature and hobbyist newsletters regarding the success and failure rate with anemonefish host sea anemones. It is apparent from these articles that some anemone species fare well in captivity while others do not usually, though this does not mean that they cannot survive in captivity. What is missing is an understanding of how to duplicate the type of environment that these anemones need to thrive. Our intention in writing this book was not only to provide a means of identifying the common tropical anemone species collected for aquariums, but to also teach aquarists and scientists exactly what anemones require to live in a captive environment. We do not wish to promote the wasteful collection of species that have a poor survival record in captivity. But we also do not want to perpetuate ignorance about these creatures. Our goal is to say something new and, hopefully, promote the captive husbandry of anemones to such an extent that captive propagation becomes the source of anemones for aquarists.

Another goal of our book is to provide a very accurate and easy to use guide for identifying soft corals commonly imported for aquariums. This was a task we knew would be most difficult, since soft coral taxonomy is about as messy as a bag of *Xenia* that's been in transit too long. Through our association with Norwegian aquarist/authors Alf Nilsen and Svein Fosså and with the invaluable help of Dr. Phil Alderslade of the Museum of the Northern Territory, in Darwin, Australia, we have managed to learn many new things about soft coral taxonomy. Additionally, soft coral researchers such as Dr. Gary Williams at the California Academy of Sciences and Mike Gawel, University of Guam provided literature plus many helpful suggestions and opinions. In the process of our research we have also discovered some new species and helped to further the scientific community's under-standing of the relationships of different groups of these fasci-nating creatures.

We set out to develop a simple method for the casual observer to identify most soft corals to genus, or to family at least, by just looking at and feeling the coral for a sense of its overall morphology. Scientific keys for identifying soft corals concentrate on the minute sand-like skeletal elements known as sclerites, which occur in the tissues. We wanted to develop a good key that could be used without the need to look at sclerites, but discov-ered early in this endeavor that the soft corals would not be so easily tamed! So we did not develop such a key. However, our descriptions and photos will help the casual observer to sort through most soft coral genera with relative ease. We also include some sclerite information for positive confirmation. Some soft corals are so distinctive that a good photograph can identify them, and we note these instances as well.

Peter Wilkens and Johannes Birkholz initiated the aquaristic community's attempts to identify soft corals and describe their care with the book *Niedere Tiere* first published in 1986. The book, now published in English under the title *Invertebrates, Organ-pipe, Leather corals, and Gorgonians* is still a popular reference because of the wealth of information it contains about the care of these creatures, and it had quite an influence on the spread of correct and some incorrect names in the hobby and on overseas exporters' availability lists.

There has been an explosion of creativity in the making of field guides for marinelife lately, in particular for marine invertebrates of the Indo-Pacific region. In the past two years we have seen the following new books: Allen and Steene's *Indo-Pacific Coral Reef*

Field Guide, Colin and Arneson's *Tropical Pacific Invertebrates*, and Gosliner, Behrens, and Williams' *Coral Reef Animals of the Indo-Pacific*, not to mention our *Reef Aquarium Volume One*. We recommend the (Caribbean) reef series by Paul Humann, with the volumes *Reef Creatures* and *Reef Corals*. Also, a new book by Helmut Schuhmacher *Niedere Meerestiere Schwämme, Korallen, Krebse, Schnecken, Seesterne, und andere*. Finally, there is the five book series in German, *Korallenriff Aquarium* by Svein Fosså and Alf Nilsen that we mentioned in volume one. It is being translated now to English in four volumes, with the title *The Modern Coral Reef Aquarium* (the first volume in English was available in September 1996). We hope that after purchasing all of these books one can still afford to buy this, our second volume in *The Reef Aquarium* series! We know at least that one cannot afford to be without the information we provide in this volume.

Of course our books are more than just field guides. The original books by Wilkens and Birkholz, our series, and Fosså and Nilsen's also offer information about husbandry techniques. This sets our books apart as belonging to the realm of aquarium science. The science of aquarium keeping has progressed rapidly in the past five years. What was once viewed as a hobby is now considered a serious discipline and a valuable research tool by scientists who study coral reefs. The links between the scientific community and the aquarium hobby have been growing stronger, greatly assisted by the ease of communication provided by e-mail and the opportunity for meeting at formal conferences such as MACNA and the International Coral Reef Symposium. Tying it all together is the enthusiasm of coral reef researchers and "coraloholic" aquarists who have networked and shared their experience. We are happy to be a part of this process, in celebration of the beauty and mystery of coral reef ecosystems.

Julian Sprung
March, 1997

Acknowledgements:

Well, this isn't name dropping, but a lot of very important people helped us make this book, directly or indirectly, and so it's only appropriate that we thank them for it here. This book would not have been possible without their kind assistance:

Dr. Phil Alderslade for many fruitful, lengthy and enlightening discussions about soft coral systematics, taxonomy and biology. Thanks for taking the time to teach us, examine our specimens, and answer our questions;

Patrick Baker for his fantastic photographs of the snail *Drupella cornus*;

Dr. Craig Bingman for making sense out of the complex chemistry and offering new insights into physical, chemical, and biological phenomena in our aquaria;

The late Dick Boyd for stimulating Julian's interest in anemones.

Rob and Robin Burr for advice on underwater photography and help with obtaining some of the photographs;

Margaret Campbell for her wonderful illustrations;

Dr. Bruce Carlson for his pioneering work with corals at the Waikiki Aquarium and his successful efforts to integrate the scientific community with the aquarium (reef-keeping) community;

Dr. J.C. den Hartog for taking the time to share his ideas in lengthy e-mail discussions about corallimopharia, and for providing very helpful reference material;

Dr. Henry Feddern for his photographs of gorgonians and anemones in the natural habitat, and for promoting the marine aquarium hobby by collecting marinelife with the greatest care;

Dr. William Fenical, University of California at San Diego, for information about and photographs of *P. elisabethae* and the cosmetic products derived from this gorgonian;

Ann Fielding for organizing the trip to the Solomon Islands on the Spirit of the Solomons live-aboard dive boat. What a great trip we all had! Many of the underwater photographs in this volume were taken there; Thanks also to Paul and Vicki who enthusiastically showed us the fantastic little details as well as the big picture at all the sites we visited, and to the crew who looked after everyone's needs with uncanny intuition;

Larry "Fireball" Jackson for his photo of the *Tubipora* sp. that looks like *Alveopora*, and for his enthusiastic support of the hobby for beginners and experts, plus his Texas-size sense of humor;

Warren Gibbons, New England Aquarium, for samples of the *Porites*-eating nudibranch;

Dr. Terry Gosliner, California Academy of Sciences, for nudibranch identification;

Paul Humann for his photographs of *Carijoa* and *Lebrunia*;

John Jackson for his friendship, networking skill, and help obtaining some of the photographs;

Jeff Macare for not doing the macarena, but for stimulating a whole lot of enthusiasm for the hobby and sharing his observations, experience, and not-too-shabby photographs;

The cartilaginous Scott W. Michael for once again helping us to obtain those last minute photos and for being such a Husker;

Dr. David Miller, AIMS, for his assistance with obtaining reprints of some recent papers on corallimorphs;

Jon Moore for his kind assistance with the *Berghia* culture reference and obtaining specimens of *Berghia*;

Gary Moss, Jack Jewell (Marine World Africa USA) and Dave Sheehy for the last minute rush to get us a photograph of *Berghia*;

Ricardo Miozzo for the pictures of his aquarium, photographed by Alvaro Povoa;

Tony Nahacky of Aquarium Fish Fiji for his hospitality, keen observational skills and sincere love of marinelife. Thanks also for the fantastic undescribed *Pseudocorynactis/Corallimorphus*;

Alf Nilsen and Svein Fosså for their superb skill at pulling together the literature, contacting experts in the field, and documenting with photographs, articles and books the complex associations of plants and animals on a coral reef and in a reef aquarium;

Doug Perrine for his photo of *Capnea lucida*;

Daniel Ramirez for his patience and friendship, for tirelessly trying to instill within us an appreciation for the importance of a deadline, and for once again designing a beautiful book;

Giovanni Recchia for his photo of the photosynthetic hydroid;

Sandra Romano, for sending us information about the evolution and systematic relationships of the Cnidaria;

David Saxby, for rushing out to meet Julian at the London airport after gathering some new soft corals for Julian from his own aquarium and from Tropical And Marine pet shop;

Phil Shane of Quality Marine, Los Angeles, California for his information about anti-viral activity in *Macrodactyla*;

Dr. J. Malcom Shick, University of Maine, for supporting our work and for sharing his extensive reference list of publications about anemones;

Terry Siegel for sharing his ideas, speculations as well as networking skill, and for his photographs of *Plexaurella* reproducing and the strange *Sinularia* that forms hard twigs (yes it really did make them!);

Elliot Sprung for his expertise with Photoshop, patience and perfectionism. This book would not have been possible to complete without your effort and skill, from composing the cover image to mastering the techniques needed to overcome the limitations of Kodak photo CD scans;

The late Allan Storace for his beautiful photographs;

To Dietrich Stüber for the tour of aquariums in Berlin, during which we shot numerous photos used in this book, and for years of sharing his ideas with us about reef aquariums;

Dr. Gary Williams for kindly allowing us to use his soft coral and sclerite drawings and for taking the time (on numerous occasions) to share his opinions about soft coral taxonomy;

Peter Wilkens for starting this (reef aquarium) madness and supporting it with new insights to the most current topics, now that aquarists finally understand what he already knew a couple of decades ago;

Joe Yaiullo and Frank Greco for their wonderful closeup photos and;

Millie, Ted, Edwin, Jean, Eddy, Mabel, Nene, Eilene, Sonny, Arlyn, Edgar, and Roger and the rest of the folks at All Seas for their support in promoting *The Reef Aquarium* and providing specimens to photograph. Special thanks to Roger who pointed out the "carpet (anemone) with two mouth and carpet with two base."

The following individuals helped with the identification and/or provided useful insights into the taxonomy and biology of the following families:

Actiniaria
Prof. D.G. Fautin, University of Kansas, USA
Dr. J.C. den Hartog, National Naturhistorisch Museum, Leiden, Netherlands

Alcyonacea
Dr. P. Alderslade, Museum of the Northern Territories, Darwin, Australia
Dr. M. Gawel, Univeristy of Guam
Dr. G.C. Williams, California Academy of Sciences

Holaxonia
Dr. F. Bayer, Smithsonian Institution, Washington D.C., USA

Corallimorpharia
Dr. J. C. den Hartog, National Naturhistorisch Museum, Leiden, Netherlands

Introduction

When we first proposed putting together a book of our experiences keeping invertebrates in marine aquaria, we thought that it would be a single volume describing the light-loving invertebrates most people were keeping at that time. However, as the project began to take shape it quickly became apparent that we could not possibly fit everything we knew into a single volume! Hence this second volume was born.

This volume contains the culmination of our efforts in gathering photos, taxonomic information, husbandry ideas and reproductive facts about the myriad soft corals, anemones, zoanthids, and coral-limorpharians available in the aquarium trade today, plus a few not so readily available. In addition, we discuss and offer new solutions for coral pests and diseases and other reef aquarium plagues.

In the period of time since volume one was published many new discoveries have been made about maintaining reef aquariums, and a lot of previously difficult to acquire corals have become readily available. New technologies have also appeared, most notably downdraft protein skimmers, calcium reactors and high Kelvin lighting.

During the process of deciding how best to organize the information in this volume we agreed that a description of additional stony coral species not covered in volume one was not something that fit naturally with the rest of this book. Therefore a third (and final!) volume is planned, which will cover these additional stony corals, some more soft corals, additional anemones, plus a few other commonly kept marine invertebrates. At this point the third volume seems like it will be a smaller project than the first two, but these things have a way of growing! We want to assure the reader and buyer of this book that our goal has always been to provide the most complete, comprehensive, and current information about the subjects we cover, with an extensive coverage of the species kept in aquaria. Despite this goal, new ideas are constantly developed and explored by the many creative people involved in our hobby, and each year new creatures are discovered or collected for the aquarium trade for the first time.

In the planning phase of volume two we also thought we might include a section about the aforementioned new techniques as an

A family of *Amphiprion percula* at home in their purple *Heteractis magnifica* on a reef slope in the Solomon Islands. J. Sprung

update of sorts to volume one's information about aquarium systems. As we neared completion of this book it became aparent that this notion conflicted with our plans to write a separate whole book exclusively about techniques, and volume two was already becoming too large. Updates about techniques will therefore be covered in our next book, *Techniques For The Reef Aquarium*.

We believe our first volume is a very complete text by itself for anyone contemplating the creation of a reef aquarium. Likewise we know that this book, our second volume, provides a complete coverage of the identification and care of soft corals, corallimorphs, zoanthids, and anemones kept in tropical marine aquariums.

Chapters one through four deal with the complex taxonomy and identification of soft corals, zoanthids, corallimorpharians and sea anemones; respectfully. We discuss their classification, polyp and colonial anatomy, nutritional needs, growth, defensive mechanisms, reproductive strategies and habitat.

Chapter five discusses methods for the legal collection, transportation and shipment of the various invertebrates described in the previous four chapters.

Chapter six provides a detailed overview of captive propagation techniques for the various invertebrates discussed in chapters one through four, with numerous practical tips.

Chapter seven discusses virtually all of the various soft corals available in the aquarium trade today, complete with photographs and taxonomic features. With this information aquarists will be better able to identify many of the soft corals using the correct scientific names. Information is also provided on the common names, colouration, distinguishing features, similar species, natural habitat, aquarium care and reproduction for each coral.

Chapter eight introduces many of the zoanthids kept in aquaria. Information is provided for the correct identification of the major genera, as well as the common names, colouration, distinguishing features, similar species, natural habitat, aquarium care and reproduction for each genus.

Chapter nine covers the corallimorpharians. Details are given on the correct scientific and common names (where known), colouration, distinguishing features, similar species, natural habitat, plus aquarium care and reproduction for each genus.

Chapter ten provides detailed descriptions for many of the anemones kept in aquaria. This includes the correct scientific and common names, colouration, distinguishing features, similar species, natural habitat, aquarium care and reproduction for each species.

Chapter eleven describes many new pests and diseases that can affect tridacnid clams, anemones, stony and soft corals in aquaria, with supplemental information about some of the pests we covered in volume one.

Chapter twelve Following what continues to be one of the most talked about features of volume one, we again present reef tanks from around the world. This chapter contains more photos of stunning reef aquaria from both public and private aquarium collections.

Ethical and Ecological Concerns About Our Hobby

Readers may wonder about the impact of our hobby on the natural environment and the populations of the creatures described in this book. We refer the reader to the introduction in volume one for a review of this subject. More about the subject of collection can also be found in chapter five in this book and in chapter eleven in volume one. Most of the creatures described in this book are known to reproduce vegetatively, and they exhibit rapid growth rates. In addition, we demonstrate in this volume vegetative reproduction for species not known to employ it.

We are confident that the level of impact on the natural habitat from collection of soft corals is quite sustainable. They are generally collected with only fragments of shells, gravel, or broken branches of dead coral, so they hardly effect any removal of solid reef substrate. Furthermore, the aquarium industry is setting up numerous mariculture operations, "coral farms," for cultivating these fast-growing species attached to mined upland rocks. Some of these operations are being set up in the island nations where collection from the wild has been practiced, thereby keeping the industry at its source, supporting the livelihood of the native people and giving them incentive to conserve their reefs.
The collection of corallimorpharia is usually also a harmless activity to the reef, involving the removal of small dead coral and shell fragments with attached, fast growing vegetatively produced disc anemones. In some cases, however, relatively large chunks of reef weighing several pounds are broken off to obtain the pretty mushroom shaped disc anemones. Collecting by fragmenting pieces larger than a couple of fists has the potential to damage the reef in

localized areas, and we do not support such activity. For the most part, large pieces are not collected because they are heavy pieces, which means they are expensive to ship via airfreight. Thus the limits of transportation cost tend to provide a means of controlling the impact on the environment. However, an exception to this was seen in the example of *Ricordea florida*, a beautiful corallimorph that was being collected along with large pieces of rock until the state of Florida banned its collection with live rock.

Zoanthid anemones are also typically collected attached to rocks, though sometimes they are peeled off the rock in large clumps. Where they occur near the shore in the Indo-Pacific it is common to find them growing on the natural volcanic rock. In some places zoanthids can be found growing on fossil reefs located in the intertidal zone. Removal of rocks from a fossil reef is not removal of a renewable resource. In such locations it makes sense to collect unattached clumps of polyps only. Collecting zoanthids encrusting dead coral branches laying loose on sand flats associated with coral reefs (their typical habitat) does not cause significant harm since the dead branches of fast growing species such as *Acropora* or *Porites* are products of about one to two years of growth, and the loose branches disintegrate with time as boring organisms perforate them.

The collection of sea anemones is a subject of some controversy now, mostly due to the public awareness of the association between anemone and clownfish. The majority of anemones are not clownfish hosts. Many reproduce vegetatively by longitudinal fission, producing large stands of clones. Still others are prolific spawners with successful recruitment producing extensive beds of anemones. The clownfish host anemones, while common, generally do not occur in large density, though there are exceptions. *Entacmaea quadricolor* and *Heteractis magnifica* are known to reproduce vegetatively by longitudinal fission, and in some localities one may find large areas covered by them. *Stichodactyla gigantea* may also be abundant in some localities too, and although it is not yet reported in the scientific literature, we report in this book (in chapter four) two modes of asexual reproduction for this species. Certainly a managed collection of anemones in areas where they are abundant is a sustainable activity. However, it is not just the collection of the anemones that puts their populations at risk. The collection of the clownfish also affects anemone populations, as we will shortly explain.

We feel there is a potential for over exploiting the resource (i.e. taking too many anemones) from localized areas, though at this time it is our opinion that for most species the level of impact has not (and will not) come close to reaching that point. A possible exception to this may be found in the example of *Condylactis gigantea*, an anemone that occurs throughout the Caribbean. This anemone is a popular "beginners anemone" because it is hardy, attractive, and inexpensive. In the Florida Keys, marinelife collectors at one time collected hundreds of these anemones per day in seagrass beds where they are so loosely attached that they can even be netted from a boat. While the species is still common throughout the Florida Keys, the super-densely populated "anemone beds" have become scarce. Florida has now set daily catch limits for this species in an attempt to reduce the size of the harvest. Worldwide no other species of anemone is collected for the aquarium industry in quantities like *Condylactis gigantea*. Perhaps a second runner-up is the Rock Anemone from Florida, *Epicystis crucifer*. It is extremely abundant in the same habitat as *Condylactis*, but requires a bit more effort to collect, and its coloration is cryptic (unlike the typical bright whitish pink of *Condylactis*) so its populations are not at all declining. Clownfish host anemones are simply not collected in large numbers like the anemones from Florida, but their resident clownfish are.

Collection of Clownfish

The collection of clownfish can affect anemone populations because the clownfish protect the anemone from potential predators such as butterflyfishes (Fautin and Allen, 1992). If the collectors leave some clownfish in the anemones instead of taking all of them, the harvest is sustainable because new clownfish recruits will shortly settle because they will have an anemone to settle in. If all the clownfish are removed, their anemones may be eaten and no more clownfish nor anemones will return.

In recent years the quality of tank-raised clownfish has improved so much with respect to colouration and size that one can no longer complain that tank raised specimens are inferior to wild caught ones. In fact tank raised fish are much safer to purchase since wild caught clownfish are extremely prone to infections that not only kill them but also may affect other fishes to which they are exposed. While recently we have seen several clownfish hatcheries go out of business due to lack of profitability, other businesses have survived and new ones have come into existence. There is now a greater diversity of tank raised species (including fish and invertebrates) available to the consumer, and this also helps the aquaculture facility by providing more potential sources of income. It seems the consumer demand for tank raised species has also been increasing, which is an encouraging sign. With regard to clownfish, the main problem is that the cost of production makes it difficult to compete with the price of wild-caught specimens. The interesting thing is that the price of wild caught specimens and the cost of wild caught specimens are not at all the same. The invoiced price must have freight added to it plus the "invisible" cost of mortality. The losses of wild caught clownfish can be quite high, so their actual cost to the importer may be much higher than their perceived cost. Nevertheless there is still demand for wild caught clownfish and the price of tank raised fish has traditionally had to be reduced to market them against the price (not cost) of the wild caught competition. Therefore aquaculture facilities have been operating without making much or any profits. An idea has been proposed to tax wild caught clownfish with the proceeds going to a fund for research in aquaculture. This would in effect elevate the price of wild caught clownfish, allowing the farms to compete and earn the money they deserve, and at the same time provide a source of money to promote more effective aquaculture. It seems like a nice idea, but of course the management of such fund collecting is where the idea becomes problematic.

The establishment of organizations whose plan is to raise not only clownfish but also other fish species and invertebrates is something which has been taking shape the past couple of years. Right now one can already have a marine aquarium with clownfish, other fish species, live rock, anemones, soft and stony corals all farm raised. We believe that in the near future this will be more commonplace as it becomes ever more economically feasible to produce the marinelife on a large scale. With the information we present in this volume our intention is to promote the marine aquarium hobby, sustainable harvest, aquaculture, and coral reef conservation.

Chapter One

The Biology of Soft Corals

What is a Soft Coral?

We must begin with a good definition of "soft coral" because the popular concept and literal meaning of the name are quite different from the actual definition. True soft corals all belong to the subclass Octocorallia. Like stony corals and anemones, the soft corals belong to the phylum Cnidaria and the class anthozoa. What distinguishes them is the number of tentacles on the polyps. All soft corals have eight tentacles on each polyp, hence the name Octocorallia. Exceptions to this rule only occur accidentally as deformities on a few polyps, individual anomalies, while the rest of the colony has normal, eight-tentacled polyps. Another distinguishing characteristic of these polyps is the presence of side branchlets called "pinnules" on each tentacle. The pinnules make the tentacles look like feathers, and they are thus called pinnate. Some soft corals have reduced pinnules or none at all, however. The construction of the polyp with eight unpaired mesenteries is also a characteristic of octocorallia.

The name "soft" coral is misleading since not all Octocorallia are soft. The "blue coral" *Heliopora coerulea* forms thick hard crusts, plates and heads of calcium carbonate with a high concentration of iron salts that stain the skeleton blue. The living animal is brown since it contains zooxanthellae. Without the polyps expanded it could easily be mistaken for fire coral, *Millepora* spp. which form similar mustard-coloured fronds and crusts. Another soft coral that forms a hard skeleton is *Tubipora*, "Pipe organ" coral. "Pipe organ" coral is a popular curio item because of its rich, deep red colour and odd structure composed of upright tubes and flat floor-like layers. The living coral is quite variable in appearance and although one species only, *Tubipora musica*, has been recognized for many years, at least four distinct species exist. In this book we show all of them. Octocorals also form a variety of skeletal elements from tiny sclerites to axial structures made of an organic material similar to horn, and from calcium carbonate. The soft coral genus *Sinularia* has a few species (including the common *S. polydactyla*) that can actually build a solid reef from fused sclerites called spiculite produced around their base. Columns of spiculite several meters high have been found on the Great Barrier Reef after storm sand movement, with live *Sinularia* colonies still growing on top (P. Alderslade, pers. comm.)! A proteinaceous axial skeleton (gorgonin) is found in all Holaxonia gorgonians and in most sea pens (Bayer, 1973).

A rare and stunning soft coral, *Siphonogorgia* sp., photographed on a reef wall in the Solomon Islands. J. Sprung

True soft corals have eight tentacles on each polyp, and the tentacles often look like feathers because of the fine side branches called pinnules. The polyps of *Clavularia* spp. are classic examples of these features that define soft corals (octocorallia). J. Sprung

Sometimes octocoral polyps develop "Siamese twin" heads with two mouths and more than eight tentacles. On occasion there are also deformities with only one mouth but more than eight tentacles. Note the polyp in the center with at least twelve tentacles. A. J. Nilsen

"Spiculite" rock made of fused sclerites by *Sinularia* spp. This photo shows the inside composition. J. Sprung

The outer surface of the same piece of spiculite is smooth and hard. J. Sprung

A finely branched *Sinularia* sp. that produces spiculite at its base, forming hardened twigs. T. Siegel

It is common to see colonial zoanthid anemones of the genera *Zoanthus*, *Palythoa* and *Protopalythoa* referred to as "soft corals" because of their soft tissue and resemblance to true stony corals. However, they are neither soft corals nor stony corals. J. C. Delbeek

When scientists discuss soft corals, they usually refer to them as octocorals, and further subdivide these into other groups such as gorgonians and alcyonaceans. When they are thus subdivided, the term "soft coral" really only refers to the alcyonaceans such as *Dendronephthya, Sarcophyton, Sinularia, Alcyonium,* etc.

Fleshy stony corals such as *Helio-fungia*, *Catalaphyllia* and *Euphyllia* are sometimes called "soft" corals because of their soft fleshy tissues, but they are true stony corals, scleractinia. *Heliofungia actiniformis* is shown here. S. W. Michael

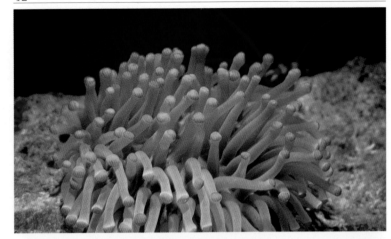

Corallimorpharians are often called "false corals" and sometimes "soft corals" because they look like corals, are soft and fleshy, and lack a skeleton. They are closely related to true stony corals and belong to the suborder Corallimorpharia. *Ricordea florida* is shown here. J. Sprung

This looks like a type of sea fan (order Gorgonacea) but in fact is a type of black coral (order Antipatharia). J. Sprung

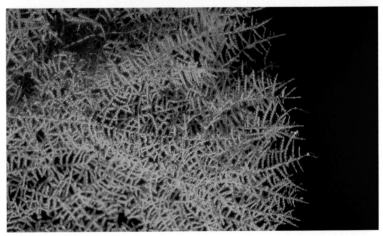

These colonial zoanthids, *Parazoanthus* spp., live in association with other invertebrates such as hydroids and sponges. They are often confused with soft corals or with black coral (antipatharians). J. Sprung

The Fire Anemone, *Actinodendron* has tentacles which look like soft coral branches, most similar to *Nephthea* spp. J. Sprung

The organ-pipe coral, *Tubipora*, is an octocoral that has a hard skeleton made of calcium carbonate and coloured red by mineral salts deposited with the calcium. Although it is considered closest to *Pachyclavularia*, it probably is most closely related to *Clavularia* spp. J. Sprung

The "Blue Coral," *Heliopora coerulea* has a dense stony skeleton composed of calcium carbonate and embedded iron salts which give it a blue colour. The live animal is brown, and has tiny eight-tentacled polyps which identify it as a type of octocorallia. It is therefore a "soft coral" with a hard skeleton. J. Sprung

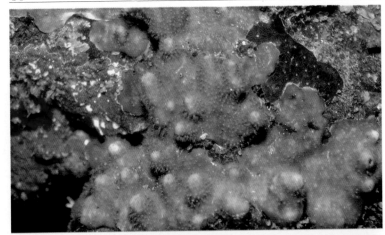

Soft corals of the genus *Dendronephthya* are what typically comes to mind for most people when they hear the description "soft coral." These soft-bodied colonies have sharp spiny sclerites that give them a tough texture. J. Sprung

Sea whips and other gorgonians are soft corals that have an axis made of a horn-like material called gorgonin. Some types also have calcium carbonate in the axis, and there are also sclerites of calcium carbonate in the rind. This is a gorgonian from the Caribbean, *Plexaurella* sp. J. Sprung

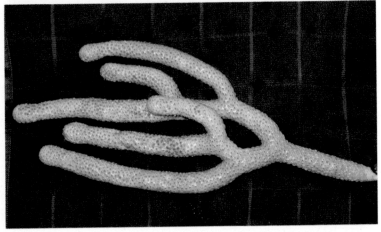

Sea pens are special types of soft corals with a foot used for burrowing and anchoring the colony in soft bottoms or sand. The "foot" is formed by the original polyp and all other polyps are produced from it by budding.
S. W. Michael

Soft corals such as *Sarcophyton* and *Sinularia* are types of Alcyonaceans with symbiotic zooxanthellae. Their tissue is tough and leathery, giving them the common name "Leather corals."
Sarcophyton (left) J. C. Delbeek

Sinularia (right)
B. Carlson

Classification and Taxonomy

It must be understood that with respect to soft corals the taxonomy is presently in a state of confusion. (Of course anyone working on taxonomy in a group of living organisms would probably get a kick out of the previous statement since taxonomy in general is full of problems, but here we concentrate on the messy state of the soft corals). Seemingly different soft corals can be forms of the same species since many soft corals vary greatly as a result of environmental factors. Furthermore, seemingly identical corals may belong to different species, genera, or even families! Positive identification is often impossible without microscopic examination of the minute, sand-like skeletal elements known as sclerites (spicules). Many species are still undescribed. Therefore,

Figure 1.1
Some typical sclerites
From Williams, 1993

A, B. *Clavularia,*
C, D. *Cladiella,*
E, F. *Lobophytum*
G, H, I. *Sarcophyton*
J, K. *Sinularia*
L, M. *Dendronephthya*

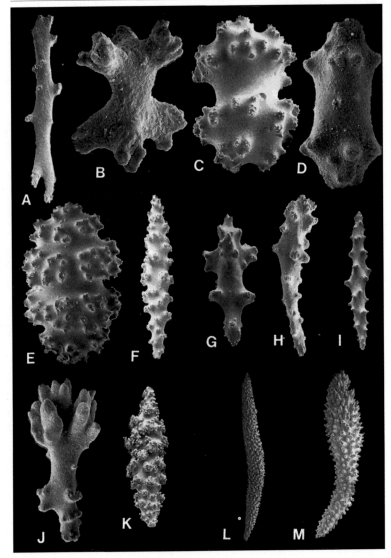

we are not always able to identify soft corals to species, and we feel that all that is really necessary to know is the genus. We have made every effort to assure the accuracy of the taxonomy we use and the names given in this book. Nevertheless future revisions of soft coral taxonomy will likely show that our book contains some identification errors. We have very deliberately avoided the unfortunate habit of some aquarium book authors who merely look at old books and copy the incorrect names found there for identification of creatures in their "new" texts. The identifications in this book involved painstaking collection and preparation of tissue samples for examination by experts in soft coral taxonomy, and lots of correspondence.

Soft coral taxonomy is based on the study of the skeletal elements known as sclerites (sometimes referred to as spicules). The plasticity of form in soft corals makes the identification to species difficult or impossible without examination of the sclerites, which are usually more uniform in structure. The sclerites are taken from both the branches and the base since they vary depending upon their location in the colony.

Preparation of Sclerites for Examination

To examine the sclerites of a soft coral one must prepare a sample by dissociating the soft tissue from the calcium carbonate sclerites. This is done by simply excising a small (approx. 5mm x 5mm) sample of tissue with a scissors or scalpel and placing it on a microscope slide with a few drops of sodium hypochlorite (household bleach or Clorox). The solution dissolves the organic material away quickly, freeing the sclerites. A coverslip may then be added and the sclerites can be observed under low power. The sclerites can be rinsed with water in a vial to remove traces of sodium hypochlorite and clear away the cloudy dissolved organic material.

In the past, many soft coral taxonomists hardly knew how living colonies actually appeared, since they usually worked with preserved specimens from collections. The new school of soft coral taxonomists study living colonies. As aquarists, our photographic records and notes may serve to benefit the study of coral biology, and may help clean up the taxonomic mess that exists with respect to soft corals. We may also provide a valuable tool to taxonomists with our techniques for keeping and growing corals in captivity. Our living collections contain numerous undescribed species, particularly of soft corals. Unfortunately, growth in captivity can produce strange anomalies in the sclerites that can easily confuse the taxonomist. For example, *Sinularia* species typically have a concentration of long spindle shaped sclerites in the base. In captivity when branches are severed for the purpose of asexual propagation of the colony, the offspring often fail to develop this concentration of spindles in the base. *Alcyonium* (Colt Coral) also is frequently propagated by making cuttings. The colonies grown this way often lack sclerites, though the original parent colony had them, particularly in the base. Sometimes the

Table 1.1

Classification of Soft Corals *After Bayer, 1981*

We have not included all genera, particularly the sea pens, but all of the genera covered in this book are shown, in addition to other related genera not covered here. Items in brackets do not have formal taxo- nomical significance, but they are sometimes used as a matter of convenience by soft coral taxono- mists, for grouping some of the genera by some common morpho- logical features.

Phylum Cnidaria (Coelenterata)
  Class Anthozoa
    Subclass Octocorallia Haeckel, 1866
      Order Helioporacea (=Coenothecalia)
        Family Lithotelestidae: *Epiphauxum* (=Lithotelesto)
        Family Helioporidae: *Heliopora*
      Order Alcyonacea Lamouroux, 1816
        [Suborder Protoalcyonaria]
          Family Taiaroidae: *Taiaroa*
        [Suborder Stolonifera]
          Family Cornulariidae: *Cornularia*
          Family Clavulariidae
            Clavulariinae: *Clavularia, Bathytelesto, Rhodelinda, Scyphopodium*
            Sarcodictyinae: *Sarcodictyon,Cyathopodium, Scleranthelia, Tesseranthelia, Trachythela*
            Telestinae: *Telesto, Carijoa, Paratelesto, Telestula*
            Pseudocladochoninae: *Pseudocladochonus*
          Family Tubiporidae: *Tubipora, Pachyclavularia*
          Family Coeologorgiidae: *Coelogorgia*
          Family Pseudogorgiidae: *Pseudogorgia*
        [Suborder Alcyoniina]
          Family Paralcyoniidae: *Maasella, Carotalcyon, Paralcyonium, Studeriotes*
          Family Alcyoniidae: *Alcyonium, Acrophytum, Anthomastus, Bathyalcyon, Bellonella, Cladiella, Lobophytum, Metalcyonium, Minabea, Malacacanthus, Nidaliopsis, Parerythropodium, Sarcophyton, Sinularia*
          Family Asterospiculariidae: *Asterospicularia*
          Family Nephtheidae: *Nephthea, Capnella, Coronephthya, Daniela, Dendronephthya, Drifa, Duva, Gersemia, Lemnalia, Litophyton, Morchellana, Neospongodes, Paralemnalia Pseudodrifa, Roxasia, Scleronephthya, Stereonephthya, Umbellulifera*
          Family Nidaliidae
            Nidaliinae: *Agaricoides, Nidalia*
              Siphonogorgiinae: *Chironephthya, Nephthyigorgia, Siphonogorgia*
          Family Xeniidae: *Anthelia, Ceratocaulon?, Cespitularia, Efflatounaria, Fungulus, Heteroxenia, Stereosoma, Sympodium, Xenia*
        [Suborder Scleraxonia]
          Family Briareidae: *Briareum*
          Family Anthothelidae:
            Anthothelinae: *Anthothela*
             Semperininae: *Iciligorgia, Semperina, Solenocaulon*
             Spongiodermatinae: *Alertigorgia, Callipodium, Diodogorgia, Erythropodium, Homophyton, Titanideum, Tripalea*
          Family Subergorgiidae: *Subergorgia*
          Family Sibogagorgiidae (=Paragorgiidae): *Paragorgia, Sibagorgia*
          Family Coraliidae: *Corallium, Pleurocoralloides?*
          Family Melithaeidae: *Melithaea, Acabaria, Clathraria,Mopsella, Wrightella*
          Family Parisididae: *Parisis (=Trinella)*
        [Suborder Holaxonia]
          Family Keroeidae (=Keroeidididae): *Keroeides, Ideogorgia, Lignella*
          Family Acanthogorgiidae: *Acanthogorgia, Acalycigorgia, Anthogorgia, Calcigorgia, Cyclomuricea, Muricella, Versluysia*
          Family Plexauridae
            [Plexaurinae]: *Plexaura, Anthoplexaura, Eunicea, Euplexaura, Muricea, Muriceopsis, Plexaurella, Psammogorgia, Pseudoplexaura*
            [Stenogorgiinae (=Paramuriceinae)]: *Swiftia, Acanthacis, Astrogorgia, Bebryce, Calicogorgia, Dentomuricea, Echinogorgia, Echinomuricea, Heterogorgia, Hypnogorgia, Lepidomuricea, Lytreia, Menella, Muriceides, Nicaule, Paracis, Paramuricea, Placogorgia, Pseudothesea, Scleracis, Thesea, Villogorgia*
          Family Gorgoniidae: *Adelogorgia, Eugorgia, Eunicella, Gorgonia, Hicksonella, Leptogorgia, Lophogorgia,Olindagorgia, Pacifigorgia, Phycogorgia, Phyllogorgia, Pseudopterogorgia, Pterogorgia, Rumphella*
          Family Ellisellidae: *Ellisella, Ctenocella, Junceella, Nicella, Riisea, Toeplitzella, Verrucella*
          Family Ifalukellidae: *Ifalukella, Plumigorgia*
          Family Chrysogorgiidae: *Chrysogorgia, Chalcogorgia, Distichogorgia, Helicogorgia, Iridogorgia, Isidoides, Metallogorgia, Pleurogorgia, Radicipes, Stephanogorgia, Trichogorgia, Xenogorgia*
          Family Primnoidae: *Primnoa, Ainigmaptilon, Amphilaphis, Armadillogorgia, Arthrogorgia, Ascolepis, Callogorgia, Callozostron, Calyptrophora, Candidella, Dasystenella, Narella, Ophidiogorgia, Paracalyptrophora, Parastenella, Plumarella, Primnoella, Pseudoplumarella, Pterostenella*
        Family Isididae
          Isidinae: *Isis, Chelidonisis*
          Muricellisidinae: *Muricellisis*
          Keratoisidinae: *Keratoisis, Acanella, Isidella, Lepidisis*
           Mopseinae: *Mopsea, Chathamisis, Circinisis, Echinisis, Minuisis, Peltastisis, Primnoisis*
      Order Pennatulacea Verrill, 1865
        Family Veretillidae Herklots, 1858
          Cavernularia

sclerites that form in captivity are malformed, or they change from the form they had when the colony was in the natural environment. While our aquariums are admittedly not the natural environment, they are similar enough to it that the sclerite changes occurring in our aquaria may also occur in the natural setting depending on environmental factors. If that is the case, then the study of sclerites may be of limited value in determining species (though they are certainly valuable for determining family and genus). At the moment such a notion is not a popular idea among soft coral biologists who specialize in learning the subtle differences between sclerites of different species.

Polyp Anatomy

The polyps of octocorals are distinctive from all other anthozoans in that they have eight tentacles per polyp. As we mentioned earlier, occasionally an exceptional "double polyp" occurs (something like a Siamese twin) that has more than eight tentacles, usually with two mouths (see photo). The tentacles tend to taper towards the end and each tentacle (usually, but not always) contains a number of short, pointed projections, usually in rows, called pinnules. These give the tentacles a feathered appearance. Sometimes the pinnules are not well developed, or are fused. In at least one species imported for aquariums, there are apparently no pinnules at all (see chapter seven, "unidentified stoloniferan number two").

Soft coral tentacles and pinnules are mobile, contractile, and hollow, their cavities being extensions of the gastrovascular cavities (Hyman, 1940). Octocoral polyps may be elongated (in some genera they extend several inches in length) and are topped with the flattened oral disc. At the center of the oral disc lies the oval mouth that opens directly into a pharynx (=actinopharynx). The pharynx can be smooth or grooved and extends down into the gastrovascular cavity. At one end of the oval shaped pharynx lies a groove lined by flagellated (=ciliated) cells known as the siphonoglyph (=sulcus) whose purpose is to drive water currents (and perhaps food particles) into the gastrovascular cavity.

There are three cellular layers that constitute the projecting portion of octocoral polyps. The outer layer, the epidermis, covers the exterior surface of the polyp and extends out over the body of the colony (coenenchyme). The epidermis that covers the polyps contains mucus cells, sensory cells and nematocysts, the last often in warts. The epidermis covering the coenenchyme contains fewer sensory cells and nematocysts (Hyman, 1940). The inner cell layer, the gastrodermis,

Figure 1.2 a
The internal anatomy of a typical octocoral polyp
After Hyman, 1940

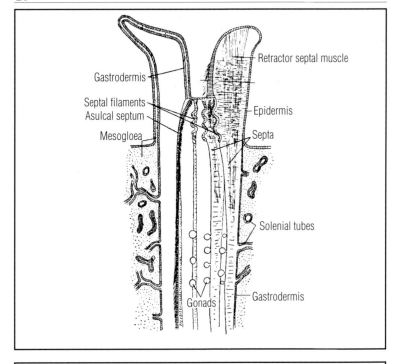

Gastrodermis

Septal filaments
Asulcal septum

Mesogloea

Retractor septal muscle

Epidermis

Septa

Solenial tubes

Gastrodermis

Gonads

Figure 1.2 b
Vertical section through the coenenchyme of *Alcyonium*, showing solenial network. Some polyps are expanded, some contracted.
After Hyman, 1940, based on Hickson, 1895

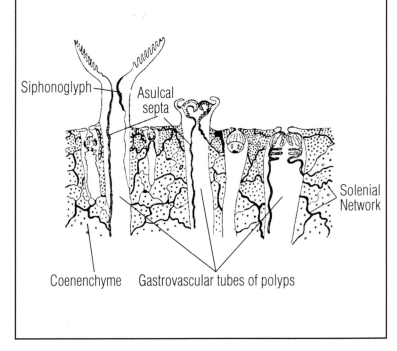

Siphonoglyph

Asulcal septa

Solenial Network

Coenenchyme   Gastrovascular tubes of polyps

lines the inside of the tentacles, pharynx, mesenteries, gastrovascular cavity and extends through the colony via the gastrodermal tubes. The gastrodermal cells are where zooxanthellae are located. Between these two layers lies the mesogloea consisting of a gelatinous matrix and this is where the sclerites (= spicules) occur. Within the polyps it forms a very thin layer, but forms the majority of coenenchyme of the colony outside of the polyp (fig. 1-2). Within the mesogloea exist the gastrovascular tubes of the polyps and a network of gastrodermis-lined tubes that connect the gastrovascular tubes of the various polyps, called gastrodermal tubes or solenia. Special cells called amoeboid cells are also found in the mesogloea. Some of them become scleroblasts responsible for the manufacturing sclerites; others are responsible for depositing gorgonin in gorgonians (Hyman, 1940).

Within the polyp itself, eight longitudinal partitions called septa (= mesenteries), extend from the body wall. In the upper portion of the polyp they extend completely across, and are joined to the oral disc and pharynx, forming eight separate compartments, each of which continues into a tentacle (Hyman, 1940). Below the level of the pharynx the inner edges of each septa are free. Along these free edges occur thickened, sinuous filaments (mesenterial filaments). The two septa directly across from the siphonoglyph (asulcal septa) bear very long filaments with lots of flagella, presumably to create upward currents. These two septa extend the furthest into the polyp. The other six septa and their filaments are shorter, contain digestive cells and do not extend as far; not all genera have these other six septa e.g. the family Xeniidae (Hyman, 1940).

The portion of the polyp that extends above the colony is know as the anthocodium. In the suborder Stolonifera, the lower portion of the anthocodium is thickened and may be heavily spiculated, forming an anthostele or calyx. The upper, soft portion can then be withdrawn into this structure. In most other octocorals the anthocodium can be completely withdrawn into the coenenchyme leaving only a small hole behind. Some genera, however, cannot retract their polyps (e.g. *Anthelia, Heteroxenia, Xenia*). In sea pens, there is one main axial polyp (primary polyp) that runs the length of the stem and all other polyps (secondary polyps) extend from it (Hyman, 1940). In gorgonians, which have a shallow layer of coenenchyme due to the axial skeleton, the polyps tend to be short.

In many octocoral genera the polyp extends well below the surface of the colony and all or some, can reach all the way to the base of the colony. This brings up an interesting possibility. By extending so

Figure 1.3

Figure 1.3
A *Clavularia* polyp showing the anthocodium and anthostele
After Hyman, 1940

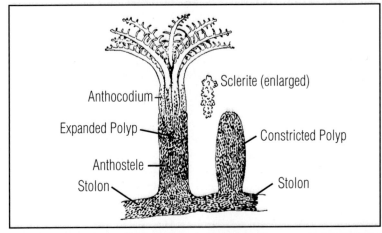

Sclerite (enlarged)

Anthocodium

Expanded Polyp

Constricted Polyp

Anthostele

Stolon

Stolon

The pinnules are clearly evident on the tentacles of *Clavularia* spp.
J. Sprung

The tentacles of "Green Star Polyp" *Pachyclavularia* (*Briareum*) spp. often have reduced pinnules.
J. Yaiullo and F. Greco

These are the polyps of the common sea fan, *Gorgonia ventalina*. J. Yaiullo and F. Greco

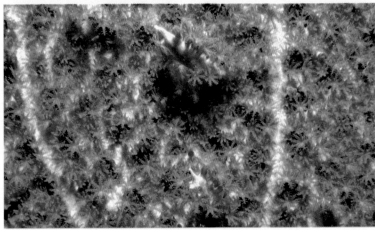

The elongate polyps of *Sarcophyton* spp. really seem to be like fibre-optic cables capable of piping light to the zooxanthellae contained in the interior. J. C. Delbeek

The commonly imported "Clove Polyp" is an unidentified stoloniferan, possibly *Acrossota* sp. (see chapter seven). It has very distinctive polyps with fused pinnules. J. C. Delbeek

The polyps in this distinctive unidentified stoloniferan from Bali, Indonesia are completely devoid of pinnules. J. Sprung

deeply into the body of a colony, these elongated tubular polyps may create a "fibre-optic" effect where they may actually "pipe" light into the deeper layers of the colony, especially in *Sarcophyton* and *Xenia* species that have highly elongate polyps.

As mentioned above, the gastrovascular tube of each polyp in a colony is connected by a series of gastrodermal tubules called solenia. In forms whose polyps arise from an encrusting sheet or stolon (e.g. *Anthelia, Pachyclavularia, Clavularia, Briareum, Erythropodium*, etc.), the solenia are limited to the base only. In most fleshy octocorals that grow above the substratum (e.g. *Sarco phyton, Lobophytum, Xenia*, etc.) however, the solenia extend throughout the colony often enclosing the bases of the gastrovas

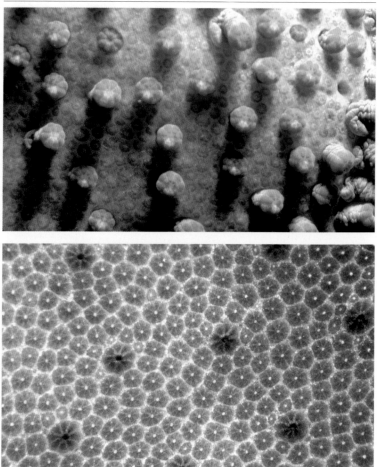

Closeup photo of *Sarcophyton* showing autozooids and siphono-zooids. In the top photo the auto-zooids are almost fully retracted, in the bottom photo they are fully retracted. J. Yaiullo and F. Greco

cular tubes of the polyps (Hyman, 1940). The function of solenia is not clear. New polyps arise when solenia approach the epidermis. They form a small chamber just below the epidermis. A small swelling appears on the upper surface and this then develops tentacles becoming the anthocodium (this can clearly be seen on the stalks of *Alcyonium* species, aka "Colt Coral" from Indonesia). The epidermis then invaginates into the chamber below forming a mouth and pharynx. Solenia may also act to distribute food and nutrients through the colony; they may allow zooxanthellae to move around the colony and infect newly developed polyps (a function reminiscent of the zooxanthellal tubule system in tridacnid clams, see volume one); or they may be involved in maintaining hydrostatic pressures in more gelatinous genera such as *Dendronephthya* or *Nephthea*.

Heteroxenia sp. exhibiting polyp dimorphism characteristic of the genus. The tentacle-bearing autozooids are large and run off the photograph. The siphonozooids are apparent on the capitulum in between the bases of the autozooids. J. Sprung

This fantastic red soft coral thriving in a behind-the-scenes display at the Monterey Bay Aquarium was collected in very deep water. It clearly shows autozooids and siphonozooids. To give an idea of scale, the autozooid polyps are 2.5 cm (1 in.) in diameter! J. Sprung

Autozooids and Siphonozooids

In some octocorals there are two distinctly different types of polyps present; these corals are said to have dimorphic polyps. *Sarcophyton, Lobophytum, Heteroxenia* and sea pens are all dimorphic. However, *Heteroxenia* (the Latin name refers to the fact there are two different types of polyps) is only dimorphic beyond a certain size (see top of next page).

Autozooids are what one would normally consider polyps. Their structure is just as we described above but they may have reduced or absent siphonoglyphs. They are primarily used for feeding, respiration, light gathering and perhaps light "piping" to lower regions of the colony. They also bear the ovaries and testes.

Siphonozooids are reduced in size and either lack or have very rudimentary tentacles. They also have greatly reduced mesenteries (usually only the two asulcal ones remain) and very well-developed siphonoglyphs. The siphonozooids do not feed and serve primarily to drive a strong water current through the coral. The fact that all branched, lobed and arborescent (tree-like) alcyonaceans are monomorphic, whereas most of the large massive forms are dimorphic, suggests that dimorphism arose out of a need to transport water more efficiently through large colonies (Bayer, 1973). In support of this idea a colony of *Heteroxenia fuscescens* does not develop siphonozooids until the colony has reached a certain diameter; their numbers then increasing as the colony gets larger (Achituv and Benayahu, 1990). In some genera (e.g. *Corallium* and *Paragorgia*) the siphonozooids bear the gonads instead of the autozooids (Hyman, 1940).

Colony Organization and Morphology

There is a wide range of colony organization in octocorals. Ranging from very simple monomorphic polyps joined together by stolonic growths, to massive forms with polyps embedded in thick coenenchyme, to advanced forms with polymorphic, highly specialized polyps. We will not go into all the different colony growth forms in this section, but will merely point out the most commonly seen types in the marine aquarium trade.

Order Helioporacea (=Coenothecalia)

There is only one species within the family Helioporidae, *Heliopora coerulea* and it is generally considered to be a relict. Although it is clearly an octocoral in anatomy, its skeleton is massive like a stony coral, and its colonial organization and growth form is similar too (Bayer, 1973). Its skeleton is composed of crystalline fibers of aragonite fused into layers (Hyman, 1940). There are two cylinders within the skeleton, one larger than the other but both blind ended. The larger one houses the polyp while the smaller ones are the solenia, connecting the polyps together. There is a thin coenenchyme on the surface that is filled with a network of solenia (fig. 1-4). As the colony grows, a transverse plate forms which effectively cuts off the upper living layer. Thus only the outer thin layer is living tissue. Growth forms are usually lobes but can also be flattened vertical plates similar to Fire Coral, or thick stubby branches reminiscent of Porites. When the tissue is removed, or when a break occurs in the skeleton the underlying blue colour of the skeleton is revealed. This colour is thought to be caused by the infusion of iron salts into the

Figure 1.4
Cross-sectional view of the surface of a blue coral, showing a polyp, the coenenchyme and the network of solenia
Modified from Hyman, 1940

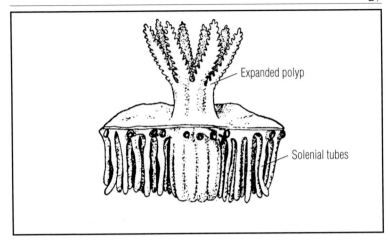

Expanded polyp

Solenial tubes

skeleton. *Heliopora* is one of the few soft corals that can contribute to reef building, sometimes forming extensive reefs e.g. in areas off the southern coast of Okinawa, Japan.

Suborder Stolonifera

Stoloniferans exhibit the simplest colony organization. Within this suborder there are also a variety of growth forms. There is no coenenchymal mass, but the polyps arise asexually from a creeping base, which may consist of separate stolons or a more or less continuous thin crust or mat (Hyman, 1940). The polyps are all interconnected by gastrodermal tubes running through the stolons or mats. The simplest growth form is found in *Clavularia* spp. (Waving Hand polyp). All the polyps are of a single type and

Creeping stolon of *Clavularia*.
J. C. Delbeek

arise singly from creeping stolons that emerge from the base of each polyp. The upper part of the polyp, the anthocodium, is thin-walled while the lower part, the anthostele, is hardened. The anthocodium can be retracted into the anthostele. A similar growth form can be found in the Xeniidae genus *Anthelia*, but there is no anthostele and the polyps cannot be retracted (see chapter seven). *Pachyclavularia* spp. (Star polyp) spread by a creeping mat, with polyps arising from it. There can also be connections between the polyps at various levels, not just at the base (Bayer, 1973). Anthosteles are present, and the polyps can be fully retracted, giving the mat a bumpy appearance when the polyps are completely retracted.

The genus *Tubipora* is unique in its growth form. The polyps arise from a basal plate and are enclosed by skeletal tubes of fused spicules, bright red in colour. These tubes are themselves intercon- nected by lateral stolons that become fused, forming platforms, and from which new polyps can arise. As the tubes increase in length the lower portions are sealed off, so the polyp only exists in the portion of the tube above the preceding platform.

Fig 1.5
Tubipora skeleton
After Hyman, 1940

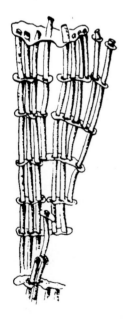

Another growth form is exemplified by the azooxanthellate genera *Carijoa* (=Telesto) and *Coelogorgia*, which has zooxan- thellae. In these genera, a single, very elongated polyp arises as a branch or stem, from a creeping base. Within this polyp lies an extensive network of solenia from which other lateral polyps arise. In *Carijoa*, lateral polyps arise along the length of a single stem. In *Coelogorgia*, the lateral polyps produce more polyps along their length, and these polyps produce polyps of their own, eventually resulting in large, tree-like growths.

Suborder Alcyoniina
Within the Alcyoniina we find the greatest variety in colonial orga- nization and shape. Alcyoniina are characterized by the presence of an extensive coenenchyme. This is formed mainly by mesogloea containing calcareous spicules. The coenenchyme is filled with tubules (solenia) that connect all of the polyps together. The anthocodium of each polyp extends above the coenenchyme and may appear to be separate, but within the coral, they are all interconnected by the solenia. New polyps arise as outgrowths of the solenia. Therefore the oldest polyps tend to be the longest, often extending all the way to the base of the colony, while the younger polyps do not. All the members of this suborder conform to this basic organization whether they are massive forms such as

Sarcophyton and *Lobophytum,* with lobes and folds or more arborescent forms such as *Nephthea* or *Litophyton.* Even in the later form, the trunks are composed primarily of bundles of older polyps whose anthocodium emerge at the tips of the branches at various levels in the colony (Bayer, 1973).

Polyps within this suborder show a wide variety of size and shape. Some can be greatly elongated while others barely extend beyond the epidermis. Some have very small spicules while other the polyps in another genera can be heavily spiculated to the point where the spicules stick out around the polyp, offering protection and support in strong currents (see Nutrition). In some genera the polyps can be completely retracted, in some they can only be partially contracted into their protective spicule sheaths while in others then are non-retractile. Finally, it is within this suborder that dimorphic polyps first appear (see above, Auto-zooids and Siphonozooids). Many of the larger more massive species are dimorphic while most of the arborescent species are not. However, this is not a fast rule. Within the family Xeniidae, there are some forms that are dimorphic and some that are not. *Heteroxenia* spp. are dimorphic but may only be so during breeding season (Gosliner et al., 1996).

There are two main growth forms in the Alcyoniina: massive fleshy colonies and arborescent colonies with a thin coenenchyme. More massive colonies have a thick coenenchyme, heavily embedded with spicules. Colonies generally consist of a stalk topped by a rounded, mushroom-like cap that bears the polyps called the capitulum. The stalk can be elongated or short while the capitulum can be smooth and rounded (e.g. some *Cladiella, Heteroxenia, Xenia),* thrown into folds (e.g. *Sarco-phyton*) or can have numerous polyp bearing lobes projecting from it (e.g. some forms of *Cladiella, Lobophytum,* and some forms of *Sinularia).* Arborescent forms fall into two groups. The Nephtheidae reach a large size but the trunk has very little coenenchyme. Instead these corals rely on abundant and spacious gastrovascular canals within their trunks to maintain their shape via hydrostatic pressure. As a result, members of the Nephtheidae can collapse and shrink to a small size when their gastrovascular canals expel water (Bayer, 1973). The arrangement of the larger branches and the polyps on the branches are used to subdivide this family. The second group is typified by the *Siphonogorgia.* They have narrower, more rigid main trunks, and the branches are subdivided to a much greater extent. These soft corals look a lot like gorgonians at first glance but lack the internal axial skeleton of gorgonians. Various terms are used to describe the colony morphologies of massive and arborescent forms (see table 1.2).

Table 1.2
Growth forms of
massive and arborescent
soft corals
After Bayer et al., 1983

Term	Description	Examples
bushy	colonies with abundant branches arising immediately above the holdfast and not forming an obvious main stem	*Plexaurella* *Stereonephthya*
capitate	unbranched colonies with a broad distal part (capitulum) on a distinctly narrower stalk	*Heteroxenia* *Xenia*
dichotomously branching	branched colonies in which the branching pattern is a repeat bifurcation	*Plexaurella*
digitate	colonies consisting of several, finger-like lobes	*Alcyonium* *Sinularia* *Lobophytum*
digitiform	unbranched, finger-like colonies	*Paralemnalia*
divaricate (colonial)	arborescent colonies that are profusely branched, with long slender branches bearing distinctly separated and diverging bundles of polyps	*Dendronephthya*
encrusting	thick fleshy layer covering the substrate	*Erythropodium* *Lobophytum* *Sinularia*
glomerate (colonial)	arborescent colonies that are sparsely branched, with numerous bundles of polyps crowded to form roundish bunches	*Dendronephthya*
lateral branching	gorgonian colonies, planar or nearly so, in which the branching originates irregularly, neither pinnate nor dichotomous	*Plexaura*
lobate	colonies consisting of several stout lobes	*Cladiella* *Sinularia*
pinnate	branched colonies in which the branching pattern is feather-like, with the branches in one plane	*Pseudopterogorgia*

planar	branched colonies in which the branches grow more or less in one plane	*Gorgonia*
reticulate	branched colonies in which the branches are joined together to form a net-like structure	*Gorgonia* *Subergorgia*
stoloniferous	colonies consisting of several polyps interconnected by stolons	*Clavularia* *Pachyclavularia*
umbellate (colonial)	arborescent colonies with numerous bundles of polyps growing together in umbrella-like groups	*Dendronephthya*
unbranched	erect colonies devoid of lateral parts	*Cavernularia*

Gorgonians

Gorgonians are predominantly arborescent in nature, though a few single unbranched stem species do occur; they are subdivided into two main groupings determined by the nature of their central supporting structure. In the Scleraxonia this is called an axis and in the Holaxonia, the central core. This structure is a product of the coenenchyme, and as such is produced by the colony, not the polyps. The Scleraxonia have a central axis composed of horny material called gorgonin, and usually, fused sclerites, while the Holaxonia central core has an horny outer layer (cortex) surrounding a chambered core of gorgonin; sclerites are not present (Bayer, 1973; Hyman, 1940). The coenenchyme can be thick in some genera (e.g. *Eunicea*) and thin in others (e.g. *Pseudopterogorgia*). It contains the gastric cavities of the polyps, solenia, axial canals and sclerites.

Polyps extend roughly half their length into the coenenchyme and are connected by solenia running throughout the coenenchyme and along the axial skeleton. In some genera the polyps are completely retractable into an inconspicuous calyx (e.g. *Plexaurella*) while in others they retract into a very pronounced

Figure 1.6
**Longitudinal and
cross-section views of a
typical gorgonian**
Modified from Bayer et al., 1983

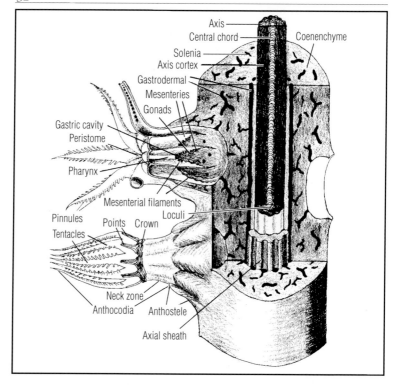

and heavily spiculated calyx (e.g. *Muricea*). The calyx can often be surround with sharp calcareous spines and lids that can cover the calyx when the anthocodium retracts (e.g. *Muricea*). Spicules often extend onto the anthocodium and can form eight sharp spines, one along each tentacle. The polyps can be distributed all over the branches, restricted to just the edges or just on one side of the branch, depending on the genus. Polyps are rarely dimorphic; most notably in the precious red coral *Corallium* (Hyman, 1940). Gorgonians are the most plant-like of corals, and their bright colours (yellow, orange, purple, red, and blue) add a brilliant touch to the underwater landscape. Colonies can be feather-like, bushy or fan-like, branching in only one plane or in several. See chapter seven for descriptions of the genera commonly kept in aquaria.

Order Pennatulacea (Sea Pens)

Sea pens represent the highest order of octocoral in terms of colonial complexity, polymorphism of polyps, functional specialization of polyps and colonial integration (Bayer, 1973). In fact, sea pens act as "super organisms" with various types of polyps performing circulatory and respiratory functions, feeding and digestion, sexual reproduction, and locomotory functions (Bayer, 1973). They tend to form fleshy colonies with a single axial polyp, from which numerous secondary polyps arise. The secondary polyps are dimorphic. The axial polyp usually lacks an anthocodium on the end and is divided into two regions. The peduncle is devoid of anthocodia and is used to anchor the colony into the substrate, usually fine sand or mud. There are no stolons or filaments on the end to anchor the peduncle but there may be a bulb-shaped swelling on the tip. The other end, the rachis, bears the secondary polyps. In the more primitive genera such as the one covered in this volume, *Cavernularia*, the rachis is a rounded cylinder that bears polyps on all sides. More advanced genera show the characteristic feather quill shape from which the common name Sea Pen was derived. For more detailed information on sea pen anatomy we recommend Hyman (1940) or Bayer (1973).

Reproduction

Reproduction in octocorals is a poorly understood topic. There have been scattered notes and papers in the scientific literature, but it was not until the early 1980's that detailed papers began to appear dealing with sexual reproduction in *Alcyonium, Heteroxenia, Lobophytum, Parerythropodium, Sarcophyton* and *Xenia*. In fact, it was only recently discovered that soft corals on the Great Barrier Reef, Australia exhibit the same type of mass spawning event in November as do stony corals (Alino and Coll, 1989).

As in all other anthozoans, octocorals can reproduced both asexually and sexually. Unfortunately, it appears the scientific community has a greater interest in sexual methods, while hobbyists are more interested in using the magnificent recuperative powers and growth rates of octocorals to propagate colonies asexually, for sale and trade among fellow aquarists. However, the vast potential of sexual reproduction for aquaculture should not be dismissed! A South Pacific species of *Heteroxenia* at the Waikiki Aquarium in Hawaii regularly releases brooded planulae that settle out all over the stony coral culture tanks and within the exhibits. Internal and external brooders offer the potential of vast numbers of planulae each year for grow-out. *Heteroxenia* is especially attractive for culturists in that it is hermaphroditic (Benayahu and Loya, 1984a). Many of these brooding corals can be made to expel planulae simply by handling.

Asexual Reproduction

The most commonly encountered form of octocoral reproduction seen in aquaria is asexual. In the wild, asexual reproduction has been recognized as an important mechanism for increasing local numbers of individuals in octocorals (Lasker, 1990). With few exceptions, all octocorals have the capacity to reproduce asexually. This most commonly occurs via colony growth and fragmentation. Other methods include budding, transverse fission and pedal laceration. Colony growth will be discussed later in this chapter.

Fragmentation

Soft corals employ many different means of fragmentation to advantage. In arborescent genera, the most common method is a general pinching-off of a branchlet with five to eight polyps by the parent

Capnella reproduces asexually by spontaneously severing branch tips, which become swollen with water for a few days just before they break free. J. Sprung

This *Plexaurella* sp. is reproducing asexually by dropping a fragment of tissue with polyps. The daughter colony produced will attach to the rock below the parent and form a new colony there. In nature this mode of reproduction produces patchy groupings or forests of clones. T. Siegel

colony. This then falls to the substrate and reattaches rapidly. In *Dendronephthya,* this is a very common occurrence (Dahan and Benayahu in prep.). The fragment attaches by means of numerous fine filaments that extend from the base. These "root" the fragment to the substrate and full attachment continues via growth, a process that takes approximately ten days in *Dendronephthya hemprichi* (Fabricius et al., 1995b). A similar process occurs in some Caribbean gorgonians. Small branchlets are produced and then through fission they are pinched off of the mother colony, to settle and grow nearby (Lasker, 1990). It is likely that this occurs in several other soft coral genera. This tendency to produce lots of fragments naturally can be used by indigenous peoples to easily collect fragments for sale. Simply placing loose rubble rock, PVC plates or ceramic tiles underneath and around colonies on the reef, would yield hundreds of fragments, ready for shipping.

Other genera such as *Alcyonium, Lemnalia, Litophyton, Nephthea* and *Scleronephthya* may encourage the growth of algae as a means of separating the growing tip of a branch. Strands of filamentous algae grow around a branchlet and constrict it until it effectively pinches off. The severed branchlet then falls to the bottom or is carried away by currents to land and reattach elsewhere. Some soft corals such as *Capnella* employ swelling of branch tips with water just before they become severed from the original colony.

Xenia and *Anthelia* species, which grow quickly and spread over substrates via vegetative budding of polyps and daughter colonies, also employ two special forms of fragmentation to help spread the colonies over longer distances. They spontaneously fragment individual polyps that are carried away in the currents. About midway down the column of each individual polyp a flattened swelling sometimes forms indicating the site of imminent fission. The separated polyps readily attach to substrates downstream and form new colonies. Other times *Xenia* spp. employ fragmentation of the colony stalk or encrusting tissue. This technique resembles transverse fission in anemones. As soon as the polyp-bearing capitulum is thus naturally severed it is apparent that the nubby stalk left behind already has some polyps branching out (Matt Rigberg, pers. comm.).

Fragmentation can also occur through the actions of predators and natural disturbances such as storms and hurricanes (called typhoons west of the International dateline). The attack of predatory worms, snails, fish, etc. on *Sarcophyton* (Leather corals), may destroy the individual colony, but produce numerous offspring from the remaining tissue. Natural disturbances would do much the same but on a massive scale. Some *Sarcophyton* spp. will also form necrotic areas on the head

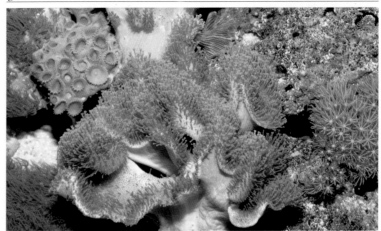

Sarcophyton spp. form necrotic areas on the capitulum and the partially severed fragments that result may drop off and form new colonies. J. C. Delbeek

A colony of *Tubipora* growing on a submersible pump at Tropicorium in Romulus Michigan. This young colony may have been produced by sexual reproduction in the aquarium. Alternately it may be the result of asexual reproduction, wherein a fragment of the stolon from another colony drifted in the water and became sucked against the intake screen of the pump, sending out new polyps and encrusting tissue from there. J. Sprung

that can cause a "flap" of tissue with polyps to separate and settle to the bottom, and a new colony may thus be formed.

Fragmentation occurs in genera with creeping stolons and runners such as *Briareum*, *Clavularia* and *Pachyclavularia* and *Tubipora*. In this case the stolon or runners, become gradually thinner and eventually sever. The stolon can also be severed by falling rocks or coral heads, and storm-tossed rubble.

Budding

In massive octocorals such as *Sarcophyton*, budding off of new individuals is not uncommon. These usually appear near the base of the stalk but can also occur just under the edge of the capitulum (see

Sarcophyton in chapter 7). If budding at the base occurs when the colony is still small, the offspring and the mother colony can grow together to form multiple stalked colonies. If they occur when the mother colony is very large, these small offspring tend to remain stunted in growth due to shading by the mother colony.

Fission

As we mentioned earlier, some soft corals such as *Xenia* spp. exhibit transverse fission, wherein the top of the colony bearing

Sarcophyton sp. budding a daughter colony from the column. S. W. Michael

Xenia exhibiting reproduction via longitudinal fission. J. C. Delbeek

the capitulum becomes severed from its base. Another form of fission occurs as soft corals develop a thick stem. Splitting of a soft coral lengthwise is most common in arborescent genera such as *Alcyonium* (Colt coral), *Lemnalia*, *Litophyton*, *Nephthea*, etc. and in *Heteroxenia* and *Xenia*. In this case, the stalk will begin to split towards the base along a vertical line between its two largest branches, eventually resulting in two equally-sized corals. While in *Xenia* spp. it may occur within as little as one week, this process usually takes several months to complete fully. Branching *Cladiella* spp. and *Sinularia* spp. are also known to split this way.

Pedal laceration

Some soft corals such as *Cladiella*, *Nephthea* and *Xenia* are known to actually move across the substrate, trailing basal tissue. This tissue can remain attached or become detached, eventually developing into a new coral.

Sexual Reproduction

Soft corals employ different modes of sexual reproduction. Some species have separate sexes, while in other species the colonies contain both male and female germ cells. When egg and sperm unite a planula larva is formed. This larva may be brooded or it may form in the water column. Many species spawn seasonally, while some spawn year round according to cues such as moon phase and tide. The vast majority of octocorals have separate male and females colonies (gonochoric /dioecious), however, a few hermaphroditic species of *Heteroxenia* (e.g. *H. elizabethae*, *H. fuscescens*, *H. ghardaqensis*) and *Xenia* (e.g. *X. viridis*) have been identified (in Benayahu and Loya, 1984a).

There are three main modes of sexual reproduction: 1) broadcast spawning with external fertilization; 2) internal fertilization with planula brooded internally in special endodermal pouches and then released through specialized structures and; 3) internal fertilization with planulae then brooded in external pouches on the surface of the polyp and then released.

Broadcast Spawning

Broadcast spawning involves the release of gametes into the water column where fertilization then occurs. Broadcast spawning has been reported in species belonging to the following genera: *Alcyonium, Cladiella, Dendronephthya, Lobophytum, Sarcophyton* and *Sinularia* (Alino and Coll, 1989; Benayahu and Loya, 1986; Fabricius et al., 1995b; Yamazato et al., 1981). It appears that this form of sexual reproduction is the most common in alcyoniids.

Gonads are located on the mesenteries of the autozooids. In studies of *Lobophytum, Sarcophyton* and *Sinularia* it was found that egg devel-

This "Colt Coral," *Alcyonium* sp., has eggs visible within its translucent branches. R. Mascarin

Figure 1.7
Longitudinal section through polyps of *Lobophytum crassum* showing the developing eggs and testes in the autozooids
From Yamazato et al., 1981

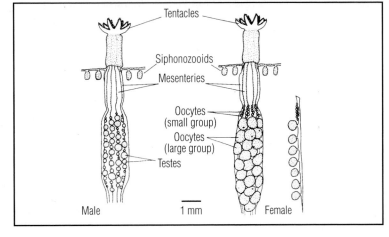

Pseudopterogorgia elisabethae, a Caribbean photosynthetic gorgonian, produces white eggs from November through December. These fall off the colony like sand grains. We have never witnessed the release of sperm in this species, nor the formation of planulae.
J. Sprung

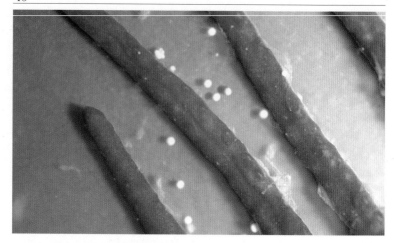

opment generally takes two years as opposed to one year for sperm (Alino and Coll, 1989; Benayahu and Loya, 1986; Yamazato et al., 1981). Therefore it is not unusual to find different size classes of eggs in the same polyp. Eggs vary in size, but they are generally much larger than stony coral eggs and can range from 625 um in *Lobophytum* spp. to 810 um in *Sinularia* spp. (Alino and Coll, 1989; Yamazato et al., 1981) Spawning usually takes place after dusk one to two weeks after the full moon, in the spring and/or summer. Fertilization occurs within a few hours, within forty eight hours planulae are formed, and one to two weeks later settlement occurs (Alino and Coll, 1989; Benayahu and Loya, 1986; Yamazato et al., 1981). Reproductively mature polyps occur on inner branches in arborescent species of octocorals such as gorgonians, and near the centers of massive soft corals such as *Sarcophyton* and *Lobophytum* (Yamazato et al., 1981). See chapter seven for further descriptions of reproduction in each genera.

Internal Brooding

In the Xeniidae family several genera have been shown to brood their planulae internally. Fertilization occurs within the gastrovascular cavity and the planulae begin to develop there. Eventually they move into pouches within the mesogloea called intersiphonozooid spaces, to complete development (Zaslow and Benayahu, 1996). Both *Heteroxenia* spp. and *Xenia* spp. employ this mode of reproduction. Most gorgonians are also internal brooders (Brazeau and Lasker, 1989). Release of mature planulae occurs a few hours after dusk in the spring and summer, usually a few days after the new moon. In some cases planulation occurs year round e.g. *Heteroxenia fuscescens*. See chapter seven for detailed descriptions of reproduction in each genera.

External Brooding

This method is very similar to internal brooding except the fertilized eggs are shed from the polyp and adhere to the side in mucus pouches where they then develop until they are released. Planulae are released a few hours after dusk. This method was first discovered in the alcyoniid coral *Parerythropodium fulvum fulvum* and has since been observed in *Briareum, Clavularia, Efflatounaria* and *Pachyclavularia*, and the Mediterranean gorgonian *Paramuricea clavata* (Alino and Coll, 1989; Benayahu and Loya, 1983; Coma et al., 1995). See chapter seven for detailed description of reproduction in these genera.

Asexual Planulae (Parthenogenesis)?

Brazeau and Lasker (1989) reported a population of *Plexaura* sp. off the coast of San Blas Islands, Panama that did not contain any male or hermaphroditic colonies, yet the females produced fertile eggs four to seven days after the full moon every month from May to July. The eggs would begin to develop just prior to or at the time of release. These observations suggest that this particular species reproduces parthenogenetically, producing planulae asexually. A subsequent study by Lasker and Kim (1996) showed that very few planulae were produced parthenogenetically. The vast majority were the product of broadcast spawning and external fertilization. Male colonies were more common at other sites than in the previous study, and were observed in aquaria to release barely discernable wisps of sperm.

Defense Mechanisms

Chemical Defenses

Octocorals produce a wide range of chemicals that play an important role in their ecology, particularly in competition for space, anti-fouling against algae, defense against predation and in enhancing reproductive success (Sammarco, 1996). Although the structures of these compounds are chemically simple, their function cannot be easily predicted from their structure (Sammarco, 1996). For example, many of these chemicals are specific in their actions i.e. they may affect certain stony corals but not others (see Sammarco et al., 1983). Also, not all species within a genus are equally susceptible. For example, *Xenia puertogalerae* was shown to allow the planula of *Acropora* spp. to settle amongst its colonies and develop (Atrigenio and Alino, 1996). However, in another study (Coll et al., 1985) showed that a species of *Xenia* severely affected the growth of *Acropora* spp. Finally, the functioning of many of these compounds now appears to be synergistic. That is on their own some appear to have little affect but when combined with other secondary metabolites, they exhibit certain abilities. Therefore it is entirely possible that these need to be tested in the presence of other secondary metabolites and perhaps in the same concentrations as found in the host tissues, in order to exhibit any bioactivity (Sammarco, 1996).

Many of the chemical compounds found in corals (both soft and stony) as well as zoanthids, sea cucumbers, gastropods, and anemones have both medical and commercial potential. For example, *Sinularia flexibilis* contains anti-cancer diterpenes such as sinularin and dihydro-sinularin. Mycosporine-GLY from stony

Figure 1.8
A summary of ecological interactions in soft corals that are mediated by secondary metabolic compounds *Modified from Coll and Sammarco, 1986*

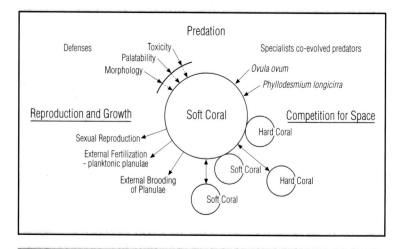

Figure 1.9
Structures of diterpenes isolated from *Sinularia flexibilis* and *Lobophytum* sp.
Modified from Aceret et al., 1995

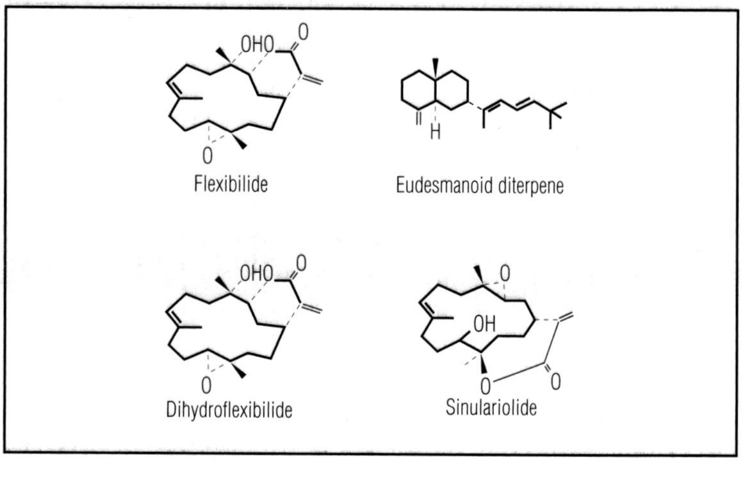

corals, and palythine and palythinol from zoanthids, are substances that absorb ultraviolet light. These have recently been synthesized and patented for use in sun-tan lotions, outdoor paints and plastics (Sammarco, 1996). Soft coral secondary metabolites are also being investigated as anti-foulants for wooden fishing boats in Indonesia. Boring organisms greatly reduce the life-span of these boats and this application has shown promising results (Sammarco, 1996). Although the majority of the work has so far been done with tropical and temperate octocorals, there has recently been a publication on a few Antarctic species that indicates that they too may possess bioactive compounds (Slattery and McClinock, 1995).

Pseudopterogorgia elisabethae, the "purple frilly" gorgonian commonly collected for the aquarium trade, occurs in some regions of the Caribbean in densities up to ten colonies per square meter. In 1986 William Fenical and his colleagues at the University of California, San Diego and Scripps Institution of Oceanography discovered that this gorgonian contains highly potent anti-inflammatory and tissue-healing agents of a novel chemical class. The combined properties have been patented by the University of California, forming the opportunity for the production of new products based on the discovery. As one might expect, concerns have been raised about harvesting these animals from coral reefs and these concerns have provided a major rationale for an extensive conservation and management program. The single major benefit of harvesting this animal is that it regrows. By clipping the animal and leaving the holdfast and some of the stem intact on the reef, it regrows quite effectively. Because of this it can be collected in large regions of the Bahamas and within sixteen to eighteen months the animals regrow to harvestable size in their original sites. The *Pseudopterogorgia* project is unique in that it provides a renewable and continuing resource for the development of skin care products. In addition the same compounds, pseudopterosins, are being developed as drug molecules for treatment of a variety of specific illnesses. The major substance under development, called methopterosin, is being investigated for treatment of skin diseases such as psoriasis and perhaps ultimately for arthritis and other autoimmune diseases.

Competition for Space

Space is at a premium on coral reefs and therefore competition can be intense. Whether it be space for coral colony expansion, for larval settlement, or just protecting space already occupied, soft corals have developed a number of mechanisms to compete.

droflexibilide and the eudesmanoid diterpene all caused inhibition of polyp activity in *A. formosa* and *P. cylindrica* (*Acropora* was the most sensitive), while sinulariolide did not. Within a few hours of exposure to levels greater than 5 ppm, zooxanthellae were expelled, followed by expulsion of nematocysts. The loss of zooxanthellae and nematocysts left the stony coral polyps unequipped to acquire nutrition, and death followed shortly thereafter (Aceret et al., 1995a). The lack of toxicity of sinulariolide was not surprising as its main function is as an anti-foulant against algae. Flexibilide exhibited the highest level of toxicity and is a known inhibitor of stony coral growth, while dihydroflexibilide is a major olfactory feeding deterrent.

Soft corals can also compete for space by inhibiting the settlement of stony coral planulae. Atrigeno and Alino (1996) showed that *Xenia puertogalerae* inhibited the settlement of stony coral planulae near it except for *Acropora* (and to a much lesser extent *Montipora* and *Fungia*), which often settled right between the *Xenia* colonies. By being tolerant of *Xenia* chemicals, this *Acropora* species has an advantage over other stony corals in colonizing new areas for settlement and growth. Studies of planula settlement showed that in areas down current from *S. flexibilis* and *Sarcophyton glaucum* the number of settled stony coral spat was significantly lower than in other areas (Maida et al., 1995). This could have been due to avoidance of the area by planulae upon detection of soft coral chemicals in the water, or of allelochemicals adsorbed onto the substratum, or once the planulae settle out they are killed by allelochemicals in the water or on the substratum; the mechanism inhibiting successful stony coral recruitment is still unknown (Maida et al., 1995). When investigating the effects of diterpenes isolated from *Sinularia flexibilis* on the eggs, sperm and embryos of *Montipora digitata* and *Acropora tenuis*, Aceret et al. (1995b) found that only eggs that were fertilized in the presence of these chemicals lost there cellular integrity and burst just a few hours after exposure. So it appears that the diterpenes can act upon the developing eggs themselves but only within the first twenty four hours.

Although laboratory studies have demonstrated the toxicity of many of these compounds to stony corals, one rarely finds evidence of local mortality or tissue necrosis on the reef itself (Coll and Sammarco, 1986). When interactions first occur between corals, tissue damage occurs very rapidly, but over the course of a few days or weeks the colonies can either grow, or in the case of soft corals, move away from each other. So one often sees colonies that have shapes indicative of avoidance behaviour (Coll and Sammarco, 1986). The fact that many soft corals such as *Nephthea* spp. can move over the substratum further helps to decrease the probability of contact with potential competitors.

Anti-Fouling

Soft corals such as *Sarcophyton, Lobophytum* and gorgonians, periodically shed a waxy film, sometimes with their epidermis in an attempt to rid it of epiphytic growths and release excess carbon (see volume one and Coll et al., 1987). Soft corals can also employ their secondary metabolite chemicals as anti-foulants to retard the persistent growth of algae. Coll et al. (1987) showed that some diterpenes isolated from *Lobophytum pauciflorum*, could inhibit the growth of the red alga Ceramium flaccidum. Interestingly, the basal portions of most soft corals contain higher concentrations of sclerites and lower concentrations of diterpenes while the tips are the opposite.

Feeding Deterrence

Soft corals are rich in nutritional substances (fats, proteins, and carbohydrates) and should serve as valuable food sources to predators, but the incidence of predation is rather low (Williams, 1993). Obviously they must have developed some mechanisms to

This *Lobophytum* sp. is shedding a waxy film to help clean its surface of growths of algae. J. Sprung

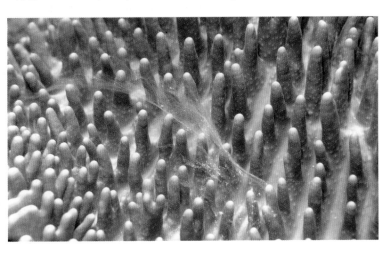

discourage predation. There are four methods by which soft corals can deter predation: the use of toxic chemicals, the use of chemicals to reduce palatability, the production of calcium carbonate spicules, and the ability to retract polyps.

sperm of this species can find the correct eggs. A similar function as recently been found for the chemicals concentrated in the eggs of *Lobophytum crassum* (Coll et al., 1995). *Lobophytum crassum* and *L. compactum* both contain isomers of cembranoid diterpenes in their eggs, (-)-epi-thunbergol and (-)-thunbergol respectively. These were shown to act as sperm attractants at very low concentrations. Since *Lobophytum* have separate male and female colonies, often separated by large distances, these attractants would play an important role during mass spawnings. Given these results it is not unreasonable to assume that the other egg specific compounds isolated from some ten other species of octocoral may also be sperm attractants (Coll et al., 1995).

One interesting observation is that the presence of secondary metabolites is highly variable. Concentrations can vary widely from species to species within a genus, and between genera (LaBarre, et al., 1986). The reproductive state also appears to play a role, with some chemicals only being present when eggs are present (Coll, et al, 1995; Sammarco and Coll, 1986). The geographic location also plays a role, with the same species showing varying levels of chemicals from one area to the next (Harvell et al., 1993; Coll et al., 1995). Finally, Leone et al.(1995) showed that moving colonies of *Lobophytum compactum* resulted in a significant increase in diterpenes, but this decreased after two months. Ongoing work at the University of Hawaii has also shown that many of the organisms that contain these defensive chemicals lose these chemicals when removed from the presence of predators (B. Carlson, pers. comm.).

Terpenes, diterpenes and other natural products of octocorals are attracting a great deal of attention and studies are now underway to investigate the possible uses of these compounds in medicine and industry. Many new natural marine products are discovered each year and they are often tested by researchers at the U.S. National Institute of Health, the U.S. National Cancer Institute and other organizations around the world. For those of you who would like to investigate these substances more closely or want to keep up-to-date on the latest findings we recommend reading The Journal of Natural Products as well as the annual reports by Dr. D. J. Faulkner published as the Natural Products Report each year.

Physical Defenses

Sweeper Tentacles

Physical defenses in other anthozoans include sweeper tentacles, sweeper polyps, acontia, and mesenterial filaments, all packed with nematocysts. Nematocysts are generally small and of a singular type in octocorals (Hyman, 1940); some families such as the Xeniidae lack them altogether. Octocorals as a rule, do not develop aggressive structures. However, there have been isolated reports of sweeper-tentacle-like structures in some genera but they have not been investigated further. To date the only octocoral that has been shown to definitely produce sweeper tentacles is the Caribbean encrusting gorgonian *Erythropodium caribaeorum* (Sebens and Miles, 1988). When colonies of this gorgonian encounter other corals, the polyps along the edges begin to transform. All eight tentacles become elongated (up to three times their normal length of 2 cm) and lose the characteristic side pinnules. They become lighter in colour and develop a bulbous tip (acrosphere) on the end; both the tentacle and the acrosphere are packed with stinging cells. These sweeper tentacles are capable of killing stony coral tissue quite rapidly, allowing for the rapid overgrowth of the stony coral colony (Sebens and Miles, 1988). We have seen other gorgonians, *Muricea* spp. for example, develop similar structures.

Sclerites

As mentioned in the previous section, sclerites afford a certain level of protection for many species of soft corals (see earlier description).

Overgrowth

Soft corals, especially encrusting forms, can quickly cover coral reef areas. In some cases toxic chemicals play a role in clearing space for growth, in others sweeper tentacles can allow for the overgrowth of stony coral colonies. Another method is illustrated by the nephthiid coral, *Nephthea brassica*. It can overgrow stony coral colonies by laying down a protective polysaccharide layer in areas close to or in contact with stony coral tentacles; and then it simply overgrows the stony coral (LaBarre and Coll, 1986).

Nutrition

Nutrition is a poorly studied area in octocorals in sharp contrast to the work done on zooxanthellae and feeding in stony corals (see volume one). As in stony corals, there are genera of octocorals who possess zooxanthellae and genera that do not (see chapter seven).

The vast majority of soft corals rely greatly on zooxanthellae for their nutrition. Some such as those in the Xeniidae family, rely almost exclusively on their zooxanthellae since they lack nematocysts and have a reduced digestive system (see Polyp Anatomy). However, recent studies have shown zooxanthellae may not be able to meet the total nutritional needs of other soft corals. Fabricius and Klumpp (1995) found that twelve of the most common photosynthetic soft coral species investigated on the Great Barrier Reef could not meet their carbon requirements by photosynthesis alone. This brings up the question of just where do they get their carbon from? Many octocorals are known as polytrophic feeders, meaning that they are capable of obtaining nutrition from more than one source (Williams, 1993). Possible sources may be one or all of the following: the direct absorption of nutrients, the ingestion of zooplankton and/or phytoplankton, or the ingestion of "marine snow" and its attached bacteria and organic material.

Members of the Xeniidae family are known to absorb organic and inorganic nutrients directly from the water column and it is possible that other soft corals have similar abilities (Schlichter, 1982a and b). In the case of *Heteroxenia fuscescens*, photosynthetically produced excess amino acids are actually released directly into the environment, thereby enriching the water (Schlichter and Liebezeit, 1991). If other such sources exist it is possible that combined they could provide enough to allow other corals to absorb and utilize these substances as an important nutrition source.

Given that octocoral polyps have few, small stinging cells (or none at all) and that their pinnules offer a large surface area, they are generally classified as suspension feeders, straining fine particles from the passing water. As such their feeding efficiency is affected by the rate of current flow, polyp and colony flexibility, and orientation. Several studies have shown that feeding efficiency generally increases up to a maximum velocity and then drops off at velocities beyond that (Best, 1988; Sponaugle and LaBarbera, 1991; Dai and Lin, 1993; Fabricius, et al., 1995b). However, the flexion of the polyps and colony can act together to increase the range of current velocities over which suspension feeding is successful (Sponaugle, 1991). The polyps themselves can actually modulate the flow around them, to enhance prey capture. In a study of the effects of flow on particle capture in the asymbiotic temperate octocoral *Alcyonium siderium*, Patterson (1991) found that at low flows (2.7 cm/s) tentacles on the upstream side of the polyps capture the most prey. At intermediate flows (12.2 cm/s) downstream tentacles within a polyp capture the most prey. In high flow (19.8 cm/s) polyps are bent downstream, eddies form over the polyp surfaces and all tentacles capture prey effectively. Prey is trapped most effectively at the tips of the tentacles compared to locations near the mouth (Patterson, 1991). We must caution readers that flow rates that provide for the most efficient feeding of octocorals most likely vary from species to species and genus to genus. No one current flow is the best for all species. For example, Dai and Lin (1993) found that three Taiwanese asymbiotic gorgonians Subergorgia suberosa, *Acanthogorgia vegae* and *Melithaea ochracea* fed over a wide range of flow rates. The ability to keep polyps open was also related to flow rates and the size of their polyps. *Subergorgia suberosa* had the largest polyps, which were deformed by the lowest currents speeds (>10 cm/s), severely hindering prey capture. In contrast, *Melithaea ochracea* which had the shortest and the least easily deformed polyps at high flow rates, could feed at the highest flow rates (40 cm/s). *Acanthogorgia vegae* had an intermediate polyp size and fed in flows of 0-24 cm/s. Although all three fed most effectively at flows of 8 cm/s, *S. suberosa* had the narrowest feeding range (5-10 cm/s) while *M. ochracea* had the widest range (4-40 cm/s) (Dai and Lin, 1993). These varying abilities to feed in various current flows is a major factor in determining distribution on reefs. *Melithaea ochracea* is the most widely spread gorgonian on southern Taiwanese reefs, occurring on the upper part of reef fronts where currents are strong. *Subergorgia suberosa*, which feeds in a narrow range of flow velocities, has a restricted distribution pattern, being found on lower reef slopes or on sheltered boulders where currents are weaker. *Acanthogorgia vegae*, which can feed in relatively strong currents, is most commonly found on the semi-exposed reef fronts or the lateral side of boulders (Dai and Lin, 1993). Therefore, water flow and its interactions with polyps and colonies, appears to greatly influence distribution patterns of colonies, colony growth, size and morphology, and rates of gas exchange (in Fabricius et al., 1995).

There have been several studies that have shown that some octocorals can feed on zooplankton, (Lewis, 1982; Sebens and Koehl, 1984; Dai and Lin, 1993). Many of these studies, however, were conducted in the laboratory, using artificial foods (*Artemia*) or concentrated natural zooplankton of unknown density (Fabricius et al., 1995b). These studies showed that octocorals tend to be highly selective for non-evasive plankton such as mollusc larvae, indicating poor capture ability of more elusive prey such as large adult copepods. This poor capture ability is most likely due to the lack of effective nematocysts, resulting in the selection of less motile prey (Fabricius et al., 1995b). In fact, Fabricius (unpubl. data) found that an inability to feed on zooplankton was widespread amongst zooxanthellate soft coral genera on the Great Barrier Reef (i.e. *Sarcophyton* 3 spp., *Sinularia* 2 spp., *Cladiella* sp., *Nephthea* sp. and *Paralemnalia* sp.). The role that zooplankton play in the nutrition of photosynthetic octocorals is as yet unclear but new information is showing that they contribute only a small portion to the nutritional budget of many octocorals (Fabricius et al., 1995a and b).

For azooxanthellate genera the capture of prey is vitally important in order to acquire nutrients. Several studies have shown that soft corals, gorgonians and sea pens can feed on a variety of zooplankton such as copepod nauplii and eggs, other invertebrate eggs, and other small items of poor mobility (Coma et al., 1994). However, there have been indications that azooxanthellate soft corals, gorgonians and sea pens may feed on other items. For many years it was assumed that octocorals fed mainly on zooplankton. However, octocorals contain few, small nematocysts and have poor ciliary and flagellar structures. When coupled with the fact that their tentacles and pinnules appear to be better adapted for feeding on small particles and/or the direct uptake of organic materials by offering a large surface area, it appears less likely that prey the size of zooplankton are a major food source (Fabricius et al., 1995b). The question remains then, if not zooplankton, what are their main prey items?

Phytoplankton is an order of magnitude more common on coral reefs than zooplankton. Studies have shown that phytoplankton is somehow depleted over corals reefs, though where it goes no one knows (in Fabricius et al., 1995b). In 1961, Roushdy and Hansen showed that the asymbiotic soft coral *Alcyonium digitatum* feeds on 14C labeled phytoplankton. In 1969 it was shown that the temperate water sea pen *Ptilosarcus gurneyi* feeds primarily on phytoplankton (Birkeland, 1969); its bright orange colour is the result of carotenoids derived from a diet of dinoflagellates (in Best, 1988). Elyakova et al. (1981), in a general survey of carbohydrases in marine invertebrates, found the presence of laminarinase and amylase in three species of the zooxanthellate soft coral genus *Alcyonium*. These chemicals are enzymes involved in the digestion of plant material. It was not until 1995 that Fabricius et al. (1995a and b) published papers that demonstrated quite clearly that the Red Sea azooxanthellate soft coral

Dendronephthya hemprichi, fed extensively on phytoplankton, gaining more than enough carbon to cover respiration and growth requirements (Fabricius et al., 1995b). Although this species also fed on zooplankton, only 2.4-3.5% of the daily carbon requirement of this coral was met by ingesting zooplankton. Three other asymbiotic Red Sea octocorals, *D. sinaiensis, Scleronephthya corymbosa* and the gorgonian *Acabaria* were also found to contain large quantities of phytoplankton in their gastrovascular cavities (Fabricius et al., 1995a). Adaptations for phytoplankton capture include the small spaces between the pinnules of *D. hemprichi*, which appear to be ideal for straining phytoplankton from flowing waters. The large spicules found in the body column and around the polyps of *Dendronephthya* spp., appear to function more in holding the column and polyps erect in strong current flows, than as protection against predation, allowing them to strain phytoplankton effectively from the passing waters (Fabricius et al., 1995b). Some of the most impressive growths of *Dendronephthya* spp. are often found on ship wrecks in the South Pacific, where structures high above the bottom and projecting into the current are often heavily encrusted! It is tempting to equate this with oyster hatcheries, where oysters are hung in cages well above the bottom and within strong currents. Both organisms feed on phytoplankton, and hence benefit from these positions by being exposed to maximal phytoplankton concentrations because of the high volume of water flowing past them. In light of this new evidence, scientists need to re-evaluate the role of phytoplankton in the nutrition of other octocorals. Several studies are now underway to determine to what extent both zooxanthellate and azooxanthellate species actually feed on phytoplankton.

Another mode of feeding may be the trapping of mucus flocs often called marine "snow". These are composed of detritus, bacteria, protozoans and possibly phytoplankton trapped in mucus. The source of the mucus flocs may be organic substances released on a regular basis by soft and stony corals to rid themselves of epizoic growths and excess carbon and fats. This material is not quickly degraded by bacteria and it is often infested with large quantities of bacteria and eukaryotes (flagellates, ciliates and diatoms) (Vacelet and Thomassin, 1991). These mucus flocs could be trapped by the spiky polyps of *Dendronephthya* spp. and used as a food source. To the best of our knowledge no one has investigated the possible role of this material in octocoral nutrition, but it is easy to see that it becomes trapped on the spiny projections of the surface of many octocoral species.

It is fully possible that octocorals employ a combination of some or all of the above feeding mechanisms, with varying degrees of importance for each (see polytrophic feeding described earlier). Further research is needed in this area and it is likely that in the next few years we will know much more about the diets and nutritional requirements of octocorals.

Growth

The growth rates of soft corals are poorly documented in the scientific literature. We know by observing them in our aquaria that many soft corals are capable of extremely rapid growth. Our experience, however, does not mean that the same growth rates occur naturally on the reefs, though we believe that the growth in our aquaria should not be very different from that in the natural setting. Fabricius (1995) studied *Sinularia* and *Sarcophyton* species on Australia's Great Barrier Reef. She found average radial growth rates of only 0.5 to 1.5 cm per year! In aquaria many *Sinularia* species grow in excess of 1 cm per month, but not all of them do, so one can not generalize about the growth rate of different members of the same genus. The growth rate also decreases as colonies approach certain size limits (Fabricius, 1995). In the wild she found that juvenile *Sarcophyton* may increase in size 28% per year while large colonies increase only 6% per year. In our aquariums *Sarcophyton* species can grow much faster, increasing in size about 25% per month, though they do so often in spurts followed by periods in which the size does not change much. Other studies have shown that when stony corals are decimated by Crown-of-Thorns seastars, soft corals (*Sarcophyton, Lobophytum* and *Sinularia* mainly) can rapidly move in and cover significant areas of reef (Benayahu, 1995). Therefore it may be possible that these corals show accelerated growth rates when colonizing new areas, but then slow as they age or grow beyond a certain size. *Dendronephthya* spp. can also quickly colonize new areas. In the Red Sea *D. hemprichi* have been know to cover man-made structures down to 240 ft (~ 80 m) growing to 12 in. (30 cm) in height in only a few months (in Fabricius et al., 1995b). Growth rates of young colonies of *D. hemprichi* can be greater than 8% of biomass per day (K.E. Fabricius, unpubl. data). This suggests that when their requirements are thoroughly understood at last, it may be possible to propagate *Dendronephthya* species in captivity.

Growth series in *Pseudopterogorgia americana* in John Haydock's aquarium, Ontario Canada.
J. C. Delbeek

Photosynthetic gorgonians grow extremely fast in nature and in aquariums. For example the sea fan, *Gorgonia ventalina* can develop into a 6 in. (15 cm) tall colony within one year after settling, and fragments of the holdfast with live tissue left on the substrate grow into new fans at the same rate (J. Sprung, pers. obs.). *Pseudoplexaura* spp. and *Pseudopterogorgia acerosa* may grow an inch (2.5 cm) per month per branch, and proliferate new branches that also grow at that rate (J. Sprung, pers. obs.). However, in a five year study of gorgonians on the southwest coast of Puerto Rico, Yoshioka and Buchanan-Yoshioka (1991) found that colony heights increased on average only 2 cm/year (0.8 - 4.5 cm/yr). The growth rate varies among genera and species, and as colonies approach their maximum size the growth rate measured as height increase is slower than for small colonies. While the height may not increase much in large colonies, branches may proliferate with rapid linear extension rates.

The fastest growing soft corals belong to the Xeniidae, including *Xenia* and *Anthelia* species. These soft corals proliferate with amazing speed and may also disappear as quickly as they come.

Growth not only pertains to growth of a single specimen but also to growth of the colony as a whole. It has long been established that soft corals are quick colonizers of space and can spread quickly through asexual reproduction and movement. A colony can easily increase its size by budding and pedal laceration, and whole colony movement is also possible (LaBarre and Coll, 1982). When coupled with their allelopathic properties many soft corals can quickly cover large areas of substratum.

Members of the suborder Stolonifera spread via growth of a creeping root-like structure called a stolon. As the stolon spreads over the surface polyps then arise from it. This stolon can take the form of tube-like ribbons (e.g. *Clavularia* spp.), sheet-like growths (e.g. *Pachyclavularia* spp.) or as sheets connecting tubes of polyps at various levels above the substratum as in *Tubipora*.

There are a number of different growth forms in the suborder Alcyoniina, which we dealt with in the colony morphology section of this chapter. Growth often involves the enlargement of the colony above the bottom, achieved via increases in the column and capitulum (e.g. *Sarcophtyon*); increases in the number of branches and column size (e.g. *Alcyonium*, *Sinularia*, Nephtheidae, Nidaliidae); spreading of the coenenchyme over the bottom from which polyps then arise (e.g. *Anthelia* spp., *Stereosoma* spp.); or a combination of these (e.g. *Xenia, Cespitularia,* some *Cladiella,* some *Sinularia* and *Heteroxenia* spp.).

This non-photosynthetic gorgonian was growing on a reef wall in the Solomon Islands, where it had ample opportunity to filter phytoplankton and organic detritus from the passing water column. Note "marine snow" trapped on its surface. While such filter feeding gorgonians grow rapidly in the natural environment, the shortage of their special food makes them difficult to grow in aquariums. J. Sprung

As we described earlier, gorgonians grow primarily by increasing the number of branches and increasing their length. Encrusting genera such as *Briareum* and *Erythropodium* grow by spreading their coenenchyme across the substratum with polyps arising from this surface.

Chapter Two

Biology of the Zoanthidea

Often called Button polyps, zoanthids are very common inhabitants of reef aquaria. Zoanthids are found throughout the world's oceans but are most widely represented in warm waters; some 300 species have been described so far (Wilkens, 1990). They can occur as single polyps or as colonies, either connected by a comon tissue or unconnected. Some genera are found in wave-swept reefs or calm shallows (e.g. *Isaurus, Palythoa* spp., *Protopalythoa* spp. and *Zoanthus* spp.) while others are found only in association with sponges, hydroids, worm tubes or gorgonians (e.g., *Acrozoanthus, Parazoanthus* and *Epizoanthus* spp.). Although zoanthids are related to stony corals, they do not produce a skeleton (except the poorly known genus *Gerardia*) but some genera do incorporate sediments into their body wall (mesoglea) giving them a rough texture, e.g. *Palythoa* spp. and *Protopalythoa* spp. (Mather and Bennett, 1993).

Despite their widespread availability and popularity with aquarists, the Zoanthidea are a relatively poorly understood, little studied order and their identification to species, and even genera can be challenging. This might seem surprising given how common they are in home aquaria and in nature, but there are many factors that come into play which affect the ease of identification. For instance, they exhibit a variety of colony and polyp morphology; they lack taxonomically significant skeletal structures like those found in stony and soft corals; and the reliance on old preserved specimens for taxonomic work makes comparisons to new samples very difficult. Furthermore the low number of studies on this group has contributed little information about this order (Muirhead and Ryland 1985; Mather and Bennett 1993). Finally, microscopic examination of internal features is often necessary to determine taxonomically important characteristics; something better left to the specialist (Mather and Bennett, 1993). However, we have included this information in the genera descriptions in chapter eight for those of you so equipped.

The characteristic contrasting oral disc colours of *Zoanthus* spp. are evident in this species.
J. C. Delbeek

Classification

Unlike the soft corals discussed in chapter one, zoanthids belong to the same subclass as stony corals, sea anemones, black corals, tube anemones and mushroom anemones; Zoantharia (Hexacorallia). As a result, they share many anatomical features, but have some distinguishing characteristics. Zoantharia exhibit a great deal of variability in polyp shape, polyp size, internal anatomy, mouth shape, number of tentacle rows . . . the list is a long one. Basically, Zoantharia are described as exhibiting characteristics that octocorals do not (Hyman, 1940), which kind of opens things up a bit! One trait that is a clear distinguishing feature is the number of tentacles. As we mentioned in volume one, Zoantharia have six tentacles or multiples of six while octocorals have eight or multiples thereof. This arrangement is mirrored internally where the body cavity is divided into six, or a multiple of six, compartments by an equal number of septa.

Of course mother nature has decided to throw a few curves at us. The order to which zoanthids belong, Zoanthidea, exhibits a few oddball traits that set it apart from all other Zoantharia. Zoanthids lack a pedal base, their ends are stalked or wedge-shaped, and their internal arrangement of septa is unlike any other anthozoan and most closely resembles that of the extinct order Tetracorallia (Hyman, 1940). It is because of this septal arrangement that zoanthids are classified into two suborders (figure 2.1). Those that have an incomplete fifth septum (i.e. it does not extend to the actinopharynx) are termed brachycnemic, while those with a complete fifth septum are termed macrocnemic.

Figure 2.1
After Hyman 1940

A. Cross section of *Epizoanthus* with macrocnemous septa arrangement.
B. Cross Section of *Zoanthus* showing brachycnemous septa arrangement..
1. Fourth and fifth septa
2. Dorsal directives

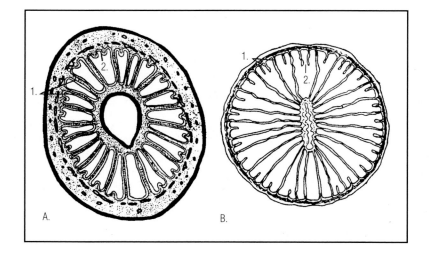

There has recently been a reorganization in zoanthid systematics as reflected in Table 2.1. Throughout this book we have attempted to use *Protopalythoa* in place of *Palythoa*, however, it is not yet

Table 2.1
Systematics of the order Zoanthidea

* We are tentatively placing *Acrozoanthus* in this family pending further taxonomic clarification.

```
Class Anthozoan
    Subclass Zoantharia (Hexacorallia)
        Order Zoanthidea
            Suborder Brachycnemina
                Family Neozoanthidae
                    Genus: Neozoanthus
                Family Zoanthidae
                    Genera: Acrozoanthus,* Isaurus, Palythoa, Protopalythoa,
                        Sphenopus, Zoanthus
            Suborder Macrocnemina
                Family Epizoanthidae
                    Genera: Epizoanthus, Thoracactis
                Family Parazoanthidae
                    Genera: Gerardia, Isozoanthus, Parazoanthus
```

possible to reassign species names to the new genus with confidence. Therefore, unless we are discussing *Palythoa caesia, P. caribaeorum, P. mammillosa* or *P. tuberculosa*, then all other references to *Palythoa* species refers to *Protopalythoa*. See chapter eight for a description of the differences between these two genera.

Polyp Anatomy

Zoanthid polyps are usually small, a few millimeters to a few centimeters in height but some can grow quite large such as *Protopalythoa grandis* and the solitary *Isozoanthus giganteus*, which can reach lengths of 19 cm (Hyman, 1940). The column of the polyp is divided into the tube-like scapus and the cap-like capitulum. Polyp walls consist of a thick cuticle that overlays the ectodermis. Between the ectodermis and the endodermis lies a

Figure 2.2
Anatomy of a typical zoanthid colony.
After Hyman 1940

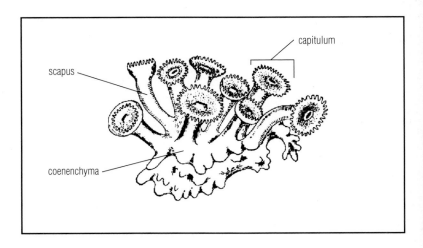

region of gelatinous tissue called the mesogloea. This layer contains numerous small canals and spaces, that link the outer layers with the gastric cavity. The function of these is unknown but they most likely aid in transport of materials throughout the polyp and perhaps act also as a hydrostatic skeleton. The canals may also be related to the transport of products of photosynthesis from the zooxanthellae, much like the zooxanthellal tubules found in tridacnid clams (see volume one), which are also associated with the digestive system. Zooxanthellae are found in these canals (Hyman, 1940) and may also be transported via these canals, allowing for the control of zooxanthellae populations by elimination via the gastric cavity and mouth. The endodermis (=gastrodermis) surrounds the gastric cavity, which contains numerous septa that extend partially or fully towards the actinopharynx. The complete septa have wing-like filaments on their upper ends, as in anemones (Hyman, 1940). The actinopharynx extends upwards towards the oral disc and opens into the small, slit-like mouth. A siphonoglyph is present and is well developed in some genera. The oral disc is surrounded by two rings of unbranched tentacles (usually) that contain nematocysts in varying numbers and types, depending on species. The second ring of tentacles is greatly reduced in some species. The oral disc has a sphincter of muscle around it that acts to open and close the polyp, pulling the tentacles inwards. The extent to which this muscle extends across the mesogloea is used as a diagnostic characteristic for some genera (see chapter eight). Zooxanthellae are found in the endodermis, mesogloeal canals and the ectodermis of some genera (Hyman, 1940).

Colony Anatomy

Zoanthid polyps can be found singly (e.g. *Sphenopus* spp.), in small unconnected groups (e.g. some *Protopalythoa* spp.), in small groups interconnected by a thin coenenchyma (*Zoanthus* spp.), or in colonies connected by a thick coenenchyma with only the oral ends protruding *(Palythoa* spp.). We will discuss colony anatomy in more detail for each genera in chapter eight.

Reproductive Strategies

The most common form of reproduction amongst zoanthids is asexual via their lateral growth over a substratum, be it the reef itself or as in the case of *Acrozoanthus, Epizoanthus* and *Parazoanthus,* over or within other organisms. New polyps can arise from a spreading sheet of coenenchyma, from creeping stolons or via budding from the base of the mother polyp, depending on the genus. It is not uncommon to find colonies several meters in diameter on reef flats; these can sometimes even be formed by hundreds of clones of a single polyp (Mather and Bennett, 1993). Extensive growths of *Zoanthus* spp. for example, are often found along shorelines, literally covering rocks with thick carpets of polyps (pers. obs. Delbeek and Sprung). Asexual reproduction via fragmentation is also common. Clumps of polyps or individuals torn from the substratum can easily reattach and form new colonies. It is these characteristics, coupled with their rapid growth that allows many of the genera to be propagated quite easily in captivity (see chapter six).

Parazoanthus sp. growing over a hydroid in the Solomon Islands. J. Sprung

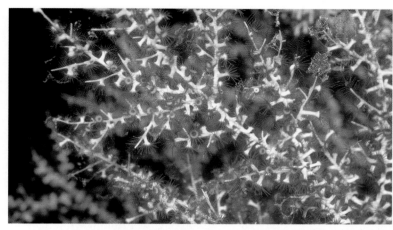

Prolific asexual reproduction results in the typical compact growth form of these *Zoanthus* spp. photographed in an aquarum. J. C. Delbeek

Sexual reproduction has not been well studied in the Zoanthidea but a few interesting facts have come to light. Studies of *Zoanthus*,

Protopalythoa, Palythoa and *Isaurus* have shown that polyps can be either gonochoristic or hermaphroditic (Muirhead and Ryland, 1985; Fadlallah et al., 1984; Ryland and Babcock, 1991). Colonies in the wild have been found to be composed of just male, just female, male and female, or hermaphroditic polyps, depending on the species and the location (see Cooke, 1976; Karlson, 1981; Kimura et.al., 1971; Muirhead et al., 1986; Ryland and Babcock, 1991; Yamazato et al., 1973). These observations raise the possibility that some zoanthid species may be protogynous hermaphrodites.

To date the species studied have been found to be external broadcast spawners, releasing sperm and eggs into the water, where fertilization then occurs. In a population of *Protopalythoa* (formerly *Palythoa*) studied on the Great Barrier Reef, ovaries were found to develop along the mesenteries. Development occurred several months before spawning and spermaries developed later in the reproductive cycle, also along the mesenteries (Ryland and Babcock, 1991). Studies in Jamaica have shown that the average diameter of the ovaries can vary from 274 um to 1885 um (Karlson, 1981). Cooke (1976) found that zoanthids in Kaneohe Bay, Hawaii, had egg diameters ranging from 75 um to 280 um, while spermaries were 50 um to 390 um in diameter. Sperm were observed to be bell-shaped, with a rounded apical end and a bulge basally, with a 50 um long tail. Egg counts in *Protopalythoa* sp. from the Great Barrier Reef ranged from 800 to 2400 eggs per full grown female polyp (Ryland and Babcock, 1991). In the Jamaican zoanthids, once fertilization occurs the larvae eventually settle out in areas of coralline algae growth and crawl along the surface till they find a suitable site, usually along the edges of shaded undersurfaces (Karlson, 1981). Although fecundity is very high in zoanthids, settlement rates appear to be low. Sexual reproduction is therefore thought to allow for dispersal and colonization over large distances, while asexual reproduction via growth and fragmentation, is more important for local colonization.

Spawning generally occurs in the spring in the Caribbean (March-April) and on the Great Barrier Reef in Australia (October - November). In Kaneohe Bay, Zoanthus pacificus was found to be sexually active all year long but the highest percentages of fertile polyps occurred in the summer, while *Palythoa vestitus* was only active from May to September (Cooke, 1976). On the Great Barrier Reef, *Protopalythoa* were found to spawn at the same time as the mass spawning of stony and soft corals. This spawning event seemed to be connected to an increase in water temperatures. Ryland and Babcock (1991) could not find any reproductive activity from January till June while sea temperatures were either rising or falling. Peak water temperature over the year was 31°C and the minimum was 22°C.

Figure 2.3
Larval stages of zoantharia
A. Zoanthina larva of *Zoanthus*.
B. Late stage Zoanthina larva.
C. Zoanthella larva of *Protopalythoa*.

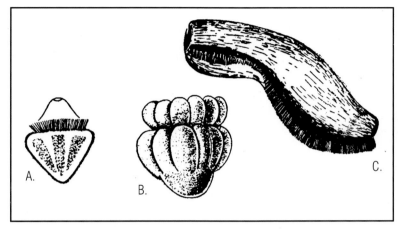

Zoanthina larvae of *Zoanthus* sp. collected in the waters off of Puerto Vallarta, Mexico. J. Sprung

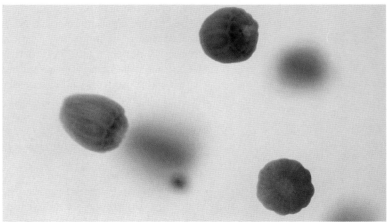

Although the complete development of zoanthids has not yet been described, larval forms of *Zoanthus* and *Protopalythoa* have been found in plankton. Zoanthina are the larvae of *Zoanthus* spp., oval in shape they have a girdle of especially long cilia near the oral end. Zoanthella are the larvae of *Protopalythoa* spp., elongated with a ventral band of very long cilia (Hyman, 1940; see Colin and Arneson 1996 for photos). The importance of sexual reproduction in zoanthids is poorly understood and further studies will be required to determine the frequency, timing, and the effects of seasonal and environmental cues on spawning.

Nutrition

As in stony and soft corals, the role of zooxanthellae in zoanthid nutrition has created some debate, not only amongst scientists but also amongst aquarists. Zoanthids can obtain nutrition in a variety ways: via the translocation of nutrients from zooxanthellae, from the capture of zooplankton, from the capture of detritus and by direct uptake of dissolved nutrients in seawater.

Zooxanthellae have long been known as providers of nutrition to their coral partners, about this there is no debate. However, the degree to which they provide nutrition is not completely known. Numerous studies have shown that the degree to which zooxanthellae contribute nutrition varies from genera to genera, and perhaps even from species to species. *Zoanthus* spp. are generally considered to derive the greatest amount of nutrition from their zooxanthellae. Steen and Muscatine (1984) found that *Zoanthus sociatus* could obtain up to 48% of its required carbon from its zooxanthellae, in what they admit may be an underestimate. Researchers have never observed *Zoanthus* spp. to feed in the wild but they have been able to illicit feeding responses to dead organic materials and amino acids such as proline and glycine (Reimer 1971; Sebens, 1977; Trench, 1974). Trench (1974) found that the internal mesenteries contained numerous cells and nematocysts that would presumably aid in digestion. Sebens (1977) showed through coelenteron content analysis that *Zoanthus sociatus* contained numerous crustacean fragments and detritus, and that numbers were higher at night. However, of 910 polyps studied during the day only 31 contained food items; the number increased very little at night.

Amongst *Protopalythoa* and *Palythoa*, zooxanthellae contribute a smaller portion to the energy budget and feeding takes on a more important role (Steen and Muscatine, 1984). Studies have shown that zoanthids from these genera actively display feeding behaviour and are capable of ingesting whole zooplanktoners such as amphipods and copepods (Reimer, 1971; Sebens, 1977). Azooxanthellate genera such as *Epizoanthus* and *Parazoanthus* obviously rely greatly on feeding to obtain sufficient nutrition.

The role that uptake of exogenous compounds plays in zoanthid nutrition is not fully understood. Reimer (1971) and Trench (1974) have both shown that *Zoanthus* spp. can actively uptake sugars and amino acids, and incorporate these into their metabolism. The fact that both *Zoanthus* spp. and *Protopalythoa* spp. are commonly found in inshore areas with greater turbidity may be explained by the higher organic levels associated with such waters, which the zoanthids could be absorbing. For example, in Kaneohe Bay, Hawaii, *Protopalythoa (Palythoa) vestitus* occurred in large numbers of up to 12,000 polyps per m^2, however, once sewage outfalls were moved further off shore, their numbers began to decline steadily. The occurrence in the intertidal zone places zoanthids where they may periodically (at low tide) be bathed in "spindrift," organic foam concentrated by the wind like a natural protein skimmer.

A general guideline for zoanthids might be that the longer and thinner the tentacles, the greater role feeding plays in their metabolism, and the hobbyist should attempt feeding on a regular basis. However, we should point out that fish feces and stray fish food are usually captured by feeding zoanthids and direct feeding may not be required. A safe rule of thumb would be to feed zoanthids that eagerly accept food. Occasional feedings will benefit them. If they show no interest whatsoever, direct feeding will probably have no benefit. See chapter eight for more information on feeding the various genera.

Growth

As mentioned previously, most zoanthids grow through extension of the tissues that connect the individual polyps. These tissues can vary in morphology depending on the conditions in which they grow. For example, on reefs in Hawaii, *Z. pacificus* develops a lamellar coenenchyme with closely crowded polyps with separate bases. In surge pools, the polyps are not as crowded and the polyp bases are often joined, while on rocky wave-washed shores, the coenenchyme can be lamellar or stoloniferous, with single polyps or groups of two or three (Walsh and Bowers, 1971).

Growth in *Palythoa* spp. involves the spread of the thickened coenenchyma over the substratum. Suchanek and Green (1981) found that *Palythoa caribaeorum* grew along its margin at a rate of 2.5 to 4.0 mm per day. Yamazato and Isa (1981) reported that the Pacific species, *Palythoa tuberculosa*, developed new polyps at the rate of 0.18 polyps per polyp per day.

Not only do zoanthids spread rapidly, they can also grow into very dense colonies. In Discovery Bay, Jamaica, Karlson (1981) found that *Zoanthus sociatus* grew in colonies of up to 671 polyps per 0.1 m^2 while *Z. solanderi* had densities up to 302 polyps per 0.1 m^2. In Kaneohe Bay, Hawaii, *Palythoa vestitus* were found to have colonies of up 12,000 polyps per m^2. Admittedly this was a unusually high density and was attributed to the higher nutrient and detrital levels in the bay at the time of the study. Very little is known about the growth rates and polyp densities of the other genera of zoanthids kept in aquaria such as *Acrozoanthus, Parazoanthus* and *Epizoanthus*; an area where hobbyists could certainly make a contribution. The rapid growth rates of *Zoanthus, Palythoa* and *Protopalythoa* should be taken into consideration when placing new colonies and when planning the aquascaping of the aquarium.

Defense Mechanisms

As we discussed in chapter one, soft corals possess numerous chemicals used for aggressive behaviour against other corals and to deter predation. Zoanthids are similar in that they too possess a host of organic chemicals and physical characteristics used for the same reasons.

Chemical Defenses

It has long been know that zoanthids such as *Zoanthus* and *Palythoa* contain toxic chemicals. Most thoroughly studied of these has been palytoxin, (PTX), considered one of the most poisonous marine toxins known to date (Mereish et al., 1991). Palytoxin acts by changing the electrical properties of the Na-K pump and causes depolarization in heart, skeletal and smooth muscle cells, and nerves resulting in paralysis and eventually death (Seyama, 1991). Gliebs et al. (1995) found this toxic substance in many of the Caribbean species of *Zoanthus* and *Palythoa* but the levels were highly variable and did not appear to correlate with their reproductive cycle or with the amount of zooxanthellae. However, Kimura et al. (1971) found that *Palythoa tuberculosa* in Okinawa possessed high levels of palytoxin during the breeding season, with the majority of the toxin concentrated in the eggs; levels reaching 100,000 MU/g, far exceeding the levels of toxin found in puffer roe. The Hawaiian zoanthid, *Palythoa toxica* contains an especially toxic chemical (most likely palytoxin) within its gastric cavity. Bowers and Walsh (1971) reported that a student collector had to be hospitalized for several days after accidentally touching a colony to an open wound on his hand. It may be that these were gravid polyps and the toxin was concentrated in the gastrovascular cavity due to the presence of eggs. The early Hawaiians were aware of the toxic nature of this zoanthid as they used to dip their spear points in them to make wounds made by them fatal. The Hawaiians named this zoanthid "Limu Maki o Hana", which means "deadly seaweed of Hana" after a location on Maui where they were commonly found in tide pools.

Figure 2.4
A molecular diagram of palytoxin
After Mebs 1989

Palythoa caribaeorum growing on and killing *Mycetophyllia danaana*. The aquarist must avoid placing *Palythoa* spp. next to stony corals because they destroy tissue as they grow, encrusting the coral skeleton. J. Sprung

Why these zoanthids should contain such a potent toxin is not clear. It may play a roll in deterring predation, especially of the eggs. However, palytoxin has been found in crustaceans (*Platypodiella* sp.) and polychaetes (*Hermodice carunculata*, fireworm) that feed on *Palythoa caribaeorum* so its role as a deterrent, at least amongst some organisms, is questionable (Gleibs et al., 1995; Suchanek and Green, 1981). Suchanek and Green (1981) observed that stony corals that were being overgrown by *P. carib-aeorum*, often exhibited areas of dead tissue several cm's from the edge of the zoanthid colony. This could have represented a "zone of death" caused by the release of palytoxin, allowing overgrowth to occur unchallenged. When combined with the rapid growth of zoanthids, these chemicals give them a distinct advantage over other organisms when competing for space on the reef. Given these facts it is somewhat surprising that zonathids do not completely cover all available substrates on a reef. Although predation by organisms such as some polychaetes, certain fish, crabs and gastropods may be a factor, this alone is not enough to explain their lack of dominance. Some stony corals such as *Agaricia* and *Siderastrea* in the Caribbean offer little resistance to *Palythoa caribaeorum* overgrowth, but others such as *Acropora* and *Montastrea* appear to be more resistant (Suchanek and Green, 1981). At this time, the mechanisms that control zoanthid population growth are not yet fully understood.

The anti-oxidant mycosporine-glycine has also been found in the tissues of *Palythoa tuberculosa* (Dunlap and Yamamoto, 1995). This is an anti-oxidant that may allow these corals to break down excess oxygen produced under high levels of illumination and can also act as a UV-B light absorber. Palythinol and palythine were discovered by Dunlap et al. (1986) in *P. tuberculosa* and have also been found to be effective absorbers of UV-B light, especially in the 310-320 nm range, wavelengths damaging to living tissue.

Physical Defenses

Sand grains embedded in the body walls of *Palythoa* and *Protopalythoa* may make them less palatable and may offer some protection against excess light and UV light. Many species of *Zoanthus* and *Protopalythoa* are often found in sandy areas where only their oral disks are visible. The sand may also protect them from excess light and their oral disks can easily retract below the surface of the sand when light becomes too strong or when disturbed.

Nematocysts

Zoanthids contain a collection of nematocysts similar to those found in stony corals. These include spirocysts in the oral disc and tentacles, holotrichs (=homotrichs), isorhizous and microbasic mastigophores (Hyman, 1940). These nematocysts can be used for a variety of purposes such as capturing and holding prey, aggressive interactions, and defense.

In the aquarium one must be careful about placing zoanthids adjacent to stony or soft corals. In general, *Zoanthus* spp. are relatively tame with respect to nettling their neighbors, and they are more likely to be stung themselves. Some species can be in contact with soft or stony corals, neither causing harm to the other. *Protopalythoa* species, in contrast, have much stronger nettling ability, and they are not safe next to most stony corals, though they are generally safe next to most soft corals. *Palythoa* species gradually kill stony corals and may affect some soft corals. A few soft and stony corals are able to sting and kill *Palythoa*, however. In general, most species of *Zoanthus* are compatible with other species of *Zoanthus*, and the different colour forms and polyp sizes of different species can be placed adjacent to each other for a nice pansy-patch effect. Furthermore, most *Protopalythoa* spp. are compatible with *Zoanthus* spp., but there are exceptions. The undescribed Indonesian genus known as "Yellow Polyps" in the aquarium trade may sting some *Zoanthus* or *Protopalythoa* species, or it may be stung by them, so it is best to keep it apart from them. It will also sting and kill stony corals and should be kept at a safe distance because of its rapid growth and ability to spread quickly over the decorations.

Chapter Three **Biology of the Corallimorpharia**

Mushroom anemones are one of the most commonly encountered anthozoans in reef aquaria. When living reef tanks first became popular in the late 1980's, these animals were considered highly unusual and aquarists often strove to acquire as many different colour morphs, species and sizes as possible. Today, corallimorphs are considered amongst the easiest anthozoans to keep in aquaria. Yet there are still aquarists who have difficulty keeping them. This chapter and chapter nine provide the information needed to make keeping them a simple task.

Classification
Corallimorpharians occur throughout the world and are found at all depths in temperate and tropical seas. However, they are a small order with only some forty to fifty species described (den Hartog, 1987). Corallimorphs are generally considered to be inter-mediate in form between stony corals and sea anemones. Although they superficially resemble sea anemones in lacking a calcareous skeleton, anatomically they more closely resemble stony corals: they lack basilar muscles, they may have tissue connections between adult polyps, they lack ciliated tracts on their mesenterial filaments, and their cnidae are similar to scleractinian cnidae (Chadwick, 1987).

If soft coral taxonomy is as messy as a bag full of rotting *Xenia* (chapter one), imagine the same mess without the bag to hold it together and you have an idea of corallimorpharian taxonomy! The organization illustrated in Table 3.1 exemplifies the taxonomy in general acceptance today. Recently, den Hartog (1987; pers. comm.) has proposed eliminating the family Sideractidae and moving the two genera into the Corallimorphidae family. He has also proposed that the family Discosomatidae replace Actinodiscidae and that all the remaining genera, save *Ricordea* be placed into it (den Hartog, 1980). This was based on the conclusion that the morphological characters being used to differentiate the genera were too vague. den Hartog further proposed that all species in the family (except *Amplexidiscus*) be placed in the genus *Discosoma* until more reliable methods were found to delineate the various genera. Although the differences between certain species of *Discosoma* and *Rhodactis* are distinct, the differences between other species are much less so (den Hartog, pers. comm.).

Corallimorpharia can exhibit fantastic fluoresent colours as seen in this *Ricordea florida*.The function of these pigments is unknown.
J. C. Delbeek

A new approach to corallimorpharian taxonomy has recently been undertaken by Dr. Allen Chen. In several papers published in the last two years, he and his co-workers have been using ribosomal DNA and RNA sequencing to try to trace the evolutionary relationships of corallimorpharians, sea anemones and stony corals, as well as between the various corallimorpharian families and genera (Chen *et al*, 1995c; Chen *et al*. 1996; Chen and Miller, 1996). Chen *et al*. (1995c) looked at several taxa from each of the scleractinians, actinarians, and corallimorpharians, and found that all the scleractinian taxa grouped by themselves. The other two groupings contained a mix of both sea anemones and corallimorpharians, indicating an unclear relationship between Actinaria and Corallimorpharia. Studies on the various genera (*Rhodactis, Discosoma* (=*Rhodactis*) placed by den Hartog (1980) into the single genus *Discosoma*, have shown that there are distinct genetic differences between them (Chen and Miller, 1996). The usefulness of these new techniques in clearing the muddy corallimorpharian taxonomy remains to be seen. Unfortunately, recently completed revisions of Indo-Pacific corallimorpharian taxonomy were not available at the time this book went to press.

Table 3.1
Classification of the corallimorpharia

Phylum Cnidaria
    Class Anthozoa
        Order Corallimorpharia Carlgren, 1940

            Family Sideractidae Danielssen, 1890
                Nectactis Gravier, 1918,
                Sideractis Danielssen, 1890

            Family Corallimorphidae R. Hertwig, 1882
                Corallimorphus R. Hertwig, 1882,
                Corynactis Allman,1846,
                Pseudocorynactis den Hartog, 1980

            Family Ricordeidae Watzl, 1922
                Ricordea Duchassaing and Michelotti, 1860

            Family Discosomatidae Duchassaing and Michelotti, 1864
                Amplexidiscus (Dunn and Hamner, 1980),
                Discosoma Ruppell and Leuckart, 1828,
                Metarhodactis Carlgren, 1943,
                Rhodactis Carlgen, 1943

Polyp Anatomy

The anatomy of corallimorpharian polyps is quite similar to that of stony coral polyps. However, there is a great deal of variation between the various families and genera, and there is no "basic" internal anatomy.

Polyps consist of three layers. The internal endoderm surrounds the interior gastrovascular cavity. This cavity contains numerous outgrowths of the endoderm called mesenteries, the gonads and mesenterial filaments. Gonads develop along the mesenteries. The mesenterial filaments are a simple cord of cnido-glandular material. All genera have an abundance of nematocysts embedded within the endoderm. A single mouth (actinopharynx) connects the gastrovascular cavity with the external environment. Some species have an indistinct siphonoglyph but most do not have one. The outer layer, the ectoderm, tends to be thin and lacks nematocysts in some genera. Between these two layers lies a layer of tissue called the mesogloea, which can be rather thin in soft and flexible genera (e.g. *Discosoma*) and thick in more rigid genera (e.g. *Amplexidiscus, Corallimorphus*).

The polyp itself consists of a base that is firmly attached to the substrate in some genera (e.g. *Corynactis, Ricordea* and *Discosoma*) while deep sea genera are often free-living (e.g. *Nectactis*) (den Hartog, 1980). The body column tends to be smooth and lacks specialized organs and can occasionally be separated into a scapus and scapulus. The oral disc can be smooth with small, bump-like tentacles (e.g. *Discosoma*) or can be covered with captitate tentacles (e.g. *Rhodactis*). Tentacles can be very reduced or elongated, sometimes with swollen tips (acrospheres) along the oral disc margins, depending on the genus and/or metabolic state of the animal. The tentacles of some species are retractile while in others they are not (see chapter nine). For more detailed descriptions of polyp anatomy of the various genera, please refer to chapter nine.

Reproductive Strategies

It is no secret that in aquaria corallimorpharians can spread quite rapidly; the same also holds true in nature. It is not unusual to find several square meters of substratum covered with (presumably) clones of one species (Fishelson, 1970; Chadwick and Adams, 1991; Chen *et al.*, 1995a). The most common method for rapid reproduction appears to be asexual. As will be explained later this offers a competitive advantage when it comes to rapidly

The blue Tonga mushroom, which is probably *Rhodactis inchoata*, demonstrates the captitate tentacles characteristic of *Rhodactis* spp. J. C. Delbeek

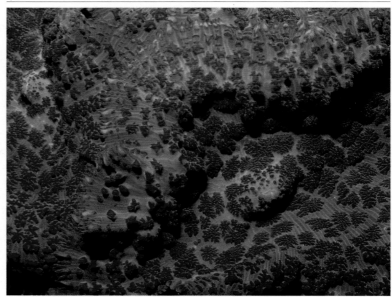

Discosoma sp. polyp showing the lack of well-formed tentacles. Note the distinct mouth and oral cone. J. C. Delbeek

colonizing areas. However, asexual reproduction does not always allow for wide dispersal and does not increase genetic variability, only sexual reproduction can accomplish this. Unfortunately there are have only been a few studies on sexual reproduction in corallimorpharia and this is something that certainly requires further research; an area where hobbyists can no doubt offer some useful observations!

Asexual Reproduction

There are a number of ways in which corallimorpharians have been observed to reproduce asexually in both the wild and in aquaria. In reviewing the literature it became obvious to us that some of the methods we have observed in our aquaria have not

Red *Discosoma* sp. exhibiting asexual reproduction. A new polyp is beginning to form from a portion of the pedal disc stretched over the rock as the parent polyp migrates (by growing). J. C. Delbeek

been reported in the scientific literature. The factors that control asexual reproduction are of equal interest, especially to those who wish to propagate these species. Chen *et al.* (1995a) studying populations of *Rhodactis indosinensis* in Taiwan, found that asexual reproduction peaked in accordance with temperature. Peak rates occurred from June to August, depending on the colony position on the reef. During the course of the study temperatures varied from a high of 28 °C (82 °F) in August to a low of 24 °C (75 °F) in January.

There are currently five forms of asexual reproduction observed in nature and mentioned in the literature and/or observed by us in aquaria. The range of methods varies from genus to genus (see chapter nine for more specific details on each genus).

Corallimorphus profundus with an asexually produced daughter polyp, photographed behind the scenes at the Monterey Bay Aquarium. This species is very similar to species of *Pseudocorynactis*. J. Sprung

The beginning phase of longitudinal fission in a *Rhodactis* sp. The mouth is open and the mesenterial filaments are clearly visible. J. Sprung

Budding

Budding of new polyps off the stalk of corallimorphs has been observed in *Discosoma* spp. and *Amplexidiscus* spp. This form of reproduction can be stimulated by an injury or tear in the stalk, but it also occurs spontaneously, independent of injury. It is most typical for very large polyps to employ this reproductive method. The resulting offspring may remain attached to the stalk or share the same pedal disc for months, it may twist and become severed from the parent, or the parent oral disc may twist and become severed from its pedal disc, leaving the new bud on the disproportionately large stalk. The bud may also "migrate" downwards and divide from the parent at the pedal disc. To the best of our knowledge this method of asexual reproduction for corallimorpharia has not been reported in the scientific literature.

Inverse Budding

Chen *et al.* (1995a) reported that *R. indosinensis* performed a form of asexual reproduction they termed "inverse budding." In this mode, a section of the pedal disc lifts upwards and the two folds

Pedal laceration is clearly demonstrated by this *Discosoma* sp. As the mother polyp migrated toward the light (a growth process) it left behind a portion of the pedal disc, here still connected by a thin thread of tissue. This fragment will develop into a complete polyp within a few weeks. J. Sprung

created fuse together forming the pedal disc of the daughter polyp. The bud is attached to the mother polyp by its oral disc, formed from the oral disc of the mother polyp. As the process proceeds, the bud alternately bends up and down until it detaches itself from the mother polyp. After detachment, the bud settles to the substratum, attaches itself with its pedal disc and forms a mouth and actinopharynx. It takes about a month to produce a bud, and another month for the bud to grow and detach. This form of reproduction may offer a means of dispersal for the colony as the buds are easily carried away by currents, and it may serve to prevent overcrowding in the original colony (Chen *et al.*, 1995a).*

Longitudinal Fission

This reproductive technique is most typical of *Rhodactis* and occurs occasionally in *Discosoma*. The polyp first splits through the mouth and then over a period of days to weeks the oral disc pinches in from the margins in the plane of the split (Chen *et al.* 1995a). Fission then progresses down one side of the split to the pedal base. During fission the polyp is completely bisected

exposing the actinopharynx and the mesenteries. Once fission is complete the torn ends of the column roll inwards and fuse (Chen *et al.*, 1995a). The result is two or more offspring that quickly develop, attaining the size of the original polyp within a few weeks. Over the course of a year Chen *et al.* (1995a) found 99 polyps of *R. indosinensis* asexually reproducing, 73 of which underwent longitudinal fission!

Chen *et al.* (1995a) described a rare form of longitudinal fission in *R. indosinensis* they termed "two-mouth" fission. In this case the mouth only divides and the polyp has two mouths for a few weeks. The oral disc then pinches in from the sides, separating the mouths but leaving the pedal disc intact. Eventually the column splits longitudinally. The whole process takes approximately two months to complete.

Pedal Laceration
Pedal laceration is a fairly simple and common means of asexual reproduction. As the polyp slowly moves over the substratum small sections of the pedal base become torn and are left behind. These small pieces of tissue then quickly form into miniature versions of the mother polyp. Pedal laceration has been observed in *Corallimorphus, Corynactis, Discosoma, Rhodactis,* and *Ricordea* and most likely occurs in the other genera too. *Pseudo-corynactis* normally reproduces asexually via longitudinal fission but probably also employs pedal laceration, though this has not been reported.

Transverse Fission
This method is common in *Discosoma* spp, and it results in short distance transport of the offspring. Transverse fission increases in frequency when the colony becomes crowded as a result of offspring produced by budding and pedal laceration. When crowded, some of the polyps extend their columns into long stalks that cause the oral disc to project upwards into the water current. The currents tend to cause the oral disc to turn and twist, forming a pinched point in the stalk. Within a few days the upper part of the polyp becomes severed from its base and floats away to reattach elsewhere. The remaining stalk re-grows the oral disc in a few weeks.

Sexual Reproduction
Records of sexual reproduction in corallimorpharia are not common in the scientific literature. Most deal only with observa-

tions of the presence of gonads or gametes in collected specimens (e.g. den Hartog, 1980, 1987; Dunn and Hamner, 1980). Only two studies have investigated sexual reproduction in corallimorpharians, Holts and Beauchamp's 1993 paper on *Corynactis californica* and Chen *et al.*'s 1995a paper on *Rhodactis indosinensis.*

Corynactis californica has been shown to be gonochoristic (i.e. they have separate sexes) but many of the colonies are either one sex or the other. It takes approximately five months to develop either eggs or sperm, and spawning takes place in late winter (Holts and Beauchamp, 1993). *Rhodactis indosinensis* differs from *C. californica* in several ways. The eggs are much larger (> 500 um vs. 120-140 um), there are separate sexes within colonies (smaller males on the periphery, larger females in the center), oogenesis takes nine months and spermatogenesis takes three to four months, and spawning takes place from May to June (Chen *et al.*, 1995a). The ovaries of *Rhodactis* were either deep blue, dark red, or pale green coloured, grape-like structures, while mature sperm bundles appeared as elongated white spirals. During non-spawning periods the egg bundles appear as small white spheres.

In a separate study, Chen *et al.* (1995b) found that within colonies of *Rhodactis*, there were definite size and sex differences. Those towards the center were much larger and were all female, while those on the outside tended to be smaller and male. In several anemone species size is dependent on environmental conditions and size is linked to sex (in Chen *et al.* 1995b). It was speculated that environmental conditions on the edges were less favourable than in the middle due to greater exposure to air, hence less energy was available for egg production, while the less energetically demanding sperm could still be easily produced. When small individuals were transplanted to the center they grew in size and became female. Female polyps transplanted to the edges became smaller and some became male. This provided evidence that a polyp's relative position within a colony was more important in determining size and sex, than is age (Chen *et al.* 1995b). These first tantalizing observations indicate that corallimorpharian reproductive biology may offer new insights into reproduction in anthozoans as a whole.

Nutrition
The discussion of nutrition in corallimorpharians can be divided into two parts; nutrition for those that lack zooxanthellae and for those that have them. Members of the families Sideractidae and

Rhodactis sp. displaying the classic onion bulb shape exhibited by feeding Discosomatidae. J. C. Delbeek

This close-up of *Amplexidiscus fenestrafer* clearly shows the nematocyst-bearing ring of marginal discal tentacles. J. Sprung

Corallimorphidae do not possess zooxanthellae and must acquire energy through feeding. As a result genera in these families have the widest variety and greatest numbers of nematocysts. The sticky tentacles of *Corynactis* spp. and especially *Pseudocorynactis* spp. are usually extended at night and are capable of capturing food items including zooplankton, small crustaceans and small fish (den Hartog, 1980). *Nectactis* and *Sideractis*, are deep water corallimorphs speculated to feed on detritus and jellyfish (den Hartog, 1987). Deep-dwelling *Corallimorphus* spp. also feed on a wide variety of small live foods and have very sticky tentacles.

Zooxanthellate families include the Ricordeidae and the Discosomatidae. The major difference between the two families is that tentacles of the members of the Discosomatidae do not possess spirocyst nematocysts (except *Amplexidiscus* which may have small numbers of them), generally felt to be indicative of their ability to capture prey (den Hartog, 1980). As in the Corallimorphidae, *Ricordea* spp. have a full compliment of nematocyst types but their spirocysts are quite small and much less numerous. As a result they are still capable of catching small prey items and the occasional feeding is encouraged in aquaria (see chapter nine). However, the presence of zooxanthellae probably accounts for a large portion of their nutritional requirements (den Hartog, 1980).

Despite the lack of spirocysts there is a wide degree of feeding behaviour observed in the Discosomatidae. It is generally agreed that given the large amounts of zooxanthellae found in the genera of this family, they are primarily autotrophic in nature (den Hartog, 1980, Hamner and Dunn, 1980; Miles, 1991). They lack nematocysts on their outer surface, but have them concentrated internally and around the mouth, and since they lack prey capturing spirocysts, den Hartog (1980) proposed that feeding played a very insignificant role in their nutrition, though uptake of dissolved nutrients directly across the body column could not be ruled out. However, subsequent studies by Hamner and Dunn (1980) and Miles (1991) have shown that some genera are in fact quite active feeders. For example *Amplexidiscus fenestrafer* (Elephant Ear polyps) feeds by enveloping its prey within a sac it creates with its body wall. The sides of the polyp move upwards and the top edge draws closed just like the purse strings on a pouch, preventing the prey from escaping. This entire process can occur as quickly as three seconds! The closing rate of *Rhodactis howesii* and *Discosoma* (=*Actinodiscus*) *fungiformis* is much slower; ten seconds to one minute. The upper margin of the body wall of *Amplexidiscus* contains marginal discal tentacles that do possess ectodermal nematocysts and these presumably function to prevent prey from escaping through the rapidly closing opening of the sac (Hamner and Dunn, 1980). Once the top is closed the mouth is opened and the prey is ingested. Similar behaviour was observed in *Rhodactis howesii* and *Discosoma* (=*Actinodiscus*) *fungiformis*, but in these species the mesenterial filaments were

Crowding is evident in this group of *Discosoma* sp. *Discosoma* spp. can rapidly cover rocks and glass in aquaria via asexual proliferation and rapid growth. J. C. Delbeek

extruded into the cavity and the large numbers of nematocysts (homotrichs) contained in these are thought to subdue the prey (Hamner and Dunn, 1980). However, *A. fenestrafer* does not extrude its mesenterial filaments and how the prey is subdued is not known. A mucus is excreted from the gastrovascular cavity into the sac and it is possible that some sort of toxin within this mucus subdues the prey. Fish left in this mucus for ten minutes or more generally do not recover even if moved to another aquarium with fresh seawater (Hamner and Dunn, 1980).

Elliott and Cook (1989) showed that the Caribbean corallimorpharian *Discosoma sanctithomae* relies on zooxanthellae for its nutritional requirements during the day but at night the polyps exhibit morphological changes designed to capture prey items. In the evening, a semi-transparent membrane along the outer edge of the polyp expands, greatly increasing the surface area of the polyp. When prey contact the discal tentacles this outer membrane folds inwards, capturing the prey against the mouth within a few seconds. Within forty five minutes to an hour the prey is ingested; again no mesenterial filaments are extruded. Undigested remains are excreted one to two days later. As in *Amplexidiscus*, the marginal tentacles possess abundant nematocysts which may aid in preventing escape or subduing the prey item.

In our experience, most Discosomatidae do not require direct feeding to do well in aquaria as they often receive enough food from stray fish food, or from planktonic organisms at night. In some cases such as with *Amplexidiscus* and *Rhodactis*, the occasional direct feeding is quite beneficial. Feeding also increases growth and the rate of asexual reproduction. A general rule with mushroom anemones is that if they have large bumps or tentacle-shaped protrusions, they may accept additional feedings. Smooth surfaced forms, however, generally obtain enough nutrition from their zooxanthellae or via mucus and ciliary feeding on bacteria, detritus and small zooplankton (see chapter nine for more detailed information on feeding the individual species).

Growth

Few studies have been conducted on growth rates in corallimorpharians. As Chen *et al.* (1995b) pointed out, it is possible that size is controlled by environmental factors such as temperature and desiccation, as it is in some sea anemones. In our aquaria, it is not unusual for colonies of *Discosoma* and *Rhodactis* spp. to spread quickly, while others such as *Ricordea* spread much more slowly. Since asexual reproduction represents the primary means by which corallimorphs spread in our aquaria it stands to reason that factors affecting this will determine the rate of colony and polyp growth. Chen *et al.* (1995a) demonstrated a significant positive relationship between temperature and the rate of asexual reproduction. It is possible that other factors such as nutritional status and perhaps light intensity will also be shown to play an important role in colony growth rates.

Aggressive and Defensive Mechanisms

Corallimorpharians share space on the reef with a multitude of other organisms. As a result, they have developed strategies for protecting or expanding their growing areas. These can include the capacity to move across substrates, to reproduce asexually and to damage or kill neighbouring organisms (Chadwick and Adams, 1991).

Movement

In one of the few studies done on corallimorpharian locomotion Chadwick (1991) showed that the temperate corallimorph, *Corynactis californica*, could move up to 14 mm a month. Not a very rapid movement, but given enough time, colonies can cover wide areas. The slow rate of movement compared to other anthozoans such as sea anemones, should not come as a surprise since, unlike sea anemones, corallimorphs lack basal muscles, thereby severely limiting their ability to move laterally. No formal studies have been done on the other corallimorpharian genera but it seems likely that movement over the substratum is not a very effective way for corallimorphs to colonize new areas.

Asexual Reproduction

As mentioned in the previous section on reproduction, corallimorpharians exhibit a variety of asexual reproduction methods. Although few studies have been performed to ascertain the frequency of asexual reproduction in corallimorpharians, Chen *et al.* (1995a) did find that up to 25% of the polyps in colonies of *Rhodactis indosinensis* were in the process of asexual reproduction in the summer months. In aquaria, the rapid spread of corallimorphs, especially those in the zooxanthellate families Ricordeidae and Discosomatidae, is self-evident. Wilkens (1990) reported that blue morphs of *Discosoma* (*Actinodiscus*) could produce 15 to 25 new polyps per year in aquaria. It is not uncommon in nature to find several square meters of reef covered by colonies of *Discosoma, Ricordea* or *Rhodactis* (Fishelson, 1970; den Hartog, 1980; Wilkens, 1990). Chadwick and Adams (1991) found that the average rate of polyp production in *Corynactis californica* was 46.1 polyps per year, while the average time required to double the number of polyps in a colony was 2 months. Given that Chen *et al.* (1995a) found that the percentage of polyps undergoing asexual reproduction was greatest in the warmer summer months it seems probable that expansion of a colony can occur quite rapidly in tropical species but much slower in temperate species due to lower water temperatures.

Aggressive and Defensive Structures

All corallimorpharians possess nematocysts. There are a wide variety of nematocysts and it is not our intent to go into detail on the different types, suffice it to say that some are specialized for capturing food items (e.g. spirocysts) while others play defensive or aggressive roles (e.g. homotrichs) (see den Hartog, 1980, for a complete description of the various types). Nematocysts can be found in tentacles, the swollen tips of tentacles (acrospheres), the mesenterial filaments and the body column, and are used as taxonomic characters for identification purposes (see den Hartog, 1980).

Figure 3.2
Some types of nematocysts found in corallimorphs
After Schmidt, 1974

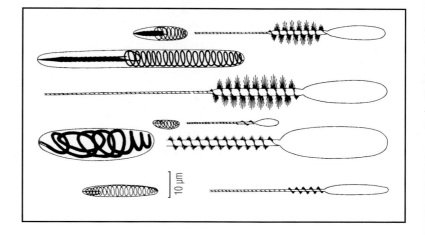

Aggressive interactions in corallimorphs have only been observed in two genera, *Corynactis* (spirocysts and homotrichs) and *Discosoma* (homotrichs). However, all genera possess at least some form of nematocysts, and these can be quite potent, especially in *Pseudocorynactis*, and is likely that further studies will bring this to light.

Mesenterial Filaments

Studies of aggression in the temperate species, *Corynactis californica*, have shown that these corallimorphs can be quite lethal to adjacent organisms such as sea anemones and corals. Upon contact with an adjacent organism the tentacles will retract and then stretch out again. After a few hours of this behaviour mesenterial filaments begin to appear from the mouth, the tips of the tentacles, the body column, or from the base of the polyp (Chadwick, 1987). The mesenterial filaments can extend from 1.0 to 42.0 mm from the polyp and completely envelop the neighbouring organism. These filaments are packed with nematocysts and digestive enzymes. Not only can they destroy adjacent coral tissue, they can also digest large prey items and then ingest them (Chadwick, 1987). *Corynactis californica* has also been observed to use these filaments to protect themselves from one of their major predators, the sea star *Dermasterias imbricata* (in Chadwick, 1987). It is possible that the Caribbean species *C. parvula* may also be able to extrude mesenterial filaments so aquarists should keep this in mind when placing other organisms close to

White stringy mesenterial filaments are clearly visible through the epidermis of this *Rhodactis* sp. viewed from below. Some of these filaments are extending towards the marginal tentacles. This specimen has lifted up its base, providing a rare glimpse of the basal structure J. Sprung

it. The aggressive behaviour of *C. californica* also acts to control species distribution in its habitat by affecting larval settlement (it eats the larvae) or by killing newly settled larvae within reach of its mesenterial filaments (Chadwick, 1991). They have also been shown to allow for greater survivability of large clam populations growing within their colonies by slowing predation on clams by sea stars (Patton, *et al.*, 1991); the sea stars presumably get "hot feet"!

Other corallimorphs have been observed to release mesenterial filaments from the mouth and distal tentacles too. Hamner and Dunn (1980) found that *Rhodactis howesii* extruded mesenterial

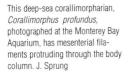

This deep-sea corallimorpharian, *Corallimorphus profundus,* photographed at the Monterey Bay Aquarium, has mesenterial filaments protruding through the body column. J. Sprung

filaments into a cavity it formed with its body wall to digest entrapped food items. Miles (1991) reported that the Caribbean corallimorph *Discosoma sanctithomae* would extrude mesenterial filaments from the mouth and through the body wall upon initial contact with other anthozoans. In addition, both species could transfer mesenterial filaments to, and out of, the tips of the distal tentacles. So it is possible that other corallimorphs have similar abilities and the aquarist should take this into consideration when placing corallimorphs near other corals. Wilkens (1990) mentioned the negative effects of proximal colonies of corallimorphs on adjacent stony corals. He speculated that this was some form of chemical attack. However, as far as we are aware, there are no records in the scientific literature concerning allelochemicals produced by corallimorphs. It is possible that the effects observed by Wilkens could have been the result of extruded mesenterial filaments or mucus. We have also observed negative effects of corallimorphs on several species of stony coral including *Acropora* and *Lobophyllia,* and on gorgonians. Lastly, it is not uncommon to see mesenterial filaments expelled from the mouth of *Discosoma* when that have been disturbed; these are usually retracted within a few hours (see chapter nine).

Specialized Structures

In 1976, while observing photos taken of *Discosoma* (*Rhodactis*) *sanctithomae* in Curacao in 1973, J.C. den Hartog noticed that stony corals adjacent to *Discosoma* colonies showed necrotic areas and that the corallimorphs possessed odd looking white vesicles on the tips of their marginal tentacles. Upon closer examination of

Ricordea yuma exhibiting elongated marginal tentacles. Note the white tips indicative of acrosphere development. To the best of our knowledge this is the first report of these structures in *Ricordea*.
J. C. Delbeek

preserved specimens he found that the swollen tips of these tentacles contained larger and more numerous homotrich nematocysts than "normal" marginal tentacles, and postulated that these were the result of aggressive interactions (den Hartog, 1977).

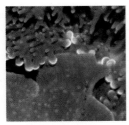

The whitening of the edges of the marginal tentacles in this *Rhodactis* sp. is indicative of an increasing concentration of nematocysts, here being used for defense against a *Discosoma* sp. J. C. Delbeek

In chapter nine we show the development of special structures in response to illumination. The extent of development of the tentacles on the oral disc, their shape and colour, is correlated to light intensity and U.V. wavelengths.

Later experiments and observations by Miles (1991) confirmed den Hartog's suspicions. When placed close to other anthozoans, *D. sanctithomae* were found to react immediately by extruding mesenterial filaments from the mouth and distal tentacle tips. Mesenterial filaments were observed to move into the distal tentacles over a period of a few days, causing the initial swelling of the tentacle tips. Acrospheres then form and give the tips an opaque appearance. The ectoderm layer of these outer tentacles then slowly thickened as it became engorged with homotrich nematocysts, furthering the swollen appearance. Miles (1991) found that once induced, these swollen tips remained. One interesting observation was that the intensity of the response varied depending on the species of stony coral involved. *Agaricia agaricites,* a relatively weakly stinging coral, invoked a slow, graded response that eventually resulted in acrosphere development. However, *Meandrina meandrites*, which would sting the corallimorphs badly on initial contact, caused the remaining *Discosoma* polyps to develop large and numerous acrospheres within a few days. Often the entire distal margin would become greatly thickened such that individual tentacles were barely distinguishable; no doubt these are the "monstrosities" referred to by den Hartog (1977), (Miles, 1991). Similar tentacular modifications can be seen in *Rhodactis* spp. kept in aquaria, where the marginal tentacles will elongate greatly and form bulbous, opaque tips. Aquarists should keep this in mind when placing members of this genus close to other anthozoans!

Chemical Compounds

As we mentioned above, we were unable to find any reference to the presence of allelochemicals in corallimorphs. However, Hamner and Dunn (1980) observed that prey appeared to be narcotized within the sac *Amplexidiscus fenestrafer* forms to trap prey. Presumably the mucus released from the gastrovascular cavity into the oral cavity during feeding contains a toxic agent that immobilizes the prey. Miles (1991) also did not observe mesenterial filaments within the sac formed by feeding *D. sanctithomae*, and could not ascertain how the prey was subdued; perhaps this chemical is also present in this species. Given the great deal of interest in chemically active compounds in marine organisms it is probable that specimens of corallimorphs have already been collected and are merely awaiting analysis.

Chapter Four

Biology of Sea Anemones

Introduction

What is a Sea Anemone?

The definition of the term "Sea Anemone" is not always clear to the average observer of marinelife. There are numerous members of the phylum Cnidaria (Coelenterata) that look like anemones, are related to anemones, but are not true sea anemones. What distinguishes true sea anemones from the rest is clearly defined for the scientist, as we shall shortly explain.

Classification

In our descriptions here we use some words not often found in everyday discussion, so we advise readers to keep a finger or book-mark in the glossary to be able to refer to it for helpful definitions.

Early descriptions of the sea anemones noted their obvious plant-like appearance, hence the name zoophyta, literally "animal plants." Now known as Anthozoa, the "flower-animals" include corals, anemones, and anemone-like creatures. Sea anemones belong to the phylum Cnidaria which was formerly known as the phylum Coelenterata, a name still in common usage. Several features distinguish sea anemones from their close relatives. Along with corals, anemones are in the class Anthozoa. They belong to the subclass Hexacorallia, which differs from all other Cnidaria and the other subclass of Anthozoa, Octocorallia, on the basis of the possession of spirocysts. Spirocysts are stinging cells or cnidae that have the distinction of being non-penetrating and glutinant. Hexa-corallia are further distinguished by never having the eight pinnate tentacles or eight unpaired mesenteries that characterize Octoco-rallia (soft corals). True sea anemones are placed in the order Actiniaria. Members of this order typically have a flat pedal disc for attachment (though not all of them do), a distinct column, and an oral disc with tentacles. The mouth is a slit-shaped opening in the center of the oral disc. At one or both ends of the mouth there is a ciliated groove called a siphonoglyph which transports water into the gastrovascular cavity. Other anemone-like creatures belong to the orders Ceriantharia (tube anemones), Zoantharia (zoanthid anemones), and Madreporaria, which includes the suborder Scler-actinia (stony corals) and the suborder Corallimorpharia ("mush-

The loveliest of the clownfishes, *Amphiprion percula*, in its host anemone *Stichodactyla gigantea*. *Amphiprion percula* living in *S. gigantea* tend to have more black pigment than those living in *H. magnifica*. This perfect portrait was taken in the Solomon Islands. J. Macare

These look like sea anemones but are actually corallimorpharians. *Corynactis* is on the left, and *Pseudocorynactis* on the right.
J. Sprung

These anemone-like creatures are also corallimorpharians. *Discosoma* (*Rhodactis*) *sanctithomae* is on the left and *Ricordea florida* on the right.
J. Sprung and J. C. Delbeek

These "colonial anemones" are not true anemones. They belong to the order Zoanthidea (Zoantharia).
J. C. Delbeek and J. Sprung

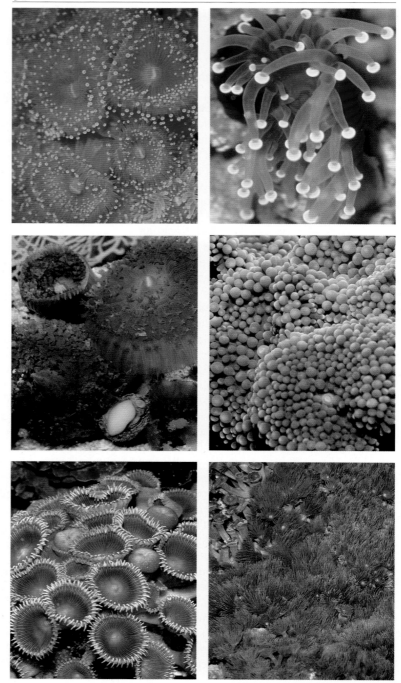

Cerianthid anemones belong to the order Ceriantharia, and are not true sea anemones. J. C. Delbeek

Several stony corals with large fleshy polyps such as *Catalaphyllia*, left and *Heliofungia*, right are easily mistaken for sea anemones.
J. C. Delbeek and S. W. Michael

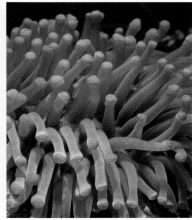

The siphonoglyphs of *Stichodactyla gigantea* are quite conspicuous. These are the objects that look like cooked barley with a pinkish groove on opposite sides of the mouth. J. Sprung

room" or "disc" anemones and strawberry anemones). The Actiniaria are separated additionally into suborders, tribes and families. While there are many genera and species of true anemones (about 1000 species), the scope of this book does not allow their description. We are only concerned with those sea anemones that are commonly maintained in tropical aquaria.

Table 4.1
Systematics of Sea Anemones
Not all species are shown. This table primarily features species covered by this text.

Phylum Cnidaria, Class Anthozoa

Subclass Octocorallia
Subclass Hexacorallia
    Order Ceriantharia
        Cerianthus spp.
    Order Madreporaria
      Suborder Scleractinia
      Suborder Corallimorpharia
    Order Zoanthidea
    Order Antipatharia
    Order Ptychodactiaria
    Order Actiniaria
      Suborder Protantheae
        Family Gonactiniidae
      Suborder Endocoelantheae
      Suborder Nyantheae
        Tribe Boloceroidaria
          Family Boloceroididae
          Family Aliciidae
            Lebrunia coralligens
            Lebrunia danae
            Phyllodiscus semoni
        Tribe Mesomyaria
          Family Diadumenidae
          Family Aiptasiidae
            Aiptasia pallida
            Aiptasia pulchella
            Bartholomea annulata
            Capnea lucida
          Family Aiptasiomorphidae
          Family Hormathiidae
            Calliactis spp.
          Family Metridiidae
          Family Acontiophoridae
          Family Sargartiidae

Family Actinostolidae
Family Halcampidae
Tribe Endomyaria
Family Edwardsiidae
Family Haloclavidae
Family Actiniidae
Actinia spp.
Anemonia spp.
Anthopleura spp.
Bunodosoma granulifera
Bunodosoma cavernata
Condylactis spp.
Entacmaea quadricolor
Gyrostoma spp.
Macrodactyla doreenensis
Family Phymanthidae
Phymanthus spp.
Epicystis crucifer
Family Stichodactylidae
Heteractis crispa
Heteractis magnifica
Heteractis malu
Stichodactyla gigantea
Stichodactyla haddoni
Stichodactyla helianthus
Stichodactyla mertensii
Family Actinodendridae
Actinodendron plumosum
Family Thalassianthidae
Cryptodendrum adhaesivum
Heterodactyla hemprichii
Thalassianthus aster

Polyp anatomy

True sea anemones are solitary polyps. Many species reproduce asexually, resulting in large stands of adjacent clones, but these stands of identical individuals are not colonies in the strict sense because they are not interconnected.

The body of an anemone can be thought of as a hollow tube, closed at one end and open at the other, kind of like a sock. The major portion of the sea anemone is formed by the column, which has at its aboral end a flattened pedal disc for attaching to the substrate, and at its other end the oral disc bearing numerous hollow tentacles.

Figure 4.1a
Sea anemone body plan.
Longitudinal section and cross
sections. *After Barnes, 1980*

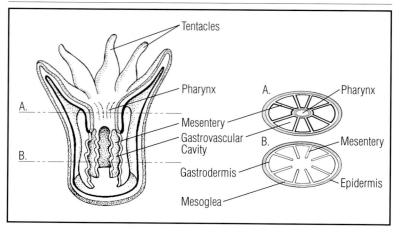

The construction of anemones is accomplished with three tissue layers: an outer ectoderm, inner endoderm, and a mesogloea sandwiched in between. The three tissue layers are essentially laminar but highly folded to form the large surface of mesenteries that partition the coelenteron. The body plan is radially symetrical, though the radial symmetry of anthozoa is properly termed "biradial symmetry" because their mesenteries occur as couples on opposite sides of a plane bisecting the mouth, actinopharynx, and siphonoglyph(s). This bilateral symmetry is related to the hydrostatic design (Pantin, 1960) and the need to ventilate the coelenteron, especially in large anemones (Hyman, 1940).

The mesenteries not only provide a large surface area for gas exchange, they are also an important site of digestion of food (see the topic feeding), and development of gametes (see topic reproduction). Descriptions of mesenteries often refer to them being "complete" or "incomplete." If one imagines an anemone cut in cross section, the mesenteries form what looks like spokes, with the body wall that forms the column in the wheel position and the pharynx located at the hub. Complete mesenteries are attached to the column wall on one side and the wall of the pharynx on the other. Their presence provides structural support that facilitates the hydrostatic skeleton achieved by muscular contraction against the water filled cavities. Incomplete mesenteries are attached to the column wall only, extending part of the way into the gastrovascular cavity, the lower part of the coelenteron below the pharynx, where prey items are digested. Mesenteries occur in "cycles" that are usually in multiples of twelve. The primary cycle

Figure 4.1b

Sea Anemone Morphology

After Shick, 1991

This diagram is based on an imaginary anemone that has features of endomyaria and mesomyaria.

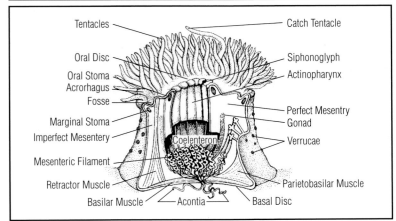

Figure 4.1c

Cross Section of an Anemone

After Hyman, 1940

Top section is at the level of the pharynx, bottom is below the pharynx.

2. siphonoglyph
6. epidermis
7. mesogloea
8. circular muscle layer
9. gastrodermis
10. primary septa
11. secondary septa
12. tertiary septa
13. retractor muscle
14. directives
15. pharynx
16. mesenterial filament

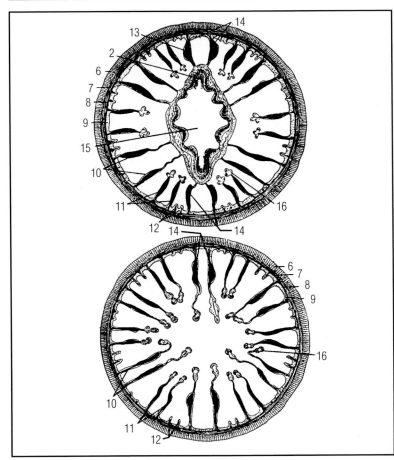

of, for example, 12 mesenteries may be complete, while secondary and tertiary cycles of mesenteries positioned between them may be complete or incomplete. In the pharyngeal region complete mesenteries have holes in them that allow water to pass through. Below the pharynx the mesenteries have a free (unattached) margin that recurves toward the column wall. This unattached margin has three lobes and is called a mesenterial filament. It is important in digestion of food. The side lobes on the mesenterial filament have ciliated cells which aid in water circulation within the coelenteron. The middle lobe is armed with nematocysts and lined with enzyme-secreting gland cells. At the base of the mesenterial filament the middle lobe may continue as a thread-like structure called an acontium. This structure serves digestive function and also a defensive role as anemones with acontia may eject the filaments through the body wall in response to a disturbance. The filaments can sting and partially digest the tissue of an attacking organism. Anemones without acontia (as well as corallimorpharia and stony corals) may also eject whitish stringy mesenterial filaments through the mouth or body wall for defense or agression.

Defensive and other notable structures

Acontia and mesenterial filaments

We just mentioned that these thread-like processes, which serve primarily a digestive function, can also be used for defense against predators or other anemones encroaching on the territory. The extrusion of these whitish threads through the mouth or column wall of an anemone is usually a sign of physical distubance such as rough handling, excessive water flow, inadequate water flow, or stinging by a neighboring invertebrate, for example. It can also be a sign that something is wrong about the temperature or water quality, but normally the disturbance is physical.

Acrorhagi

These structures are finger-like projections forming a collar on the upper column just below the oral disc. They are loaded with potent nematocysts and anemones use them in aggressive interactions with other anemones.

Verrucae

Similar in appearance to acrorhagi but extending down the column, these bump-like structures serve an adhesive function,

The verrucae of an uncommon purple morph of *Macrodactyla doreensis*. J. Sprung

The verrucae of this *Stichodactyla mertensii* adhere to the rock, helping to maintain the open-face position of the oral disc in strong water motion. J. Sprung

tending to hold the flattened oral disc down against the substrate. The presence or absence of these structures is an important dignostic character in anemone identification.

Cnidae

Cnidae are special structures (organelles) produced by cells called cnidocytes in the tissues of members of the phylum Cnidaria. They are capsules ranging in size from ca. 10 to 100 micrometres in length, and contain a needle-like eversible tube. The capsule and tube are secreted by the Golgi apparatus (another organelle in the cell). The tube is inverted into the capsule by an unknown process (Shick, 1991).

Cnidae serve several functions and they come in different types that have different functions. Some are for capture and envenomation of prey, some for defense, others are merely adhesive (glutinant), and some (as in cerianthid anemones) help to build a tube in which the anemone dwells. A particular type may serve more than one function. Function is also related to location on the anemone.

Different types of cnidae have been described and their structure is useful in taxonomic classification of Cnidaria (see Shmidt, 1974, Doumenc and Foubert, 1984, and Fautin, 1988). There are three major types of Cnidae: spirocysts, ptychocysts, and nematocysts. Anthozoans produce all three types. Spirocysts occur in Hexacorallia only. Ptychocysts are found in Ceriantharia (tube-dwelling anemones) only, and the fired remains of them form a mesh with which cerianthids build their tube. The nematocysts of actiniaria, the most diverse order of Anthozoa, are likewise highly varied (see Shmidt, 1974). Nematocysts occur in two basic categories (Weill, 1934): haplonemes and heteronemes. In haplonemes neither the tube nor its armature are divided into distinct regions (though gradual tapering is typical). In heteronemes, which always have spines, a distinct basal shaft is distinguished from the distal tube by its abruptly larger diameter, bigger spines, or both (Shick, 1991). Haplonemes include rare atrichs that lack spines, and holotrichs that have spines. The holotrichs may have spines of similar diameter and concentration along the entire length of the tube, in which case they are called isorhizous. If they have a gradual but obvious change in the spine diameter or concentration along the length of the tube they are called anisorhizous. Heteronemes are also divided into two types: p-mastigophores and b-mastigophores. The p-mastigophores, sometimes called p-rhabdoids, have a shaft that is always thicker than the thread (distal tube), and they meet at a distinctive funnel-shaped junction (Shick, 1991). There are further classifications of p-mastigophores! If the undischarged shaft is longer than the capsule and therefore folded inside it, the nematocyst is called a macrobasic p-mastigophore. If the shaft is shorter than the capsule and therefore unfolded, it is a microbasic p-mastigophore. Amastigophores are p-mastigophores in which the terminal portion of the distal tube may break off and remain inside the capsule after discharge. Finally, the b-mastigophores, also known as basitrichs or b-rhabdoids, have the undischarged shaft inside the capsule lying like a straight harpoon, tapering into the spiny thread that usually coils evenly around the shaft (see Figure 4.3). Learning the structures of

Figure 4.2
Some cnidae of sea anemones
After Schmidt, 1974

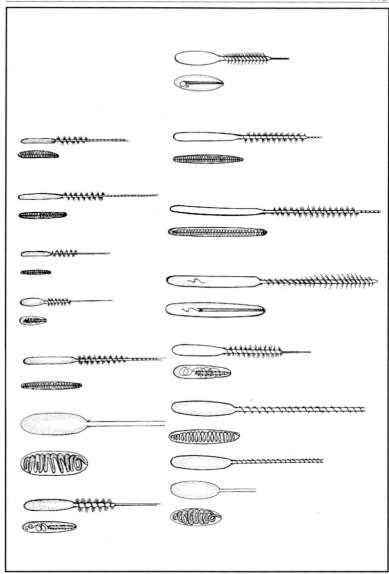

the different cnidae is an exercise reminiscent of the memorization of different types of sclerites in soft corals. It seems to be only for the most patient among us! If you really want to explore cnidae some more, an interesting review of different types of cnidae and their importance in taxonomic relationships was given by Schmidt, (1974).

The production and maintenance of the cnidae are major energy consuming aspects to the metabolism of an anemone. Adenosine Triphosphate (ATP) is known to be important for the maturation and maintenance of cnidae (Shick, 1991, Greenwood, Johnson and Mariscal, 1989). For this reason anemones in captivity which do not have adequate sources of food eventually are unable to maintain their cnidae. First they shrink in size as they consume their own body mass for maintenance energy requirements, then they lose their "stickiness" and hence their ability to capture prey.

Table 4.2
Prey items found in anemones
After Shick, 1991

Crustaceans
- Amphipods
- Barnacle remains
- Carcinus appendages
- Copepods
- crustacean fragments
- cypris larvae
- Euphausids
- Gnathia
- Isopods
- large and small decapods
- Mysid
- Nauplii
- Ostracods

Molluscs
- Mussels
- Bivalves
- Gastropods
- Chitons
- Lamellibranchs
- Opisthobranchs

Odds and ends
- Algal detritus
- Fish
- Fish eggs
- Fish scales
- Insects
- Medusa
- Polychaetes (and fragments)
- Asteroid bipennariae
- Bryozoan fragments
- Cyphonautes larvae
- Detritus
- Echinoderm larvae
- Echinoid spines
- Fecal pellets
- Flatworms
- Foraminiferans
- Hydroid fragments
- Nematodes
- Seagrass fragments
- Scyphozoans
- Sipunculids
- Sponge spicules

Conversely, it is important to note that well fed anemones also lose "stickiness," but this is a temporary condition. This satiation effect and inhibition of discharge was studied by Sandberg (1972), Mariscal (1973), Bigger, (1982), and Shelton (1982). The causes are not fully understood but may relate to the anemone (or its tentacles) becoming flaccid after eating (Bigger, 1982, Shick, 1991), which reduces the sensitivity of the cnidae - (see description of ciliary cone complex under the next topic feeding). Other possibilities for the temporary inhibition of cnidae discharge in well fed anemones include detection of body column distension (when it is full of food) by stretch receptors, or detection of digested food products by endodermal chemoreceptors. The advantage to the anemone of such satiation-inhibition is that it prevents wasteful discharge of (metabolically expensive) cnidae to capture excess food which could not be ingested (Mariscal, 1973). It is interesting to note here that aquarists have observed captive *Entacmaea quadricolor* elongate their tentacles when they are "hungry" and then shorten them into the typical "bubble-tipped" shape when they are satiated (Jakubowski, 1995).

Nutrition

Anemones in general are able to make use of many different food sources, and they are thus called "polyphagous opportunists," (like certain people we know!) We commonly think of anemones as predators with a powerful sting that is deadly to most fish and other small creatures that come in contact with the tentacles. Many anemones fit this description, but many also utilize particulate matter or dissolved organic and inorganic compounds as food. Of course those anemones which harbour zooxanthellae also have a built-in source of food and nutrient recycling, just like the hermatypic corals and giant clams.

Diet

Although anemones are opportunistic feeders, the majority of prey items captured are various types of crustaceans, due no doubt to the abundance and diversity of crustaceans in their environment. Insects may even be taken occasionally (Ayre, 1984). Fish, worms, and algal fragments are among other prey items. Although gastropod molluscs are not common prey for most anemones, they are a major component of the diet of some sand dwelling anemones such as *Heteractis malu* (Shick, 1991), and may be important for other sand dwellers such as *Stichodactyla haddoni, S. gigantea,* and *Macrodactyla doreensis.* It is interesting to note that the bottom dwelling anemone-like Caryophyllid coral *Catala-phyllia jardinei* has been observed to capture and eat herbivorous snails that contact its tentacles in aquaria (J. Sprung, pers. obs.), and this habit leaves piles of shells around the coral. Such behaviour serves a function in addition to nutrition for the coral. The pile of shells that accumulates around the base helps to stabilize the coral's position when it lives in a soft-bottom muddy environment. Snail-eating anemones may gain a similar advantage. Some anemones are suspension feeders (Barnes, 1980) that captures plankton via nematocysts and mucus on the surface of the oral disc, passing the trapped food via cillia and tentacle movement to the mouth. Such food can be duplicated in captivity with *Artemia* nauplii or liquid invertebrate suspensions. Table 4.2 provides a list of typical prey items for anemones.

Feeding

Discharge of Cnidae

The capture of prey by anemones usually involves the use of cnidae to seize the prey. In most anemones thus far studied the cnidome (complement of cnidae) consists of only three types: spirocysts that are glutinant and hold the prey; microbasic p-mastigophores that penetrate and capture the prey; and b-mastigophores that are used both to penetrate and capture the prey and for defense (Shick, 1991; Mariscal, 1974b). Toxins injected into the prey also help to immobilize it.

The discharge of nematocysts is triggered by a structure called the ciliary cone complex, which is sensitive to mechanical and chemical stimuli. The structure consists of a nematocyte that contains microvilli and a kinocillium, the former contributing mostly to chemical reception and the latter to mechanical reception. Additionally, cells around the central cillary cone complex may also have microvilli. The microvilli can be imagined as being like taste buds on our tongues while the kinocillium is reminiscent of the hair cells in the vertebrate ear (Shick, 1991).

Food Capture

Since they are sessile creatures, sea anemones depend on water motion (or gravity or the blundering motion of motile prey) to carry food to them. Shick, 1991, notes three basic modes of prey cature: 1.) Planktonic prey caught in the tentacles are passed to the mouth by muscular action or sometimes by the action of cilia (on the oral disc or the entire ectoderm in some species). 2.) Motile prey accidentally contact the tentacles or sessile prey pieces torn loose by wave action or foraging predators wash into the tentacles. 3.) Specialized corallimorpharians such as *Rhodactis, Actinodiscus, Discosoma, Amplexidiscus* can capture large prey by enveloping them with the entire disc like a Venus Fly Trap (see chapters 3 and 9, and also Hamner and Dunn, 1980 and Elliott and Cook, 1989).

Another mode of feeding by prey capture that does not belong to the three basic modes described by Shick involves the presence of commensals. Anecdotal reports of symbiotic clownfish carrying food to the anemone (observed in aquariums) suggests that the host may obtain food this way. In most instances it seems that an overeating clownfish takes more than it can chew back to its host and simply lets go as the tentacles tug the food away. This has never been observed in the natural environment and appears to be an artifact of captivity (Fautin and Allen, 1992). In other instances it appears that the fish is actively feeding the host, sometimes by capturing live fish and dragging them into it! (aquarium observations again) In addition, when the anemonefish defecates, the fecal matter often falls on the anemone and may be consumed, thus providing a source of nitrogenous compounds and some phosphate, among other nutritious compounds.

Uptake of Dissolved Inorganic and Organic Matter

We just mentioned that the host anemone may eat the clownfishes' solid waste. The clownfish also provide an on-site source of dissolved inorganic nitrogen (via ammonium excreted from the gills), and this benefits the symbiotic zooxanthellae. Of course the vast quantity of water passing over an anemone carries with it small quantities of dissolved inorganic nutrients, so with proper water flow an anemone has all the food it needs brought right to it. Anemones capture organic matter as well and transport it via cillia on the oral disc to the mouth. It is possible that the mucus on the surface of the tentacles, oral disc, and column may serve a function like that known for soft corals of the genus *Xenia*. The mucus in *Xenia* is described as a "molecular net" because of its ability to trap organic compounds from the water. It is tempting, then, to equate the pumping behaviour of *Xenia* polyps to the curious "vibrating" of tentacles in *Stichodactyla gigantea* and *S. haddoni*. This behavior certainly serves a light flashing function, but it may also be involved in the capture of dissolved organic compounds under conditions of low water velocity.

Absorption of DOM by sea anemones was first suggested by Pütter (1911), and the topic has been further examined by Schlichter (1980) and Schlichter et al. (1987). The large surface of sea anemones is amplified at least tenfold by microvilli on ectodemal cells (Schlichter, 1980). These finger like projections on the cells are characteristic of absorptive epithelia. Strong water flow therefore is important not only for providing the exchange of repiratory gases, but also for supplying dissolved organic food. The anemones are feeding all the time, even though we typically think of feeding in the sense of food caught by the tentacles and passed to the mouth. Dissolved organic material is a major supplemental food source during periods when no solid food is taken (Shick, 1975), and it may be especially important for burrowing anemones which are exposed to high concentrations of DOM, or for small anemones with proportionally high tentacle surface areas (Robbins and Shick, 1980). The capture of DOM including free amino acids on the surface of the anemone is thought to benefit the ectodermal tissues in particular, which are partially isolated from nutritive endodermal tissues by the mesoglea in between that presents a barrier to free diffusion of glucose and amino acids (Shick, 1991; Schlichter, 1973; Chapman and Pardy, 1972; Bradfield and Chapman, 1983).

Extracellular Digestion

The role of mesenteric filaments of anemones in extracellular digestion was demonstrated by Nicol (1959) in *Calliactis parasitica*. Components of the food caused the filaments to release extracellular digestive enzymes. The filaments envelop the prey and thus concentrate the enzymes in a small volume right on the food mass. Digestion occurs at the interface of mesenterial filaments and food. Ishida (1936) believed "slime" aided extracellular digestion, and Krijgsman and Talbot (1953) observed a mucus coating on the ingested prey of *Pseudactinia flagellifera*. They suggested that the coating concentrated extracellular digestive enzymes such as protease and lipase on the food (Shick, 1991).

Another mode of extracellular digestion occurs when the food is snared by the tentacles. Such "pre-oral digestion" has been described for *Cerianthus* (Tiffon, 1975) and *Heteractis magnifica* (Schlichter, 1980). Microvilli on the ectodermal cells may absorb the products of this digestion (Schlicter, 1980) or the digested material may be taken in via pinocytosis (Tiffon and Daireux, 1974). One can imagine that phagocytosis is possible here too, though large food items typically pass into the mouth and phago-cytosis occurs via endodermal cells in the coelenteron. It is also possible that bacteria are digested by enzymes on the surface of some anemones. Tiffon (1975) observed strong trypsin produced by the ectoderm on the column of *Metridium senile*, and postu-lated that it played a bacteriostatic role. This could serve functions of nutrition as well as defense against pathogenic bacteria.

Absorption

As we just mentioned, absorption of dissolved food and pre-orally digested material can occur through the surface of the anemone, but for large prey items digested in the coelenteron it occurs through phagocytosis via endodermal cells throughout the mesenteric filaments. Absorption occurs here for sugars and free amino acids liberated by the digestive process accomplished by extracellular protease enzymes. Pinocytosis and phagocytosis carry the extracellularly digested material into the cells where futher digestion occurs. Intracellular digestion involves the use of various lysosomal enzymes and amylase (Shick, 1991). Lipids and colloidal proteins are digested primarily intracellularly, though some extracellular digestion of triglycerides has been noted (Shick, 1991; Krijgsman and Talbot, 1953). Van-Praët (1981, 1982) observed phagocytosis of bacteria and cyanobac-teria in Actinia equina, supporting the notion that anemones are not strictly carnivorous.

Storage

Lipids are the primary stores of energy for most sea anemones, and may make up about half the anemones dry weight (Shick, 1991). Studies of glycogen storage in the endoderm show that it may serve quick reserve fuel and long term storage functions, but that its dry weight abundance indicates it is a minor storage product (Shick, 1991). Phagocytes in the endoderm appear to synthesize glycogen in addition to storing temporarily the prod-ucts of intracellular digestion (Van-Praët, 1982a).

Translocation

We mentioned that the ectoderm is partially isolated from the endoderm by mesoglea, and that absorption of dissolved food over the surface of the anemone is an important source of nutri-tion for the ectoderm. In fact some of the products of digestion of large prey taken into the in coelenteron do migrate across the mesoglea to supply nutrition to the ectodermal cells. The products of digestion in endodermal cells may reach the ectoderm by difusing across the mesoglea (Chapman and Pardy, 1972; Schlichter, 1974) or they may get there through the migration of mobile cells rich in glycogen and lipid that are especially abundant in the digestive region of mesenteric filaments. These mobile cells are more numerous in anemones with thicker mesoglea (Van-Praët, 1982a), indicating a transport role (Shick, 1991). Boury-Esnault and Doumenc (1979) described mobile cells rich in glycogen that migrate to sites requiring energy during gametogenesis, regeneration from injury, or asexual reproduction (Shick, 1991). They may also transfer stored materials to developing eggs in the mesoglea (Van-Praët, 1982a).

Egestion

After a prey item is taken into the mouth and digested in the coelenteron by the action of mesenterial filaments it becomes what is known as a "bolus," basically a mucus covered ball of partially digested food. It is common for the anemone to egest one or more of these yucky brownish globs several hours after ingestion of the prey. In the natural environment the currents transport the bolus away from the anemone. In the aquarium if

The zooxanthellae are clearly visible inside this young *Entacmaea quadricolor* that was spawned and reared in captivity.
J. C. Delbeek

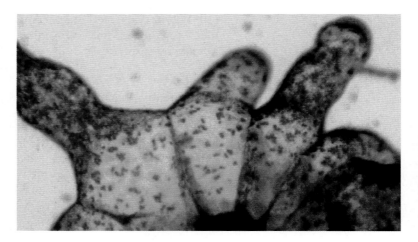

the water motion is not sufficient the bolus may stay among the tentacles or land next to the column where it could stimulate a bacterial infection. Often the bolus is bouyant, so it floats away. When various scavengers such as serpent stars or hermit crabs are included in the aquarium the bolus is quickly devoured.

Feeding by anemone larvae

Anemone larvae are free swimming planulae which may ingest copepods, chaetognaths, or the larvae of other cnidaria, but the majority of the food taken in may be unicellular algae, including dinoflagellates (Widersten, 1968, Siebert, 1974). It is suggested that this feeding mode may be the way that symbiosis with zooxanthellae is initially established (Shick, 1991).

Algal symbiosis

The symbiosis with photosynthetic dinoflagellates called zooxanthellae in certain species of anemones gives them a "built-in" source of food. These zooxanthellae are microscopic round golden brown single-celled organisms that live in the cells of the tentacles and oral disc of the anemone. The clownfish host anemones all possess zooxanthellae, as do most of the species covered in this book. Therefore they require light of sufficient intensity and spectral quality in order to maintain this symbiotic relationship and to survive (see chapter 8). The relationship between anemones and their symbiotic zooxanthellae is similar to the relationships between corals and zooxanthellae or tridacnid clams and zooxanthellae (see discussion in volume one). The dinoflagellates leak the products of photosynthesis (oxygen, sugars, and amino acids) to

This anemone in a tidepool has withdrawn its tentacles and is being shaded by the gravel attached to its column. The shading helps protect the anemone from being over-illuminated. J. Sprung

their host and in turn take in some of the dissolved products of respiration and digestion (carbon dioxide and ammonia) from their host.

Anemones can regulate the amount of light they receive by expanding or contracting the oral disc, or by withdrawing into the sand or a crevice in the rocks. Some anemones have gravel attached to their column by the sticky verrucae, and when they want to reduce illumination they withdraw their tentacles and expose the attached gravel, which shades the column and withdrawn tentacles. The regulation of light is important for the anemone since photosynthesis by the zooxanthellae under extreme illumination has the potential to generate toxic superoxide radicals faster than the anemone can detoxify them via enzymes (Lesser and Shick, 1989 a & b, Lesser and Shick, 1990, Shick, Lesser, and Stochaj, 1990). In the natural environment the passage of clouds provides rest periods (of reduced light) in photosynthesis. Changes in water column height and turbidity due to tidal flow also alter the light intensity. See the discussion of lighting in chapter 8. When they receive too much light, particularly with UV wavelengths, toxic superoxide radicals build up in their tissues and anemones may "bleach." They expel some of their symbiotic zooxanthellae and as a result appear paler because they have lost some of the dark brown pigment of their symbionts.

Reproduction

"Ignorance about their reproductive biology, combined with difficulty in maintaining them, preclude aquarium breeding of these actinians..."

----- Dr. Daphne Fautin, in Fautin and Allen, (1992).

Sexual

Sea Anemones have a variety of modes of sexual reproduction, and they vary not only among species but also within the same species depending on latitude and environmental influences. Sea anemones may be hermaphrodites (individuals producing both male and female gametes) or they may be dioecious (individuals are either male or female). Hermaphroditic species are protandric, the sex cells usually maturing at different times.

The sex cells are interstitial in the gastrodermis and ripen in the mesoglea. When ripe they may be released into the water column for fertilization and development. In some species however, only the male gametes are released and fertilization occurs internally. The larvae are "brooded" and develop inside the anemone in interseptal chambers (among the mesenteries), sometimes to the stage of young anemones with tentacles. There are arctic and antarctic anemones that form external "brood pouches" where the larvae develop. The pouches are sacs formed by invaginations of the body wall.

Entacmaea quadricolor larvae collected after an aquarium spawning event at the Waikiki Aquarium. A colony maintained there consisting of several male and female anemones spawns each April at 7 AM, two days after the full moon. Planulae develop within 24 hours after fertilization, and settle out on a variety of substrata. The newly settled anemones are already self-sufficient as they are packed with zooxanthellae.
J. C. Delbeek

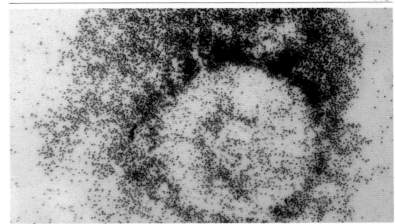

Young aquarium-spawned *E. quadricolor* photographed at the Waikiki aquarium. J. C. Delbeek

The young *Entacmaea quadricolor* clearly had zooxanthellae.
J. C. Delbeek

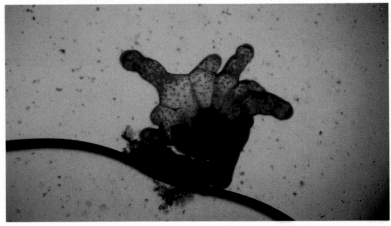

Fig. 4.3
Sexual reproduction Modes.

Modified after Barnes

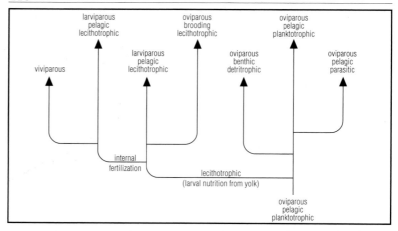

This large specimen of *Stichodactyla mertensii* was releasing great plumes of sperm during a coral mass spawning event after the November full moon in the Solomon Islands. Divers observing the anemone shined their underwater lights on it, which seemed to stimulate the anemone to erupt! Photo: Julian Sprung

Spawning usually begins with male anemones releasing sperm into the water. The sperm exits via the mouth usually, but depending on the species of anemone it may also be released from the tips of tentacles or through pores in the column. The release of sperm is detected by females of the species, and they may release eggs into the water. In some species the eggs are not released, but water-borne sperm fertilize the eggs within the gastric cavities of anemones downstream.

Anemones may respond to environmental cues that trigger mass spawning of populations, much like reef building corals do. Such cues include moon phase and (related) tide cycles. Temperature and salinity changes may also stimulate spawning. It is possible even that the mass-spawning by other marinelife such as corals (and therefore high concentration of eggs, sperm, and hormones in the water) could stimulate spawning in anemones. There are times when the reef seems to be involved in one big orgy.

Asexual

Asexual reproduction in anemones is usually accomplished by some means of vegetative propagation, but it can also occur through parthenogenetic development of individuals from unfertilized eggs. Asexual proliferation is viewed as a mode of growth

Figure 4.4
Asexual reproduction methods
After Shick 1991

Top (L) budding from tentacle
Top (R) budding from oral disc
Middle (L) Pedal laceration
Middle (R) Pedal laceration
viewed from below on glass
Bottom (L) Longitudinal fission
Bottom (R) Transverse fission

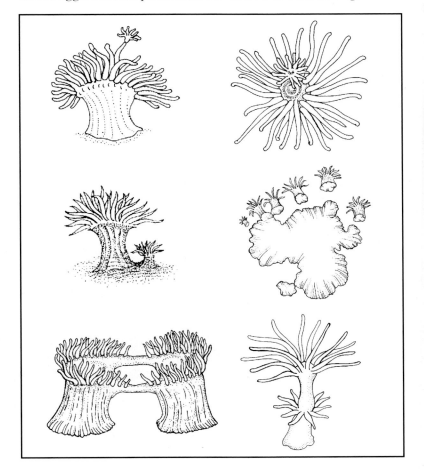

rather than reproduction since the offspring are genetically iden
tical. Chia (1976) provides a summary of the different modes of
asexual reproduction in anemones.

Table 4.3
**Asexual Reproduction
Modes in Anemones**
(Actiniaria) *After Shick, 1991*

Note: In this book we report
budding in the tribe Mesomyaria
(In *Bartholomea annulata*) and in
the tribe Endomyaria (in
Stichodactyla spp.).

Suborder Protantheae		
	Transverse fission	
	Regeneration of fragments	
	Longitudinal fission	
Suborder Nyantheae		
	Tribe Boloceroidaria	
		Budding
		Tentacular autotomy and regeneration
		Pedal (basal) Laceration
	Tribe Mesomyaria	
		Pedal (basal) laceration
		Longitudinal fission
		Transverse fission (rarely)
		Parthenogenesis
	Tribe Endomyaria	
		Longitudinal fission
		Transverse fission (very rare)
		Parthenogenesis
		Vegetative (somatic) embryogenesis

Pedal Laceration (also called basal laceration)
The simplest form of asexual reproduction occurs by the severing of
small bits of tissue from around the foot of the anemone. These little
fragments grow tentacles and develop into complete anemones within

An *Aiptasia* sp. on the glass wall of
an aquarium exhibiting the formation of daughter anemones by pedal
laceration. J. Sprung

*J. Sprung observed a group of three H. magnifica on a reef near Bequa, Fiji. Two were of equal size and obviously clones produced by longitudinal fission. The third was very small and only partially developed, and was still attached to the column of one of the larger individuals by a string of tissue. It may simply have been a late, and small product of the longitudinal fission, or else it was an example of pedal laceration.

just a few days. In clownfish host anemones this mode of reproduction is not reported and generally does not occur, but it may occur sometimes.* The anemones in aquaria that typically exhibit this mode of reproduction include *Aiptasia* and *Bartholomea*. Corallimorpharians also employ pedal laceration as a common mode of reproduction.

Budding

The formation of daughter polyps by budding is a rare occurrence in sea anemones. It is a common mode of reproductions for corallimorpharia such as *Discosoma* and *Amplexidiscus*, as well as for scleractinians such as faviidae, fungiidae and caryophyllidae. An extremely unusual mode of budding is known in the anemone *Boloceroides* (Okada and Komori, 1932). This anemone has a sphincter at the base of each tentacle, and constriction of the sphincter can cause the tentacles to be shed, severing them just below the point of the sphincter. A whole anemone can regenerate on tentacles at the severed junction. This mode of reproduction may have evolved in response to predation by nudibranchs (Lawn and Ross, 1982a), offering a means of creating several survivors, via autotomy, when the original anemone is attacked. *Boloceroides* is also capable of swimming (Lawn and Ross, 1982a, Robson, 1966), and can therefore get away when attacked.

One of the authors noticed a possible example of budding in *Stichodactyla mertensii*, which is not known to reproduce asexually. A 1 inch (2.5 cm) ball of tissue with tentacles was partially pinched off on its oral disc. If such budding does occur it is easy to understand why it may be overlooked. The bud blends

Aquarists have reported the production of very small offspring from *Entacmaea quadricolor*, the offspring not resulting from the usual longitudinal fission. It is possible that such offspring are produced by pedal laceration, but they may also be the product of parthenogenesis or vegetative (somatic) embryogenesis. *Entacmaea quadricolor* has also spawned in captivity, producing large numbers of offspring. This photo shows a juvenile *E. quadricolor* probably produced asexually, below its parent. It was photographed at the Bochum Tierpark in Germany. J. Sprung

In the Solomon Islands Julian Sprung found this specimen of *Stichodactyla mertensii* with a possible bud on its oral disc. What is this swollen knob of tissue with tentacles? Could it be the product of an injury? an abnormal growth of tissue? or is it a rare example of budding? J. Sprung

This form of budding occurs in *Stichodactyla gigantea*, and is probably the same basic technique shown in the photo of *S. mertensii*. A portion of tissue on the oral disc (or upper margin of the column) becomes differentiated, develops a pedal disc, an oral disc, and eventually severs from the parent. The formation of the mouth and internal structure presumably progresses while the bud is still attached.

Another specimen of *Stichodactyla gigantea* was found in which the bud was on the oral disc adjacent to the mouth of the parent. It was a perfectly formed anemone with a pedal disc and oral disc but no mouth, and was attached to the parent by a small section of its oral disc.
J. Sprung

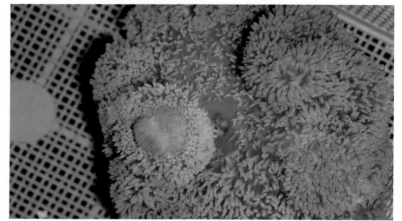

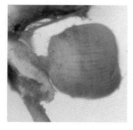

Transverse fission in a zoanthid. The polyp is pinching off.
J. Sprung

perfectly with the rest of the oral disc and is really inconspicuous. Formation of "satellite balls" in *Goniopora*, many faviidae, and other scleractinia proceeds this way. Perhaps it is a rare or simply rarely observed event for some actinians.

Subsequently a specimen of *Stichodactyla gigantea* exhibiting budding was found at All Seas Fisheries, Miami Florida, which imported the specimen. The bud developed as a new pedal disc at the margin of the oral disc. Again, it requires a sharp eye to notice this bud since it blends so well with the parent (see photo).

Transverse fission

The primitive anemone *Gonactinia prolifera* regularly reproduces by this method. A ring of tentacles develops about midway on the column and the column constricts above the tentacles until it is severed, forming two anemones as a result. Sometimes the constriction forms below the tentacles, producing two strange offspring: one is a free floating anemone with two oral ends and the other is an attached column with no tentacles. The attached column soon forms tentacles and the "two headed" anemone eventually forms a constriction in the middle to separate into two anemones (see Hyman, 1940).

Most tropical sea anemones, zoanthids, and corallimorpharia have the ability to regenerate an oral disc when severed in half transversely through the column, or when the oral disc is eaten by a predator (such as a nudibranch or bristle worm). The damaged tissue on the oral end of the attached column heals quickly and formation of tentacles there commences within a few days. The severed oral disc (if it isn't eaten) may form a new pedal disc or it may die. In some cases a severed oral disc can develop another oral disc in place of the pedal disc, forming a "two headed" anemone with no way of attaching! In an experiment the oral disc of *Condylactis gigantea* was severed from its column and the column developed a new complement of visible tentacles within one week, functional (though stubby) tentacles within two weeks, and normal length tentacles within two months (J. Sprung, pers. obs.). The severed original oral disc meanwhile died within a few days. A free floating severed oral disc can sometimes recover from the injury, forming a new pedal disc, but often it dies from bacterial infection before it can heal. In corallimorpharia this is not the case. Transverse fission is common and the severed disc recovers quickly and re-attaches within a few days (J. Sprung, pers. obs.). In zoanthids the severed oral disc is also quite hardy, heals rapidly, and is likely to survive if it can attach to a suitable substrate before it is eaten (J. Sprung, pers. obs.). Transverse fission occurs naturally, though it is not common, in the genus *Zoanthus* (J. Sprung, pers. obs.). By contrast it is a very common mode of reproduction for *Discosoma* sp. "mushroom" or "elephant ear" corallimorpharian anemones. In these cases the column forms a constriction at about the midway point, though there is no pre-formed circle of tentacles there as in *Goniactinia*. The currents twist the oral end around until it severs from the attached column. Once the polyp is severed the new oral disc forms rapidly. Transverse fission requires unequal regeneration of structures not shared by the two halves produced, and this may prevent it from occuring in large anemones that are more differentiated along the oral-aboral axis (Shick, 1991). By contrast, more "symmetrical" splitting of parts can occur via longitudinal fission, and this mode of vegetative proliferation is more widespread among anemones.

Longitudinal Fission

Longitudinal fission occurs when the anemone divides through the oral disc and pharynx, thus forming two or more daughter polyps each with a portion of the tentacles and mouth from the original solitary anemone. New septa and tentacles form in relation to the existing ones. This mode of reproduction is known in *Entacmaea quadricolor, Stichodactyla helianthus, Heteractis magnifica,* and also occurs in many other species. In some species it happens spontaneously quite frequently, in others it occurs only rarely or as a result of injury. In some species certain populations readily reproduce by longitudinal fission while other populations seldom if ever do so (Fautin and Allen, 1992). We believe that although only certain clownfish host anemones are known to reproduce this way, it is likely that under carefully controlled artificial conditions all of them can be successfully divided this way. The techniques of achieving this success have not yet been worked out so it is at present speculation on our part that it can work. We believe that the use of antibiotics to prevent infection will be the most critical factor in achieving success. Furthermore it is possible that certain species must be cut along a limited range of axis through the mouth. For example, it may be critical that both sides of a divided anemone retain one of the siphonoglyphs, or that they each retain part of BOTH siphonoglyphs. Although it is unfortunate that some anemones would necessarily be sacrificed to do the experiments, we feel that there is a worthwhile potential to learn how certain anemones might be propagated in captive culture.

Dr. Fautin points out analogously that we cannot at present expect to be able to regenerate a whole human being by cutting off and culturing an arm (pers. comm.). Nevertheless, there are species of anemones (*Aiptasia*, for instance) that can regenerate a whole animal from the tiniest spec of tissue severed. These animals are structurally quite simple and regeneration in them is not nearly as complex as it would be for a mammal, or for a larger and more complex anemone. Our interest lies in the following question: If one species in a particular genus can readily divide to form new anemones by asexual means, why should another species in the same genus be unable to do so? Moreover, why are certain individuals of the same species unable to reproduce vegetatively while other individuals are able to do so? We do not believe that the answer is that those species or individuals which don't divide are somehow more advanced and complex. How should they belong to the same genus or species if that were so? What we think causes this inability to survive fission is an inability to ward off invasion of the tissues by pathogenic bacteria, or a reduced capacity to regenerate at a sufficient rate before pathogens make a killing. We believe these factors can be artificially manipulated to produce anemones vegetatively in aquaculture.

In our opinion, that Dr. Fautin has not observed small individuals of certain host sea anemones, for example of *Stichodactyla mertensii* and *S. gigantea,* also suggests asexual reproduction could be important for them. Although Fautin notes that one does not find patches of apparent clonemates of these two species (as is common, by contrast, for *Entacmaea quadricolor* and *Heteractis magnifica*), she does note that *S. gigantea* "may be extraordinarily abundant" in some localities. What distinguishes the abundant individuals from mixed clonemates of a few parent anemones? That they are all large may simply reflect the production of still-large offspring from the division of large individuals. Furthermore, the resulting offspring may have rapid growth. The related Caribbean species, *Stichodactyla helianthus*, readily divides and forms large stands of cloned individuals, their origin made obvious by their proximity to each other. Perhaps the other species do not form such stands but instead separate and travel. We would like to test the hypothesis that these anemones can reproduce asexually by artificially dividing individuals and noting their survival and subsequent growth. Pedal laceration, though unlikely to work, is another possibility to test. Of course success or failure in these experiments has no bearing on whether such asexual reproduction actually occurs in the natural environment. We only intend to show by any successes that it is possible for these anemones to reproduce asexually, or by the failures that it may be unlikely.

As we were preparing this book for printing a fortunate last minute discovery allowed us to complete the story. Without modifying our just stated cautionary remarks and progression of argument, we announce here the discovery of *Stichodactyla gigantea* in the process of longitudinal fission. This specimen was also imported by All Seas Fisheries. It was received in the same shipment as the earlier mentioned specimen with a daughter polyp budding off the edge of the oral disc. In the same shipment there was also a third (completely healthy) specimen in which the mouth was at the edge of the oral disc. Clearly it had just divided. It is likely that the collectors found a population of *S. gigantea* in which asexual reproduction is common, but this has never before been reported in the scientific literature. Furthermore, the importer assures us that this is a common occurrence. They did

This specimen of *Stichodactyla gigantea* is in the middle of the process of longitudinal fission that, in a short period, produces two offspring of nearly the same size as the original parent. Note that two pedal discs have already formed. Interestingly, one of the mouths has two siphonoglyphs while the other mouth is less developed. The anemone remained in this condition for about one month and then, over the course of just 48 hours, the two halves pulled apart. The points of separation were closed, leaving no trace of injury!
J. Sprung

not realize it was of any significance, believing the specimens to be "two-headed siamese twins," not realizing that these are temporary double-headers in the process of reproduction.

According to Millie and Jean Chua of All Seas Fisheries (pers. comm.) this occurrence is not rare, and it also occurs, less often however, in "Long Tentacle" anemones, *Macrodactyla doreensis.*

Longevity

"...it is likely that most individuals of the 'gigantic' sea anemones we have encountered during our field work exceed a century in age."
----- Dr. Daphne Fautin, in Fautin and Allen, (1992).

We do not doubt that these structurally simple creatures are capable of living for centuries. However, we do not believe that this means that large anemones are necessarily old individuals. *Heteractis magnifica,* one of the largest of all anemones, readily reproduces asexually by dividing, producing two large anemones capable of attaining the size of the original individual within a few months. Therefore it can be demonstrated that it is possible for very large anemones to be less than one year old, not more than 100 years old (though they may be genetically the product of truly ancient parents originally produced sexually). By contrast, the other very large host anemone, *Stichodactyla mertensii,* is not known to reproduce asexually (except possibly reported for the first time in this book, see earlier comments and photo). If sexual reproduction is the only mode of reproducing for this species then it is likely that large individuals are quite old. How old they are is presently impossible to guess. Based on observed growth rates of anemones in captivity it seems probable that the minimum age of such large anemones is several years. The maximum age is indefinite. Most anemones probably have no natural life span or senescence. They cease to exist as individuals when they divide, when some accident befalls them or a predator succeeds in eating them.

Symbiosis

Anemones are well known for living together with many other types of organisms. In the earlier discussion of nutrition we mentioned symbiosis with single celled dinoflagellates called zooxanthellae that live in certain anemones' tissues and leak products of photosynthesis to their host. Other creatures associated with anemones are found giving the anemone a ride, crawling or swimming among the tentacles and around the column, or occasionally venturing into the mouth. These symbiotic partners are commensals, and they include mostly well known fishes, shrimps, and crabs, but there are likely to be other creatures associated with anemones that have not been described.

Fishes

The well known "clown" or anemonefishes of the genus *Amphiprion* and *Premnas* are the most readily recognized creatures associated with anemones. Their lives are so intimately tied

The clownfishes are the best known creatures associated with sea anemones. Here the Blue-Stripe Clown, *Amphiprion chrysopterus*, is living with *Heteractis crispa*.
J. Sprung

to their hosts that they are nearly never found without an anemone in the natural environment,* though they live perfectly well without one in captivity. Captive anemonefishes often choose a substitute host, such as the anemone-like soft coral *Sarcophyton*, the crown of "feather duster" sabellid worms, the tentacles of various *Euphyllia* spp. corals, or the elongate tentacle-like polyps of the stony coral *Goniopora*.

* An anemonefish was seen among the tentacles of the anemone-like coral *Euphyllia* at a site called "Ghavudu" in the Solomon Islands. This is a common occurrence in home aquariums, but rare in the natural environment.

Clownfish behaviour and their association with anemones are fascinating to watch and scientifically interesting. Their "immunity" to the stings of the host is not entirely explained, though much has been written about it. Chemical and behavioural aspects of the association have been studied. Actually clownfish are not "immune" to the stings- they are merely protected from stings by their mucus coating. Without the coat they are stung like any other fish. It is the mechanism of the protection and its origin that remain to be fully explained. The current belief is that clownfish have evolved to have mucus chemistry that greatly suppresses or does not stimulate nematocyst discharge. Since they live among the tentacles of the anemone they furthermore pick up some anemone mucus on their surface, just as anemone mucus can be found on other surfaces that the anemone contacts (Fautin and Allen, 1992). In this way the clownfish becomes chemically "invisible," seeming like part of the anemone.

What benefits do the clownfish get by their association? The most obvious one is protection from predators. Clownfish are slow swimmers and the anemone is a safe home for them from which they do not stray very far. Watching clownfish among the tentacles

The hybrid clownfish known as *Amphiprion leucokranos*, here living among the tentacles of *Heteractis crispa* in a bed of encrusting soft coral, *Sinularia* sp. Fish with *A. leucokranos* characteristics are produced by crosses between *Amphiprion chrysopterus* and either *A. sandaracinos* or *A. perideraion*. This fish is likely the offspring of a cross between *Amphiprion chrysopterus* and *A. sandaracinos*. This specimen is unusual because it has a complete headbar, an uncommon feature that makes it look like *Amphiprion nigripes*. Photo taken in the Solomon Islands. J. Sprung

For additional information about *Amphiprion leucokranos* see Carlson, 1996 and Nosratpour, 1997.

of their host one cannot help but notice that they seem to derive "pleasure" from the tactile stimulation. A clownfish in its carpet anemone is "snug as a bug in a rug." The tactile stimulation may do more than stimulate cozy feelings, it may cause the clownfish to secrete more of its protective mucus (Brooks and Mariscal (1984). Specimens of *Amphiprion clarki* kept with artificial anemones made of rubber bands required less time to acclimate to a real anemone than specimens maintained without such surrogate hosts. The term "acclimation" refers here to the period of time when the clownfish first approaches a new anemone. The fish exhibits a behaviour wherein it gradually comes in contact with the anemone, touching it only briefly until it finally is able to "dive right in." We have noticed that very often newly imported clownfish or ones already with a host anemone do not exhibit any acclimation period when presented with a new host, even if the host is a different species of anemone. They fearlessly swim right among the tentacles of new anemones without a pause.

There are some odd behaviours clownfish exhibit in this relationship with their host that have not been fully explained. For example, clownfish commonly suck on the tips of the tentacles, sometimes biting them, causing them to deflate and taking them in and out of the mouth with each "breath." It is possible that this behaviour is associated with ingestion of anemone mucus, but we cannot rule out the potential for tactile stimulation (and enjoyment) here, or that the firing of some nematocysts might cause a sensation for the fish like hot chili peppers! A further extension of this behaviour is eating of tentacles. We have seen clownfish during acclimation with *Stichodactyla gigantea* take

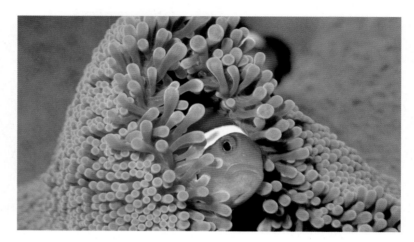

This *Amphiprion ocellaris* is certainly comfortable in among the tentacles of its host anemone, a brilliant green *Stichodactyla haddoni*. Photographed at the Baltimore Aquarium. J. C. Delbeek.

tentacles into their mouth, spin around, tear them off, and swallow them. The fish would eat a sufficient quantity of tentacles in such a "session" to become noticeably fat. These were not starved fish, so their behaviour is not an artifact of hunger. It seems their may be some nutrition that the fish gains from its host, or that acclimation may sometimes involve ingesting anemone mucus and tissue.

For further information about clownfish and their hosts please see the list of references and suggested readings. The book *Field Guide To Anemonefishes And Their Host Sea Anemones* by Daphne G. Fautin and Gerald R. Allen is a most valuable source of information about anemonefishes and their hosts, and a new book, not yet but soon to be published as we write this, *Clownfish: A Guide To Their Captive breeding, Care, & Natural History*, by Joyce D. Wilkerson will certainly be an extremely valuable reference. Joyce has contributed a great deal to aquarists' appreciation of anemonefish and anemones. She has also widely promoted anemone conservation and the understanding of rearing techniques that can be employed by private aquarists for producing captive raised fish and other marine creatures.

What benefit do the anemones get from the association with clown-fish? Clownfish protect anemones from predators (Fautin and Allen,

1992). For *Entacmaea quadricolor* in particular the presence of clownfish prevents the anemones from being devoured by butterfly-fishes. Certain clownfish host anemones have very wide oral disc that cannot retract and close. Since these anemones have lost the ability to close, they are afforded protection by clownfish which chase away potential predators. In the absence of these predators the anemones are able to thrive without clownfish.

As we mentioned under the topic nutrition, clownfish provide a concentrated source of nitrogen for their host, which benefits the host by stimulating the growth of the zooxanthellae that in turn provide food for the host via the products of photosynthesis. While this extra fertilizer from the fish is not required, there can be no doubt that the anemone benefits from it. No controlled studies have been done to determine whether such nitrogen input encourages more rapid growth or promotes proliferation of the anemones, but it may well do so. The presence of clownfish seems to stimulate the development of bubble-tips in *Entacmaea* (Fautin and Allen, 1992), and this may relate to the nutrition state of the anemone. Clownfish also stimulate the host, their swishing fins providing circulation of water over the tentacles, facilitating the removal of waste, as well as exchange of respiratory gasses.

Other fish associate with sea anemones, including *Dascyllus trimaculatus*, *D. albisella*, and *D. strasburgi*, the so called "Domino Damselfishes." These relatives of the clownfish can often be found in schools hovering over various anemones, and they retreat into the anemone when threatened. Some juveniles of a few species of wrasse such as *Thalassoma amblycephalus* may be found associated with sea anemones, but they are not as closely dependent on the anemone, making brief contact only and leaving their host completely as they mature.

Crabs

The well known "boxer crabs" *Lybia edmondsoni* and *L. tessellata* carry anemones of the genus *Bunodeopsis* in their claws, waving them at predators for defense. Several "Porcellain crabs" (actually more closely related to squat lobsters than crabs) live on anemones, particularly anemones of the genus *Stichodactyla*. *Neopetrolisthes maculata*, the Spotted Porcellain Crab, is the most common one available in the aquarium trade. Other crabs may also be found living around the bases of various anemones, including *Mithrax* spp., *Lissocarcinus laevis*, as well as some pea crabs, Pinnotheridae.

These are *Amphiprion percula* living in *Heteractis magnifica*. Photo taken in the Solomon Islands. J. Sprung

Hermit crabs have long been known to associate with anemones. The anemones are attached to the shell in which the hermit crab dwells, providing protection to the crab. In return the anemone has a safe substrate that moves to new sources of food as the hermit crab scavenges (hermit crabs are messy eaters), but stays in a habitat within suitable parameters for the anemone's survival. Calliactis species are well known anemones that associate with hermit crabs. When they move into a new, larger shell, the crabs are careful to remove the anemones from the smaller discarded shell and re-attach them to new shell that they have selected. The European hermit crab *Eupagurus prideauxi* and the anemone *Adamsia palliata* have a special relationship. The anemone completely envelops the shell and actually extends the lip of the

Porcellain crabs are commonly available to aquarists. This specimen is living with *Stichodactyla haddoni*. J. Sprung

shell opening with its basal disc, secreting a new lip with an organic horny matrix so that the shell grows as the crab grows. This eliminates the hermit crab's need to find new shells as it grows (see Barnes, 1980, Ross, 1974a and b). Furthermore, there are deepwater anemones that actually create a complete shell from scratch out of a secreted organic matrix! This shell-building ability is an advantage in a habitat where calcium carbonate normally dissolves quickly due to the high concentration of carbon dioxide in the deep sea. The anemone builds its own substrate, which happens to be the perfect domicile for a hermit crab.*

*see Dunn, Devaney, and Roth, (1980) for information about shell building anemones

Periclimenes brevicarpalis is a common inhabitant of *Cryptodendrum adhaesivum.* J. Sprung

Shrimps

Members of the genus *Periclimenes* are common commensals on sea anemones and other cnidarians. *Periclimenes yucatanicus* and *P. pedersoni* are common inhabitants of Caribbean sea anemones such as *Bartholomea annulata, Condylactis gigantea*, and *Stichodactyla helianthus*. *Periclimenes brevicarpalis* is a common inhabitant of Indo-Pacific anemones, particularly *Cryptodendrum adhaesivum*. There are numerous other less well known *Periclimenes* species. The fascinating "sexy shrimp" *Thor amboinensis* occurs in the Caribbean and Indo-Pacific, associated with anemones such as *Lebrunia, Bartholomea*, and *Actinodendron*, as well as other cnidaria, including corals. It waves its abdomen up and down rhythmically, hence the name.

These shrimps obviously gain protection from predation because of their host, but they also may be partly dependent on the host for food. The shrimps will take scraps of food and mucus from their host's oral disc, but in the absence of such food *Periclimenes brevicarpalis*, for example, may also eat tentacles (Daphne Fautin, pers comm.) In the latter sense they may seem like parasites, but they really only exhibit harmful behaviour when starved and maintained with an anemone that is also not receiving adequate nutrition. In that case their presence may result in consumption of the host, something which does not happen with their relationship in the natural environment.

Symbiosis in anemones is one of the most wonderful natural associations to observe. We hope that with the help of this book you too can learn to "live together" with anemones, in an environmentally sound and responsible manner. In this way you may add to the body of knowledge about these delicate creatures while you observe them in the natural environment and at home in an aquarium.

Chapter Five

Collection And Transportation

We discussed much of the pertinent information regarding the collection and transportation of marinelife in chapter eleven of volume one of *The Reef Aquarium*. Please refer to this chapter for information regarding permits and general information about holding and shipping collected specimens.

Collection Versus Captive Propagation

In the three years since we published the first volume we have witnessed a proliferation of businesses cultivating invertebrates for sale to the marine aquarium hobby. Some have come and gone, but each year there are more companies succeeding in the effort to provide captive raised marinelife to the marine aquarium trade, including soft corals, stony corals, zoanthids, and corallimorpharia. The captive propagation of clownfish host anemones has not become widely practiced yet, although some operations have been able to produce *Entacmaea quadricolor* clones, not surprising since that species readily divides in the natural environment. Other anemones are more difficult to clone, but it is not impossible to do so, and spawning anemones to produce offspring is also possible, of course (see chapter four). We believe that in time the collection of anemones from the wild will hardly be necessary. With this bold prediction we proceed to describe methods for collection and transportation of marinelife. It is our goal to encourage proper handling of the animals and minimal impact on wild populations.

Anemones

Sea anemones present several challenges for the collector. They are soft bodied so care must be used to avoid tearing the tissue when collecting them. They have the ability to contract rapidly, which may result in them disappearing into a crevice in the coral or a hole in the sand. Sand dwelling anemones are generally easiest to collect. They often attach to a small solid object such as a shell buried in the sand, and can be removed intact simply by excavating the sand. Anemones attached to large rocks present a greater level of difficulty, but they may be collected by lifting or pushing up an exposed portion of the pedal disc, being careful not to tear the tissue (that's the difficult part). Once a portion of the pedal disc is lifted off the rock, the rest of it comes off more easily, but one must proceed slowly to avoid tearing the disc.

Dendronephthya spp. include some of the most beautiful soft corals. Unfortunately they do not thrive in captivity. Until the proper captive husbandry techniques are determined collectors should avoid taking them. This photograph was taken in the Solomon Islands. J. Macare

Invariably tiny fragments of tissue will remain on the rock and for some species these can grow into new anemones. The most difficult anemones to collect are those which live in crevices or in porous or branchy coral rock. The only way to collect these is to break the rock, something we do not encourage. It is better to search for specimens located in such a way that they can be collected without causing destruction.

Shipping anemones is not always easy. Some species do not suffer from staying in a bag for several days, while others seem to become prone to fatal infections after this treatment or worse, they die in the bag. The principal cause for problems with shipping anemones has to do with the anemones' rate of metabolism and respiration. Since the anemones are packed in boxes, they are kept in the dark during transit, which means that both the anemone and its symbiotic zooxanthellae are consuming oxygen. In the confines of a bag the anemone may quickly consume all dissolved oxygen in the water. In response it may swell, taking in the oxygen depleted water, to expose as much of its surface to the air or oxygen sealed in the bag. If it is a long trip (and a large anemone) this oxygen may also be used up, particularly if the bag collapses. The stress of shipping also makes some species secrete copious mucus, which promotes the proliferation of bacteria that also consume oxygen. When exporters ship a large fish it is typically given plenty of room and lots of water. Anemones, by contrast, are sometimes mistakenly placed in a bag just large enough to fit the animal. Given more room anemones have more oxygen available to them.

Exporters have tried different methods of shipping with various anemones. The following is what they have found works best. For the carpet anemones, Stichodactyla gigantea, S. haddoni, and S. martensii it is best to ship the anemone in a bag without water (beyond what the anemone retains in its coelenteron). For *Heteractis malu* and *H. crispa* ("Sebae" anemones), and *Macrodactyla doreensis* ("Long tentacle" anemone) the dry method is also used successfully. *Heteractis magnifica* ("Ritteri" anemone) is a problem species. Sometimes it is sent with a large volume of water, other times it is shipped dry. In either case survival is not very good. Large specimens of *Entacmaea quadricolor* also do not ship very well. They are sometimes shipped successfully with a large volume of water, sometimes without water. Small specimens shipped in a large volume of water, however, seem to do quite well. Small 5 cm (2 in.) clones of the especially beautiful

"Rose Anemone," a pink form of *E. quadricolor*, are sometimes shipped all together in a single full size bag in a styrofoam box.

If the exporters hold the anemones for several days after collection to give them a chance to recover from any injury before shipment the success rate improves. Holding them first this way also tends to reduce the quantity of mucus produced in the bag by the anemone, which reduces problems with pathogenic bacteria. The future of anemone shipping will likely include other procedures to reduce pathogenic bacteria, such as antibiotic treatment. Other things that help insure better survival include shorter flight connection times and avoiding excessive heat in transit to the airport (difficult in the tropics).

A new type of plastic bag has been promoted lately by the company Kordon, which uses it for packaging their live foods. The bag is supposed to allow excellent gas exchange through the plastic (without leaking!). We do not know if such a material would offer advantages for shipping anemones, but we suspect that it might.

Holding Sea Anemones

At importers' facilities the anemones must be held in such a way as to maximize their survival and minimize difficulties in handling them. An intelligent solution has been devised for holding them in aquaria. The tanks are built wide and shallow, making it easy to provide good water circulation and gas exchange. The water feed may be directed across the overflow surface drain in such a way as to prevent anemones from approaching and blocking the drain. If underwater drains are used, a sheet of foam-like mechanical filter media prevents the anemones from getting pulled into the drain. Another technique has the water feed so slow that it in effect is like a slow water change, and the surface overflow drains are used with a foam cartridge to keep anemones from covering the drain. In some designs the water feed is strong and the overflow drain runs the width of the tank, minimizing the chance of it becomong blocked. The sides and bottom of the tanks are covered with a short dense industrial carpeting that prevents the anemones from sticking to the walls, thus facilitating the process of removing them for shipping. Flat plastic spatula's are typically employed for gently lifting the pedal disc off the carpet while avoiding contact with hands.

Anemones can be transferred to a plastic bag in several ways. They can be netted and rinsed in clean seawater before being gently released into a large bag. Another possibility is to use the technique developed by dog owners for no-mess pick up of their dog's poop: turn the bag inside out, insert one's hand in it, grab the anemone with the bag and pull it in as the bag is turned right side out again. Picking the anemone up by hand and sliding it into the bag is possible but not recommended. Anemone stings can be painful, particularly if you have thin or sensitive skin, but worse than this you might injure the anemone! *Stichodactyla gigantea* and *S. haddoni* are extremely sticky, like flypaper, and tentacles will be torn off as you try to free your fingers from their grip.

Zoanthids

Zoanthids may be collected from a variety of habitats, including intertidal rocky shores, coral reefs, seagrass beds, and reef flats. Where they occur on rocks in the intertidal zone they may be collected along with the rock, if such collection is legal. In many regions collection of the rock is not legal. If the rock cannot be removed but the marinelife can be taken, one may feel the colony of zoanthids to find a loose clump which can be peeled off. Often this will be a portion of the colony growing on a clam or oyster. In areas where the growth is thick, particularly for *Zoanthus* spp. rather than *Protopalythoa* or *Palythoa*, loose clumps of polyps may be found washed ashore or laying in the sand around the rocks. Peeling clumps of polyps off the rocks is another option. For *Palythoa* spp. it is best to find a small colony, or a large one that has divided into many small, separate patches. If one attempts to peel a large section of *Palythoa* off the rock it is sure that a tear will form through some polyps, which may lead to a fatal infection for the colony. Small round patches of not more than 15 cm across are easy to pry off the rock, particularly in sandy hard-bottom areas. For *Protopalythoa* and *Zoanthus* peeling clumps of polyps off the rock may be assisted with a flat blade or screwdriver used to lift some tissue at the edge of the colony. Then one may push and lift to peel up a flap of living polyps.

We must offer a word of caution about zoanthids. Some of them are known to generate toxins which could produce reactions in sensitive people. For example, *Protopalythoa toxica* from Hawai'i was used for making poison for fish spears (see chapter two). *Palythoa* species are also known to produce so-called palytoxins that are extremely toxic. While we have never had any sort of reaction from handling zoanthids with our bare hands, it is possible that some people could develop serious reactions, particularly if there are any breaks in the skin. It is always wise to wear gloves when collecting or handling zoanthids and to wash your hands afterwards.

Shipping zoanthids is generally easy. Most species are best shipped by the "dry method." Rinse the zoanthids with a stream of saltwater to flush out excess sand and remove any large attached sponges that could foul. The zoanthids may be wrapped in plastic strips or a layer of paper or absorbent cloths such as Wipe-Alls™ and placed in the plastic shipping bag. The bag is then filled with seawater temporarily to wet the plastic or paper wrapping, and then the water is completely poured off (see photographs in Volume One chapter eleven). A small amount of oxygen is then injected (as a boost to the air present) before sealing the bag.

Cerianthid anemones

Cerianthids are found in sand or mud in areas of seagrass or sandy plains between reefs. They can be collected by carefully excavating around their tube to free it up from the surrounding sand or mud.

Shipping cerianthid anemones does not present too many problems. In general they are best shipped with enough water to cover them and the rest of the bag volume should be filled with pure oxygen before sealing. There may be quite a bit of interesting life on their tube and it is nice to keep this community alive together with the cerianthid anemone. Careful collecting technique and handling will insure that the tube is not damaged and the cerianthid stays in it.

Corallimorphs

Mushroom anemones and their allies typically occur on hard substrate in turbid water or on coral reefs in shady regions. Sometimes they occur on the skeletons of branchy or platy corals such as *Porites* or *Acropora* spp. and *Pectinia* or *Pavona* spp. When they occur this way collecting them is simply accomplished by taking a piece of the dead coral (where with CITES permit this is legal), which is usually loosely attached, in sand or among other branches. Some corallimorphs, such as *Ricordea florida*, occur mainly on solid ground, so one is unlikely to find a loose piece. In Florida the collection of this species with the rock has been outlawed since it involved the chiseling off of substantial pieces of rock from reef areas. Some collection of this species continues wherein single polyps are carefully scraped off the hardbottom without removal of rock.

The non-photosynthetic corallimorphs *Pseudocorynactis* spp. live as solitary polyps generally, and collecting them is best accomplished with a geological hammer or hammer and chisel used to take a thin sliver of the rock with them (where this is legal). If the base is accidentally torn it is not a problem; the polyp will recover. Given the substantial regenerative powers of this genus, it is possible to simply cut the polyp off at the base of the column, and it will re-grow a base. The remaining base and portion of the column left on the reef will re-grow an oral disc.

Photosynthetic species may also be collected with a scissors. If the polyps are crowded and are cupping up so that one can have a clear shot at the stalk, a quick cut to sever the disc produces a live polyp for the collector and leaves a live base that will develop into a complete polyp again within a few days and achieve the size of the original within weeks to months.*

Shipping Corallimorphs
In general corallimorphs are best shipped with just enough water to cover the polyps. Their metabolism is slow, so not much water is needed. Either air or pure oxygen is used to inflate the bag. We have seen *Discosoma* spp. shipped without water in the bag from Indonesia, with a transit time in excess of 36 hours. Corallimorphs are sensitive to heat, so exporters often pack them with ice in the box to keep them cool. The Indonesian *Discosoma* and *Rhodactis* species seem to tolerate cold weather quite well. Shipments delayed in transit during winter often arrive very frigid and the corallimorphs seem to survive this just fine.

Soft Corals

Gorgonians
Collecting gorgonians can be done successfully and easily in three ways. One can use a geological hammer to take a bit of rock along with the base,[1] or one can grasp the stalk and pull or snap the gorgonian off the bottom, or one can use a scissors to simply cut off branches from large colonies.[2]

The technique used to snap a gorgonian off the bottom is not as obvious as it may seem. Gorgonians are attached to the bottom by a holdfast. The holdfast is composed of extensions of the coenenchyme, including gorgonin, sometimes calcium carbonate, and it is usually covered with live tissue. If the collector grabs the central stalk and pulls upward, the result is normally that the tissue on the stalk becomes damaged, bunched up and torn from

*Julian Sprung tried to get a federal grant to demonstrate the viability of using this novel non-destructive collecting technique as part of a mariculture project to grow colonies of *Discosoma* (*Rhodactis*) sanctithomae and *Ricordea florida* for the aquarium industry. The grant was rejected on the basis of the criticisms of only one of the reviewers. This reviewer criticized the idea largely because (he/she) did not see any references to published literature about the technique! (Here you have it, whoever you are).

[1] In Florida recently a law was passed limiting the size of the base of collected gorgonians to not more than one inch across in any direction. This law was intended to prevent collection of live rock (now outlawed) with gorgonians. Imagine the paranoia about live rock removal which necessitated making the bases of collected gorgonians not larger than an inch across! Fortunately aquarists can use underwater epoxy to attach gorgonians to rock and thereby provide a stable support for them.

[2] Cutting off branches with a scissors is a completely non-destructive technique in that the gorgonian colony is not removed from the environment and it quickly grows new branches.

the axis, but the holdfast holds firm to the bottom. However, if the collector holds the stalk lightly and pulls sharply sideways, the strength of the holdfast is normally compromised and the gorgonian breaks free. This is why strong waves effectively sever gorgonians from the bottom. The flexibility of the gorgonians allows them to disperse the wave energy most of the time, but some types of waves are able to shear them off. This means death for some of them if they get washed ashore, but many end up

Santiago Gutierrez looks at a pile of dead gorgonians washed up on shore on the island "Caja de Muertos," just south of Puerto Rico. The gorgonians were piled over a foot thick and more than a yard back to front forming a dark belt-like strand for quite some distance along the shore. This gorgonian massacre is a natural process caused by wind and waves during storms breaking and tossing the gorgonians from the sea. Recently Puerto Rico passed legislation banning the collection of gorgonians for sale to aquarists. We believe that such laws are as ludicrous as banning people from cutting their grass! Gorgonians are a completely renewable resource, growing from larva or fragment to marketable size in one to two years. We agree that it is prudent to pass laws regulating the collection of gorgonians, but a ban on their collection does not make sense. J. Sprung

getting stuck by their branches in crevices, and stay fixed there long enough to reattach and begin growing in a new location.

Shipping Gorgonians

Most Gorgonians are shipped in sealed plastic bags with enough water to cover them and pure oxygen over the water. For large specimens this often means quite a bit of weight. Many (but not all) species tolerate "dry" shipping, in which case they are wrapped in paper towels or plastic strips damp with saltwater (as we described in Volume One, chapter eleven). We have noticed that it is best to use air or oxygen diluted with air, not pure oxygen, when shipping gorgonians without water. When pure oxygen is used photosynthetic gorgonian species expel their zooxanthellae. When they are packed in water, however, pure oxygen must be used to insure they don't suffocate. One can place more than one specimen in a bag, but it is important not to include too many, to prevent suffocation. Also, it is best to keep only one species per bag. It is possible to mix certain species, but this takes experience to learn which ones are compatible. It is best to hold the gorgonians in a healthy aquarium with good water motion for several days after they are collected before they are shipped. This will allow them time to recuperate from damage caused by handling. Gorgonians suffer from bacteria that invade the tissues during shipping, and they may suddenly fall apart a day or two after they arrive at their destination. This decomposition is the rapid tissue-ravaging affect of bacteria (probably *Vibrio* spp.) which also kill other soft corals, anemones and stony corals. For this reason it can be advantageous to treat the shipping water with antibiotics. Unfortunately, at the time of this writing such treatment is only an idea and not well practiced so we have not developed a protocol.

Leather corals and other Alcyonaceans

The collection of Leather Corals, *Sarcophyton*, *Lobophytum*, and *Sinularia* spp. for the aquarium trade is primarily done in Indonesia and Singapore, but also in Fiji, Tonga, the Solomon Islands, and a few other localities to a lesser extent. Collectors generally find places where these corals are growing on loose pieces of shell, gravel, or dead coral, so that collecting involves nothing more than picking the colonies up off the bottom like collecting fruit from beneath a tree. Other species such as *Nephthea*, *Capnella*, *Alcyonium*, and *Cladiella* are collected in a similar fashion. This activity is harmless to the environment as the collected colonies are small, asexually produced offspring (practically always), from larger colonies left in the habitat. Some work has been done in the Philippines, the Solomon Islands, Palau, and East Africa to demonstrate the viability of sea farming these creatures by taking cuttings from parent stock on the reef and attaching them to upland rock, allowing them to grow-out in a protected lagoon location or in shore based aquaria. Whether the "farming" is done actively as such, or passively by collecting naturally produced colonies, the effect on the natural environment is minimal. It is of course quite possible to create parent stock from these fast growing cuttings, thereafter having zero impact on wild populations. It may seem like the ultimate goal to promote such captive aquaculture based in the USA or Europe; from an economic standpoint it certainly makes sense. However, removing the aquaculture activity from the country of origin for the cultured corals is in effect robbing the people there of a livelihood. Aquaculture or non-destructive collection of small live corals for the aquarium trade, when done by the native people, is also a positive way to encourage coral reef conservation. The people protect the reef because their livelihood depends on it.

A view of the soft coral fauna close to shore in a deep channel protected from strong surge in the Solomon Islands. A great diversity of leather corals such as *Sinularia*, *Sarcophyton* and *Lobophytum* spp. occurs here, and offspring can be harvested without impacting the large stands of parent colonies. J. Macare

Shipping Leather corals

Shipping of these alcyonaceans essentially mirrors what we've already said for gorgonians. We would like to emphasize the importance of holding them for several days before shipping to allow them to be in good (not stressed) condition. In addition we should mention that in general, large specimens of *Sarcophyton*, *Lobophytum*, *Sinularia*, etc. ship poorly, so it is best to ship small specimens only. They do grow quickly in captivity.

Xenia

We described the technique for shipping *Xenia* species in Volume One. It basically involves floating the *Xenia* and attached rock by attaching a small piece of Styrofoam with a rubber band. This keeps the *Xenia* moving up in the water and helps to prevent it from suffocating on the bottom of the bag. It is likely that the use of antibiotics in the shipping water or treating colonies with antibiotics before shipping would improve their survival.

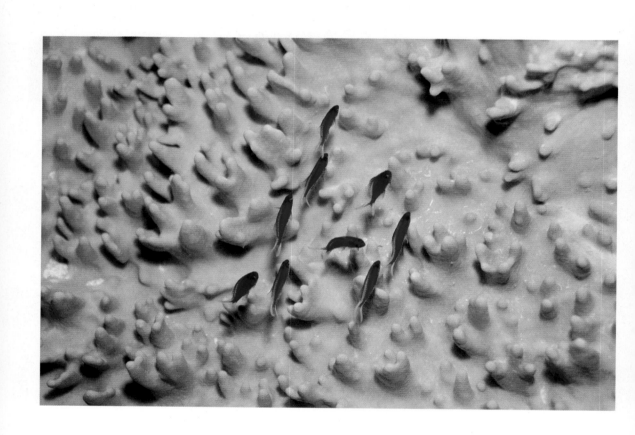

Chapter Six

Propagation Techniques

When we speak about propagating soft corals, anemones, coral-limorphs, and colonial zoanthids in captivity, we refer primarily to vegetative means of reproduction for mass propagation. While it is true that many species can and do reproduce sexually in captivity, by far the more common mode is by asexual means, and this capacity can be assisted with skill and imagination to produce large quantities of certain species in an aquaculture-farm facility or in one's own private aquarium.

There is a common joke among tropical fish farmers that goes something like "the way to make a small fortune in the aquaculture of ornamental species is to start with a big fortune!" When one sees the retail value of the tropical invertebrates offered for sale in pet stores it appears as if a fortune could be made by mass culturing high-value species. In fact, one can earn a living by culturing marinelife for the aquarium trade. It takes careful planning, enormous amounts of time, and a big dose of creativity and marketing savvy to really succeed; not to mention knowledge of the market and the biology of the marinelife cultured. We can't teach the reader all of these things, but we can offer some practical tips about ways to divide creatures and yield a good number of offspring. The design of holding and grow-out facilities, business plans, marketing strategies, funding, and motivation belong to the chapters of a different kind of book.

Before we discuss the various methods used to artificially propagate octocorals and other cnidarians, we need to mention one very important caveat. Do not attempt to propagate any coral that is not healthy and thriving. If you attempt to propagate a weakened specimen, the stress induced may kill the parent colony. Only propagate healthy, growing colonies. There are of course exceptions to this rule. For example if a specimen is badly infected by disease, propagation may used as a last resort to salvage portions of the main colony.

A school of Purple Queens, *Pseudanthias tuka,* soars in formation past an encrusting *Sinularia* sp. J. Sprung

Tools of the Trade
A Sharp Scissors, thread, monofilament line & thin rubber bands. Cyanoacrylate, hot melt glue and underwater epoxy.

Underwater Epoxy

There are some things that need mentioning regarding the use of underwater epoxies. First of all, although they are not toxic to marinelife, they do initially leach organic compounds into the water while curing. Once cured they do not leach anything into the water. The substances leached into the water are harmless, but they do tend to make a protein skimmer foam more than usual. For that reason we recommend turning the protein skimmer off or reducing the air input to the skimmer for 24 to 36 hours after using the epoxy. One may increase the use of activated carbon for a few days to remove leached substances, but it is not necessary to do so.

Proper use of underwater epoxy requires understanding, practice, and of course patience and planning too. Underwater epoxies are NOT superglues! Many aquarists have the impression that the epoxy will bond on contact and hold a heavy object in place, but these epoxies do not work that way. They work more like concrete than superglue, though the consistency of the stick format types is like clay or putty. Sometimes it is possible to position the drying bond out of water until it hardens. This results in a much stronger bond than if the epoxy dries underwater (J. Brandt, pers. comm.).

The thick (as opposed to runny) consistency of the stick format epoxies makes them the perfect solution for attaching gorgonians. Simply find a hole to insert the gorgonian base or stem in, and then push epoxy into the hole and around the stem to secure it in place. This exercise demonstrates the best use of underwater epoxy: to surround a stem or peg, like concrete does around iron reinforcing bars. To create a natural projecting position for a large piece of coral, one should first insert a wooden or plastic rod into the base of the coral to make a peg. Insert this peg into a hole in the rockwork, using epoxy between the coral and rock to cement the piece in place. For small coral fragments one can simply surround the base with epoxy and push the blob and coral fragment onto a rock, preferably into a depression in the rock.

It is also possible to attach lightweight corals to the glass with underwater epoxy. Thin, flattened pieces work best as they offer a large contact area for bonding. A flattened base on a lightweight gorgonian or other soft coral is also relatively easy to attach. The glass should be cleaned first with a razor blade to remove algal films and expose clean bare glass. Place a sufficient quantity of epoxy on the center of the base to spread flat and cover most of it when pressed against the glass. Hold the object steady with light pressure for about two minutes, which can seem like an eternity! If the piece is small and not heavy it may be released after the two minutes without additional support. If it is heavy it may need to be supported much longer, until the epoxy cures, which takes several hours. One must devise a system for holding the object in place until the epoxy cures. Magnets used for cleaning algae off the glass (one inside below the object and one outside) are one possibility for holding the object in place. Supporting the object first with just enough Styrofoam to make it neutrally buoyant is another possibility. Pieces of straight PVC can also be used to prop pieces into place and hold them there; 24 hours is usually sufficient.

This gorgonian was attached to the wall of the aquarium using under-water epoxy. The effect creates a very natural look and position for the gorgonian. J. Sprung

Cyanoacrylate (Super) Glue

As described in *The Reef Aquarium* Vol. One, cyanoacrylate glues are very useful for attaching small coral fragments to rock. They can be used underwater, but work best when the surfaces being bonded can be at least partially dried. The drawback to cyano-acrylate is that the bond does not have much elasticity, so it will sheer and separate if it is agitated or jarred strongly before the coral has had time to grow new tissue down over the rock. The beauty of cyanoacrylate glue is that it allows one to spot glue tiny bits of soft tissue, which is most useful for aquaculture of soft corals and anemones. LeRoy Headlee of Geothermal Aquaculture Research Foundation in Boise, Idaho told us about his experi-ences with using cyanoacrylate for attaching *Xenia* and other soft corals. LeRoy prepared an article about using cyanoacrylate in his aquaculture for *SeaScope* (Headlee et al., 1996). In our experience the techniques work well, but sometimes the polyps or cuttings of soft bodied creatures such as soft corals or zoanthids will separate from the glue after a day, before they can grow and form a natural bond with the rock. Small stony coral fragments glued with cyano-acrylate, however, usually stay put, so the method is a good time saving technique for working with them.

These zoanthid polyps were attached to the shell using cyano-acrylate gel. J. Sprung

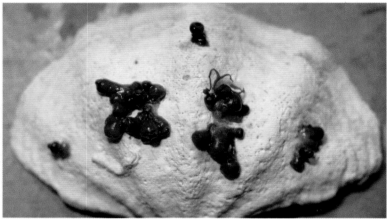

In order to make the zoanthids adhere to the rock when using cyanoacrylate gel, it is necessary to partially dry them first. Here they have been patted dry with a towel. J. Sprung

Hot Melt Glue

Hot Melt Glue administered by an electric heating gun is another alternative for attaching corals to rock temporarily held outside of the aquarium. Caution: Do not insert the gun or its tip underwater! Hot melt glue works well for small coral fragments and has better elasticity than cyanoacrylate. It can also be used for attaching larger corals to rocks, but as with underwater epoxy, it is best to

Hot melt glue is effective for attaching small stony coral fragments to rock. J. Sprung

incorporate plastic or wooden rods to help provide a more structural attachment to the rock.

Quick setting cements such as Thorite were also mentioned in *The Reef Aquarium* Volume One and in a recent *SeaScope* article. These cements are most useful for building strong structures with limestone or live rock. Quick setting cement can support heavy pieces, unlike epoxy. However, while the epoxy can be used in an established aquarium, the quick setting cements are best used when the aquarium is first set up, during the construction of the aquascape, as they are best applied to a dry or semi-dry surface. They can be used of course for attaching a piece of coral to a rock

This artificial rock is made from plaster-like material by Mr. Torsten Luther in Germany. J. Sprung

The manufacture of lightweight, porous, inert materials as artificial rock provides a means of standardizing the aquaculture product or custom forming special modules for aquariums.

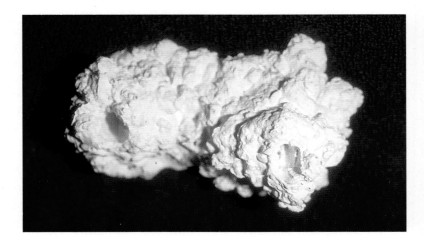

outside of the aquarium, which can be placed in the aquarium after the cement has cured. A temporarily lowered water level could also be employed. It is important to periodically splash the area being cemented while it hardens in order to cool it, since the reaction is exothermic (generates heat)! Thorite can also be used to attach rocks together. It can be given a rock-like texture by using a damp, large-pore sponge to shape the surface while it is still workable.

Treatment of Severed Tissue Fragments

Any time a coral is damaged, either accidentally or on purpose during propagation, it is susceptible to infection. For this reason it is wise to treat the severed ends with antibiotics in order to prevent possible infections.

Antibiotics

The use of 5 to 10 ppm Streptomycin or Neomycin can help prevent bacterial infection in the severed piece. Other types of antibiotics may also prove beneficial during the production of small cuttings or division of polyps. The future of tissue culture of corals and anemones will involve the discovery of procedures using antibiotics. We must warn the reader that the casual use with expo-sure to antibiotics can be hazardous to one's health. Wear gloves and take precautions (e.g. work in a well ventilated area close to running water. For some antibiotics (e.g. Chloramphenicol) it wise to wear a dust a mask too for additional protection (see the topic RTN for additional information about antibiotics).

Probiotics

If the cuttings are placed in well-established aquaria with live sand, live rock and a teaming diverse community of microorgan-isms they are less likely to be affected by bacterial infections than if they are placed in a clean lifeless environment. Nevertheless, the use of antibiotics in sterile culture systems provides a better margin of control for the mass production of offspring through asexual divisions. It is possible that a future protocol might involve high doses of a friendly bacteria strain to out-compete bacteria that attack severed tissue fragments. This is the essence of the probiotic method.

Water Motion

When cuttings are made, particularly from soft corals, the frag-ments respond by producing copious mucus. This mucus produc-tion can suffocate the fragment because it effectively isolates it from the water, blocking gas exchange. The mucus and injured tissue also promote the growth of bacteria and invasion by pathogenic organisms such as protozoans. Placing fragments on the bottom of an aquarium with little water motion therefore greatly reduces their chance for survival. Strong water motion removes the excess mucus and reduces the chance of bacterial infection. Of course the fragment must first be securely attached or else you will have some pretty mobile soft corals!

Soft Corals

Sinularia
The propagation of *Sinularia* and other branched soft corals simply involves the use of a scissors to sever branches. The severed piece must be handled carefully to avoid losing it to an infection. If the piece is a large lobe, it may be attached to a rock by inserting a plastic toothpick into the base and then sliding the projecting part of the toothpick into a hole in a rock. Underwater epoxy can help to hold the toothpick in the hole in the rock. Within a few weeks the coral tissue will form attachments to the rock. Small pieces of *Sinularia* can be attached to rock with Cyanoacrylate gel glue. For more massive or encrusting species, a razor blade can be used to cut off small sections.

Daniel Knop (Knop, 1997) proposes to insert a thin plastic or wooden toothpick sideways through the stem of the severed fragment about 10 mm above the cut in such a way that the toothpick protrudes through both sides. Then place the soft coral fragment on a rock substrate with the severed base inserted into a depression on the rock, so that the ends of the toothpick are flush with

Sinularia being propagated by making cuttings with a scissors. J. C. Delbeek

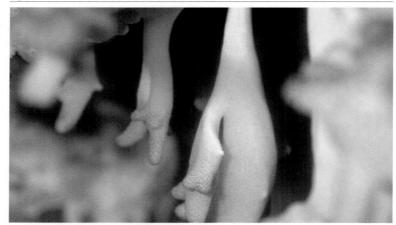

This soft coral is producing offspring which will drop off spontaneously and attach to the gravel or rocks. J. Sprung

These soft corals were propagated by Joseph Yaiullo at the New York Aquarium for Wildlife Conservation. He put them in shallow cups with gravel to keep them from drifting around and give them something on which to attach. J. Sprung

the rock surface. The end of the soft coral should not be inserted with pressure or pressed against the rock, just loosely held there. Tie the ends of the toothpick to the rock with rubber bands or nylon thread. Daniel has used this method since 1988 and reports great success with nearly all soft coral species.

It is often a good idea to isolate the newly propagated colony to protect it from drifting away or being dislodged by snails, crabs or urchins. This can be achieved by placing it in a small plastic cup or by placing a narrow piece of PVC pipe over the attachment site (see photos).

Sarcophyton and *Lobophytum*
These capitate corals can be propagated in a manner similar to *Sinularia*, by using a scissors and attaching cut pieces to rock.

These photos show the effect of severing the capitulum of a *Sarcophyton* sp. Top photo immediately after severing the capitulum. Note the tubes that look like xylem and phloem in plants. These are extensions of the polyps (autozooids and siphonozooids) and they function in maintaining hydrostatic pressure, gas exchange, transport of zooxanthellae, and possibly fibre-optic "light piping." Middle photo one day later the wound is healed. Within a week new polyps appear on the stalk, bottom photo. The severed "head" (capitulum) quickly reattaches to rock when treated properly. J. Sprung

The crown may be severed completely or partially. The most successful method appears to be a two step technique. First cut into the crown to divide it into pie shaped sections without completely severing them. Provide strong water motion and good environmental conditions to allow the colony to heal from the injuries. Then, once the cut tissue has healed it is a simple matter to completely sever the pieces of the pie, leaving only a small area of cut tissue to heal. It is common to find small stalks complete with capitulum and polyps growing from the stalk of a *Sarcophyton*. In this case it is a simple matter to sever the offspring with a scissors or razor blade.

Xenia and *Cespitularia*

These soft corals are among the fastest growing. Culturing them is an art. In general they can be cultured by just letting them grow onto new substrates such as rocks or shells, but the active intervention by making cuttings greatly increases the yield. The following suggestions for *Xenia* apply in general to the closely related *Cespitularia* and *Heteroxenia* as well, and also to *Anthelia* to a lesser extent.

Xenia utilize dissolved organic substances as food. Therefore rapid removal of this food source from the water may inhibit their growth While the primary source of nutrition in *Xenia* is supplied by the photosynthetic products of the symbiotic zooxanthellae, this specialized soft coral also traps organic compounds from the water for food. The copious slimy mucus it produces has been described as a molecular net for capturing dissolved organic compounds. So, one can see that it is possible that water that is very efficiently filtered by activated carbon and skimmed by a protein skimmer could slow the growth of the *Xenia*. Readers should not misinterpret our meaning here...we are not saying to stop using these filters. On the contrary, they should be used. However, take care not to overdo it, or if you must overdo it, be sure to feed enough to make up for it!

Crowding that occurs when the *Xenia* colony grows into many stalks tends to concentrate mucus in a way that can smother the individual stalks or promote protozoan infections that clear out the "forest" like a fire. When the colony becomes dense it is time to prune out some of the central stalks.

On the subject of pruning, one way to thin out the parent colonies without the trouble of trying to attach the loose cut pieces is to

Xenia cutting placed in a plastic ring to keep it from drifting away. J. C. Delbeek

place thin (dead) coral branches or small pieces of live rock among the *Xenia* stalks. Within days the stalks will attach to the branches and then it is a simple matter to cut the stalks away from the parent colony while carefully leaving the new attachment to the coral branches. The process is, by analogy, like touching an unlit candle to a lighted one fixed in position, and using the newly lighted candle to light another candle and so on. Actual pruning will still be needed once in a while, and one may just cut stalks with a scissors. Place the severed pieces into depressions on the rock in an area with very light water motion, or on gravel with slight water motion, or among algae. If there is no water motion, the cut *Xenia* may succumb to infection by bacteria that feed on the copious mucus emitted as a result of the injury. If there is too much water motion the cut *Xenia* will blow away and land behind or underneath a rock, with a tendency to gravitate to the one place where one absolutely could not possibly retrieve it. If it doesn't land there right away the only other possibility is for it to get sucked into a power-head and blown out shredded, which would not kill it except that after it goes through the powerhead it will then seek that place beneath the rocks where you can't get it. From this scenario it should be apparent that the cut pieces of *Xenia* are best housed in a separate aquarium until they are firmly attached.

The use of cyanoacrylate glues vastly simplifies the problem of wandering severed *Xenia*. The severed pieces can be glued to rocks quite easily (Headlee et al., 1996). In our experience it is best to use dry rocks and to lightly pat the stalk of the *Xenia* to partially dry it. The thick cyanoacrylate gel is placed as a drop on the rock and the stalk of

Xenia pressed onto it for a few seconds. The technique requires practice, as *Xenia* is slimy and tricky to handle. Once the stalks are glued to a rock, the piece is placed in an aquarium with sufficient water motion to prevent the slimed up *Xenia* from suffocating, but not so much water motion that they get blown off the rock. In the first few days there is the possibility that the *Xenia* will fall off the rock, breaking away from the patch of dead tissue adjacent to the cyanoacrylate linking it to the rock. If the *Xenia* stays in place, it will grow and form new attachments with the rock. The cyanoacrylate merely tacks it in place until such growth makes a sturdier attachment.

To enhance the growth of propagated pieces we advocate the use of trace element supplements. There is a positive effect on *Xenia*

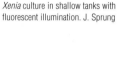

Xenia culture in shallow tanks with fluorescent illumination. J. Sprung

Xenia culture. The colonies are being propagated onto bare chunks of broken coral and limestone. J. Sprung

growth from the addition of iodine (as potassium iodide, iodine dissolved in potassium iodide, or organic extracts containing iodine). The reasons for the beneficial effect are not entirely understood, and probably are plural. Full spectrum supplements containing iodine also afford excellent results, often better than just potassium iodide.

Photoperiod

Culturing *Xenia* and other soft corals under artificial lighting allows one to extend the photoperiod. It is even possible to grow them with no dark period at all, and for some species this may increase the yield.

pH

High pH, which can be attained with the addition of kalkwasser or via the growth of macroalgae seems to promote healthier *Xenia*. Most soft corals appear healthiest when the pH ranges between 8.2 and 8.5. When the pH is less than 8.1 soft corals often fail to expand fully and *Xenia* species lose coordination of pumping or show degeneration of pinnules.

Colt Coral (Alcyonium)

Alcyonium can be propagated like *Sinularia,* by cutting off branches with a scissors. The tricky part is to get the slippery cutting to attach to something. Several ways have been devised to achieve that end, but by far the best one is the use of cyanoacry-late glue. In our experience, severing really large branches is problematic in that they frequently suffer from bacterial infections. Once severed they flop over and secrete mucus, and may be lost in a few days. The treatment with antibiotics should solve that problem, but an alternative is to sever only small branches, approximately one inch (2.54 cm) long. These are easily attached to rocks with cyanoacrylate gel, and if water flow is directed over them they are unlikely to be destroyed by bacteria.

Nephtheids

Nephthea and *Capnella* species readily reproduce by dropping daughter colonies formed by natural separation of branch tips.

Given strong light and water motion these colonies rapidly grow and produce offspring with little intervention required. The aquarist may speed up the process by cutting branches with a scissors. The cuttings may be attached to small stones or dead coral branches with cyanoacrylate gel.

Star Polyps, Clove Polyps and *Anthelia*

These soft corals grow like algae, rapidly advancing over the substrate with root-like stolons or sheets of tissue bearing the polyps. Placed next to bare substrate they spread and encrust it in a short period of time. *Clavularia* species grow like *Caulerpa* spp. algae, with palm tree-like polyps in place of the leafy fronds of *Caulerpa*, and on similar looking root-like stolons. When allowed to grow on glass, the stolons can be peeled off and attached individually onto new substrates with cyanoacrylate or by tying them with thread, monofilament line or thin rubber bands. Star polyps may also be grown on glass. This way the advancing sheets of growth are easily peeled off. They may be attached to rock with rubber bands, used to hold the sheet in place until it grows to form natural attachment with the stone.

Gorgonians

Gorgonians are easily propagated with a scissors. Simply cut off branches and attach them to rock by inserting the cut end into a hole and surrounding it with underwater epoxy to secure it in place. In some cases it may be necessary to trim (or scrape) off tissue from the cut end, exposing the bare axis of gorgonin. This exposed rod can then be inserted into a hole with epoxy, offering a firmer bond than epoxy on living tissue. For thick-tissue species such as *Eunicea* and *Plexaurella* this must be done because covering the tissue with epoxy can cause an infection that may spread and kill the colony.

These gorgonian cuttings have been cut from parent colonies by means of a scissors, and they can be attached to a rock with underwater epoxy. J. Sprung

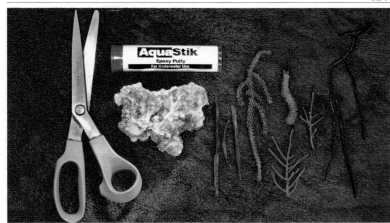

Here is the composed rock with gorgonians attached. J. Sprung

Zoanthids

Zoanthus, Isaurus, and *Protopalythoa,* as well as "yellow polyps"
These lovely colonial anemones can be cultured two ways: actively and
passively. The passive way involves allowing the anemones to creep
onto new substrates as the colony increases in size by natural asexual
division (budding). All that is required is sufficient light, water motion,
and in some cases supplemental food to stimulate more rapid growth.
The active way of propagating zoanthids involves peeling or cutting off
clumps of polyps and attaching them to stones, shells or other substrates.
The way to attach the polyps depends on how many there are. If the
clump of polyps is large enough, it can simply be tied to the rock with
monofilament string or held in place with a thin rubber band. If the
clump of polyps is small, or if one is attaching single polyps to a
substrate, cyanoacrylate glue works very well. It is best to use gel type
cyanoacrylate glue. The procedure is as follows: Use a dry substrate for
attachment. Prepare the polyps in a shallow dish for easy access. Dab the
polyps on a dry towel to remove excess water. Squeeze a drop of cyanoacrylate gel onto the substrate and gently push the polyps in place on it.

Palythoa

Propagation of members of this sheet forming genus is not as easy as
for the other zoanthid species. The polyps are not easily separated
since they are imbedded in a thick tissue matrix. Cutting through the
sheet invariably results in cutting through polyps longitudinally, which
leaves them very prone to infection. Treatment with antibiotics and
strong water motion can help prevent infections, so it is possible to
propagate these colonial organisms asexually. The severed pieces can
be loosely tied to rock with monofilament until they attach naturally.
Cyanoacrylate gel may also be used to form a bond with the rock.

Corallimorpharians

Corallimorpharians have a very powerful capacity for regeneration.
Tiny fragments of tissue are capable of growing into complete polyps
under the right conditions, though this capacity varies among the
species. We offer information here and in chapters three and nine
about some of the natural asexual reproduction methods known for
the various genera. Aside from these natural processes, one can inter-
vene and artificially mass propagate them, taking advantage of their
regeneration capacity and fast growth rate. Polyps can be cut off of the
rock by slicing through the column with a scissors, leaving the pedal
disc attached. The pedal disc will grow a new oral disc and the severed
polyp will heal and can re-attach within a few days. *Discosoma* and
Rhodactis species may offer interesting potential for commercial aquaculture using mass propagation via tissue culture techniques.

Discosoma

Members of the genus *Discosoma* readily reproduce by pedal laceration, budding, transverse fission, and longitudinal fission. Their diverse
asexual reproductive capacity is a good indication that most fragments
of their tissue are capable of regenerating a complete animal.

Ricordea

The genus *Ricordea* reproduces like *Discosoma*, though seldom does it
naturally reproduce by transverse fission. Its growth rate is a bit slower too.

Rhodactis and Amplexidiscus

These two genera differ slightly from *Discosoma* and *Ricordea* in
their most typical modes of asexual reproduction. Both reproduce
by pedal laceration. *Amplexidiscus*, like *Discosoma*, occasionally
forms daughter polyps by budding them off of the column,
whereas *Rhodactis* nearly never does so. *Rhodactis* often spontaneously divides the polyp like a pizza into several slices that
become new individual polyps (longitudinal fission). This technique can be enhanced artificially by making the cuts with a blade
instead of waiting for it to happen spontaneously.

Pseudocorynactis

These corallimorphs reproduce by longitudinal fission and pedal
laceration. They have amazing regenerative powers. Although
they do not spontaneously reproduce at a rapid pace, the active
propagation of them via planned cutting can yield large numbers
of offspring. These corallimorphs do not have photosynthetic partners and so must be fed to stimulate rapid growth.

Sea Anemones

We did not develop a protocol for the mass propagation of clownfish host anemones before writing this book. Nevertheless we are
sure that it can be done. Chapter four on the biology of sea
anemones shows examples of offspring produced by sexual and
asexual means. We hope to encourage research in this field in
order to promote the aquaculture of anemones as an alternative to
removal of anemones from the wild. Our book demonstrates that
the anemones can and do reproduce asexually, so it is simply a
matter of time before the techniques are worked out for chopping
them up to produce clones. The major obstacle now is preventing
bacteria from destroying the injured tissue. As we learn more
about anemone biology it is also likely that sexually produced
offspring will become an important means of culturing large
numbers of anemones.

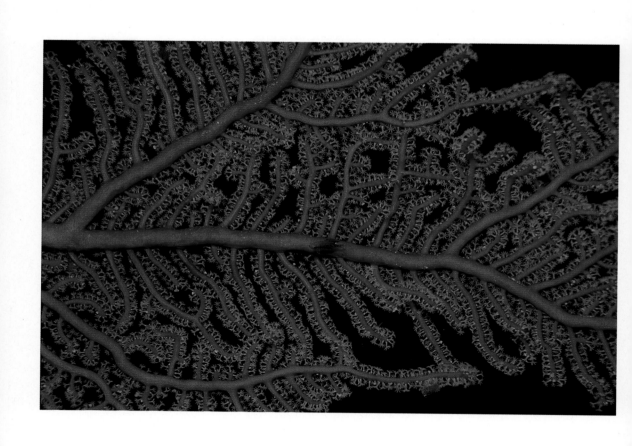

Chapter Seven

The Identification and Care of Soft Corals

Introduction

The eight tentacled cnidaria encompass a broad range of forms that captivate the observer with their movement and palette of colour. While a handful of scientists attempt to classify them, which is no easy task, others are analyzing them for natural products chemistry in the search for new medicines (see chapter one). Meanwhile aquarists have been growing the lovely soft corals of the tropical reefs at home in miniature reef aquariums where they thrive just like flowering plants in a garden.

To understand the distinguishing characteristics for the different families and genera one must have some definitions for the terms used to describe the various structures of the colonies, skeletal elements, and their growth forms. Please refer to the glossary for these definitions.

Selecting Healthy Soft corals

While soft corals are generally very hardy and easy to grow or propagate in captivity, they are easily injured by improper handling in transport. An aquarist must learn to distinguish a healthy specimen from one that is marginally unhealthy. To the novice there does not appear to be much difference between a dead soft coral and one that has simply contracted, expelling water and shrinking as it does so. A dead soft coral can foul a small aquarium. An injured soft coral may rapidly succumb to an infection as if consumed by gangrene. While we cannot explain in a few pages what years of observation teach, we present here some specific things to look for in special organisms.

Gorgonians

A spectacular sea fan, *Semperina* sp. photographed in the Solomon Islands. J. Sprung

Shedding is usually OK. Gorgonians shed a thin, waxy film, often the same colour as the branches, the colour imparted by embedded sclerites. This shedding process removes algae and other organisms that settle on their surface. However, when tissue sheds off, exposing the rod-like skeleton underneath, this is a sign that the branch or whole colony is dead. It is best to choose gorgonians that have the polyps expanded. If the gorgonians have just arrived in a fresh shipment, wait a few days before purchasing them, if possible, since colonies that have died in transit may not begin to rot for one or two days. If the dealer allows it, shake a colony gently underwater— does the tissue remain intact? If tissue (not just the thin waxy film) falls off of the branch, exposing the skeleton, or if the water rapidly turns cloudy brown, avoid the specimen. It is not necessary to "test" colonies that are fully expanded and obviously healthy.

Pterogorgia species commonly shed a waxy film to rid the surface of attached algae. This is a normal process and not an indication of poor health. J. Sprung

Leather corals

For *Sarcophyton* spp. beware pale sloughing areas or "brown juice" release upon handling. Ideally the colony is expanded with polyps expanded as well. Avoid a colony that is shrunken and bent over with the crown facing down and touching the rocks or bottom. Look carefully for flatworms, which look like brown freckles. Also look for egg masses from parasitic snails or nudibranchs.

Sarcophyton spp. normally shed a waxy film to rid their surface of attached algae or detritus. They may remain closed for a few days before shedding this film. This is a normal process. Strong water currents assist with sloughing the film. J. C. Delbeek

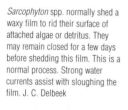

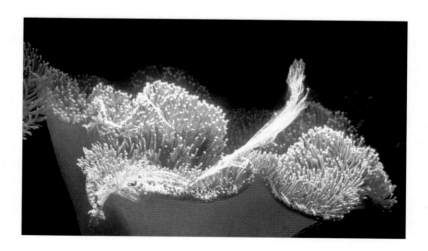

These snail eggs deposited on the underside of the umbrella-like capitulum of *Sarcophyton* are from a snail, probably *Calpurnus verrucosus* (Linnaeus, 1758), which feeds on the coral. J. Sprung

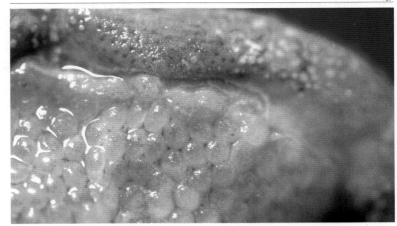

These eggs on the base of a soft coral are from a nudibranch, Family Tritoniidae, which eats *Sarcophyton* and other Alcyonaceans. J. Sprung

This "hot spot" is a kind of sore common in *Sarcophyton* and *Lobophytum* species. Its cause is unknown but it is probably of bacterial origin or possibly from other microorganisms attacking the tissue. It is generally not fatal and heals spontaneously when strong currents are directed over the area. Sometimes large yellow sores indicate the attack of nudibranchs such as *Tritoniopsis* that feed on leather corals. See Volume One, page 304. J. Sprung

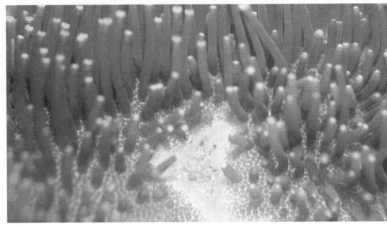

For *Sinularia* spp. beware of black areas. Blackened tips or base indicates necrosis and, while not necessarily fatal to the whole colony, it is an indication that the colony has been injured. Injured specimens are prone to infections that can kill the whole colony.

For *Xenia* and *Anthelia* spp. avoid limp colonies. Only choose robust, expanded colonies. Beware of yellowish areas on stalk (often the site of an infection).

Why "evolve" to a stony coral tank?

There is a bothersome psychological tendency among reef aquarists lately to aspire toward the challenge of "a stony-coral-only tank." We're confident that once the challenge is met most aquarists will miss the (usually) less challenging soft corals that happen to be more interesting and generally more beautiful with their fluid motions. Why people get hung up on creating a soft coral only or stony coral only tank is a bit of a mystery. We suppose it has to do with the belief that one must choose only between these two options because of chemical warfare between soft and stony corals. Nevertheless those aquarists who try to mix a nice population of both soft and stony corals usually meet with success. While it's true that one must be careful to provide enough room for growth and not allow certain soft corals to grow onto or next to stony corals, they can coexist in the same aquarium without problems. The use of protein skimming and activated carbon manages to prevent any harm caused by the substances released into the water by these creatures. Difficulties with mixing soft and stony corals generally arise only in extreme conditions, as when a single stony coral is placed in an aquarium overgrown with many species of soft corals or vice versa.

The Identification and Care of Soft Corals in Aquariums

Phylum Cnidaria (Coelenterata)
Class Anthozoa
Subclass Octocorallia Haeckel, 1866
Order Helioporacea (=Coenothecalia)

Family Helioporidae

Scientific Name: *Heliopora coerulea* (De Blainville, 1830)

Common Name: Blue coral, blue fire coral

Colour: Brown when alive, blue skeleton.

The appearance of living
"Blue Coral," *Heliopora coerulea.*
J. Sprung

Distinguishing Characteristics: This monotypic "soft coral" has a hard skeleton made of calcium carbonate and colored blue by special iron salts. This brown lumpy living colony is seldom collected as a target specimen for the live coral trade, but instead usually comes into the aquarium hobby along with other targeted creatures such as "Star Polyps" (*Pachyclavularia* or *Briareum* spp.) and "Button Polyps" (*Protopalythoa* spp.) that encrust over it.

Natural Habitat: *Heliopora* lives in very shallow water, often becoming exposed at extreme low tides. It occurs under a variety of lighting and water flow conditions, but grows most prolifically in very bright light with strong water motion. On reef slopes it may form flat sheets, particularly in shaded locations as in grottoes.

Similar Species: *Montipora spongodes* and *Millepora* spp. resemble *Heliopora. Heliopora* has eight tentacles on each polyp.

Aquarium Care: Give strong light and water motion and this coral will encrust adjacent rocks and glass and grow rapidly. It requires adequate calcium and alkalinity to form a good skeleton, and sufficient iron to develop the blue colour of the skeleton.

Reproduction: Blue corals are dioecious (separate sexes). Fertilization takes place internally and the eggs are brooded externally (see chapter one) (Babcock, 1990). Sexual reproduction has not yet been reported in aquaria.

Order Alcyonacea
Suborder Stolonifera Hickson, 1883

Family Clavulariidae Hickson, 1894

Subfamily Clavulariinae

Genus: *Clavularia* Blainville, 1830

Synonym: *Hicksonia* Delage & Herouard, 1901

Etymology: Name derived from the Latin word for club, *clavula*. The suffix -*aria* means like. The name refers to the club-like appearance of the calyces when the polyps are retracted.

This *Clavularia* sp. from Indonesia has very large polyps which are usually light brown. J. C. Delbeek

This is *Anthelia*. Compare its appearance with *Clavularia*. J. C. Delbeek

Distinguishing Characteristics of Genus: Cylindrical upright calyces sprout from a common ribbon-like creeping stolon that adheres to the substrate. The calyces may be club shaped or tubular and are longer than wide. Solitary polyps (i.e. polyps sprout from stolon, and do not bud from other polyps) are monomorphic. Anthocodiae can completely retract into the calyces, leaving a cluster of knobby tubes or clubs. Tentacles usually large and feathery with distinct pinnules. The sclerites from the calyx walls are irregularly shaped radiates. Sclerites from the anthocodiae are rods or spindles usually, but variable. Colour of the stolon is usually cream, brown, or gray. The anthocodia is most often whitish gray, but may be brown, green, fluorescent yellow or orange, or (in one species at least) bright blue. There are more than 40 species. References: Tixier-Durivault (1964); Weinberg (1986); Williams (1992)

The stolons of *Clavularia* spp. are reminiscent of the root-like stolons of green algae of the genus *Caulerpa*, and they grow almost as quickly! J. C. Delbeek

Scientific Name: *Clavularia* sp.

Common Name: Clove Polyp, Glove polyp, Waving hand polyp, or *Anthelia* (especially in Germany)

The origin of the common name "Clove Polyp" used by Indonesian exporters is a mystery. It could be a typographical error of a potentially good name for the coral, Clover Polyp. Glove polyp seems to be a variation of clove polyp, but it could also be a variation of a common name sometimes used for *Xenia* spp., Waving Hand Polyp. There is also the possibility that the smell of this soft coral reminded someone of cloves.

In Germany the common name for this coral is *Anthelia*. The polyps are quite similar to those of *Anthelia*, so the confusion is understandable. We hope that this common name falls out of use as it is misleading. Similarly the common name *Xenia*, often used in the USA for this and other corals and zoanthid anemones should be rejected. *Xenia* is the correct Latin name for a distinct group of soft corals.

Colour: Usually pale brown or gray.

Distinguishing Characteristics: A tough creeping stolon with spicules, and very tall, large polyps with feathery tentacles. The polyps are approximately two inches tall when retracted, and nearly twice that height when open. The diameter of an open polyp is typically two inches or more. The center portion of the polyp is only about 1/16 to 1/8 inch in diameter.

Similar Species: *Anthelia* cf. *glauca* has nearly identical polyps, and the two are often confused. *Anthelia* does not have large sclerites like *Clavularia* (see photo), and, although *Anthelia* can deflate, it cannot retract its polyps the way *Clavularia* does. When *Clavularia* is closed one sees the round heads of each closed calyx. When *Anthelia* is closed one can still see the tentacles of the polyps, though they are greatly reduced in size when deflated. One form of pipe organ coral, *Tubipora* sp. has giant polyps nearly indistinguishable from this species of *Clavularia*.

Natural Habitat: Reef slopes with bright light and tidal currents. Probably also occurs on coral rubble or gravel in lagoon areas

This *Clavularia* sp. photographed on a reef slope in the Solomon Islands had enormous polyps and grayish colour. The polyp diameter was about 5 cm (2 in)! J. Sprung

with heavy sedimentation, based on the attached gravel pieces in newly imported specimens.

Aquarium Care: Prefers strong illumination and a gentle current, which makes the polyps sway. This species fares better under metal halide light. It grows quickly, spreading over adjacent rocks, glass, and other invertebrates. With strong light and regular additions of trace elements it is hardy. In dimly lit aquaria without much trace element additions it usually spreads nicely for about four or five months, and then becomes brittle, gradually disintegrating. Also beware that hair algae easily attach to the sclerites, allowing growths to become established between the polyps. Don't let this happen! Hair algae can smother the coral. *Clavularia* species irritate and kill adjacent zoanthid anemones, including *Palythoa* spp., *Protopalythoa* spp., *Zoanthus* spp. Since *Clavularia* spp. grow rapidly and zoanthids multiply rapidly, one should plan to keep adequate distance between these groups. The polyps do not capture prey, so trying to feed them is useless.

Reproduction: The most common form of reproduction is asexual, as new polyps arise from the creeping stolon.. In the wild *Clavularia hamra* in the Red Sea and *C. inflata* on the Great Barrier Reef have been shown to be dioecious external brooders (see chapter one) (Alino and Coll, 1989). The white planulae stick to the polyp calyces within a mucus sheath. On the GBR, spawning occurs between 22 and 24 days after the full moon in November, at 9 AM (Alino and Coll, 1989). Sexual reproduction in aquaria has not yet been reported.

Scientific Name: *Clavularia* sp.

Common Name: Clove polyp, glove polyp

Colour: Usually whitish gray, not as brown as the previous species. Sometimes green or yellow, rarely orange.

Distinguishing Characteristics: Polyps not as large as the previous species, only one inch across (2.5 cm) maximum, and with very densely spaced pinnules. Polyps appear like snowflakes. Structure of colonies is essentially the same as the previous species, creeping stolons with spicules, but the polyps and stolons are thinner (about half as thick usually), while the centers of the polyps are larger, about 1/4 inch in diameter.

A beautiful *Clavularia* sp. with fluorescent yellow stripes.
S. W. Michael

A distinctive species of *Clavularia* from the Solomon Islands.
J. Sprung

Natural Habitat: Forms thick, "pillow" colonies on sand and gravel, but also is common among live corals on reef slopes, where it forms smaller, creeping rows of polyps. J. Sprung observed this species in clear water on the outer barrier reef in Australia, at the base of a high profile reef in 40 feet (13 meters) of water. It was encrusting dead coral rubble and living freely on sand and gravel, in the shade and in the open, but completely protected from currents. The light at this depth was bright and spectrally very blue. The polyps were expanded and motionless. At this site it did not occur in shallow water where the light and currents were more intense. It is likely that this species also occurs in lagoons. Similar and quite colourful species occur in the Solomon islands on reef slopes in clear water.

The spectacular green morph of this *Clavularia* species was quite common in some areas in the Solomon Islands. It does not survive shipping and so has yet to become established in the aquarium trade. If small fragments were collected instead of larger colonies it might be possible to ship this species more successfully. J. Sprung

Another colour variety of *Clavularia* from the Solomon Islands. J. Sprung

Aquarium Care: This species fares well under fluorescent or metal halide. Place it in a spot where it will receive strong light and moderate current. It sends out stolons like plant runners in every direction, and quickly spreads to adjacent rocks and glass. The polyps do not capture prey, so trying to feed them is useless. It is beneficial to have strong currents intermittently to prevent the colony from trapping dirt that might stimulate algae to grow on it. The stolons do not seem to bother most stony corals, though the rapid growth of this species can shade the coral and therefore smother it.

Reproduction: The most common form of reproduction is asexual, as new polyps arise from the creeping stolon. Sexual reproduction has not yet been reported but is likely similar to that reported for other *Clavularia* spp., (see previous description).

Order Stolonifera Hickson, 1883

Family Clavulariidae Hickson, 1894?

Scientific Name: *Acrossota* sp. ?

We were unable to get a positive identification for this soft coral, which is a close relative of *Clavularia* spp. It may be *Acrossota,* but this needs careful investigation and examination of the original specimens of that species for positive confirmation (P. Alderslade pers. comm.). We don't know if it belongs in the family Clavulariidae, but suspect it does. For now we call this "Unidentified Stoloniferan Number One." Fosså and Nilsen refer to it as "KA4-Stol-07" on page 115 and "KA4-Stol-11" on page 116 in their book *Korallenriff-Aquarium Band 4.*

This soft coral sold under the common name "Clove Polyp" comes from Indonesia. It has not been identified positively, but may belong to the genus *Acrossota.* J. C. Delbeek

Common Name: Clove polyp, Glove Polyp, Star polyp, *Xenia, Anthelia,* Unidentified Stoloniferan number One

Colour: Brown with yellow, white or green centers.

Distinguishing Characteristics: The polyps look similar to "brown star polyp" *Pachyclavularia* (*Briareum*) *violacea* because they have large green, white or yellow centers, but the tentacles are distinctive, being flattened, paddle shaped and about 1/16 to 1/8 inch wide. The pinnules are fused. This coral encrusts with creeping stolons like *Clavularia* instead of sheets as in *Briareum.*

Natural Habitat: Found on coral rubble in shallow lagoon and reef slope areas where there is good coral growth. This species encrusts the dead, broken branches of *Acropora* and other fast-growing branchy species.

Aquarium Care: This species fares best under bright light, either metal halide or sufficient intensity of fluorescents. It grows quickly, spreading over adjacent rocks, glass, and other invertebrates. With strong light and regular additions of trace elements it is hardy. In dimly lit aquaria without much trace element additions it usually spreads nicely for about four or five months, and then becomes finer, gradually disintegrating. It is easily overcome by the growth of filamentous algae. One must prevent this from happening by including sufficient numbers of herbivorous tiny hermit crabs and snails. Strong water motion helps prevent the stolons from collecting detritus that would promote algal growth on them. The polyps do not capture prey, so trying to feed them is useless. Beware that when this coral is healthy the growth is vigorous and it can smother stony corals. This species is beautiful in really small aquariums 20 L (5 gal) or smaller with adequate light.

Reproduction: The most common form of reproduction is asexual, as new polyps arise from the creeping stolon. Sexual reproduction in aquaria has not been reported but is likely similar to that reported for *Clavularia* spp., (see previous description).

Order Stolonifera Hickson, 1883

Family Clavulariidae Hickson, 1894?

Genus: Unknown

Scientific Name: Unknown

Common Name: Clove Polyp, Unidentified Stoloniferan Number Two

Colour: Light brown to copper.

Distinguishing Characteristics: Tentacles cylindrical, without pinnules. Polyps on creeping stolons like *Clavularia* spp. Most similar to the previous species (*Acrossota?*) and may possibly belong to the same genus. For now we call this species "Unidentified Stoloniferan Number Two."

"Unidentified Stoloniferan Number Two." This new stoloniferan has polyps similar to *Pachyclavularia violacea* and the variety of *Tubipora* with pinnule-less tentacles. The polyps are uniformly brown and completely devoid of pinnules. The colony spreads on well developed stolons most like those of *Clavularia* spp. and "Unidentified Stoloniferan Number One."
J. Sprung

Natural Habitat: Indonesia (probably Bali) on reef slopes and possibly in lagoons.

Aquarium Care: Provide strong, indirect illumination and moderate currents. Does not take food. Subsists on the photosynthetic products of its zooxanthellae and probably also feeds on dissolved organic and inorganic matter.

Reproduction: The most common form of reproduction is asexual, as new polyps arise from the creeping stolon. Sexual reproduction has not yet been reported but is likely similar to that reported for *Clavularia* above.

Order Stolonifera Hickson, 1883

Family Clavulariidae Hickson, 1894?

Genus: Unknown

Scientific Name: Unknown (*Cervera* sp?)

Common Name: *Xenia, Anthelia,* Unidentified Stoloniferan Number Three.

Colour: Brown and gray

Distinguishing Characteristics: Polyps with pinnules are on creeping stolons. Polyps look like miniature *Clavularia* polyps, only 2-3 mm in diameter. The stolons are very fine, about 0.25 mm thick.

"Unidentified Stoloniferan Number Three." This delicate looking soft coral seems like a miniature *Clavularia* species but it belongs to a different genus, probably even a different family. J. Sprung

This tiny stoloniferan from Indonesia, "Unidentified Stoloniferan Number Four," is a similar species to "Unidentified Stoloniferan Number Three" and probably belongs to the same genus. It has distinct polyps only a few mm tall. A. J. Nilsen

Drawing of a *Cornularia* colony. After Bayer, 1973

The two unidentified stoloniferans on this page may be *Cornularia* spp. This genus is characterized by very small polyps connected by stolons, with no sclerites. Polyps and stolons are protected by a horny perisarc. Phil Alderslade, based on examined specimens, advised us that these two stoloniferans are probably *Cervera* spp., which have been confused with *Cornularia*.

Similar Species: Similar to *Clavularia* but much smaller. There is another similar small species (Unidentified Stoloniferan Number Four) with quite different polyps. It has pinnules, but they are more like the pinnules on *Briareum* than like *Clavularia* (see photo). The general description for the genus *Cornularia* reminds us of these two species, but we have not been able to get a positive identification for them.

Natural Habitat: Indonesia on live rock, coral rubble, or gravel. Cryptic. Quite common but inconspicuous because of its small size and rather sparse colonies.

Aquarium Care: This species (and the similar "Unidentified

Stoloniferan Number Four") is not generally offered for sale, but it finds its way into our aquaria as a hitchhiker on other purchased pieces. It is commonly associated with other stoloniferans such as *Clavularia* spp, growing among them. It is also common on the bits of coral rubble attached to *Sarcophyton* or *Nephthea* spp. It readily spreads to adjacent rocks, glass, or onto sand and gravel by sending out rapidly proliferating stolons. Provide strong, indirect light and moderate water motion. This species is ideal for really miniature aquariums!

Reproduction: The most common form of reproduction is asexual, as new polyps arise from the creeping stolon. Sexual reproduction has not yet been reported but is likely similar to that reported for *Clavularia* above.

Family Clavulariidae

Subfamily Telestinae

Genus: *Carijoa*

Scientific Name: *Carijoa* sp.

Common Name: none

Colour: Pale brown or pinkish with white polyps. Often the stalks are encrusted with a commensal sponge that makes the colonies brilliant orange, yellow, or purple. The polyps are always white, and do not contain zooxanthellae.

Carijoa riisei from the Caribbean sifts the water with its lovely polyps. P. Humann

Figure 7.1
Carijoa
After Bayer, 1961
Carijoa has tall axial polyps
that form branches with
smaller daughter polyps
budding off the sides.
Coelogorgia has pinnate
branches without distinct
axial polyps.

Distinguishing Characteristics: A root-like stolon attaches the branches to the substrate. Stalk-like branches are formed by the extended growth of a single axial polyp off of which daughter polyps bud. The daughter polyps do not bud off of other daughter polyps. Stalks are mostly singular with infrequent branching. Colonies are composed of clusters of upright branches connected by the root-like stolons from which new axial polyps emerge.

Similar Genera: *Coelogorgia* is easily confused with *Carijoa*. In *Coelogorgia* new polyps often bud off of other polyps, thereby forming many new branches. The species of *Coelogorgia* seen in the aquarium trade contains zooxanthellae and is quite hardy.

Natural Habitat: *Carijoa* spp. are found throughout the Indo-Pacific and in the Caribbean. They are considered a "fouling organism" in that they rapidly colonize shipwrecks, jetties, dock pilings, the undersides of boats, and old tires used to prevent boats from hitting the seawall. *Carijoa* is common therefore in polluted harbours, but also occurs on reefs in clear water, usually in caves or under ledges where there is considerable surge or strong currents.

Aquarium Care: *Carijoa riisei* will grow with or without illumination. It prefers but does not require strong water motion. It does require feeding to really thrive. It will take particulate food such as crushed flake food mixed with Selco, or zooplankton such as copepods and *Daphnia*, but it may also consume phytoplankton. Crushed *Spirulina* flakefood or green-water microalgae cultures can be used to substitute phytoplankton food. In the natural habitat *Carijoa* grows strongly for several months and then dies back. It does the same in aquaria too. If it is healthy the colony will send branched stolons rapidly all over the substrate. When the polyped stalks die back the stolons may remain, and new stalks may grow from them periodically. This built-in senescence is not well understood, but may serve an asexual reproductive function, or it may prevent fouling algae from smothering the colony.

Reproduction: The most common form of reproduction is asexual, as new polyps arise from the creeping stolon. Nothing is known about sexual reproduction in this genus.

Family Coelogorgiidae

Genus: *Coelogorgia*

Scientific Name: *Coelogorgia* sp.

Common Name: None

Colour: Pale brown, lavender or pinkish with white or brown polyps.

Distinguishing Characteristics: A root-like stolon attaches the branches to the substrate. New polyps arise from stalks, and bud off of other polyps. According to the literature the polyps contract but are not retractile, but this may be an artifact observed in preserved specimens only, since live colonies seem to be able to retract the polyps into the calyces (pers. obs. and G. Williams, pers. comm.). Colonies are composed of numerous upright branches connected by their root-like stolons. Main stalks with frequent branching, pinnate in one plane generally, though growth in the aquarium can alter this.

This *Coelogorgia* sp. was photographed in the aquarium of Klaus Jansen. It greatly resembled the alga *Laurencia*. J. Sprung

Julian first observed this species in the aquarium of Klaus Jansen, Cologne, Germany, when traveling with Alf Nilsen and Svein Fosså. Upon first notice it appeared to be a clump of the alga *Laurencia* sp. The colour of the small colony (pale purplish) was like the alga and the shape of the blunt closed polyps was extremely similar to the blunt ended branchlets in *Laurencia*. It was only when some of the polyps began to open up that we realized this was a soft coral. On another trip with Fosså and Nilsen Julian saw a large colony *Coelogorgia* at the Löbbecke Aquarium in Düsseldorf, where it was proliferating nicely.

Similar Genera/Species: *Coelogorgia* is easily confused with *Carijoa* and *Telesto.* In *Carijoa* individual branches are formed by a tall axial polyp with many short lateral polyps budding off the side. In *Coelogorgia* new polyps often bud off of other polyps, thereby forming new branches (P. Alderslade, pers. comm.). The branching in *Coelogorgia* is denser than in *Carijoa*, and it is often pinnate. The species of *Coelogorgia* seen in the aquarium trade contains zooxanthellae and is quite hardy, compared to the similar looking *Carijoa riisei*, which does not contain zooxanthellae. The type species is *Coelogorgia palmosa*, and we are aware of another species, *C. repens*, which differs by having larger spicules and therefore a rougher texture (Fosså and Nilsen, 1985).

Natural Habitat: Common in polluted harbours, but also occurs on reefs in clear water, on reef slopes where there is considerable surge or strong currents. The specimen photographed in Klaus Jansen's aquarium originated from the Red Sea. The specimen we saw at the Löbbecke Aquarium in Düsseldorf was identical to the species described as *Carijoa* sp. 2 in the book *Coral Reef Animals of the Indo-Pacific* by Gosliner, Behrens and Williams. It is described as "KA4-STOL-15" in the book *Korallenriff-Aquarium Band 4* by Fosså and Nilsen. That species is widely distributed in the Indo-Pacific (G. Williams, pers. comm.).

Aquarium Care: Strong light and moderate to strong water motion.

Reproduction: The most common form of reproduction is asexual, as new polyps arise from the creeping stolon. Nothing is known about sexual reproduction in this genus.

Family Tubiporidae

Scientific Name: *Tubipora musica* (Linnaeus, 1758)

Common Name: Organ-pipe coral, Pipe-organ coral

Colour: Red to maroon skeleton with white, gray, brown or green polyps.

Distinguishing Characteristics: Skeleton is distinctive, being composed of long tubes with connecting terraces. The polyps of the different forms may easily be confused with the different *Clavularia* spp. and *Pachyclavularia* (*Briareum*) spp. One form that lacks prominent pinnules has polyps essentially identical to those of the stony coral *Alveopora*, distinguishable only by the fact that *Alveopora* has twelve tentacles and *Tubipora* only eight. Another form has flattened tentacles that look like paddles. Although *Tubipora* is considered monotypic, it is likely that the different forms are different species. There are four nominal species, but scientific consensus presently recognizes only one species as valid (Veron, 1986). Nevertheless, we feel that the differences in skeleton and polyp structure, and relative ease of aquarium care between the forms is so significant that at least three, and possibly four species should be recognized.

Natural Habitat: Wide ranging, but most abundant in shallow lagoons in turbid water. Also found on reef slopes, and in deep water in clear or turbid areas. In shallow backreef locations it forms really large isolated heads in sand or coral rubble. On the reef flat the heads are smaller and encrusting.

Aquarium Care: Different forms have greater or less demanding requirements. The easiest form to keep has large polyps that are indistinguishable from the larger polyped *Clavularia*. The most difficult form to keep has tiny polyps. *Tubipora* spp. appreciate very strong illumination, and gentle to strong currents. Trace elements are very important for long-term success with *Tubipora*, particularly iron. Hair algae is an enemy of course, so it should not be allowed to grow on it. Newly imported specimens often have sponges growing throughout the skeleton of the coral. This is not a problem as long as the sponge is alive. If the sponge is damaged in shipping, it may die, rot, and kill the coral.

Reproduction: The most common form of reproduction is asexual, as new polyps arise along the interconnecting stolons. Nothing is known about sexual reproduction in this genus.

Two colour morphs of the small polyp variety of *Tubipora*.
J. C. Delbeek

The small polyp variety of *Tubipora* photographed on the reef. Under different lighting conditions (usually partial shade) the tentacles and oral disc may become broad.
S. W. Michael

This variety of *Tubipora* has medium sized polyps.
J. C. Delbeek

Compare the large polyp variety of *Tubipora* with the small polyp variety. A. J. Nilsen

This "paddle tentacle" variety of *Tubipora* is quite distinctive. The pinnules are fused. Compare the polyps with those of the species we called "*Acrossota*," which also has fused pinnules. This variety of *Tubipora* is likely a distinct species from the varieties with pinnules. J. Sprung

This highly unusual variety of *Tubipora* is probably another distinct species. It has no pinnules at all and the polyps are remarkably similar to those of the stony coral *Alveopora*. Compare the tubular pinnule-less tentacles of this species with those of the "Unidentified Stoloniferan Number 2." The photo was taken in the Solomon Islands. L. Jackson

[1]The genus *Briareum* is presently classified as a gorgonian under the suborder Scleraxonia. Many soft coral taxonomists consider *Briareum* synonymous with *Pachyclavularia*, which is classified as a genus in the family Tubiporidae. We agree that *Briareum* and *Pachyclavularia* seem very close, probably synonymous, and that is why we have put the genus *Briareum* here. However, the position in the family Tubiporidae, while intuitive based on the reddish-purple encrusting growth form *Pachyclavularia* shares in common with *Tubipora*, seems erroneous when one compares the polyps of *Tubipora* to other Stoloniferans. *Tubipora* seems to be more similar to *Clavularia* species and the related unidentified stoloniferans shown in this book than to *Pachyclavularia*. A revision of the group may eliminate some families and subfamilies or create new ones.

[2]There may be more than one species of *Briareum* in the Caribbean, in addition to the similar-looking but unrelated *Erythropodium*. See comments under *Briareum asbestinum*.

Family Tubiporidae[1]

Genus: *Briareum*

The Genus *Briareum* was formerly considered a type of gorgonian, suborder Scleraxonia (see table 1.1 in chapter one). Some *Briareum* spp., *B. asbestinum* from the Caribbean for example, form upright branched colonies without a central axis made of gorgonin, but with a medulla instead. The same species[2] may also form encrusting sheets on hard or soft bottom, or it may encrust and kill gorgonians, using the remaining axis for support and giving the impression of being the gorgonian that formed the axis. Some members of this genus in the Indo—Pacific were until recently assigned the genus *Pachyclavularia*. It is now gaining acceptance that there is little difference between *Briareum* and *Pachyclavularia*, and many soft coral taxonomists consider the two genera synonymous.

Scientific Name: *Briareum* spp.

Formerly called *Clavularia viridis* in the aquarium literature, but this is incorrect. See for example Wilkens, 1990. *Clavularia viridis* Quoy & Gaimard in Milne Edwards & Haime, 1850 is the type species for the distinct genus *Clavularia*. The name *Pachyclavularia viridis* is a compound mistake, a make-believe name by aquarists who know the genus is *Pachyclavularia*, linking it with the specific name Wilkens gave.

Common Name: Green Star Polyp, Star Polyps, *Xenia*

Closeup of the polyps of Green Star Polyp, *Briareum* cf. *stechei*. Note the reduced pinnules. J. Yaiullo

Color: Encrusting pale purple sheets with fluorescent green polyps. Sometimes polyps are brown, gray, bluish or silvery. Centers of polyps may be white, yellow, or green, often (but not always) contrasting with the tentacles, giving the effect of a starburst, hence the common name. There are several distinct species that are very similar to each other. *Briareum* cf. *stechei* (Kükenthal, 1908) is one of the species imported from Indonesia and may be the Green Star Polyp most commonly imported, aside from green forms of *Pachyclavularia* (*Briareum*) *violacea*.

Distinguishing Characteristics: The form most commonly called "green star polyp" usually has brilliant green polyps with small (less than 1/16 inch), pale green or whitish center. Polyps occasionally just brown or gray. Encrusting sheet is usually deep purple, but fades in captivity to a lighter colour. Sometimes encrusting sheet is brownish, and other species form light tan encrusting sheets. *Pachyclavularia* (*Briareum*) *violacea* ("Brown Star Polyp") is easily distinguished. It has a very large bright center on each polyp (ca. 1/16 to 1/8 inch), and when the polyps close they leave tall projecting tubular calyces that are dark purple (a synonymous name is *Pachyclavularia erecta*). When the similar "Green Star Polyp," *Briareum* sp. closes, the calyces are only slightly projecting. Either species can have brown, green, or gray polyps. There are also several other similar species that may have brown, gray, or green polyps, with a brown or purple encrusting sheet, but with polyps bearing distinct fine pinnules. One type has a lighter coloured stripe running down each tentacle, and greatly resembles the Caribbean species, *B. asbestinum*. A few species have creeping stolons that may fuse to form sheets, some with very tiny polyps. The Caribbean has two genera, *Erythropodium* and *Briareum*, which resemble Indo-Pacific star polyps. There are *Erythropodium* species in the Indo-Pacific as well, including temperate species. Future revision of soft coral taxonomy will probably place *Pachyclavularia* together with *Briareum*, and new books have already included this change (see for example Allen and Steene 1995, Nilsen and Fosså 1995, Colin and Arneson 1995). This change is a bit problematic since the genus *Briareum* is currently classified as a type of gorgonian, under the suborder Scleraxonia, based on the structure of its medulla, while *Pachyclavularia* is classified as a stoloniferan in the family Tubiporidae. This is not such a big problem; when one looks at species in all of the different groups it is apparent there are continuities (intergrading forms) between the taxa, with the exception of Pennatulacea. Verseveldt (1940) recognized the link between Alcyonacea

This *Briareum* sp. from Indonesia forms encrusting tangles of "twigs" instead of the more typical mats. The polyps are bright green. J. Sprung

The polyps of this unidentified Indonesian species look like *B. asbestinum* from the Caribbean, though they often have a greenish hue never found in *B. asbestinum*. The encrusting sheet of tissue has a unique form. It is usually perforated, composed of fused creeping stolons. J. C. Delbeek

Closeup of encrusting sheet of the same unidentified species. J. Sprung

Shortly before this book went to press we received word from Dr. Phil Alderslade, who examined the specimen shown here, that this is not a *Briareum* species, but a very unusual *Erythropodium* sp! Although the polyps resemble those of *Briareum*, the two genera are not closely related. See the description for *Erythropodium* later in this chapter.

and Gorgonacea in the example of Briareidae, and he proposed moving Briareidae to Alcyonacea (Bayer, 1981).

Natural Habitat: Green Star Polyp is frequently imported from Indonesia and nearby localities in the Indo—Pacific, where it grows on outer reef slopes and in lagoons and bays, encrusting coral rubble and live corals.

Aquarium Care: Green Star Polyp is a popular, hardy soft coral that can be recommended even for the novice aquarists. The only problem one might encounter regards filamentous algae, which can easily smother this coral. Star polyps should not be added to the aquarium until it is free of these algae. If filamentous algae begins to grow on it, twirl a wooden toothpick in the algae to draw it off, and then apply several algae eating snails directly on the colony to polish off the short turf that remains. Star polyps like bright indirect illumination. Under metal halide light it is best to place green star polyps lower down in the tank as very bright light makes the colours paler. Their colors are best shown off under a combination of daylight and blue fluorescent tubes. When the blue tubes are on alone, the green color is brilliant. Strong currents stimulate polyp extension and enhance growth of the colony. Occasional blasts with a powerhead or fanning by hand will help wash away detritus that may accumulate around the base (Wilkens, 1986). Be careful not to allow this fast growing species to overgrow stony corals! It will kill them. It is therefore best to avoid placing this species on rocks where it can encroach on stony corals. It can be placed instead on sandy bottom or where it will encrust on the walls of the aquarium. It's growth is easily managed when it encrusts over glass, acrylic, or sand by simply lifting up the sheet and cutting with a blade or scissors. When it encrusts on rock it is nearly impossible to control. It may be brushed with a bristle brush to keep it away from stony corals, a real task. In a soft coral-only aquarium it can safely encrust the rocks as it seldom causes harm to other soft corals.

Reproduction: The most common form of reproduction is asexual, as new polyps arise from the creeping stoloniferous mat. On the GBR, *B. stechei* was found to be a dioecious external brooder, with the developing planulae residing just beside the mouth. The reddish-brown planulae were released between 11 and 13 days after the full moon in November, at 10 AM (Alino and Coll, 1989). The colour of the planulae suggests the presence of zooxanthellae. Sexual reproduction in aquaria has not yet been reported.

This is the green colour morph of
P. violacea. J. C. Delbeek

The common brown form of
P. violacea. J. C. Delbeek

Scientific Name: *Pachyclavularia* (*Briareum*) *violacea*

Common Name: Brown Star Polyp, Green Star polyp (green form)

Colour: Brown, gray, or green polyps with white, green, or yellow centers. The encrusting sheet is purple or reddish.

Distinguishing Characteristics: Purple encrusting sheets with brown or green polyps. The 1/16 to 1/8 inch centers of the polyps are bright white, green, or yellow. When the polyps close, the projecting calyces are approximately 25% larger than those of the just previously described *Briareum* sp. Polyps have some indistinct pinnules.

Similar Species: *Briareum* sp., distinguished in the previous description.

Natural Habitat: This is a common import from Indonesia. J. Sprung observed it on coastal reefs in Australia, in turbid water approximately 5 meters deep encrusting dead coral, hardbottom, and algae. It formed vast mats several meters across. All colonies observed in Australia were brown. Hobbyists in Australia report no green-polyped colonies of this species. Wilkens (1986) found star polyps from extreme shallows to at least 8 meters depth in the South China Sea and Central Java Sea, where most aquarium specimens originate. J. Sprung observed this species on reef slopes in the Solomon Islands, where it was very common, usually brown but occasionally with a slight greenish hue. The bright green varieties seem to be uncommon and are imported mostly from Indonesia.

Aquarium Care: Same for Green Star polyp, except this species tolerates stronger light. Strong currents stimulate polyp expansion. Polyps do not take food. Be careful not to allow this fast growing species to overgrow stony corals! It will kill them.

Reproduction: The most common form of reproduction is asexual, as new polyps arise from the creeping stoloniferous mat. On the GBR, *P. violacea* was found to be a dioecious external brooder, with the developing planulae residing just beside the mouth. The reddish-brown planulae were released between 11 and 13 days after the full moon in November, at 10 AM (Alino and Coll, 1989). The colour of the planulae suggests the presence of zooxanthellae. Sexual reproduction in aquaria has not yet been reported.

Scientific Name: *Briareum asbestinum*

Common Name: Corky Sea Fingers, Encrusting Gorgonian, Briareum

Distinguishing Characteristics: *Briareum* is a beautiful soft coral from the Caribbean that may form flat crusts, knobby crusts, upright branches like a gorgonian but without a horny skeleton, or it may encrust (and kill) other gorgonians, using the skeleton for support. The appearance is similar to the "star polyps" from the Indo—Pacific, see earlier comments on the re-classification of these. The polyps, which often have a white streak down the center of each tentacle, resemble *Xenia* polyps to the casual observer.

Similar Species: *Erythropodium* spp., *Anthelia* spp., *Xenia* spp. There are two forms (probably species) of *Briareum* in the

Briareum asbestinum.
J. C. Delbeek

These are two varieties of *Briareum asbestinum* collected in Florida. There may be more than one species, see text. The top specimen is the non-encrusting reef form which forms upright branches with a stiff medulla. The bottom specimen growing on *Halimeda* is the inshore encrusting form, which also occurs on reefs. In deep or turbid water it develops especially large polyps. Note how the calyces in the bottom specimen resemble those of *Pachyclavularia*. J. Sprung

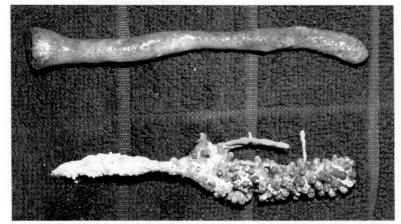

Two more examples of the same two forms from Florida. The left specimen is the non-encrusting reef form which forms upright branches with a stiff medulla. The right specimen is the inshore encrusting form, here growing over the axis of another gorgonian. J. Sprung

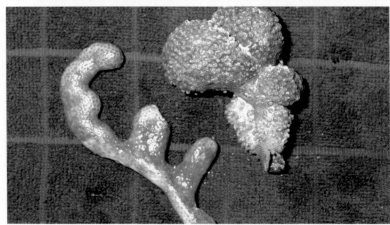

This *Briareum asbestinum* is the encrusting form. Here it has grown over and killed a gorgonian.
S. W. Michael

Compare the appearance of *Briareum* (L) to *Erythropodium* (R).
J. Sprung

Caribbean, one basically encrusting; the other forming upright branches that have not encrusted over another gorgonian. The sheet or encrusting form has erroneously been given the name *Erythropodium polyanthes* Duchassaing and Michelotti (see Bayer, 1961). It is also possible that there is more than one encrusting species in the Caribbean as there are differences in the size and colour of polyps and pinnule development, as well as the thickness and consistency of the encrusting sheets (J. Sprung, pers. obs.). See West, Harvell, and Walls (1993) for additional information about variability in this species and the possibility of undescribed species.

Natural Habitat: *Briareum asbestinum* prefers areas with strong currents or some wave action. The erect, non-encrusting form occurs on reefs and hardbottoms in clean water only. It also grows in deep water, where currents can be slight. In deep water the polyps are much larger than in shallow water. The encrusting form grows in bays and on reefs. In deep or turbid water it also develops very large polyps.

Aquarium Care: In the aquarium *Briareum* likes currents that help it shed the waxy film that it occasionally forms to clean off algae growing on its surface. Colonies of finger-like branches often have the polyps at the growing tip closed, giving the appearance of a bald spot. This may be a response to light intensity, ultraviolet radiation (and buildup of photosynthetically produced active oxygen), or simply a growth response. This coral does not appear to capture prey, so feeding particulate matter is not necessary nor useful.

Reproduction: The most common form of reproduction is asexual, as new polyps arise from the creeping stoloniferous mat. Sexual reproduction in aquaria has not yet been reported.

Suborder Alcyoniina

Family Paralcyoniidae (=Maasellidae, =Fasciculariidae)

Genus: *Studeriotes*

Scientific Name: *Studeriotes* sp.

In aquarium literature mistakenly identified as *Sphaerella krempfi* (Hickson). See for example Wilkens, 1990. The commonly imported Christmas tree coral may be *Studeriotes longiramosa* Kükenthal.

Common Name: "Christmas tree" coral, "French Tickler", *Sphaerella krempfi*

Colour: Brown, with pale base.

Distinguishing Characteristics: A pale, off-white column with large sclerites on the outside. The polyparium, consisting of straight branches with polyps on opposite sides, may be completely withdrawn into the column much like an anemone retracts its tentacles. Polyps are brown but do not contain zooxanthellae.

Natural Habitat: Found on sandy, muddy, or gravel bottoms with the column partially buried and polyparium expanded when there is strong water motion.

Studeriotes is a peculiar soft coral with a column into which the polyparium can be withdrawn.
J. Sprung

Aquarium Care: Although this species has brown polyps, it does not contain symbiotic zooxanthellae, so it does not need light. Do not place it on rock. Inexperienced aquarists often make this mistake, and the *Studeriotes* then flops over and rapidly dies. It should be placed on the bottom in a thick sand or gravel layer where it will anchor itself with root-like tendrils. It will expand the polyparium and polyps when it receives strong water currents. Feed with *Artemia* nauplii, *Daphnia*, or pulverized food suspension when the polyps are expanded. In general this species does not thrive in captivity. Dedicated aquarists who take the time to feed it can grow this coral, however. It is hardy, ships well, and is very resistant to infections or injuries that can kill other types of soft corals. Avoid keeping large or nippy fishes with this coral that might discourage it from expanding and thus prevent it from feeding.

Reproduction: This is one soft coral for which asexual (vegetative) reproduction is not well known. Reproduction of this species in captivity (by sexual or asexual means) has not been reported. It is possible that the tendrils that anchor this species in the substrate may develop into new colonies, but this has not been observed. Sexual reproduction has not yet been reported in aquaria.

Family Alcyoniidae Lamouroux, 1812

The family Alcyoniidae includes soft corals in which the polyps are contained in fleshy, membranous, or lobed masses. Polyps are dimorphic in some genera and monomorphic in others, and they are mostly evenly distributed, though they may be confined to a polyparium or capitulum that is separate from a polypless stalk. There are approximately twenty genera worldwide. See chapter one for more information on colony organization and shapes.

Genus: *Alcyonium* Linnaeus, 1758

* Formerly known as *Cladiella* in aquarium literature. *Cladiella* is a separate but similar genus. The origin of the name *Alcyonium* is derived from the coral's resemblance to a type of sponge, Alkyonium, which was named for its resemblance to the nest of the Kingfisher bird, Alkyon, from the Greek (Williams, 1993).

Common Name: Colt coral, Broccoli coral, Cauliflower coral

Colour: Pale brown, dark brown, or gray. The polyps are darker than the pale stalk. Occasionally colonies have green or blue hue.

Distinguishing Characteristics: *Alcyonium* are slimy to the touch, and have polyps that appear to be generated on the lower portions of the stalk, developing as they migrate upward. The distinction between some species of *Alcyonium* and some species of *Cladiella* is quite blurry based on gross morphology. One must examine the sclerites to be certain.

Similar Genera: *Alcyonium* is quite similar to *Cladiella*, so it is not surprising that confusion exists between these genera. Some slimy species of *Sinularia* are also quite similar to *Alcyonium* when expanded. Some expanded *Alcyonium* could be confused with *Nephthea*, *Lemnalia*, or *Capnella*, but *Alcyonium* is slimy to the touch while the three mentioned nephtheids have a rough texture because of their abundant large sclerites.

This *Alcyonium* sp., "Colt Coral," in the aquarium trade, has beautiful bushy polyps and a pale stalk. J. C. Delbeek

Another variety of *Alcyonium* known as Colt coral. J. C. Delbeek

Alcyonium is a very diverse genus; some species are nearly identical to each other while others are so different they seem like other genera. J. C. Delbeek

These varieties of *Alcyonium* are quite similar to *Cladiella*. They may have the ability to sting thin skin areas such as the underside of arms, a rare ability in soft corals. J. C. Delbeek

This rare variety of *Alcyonium* forms dark brown encrusting mats with short soft branches that are beautifully fluid in strong water motion. It is similar to low encrusting *Cladiella* species, but does not become stiff nor blush white when the polyps close. J. Sprung

Natural Habitat: *Alcyonium* occur most prolifically on reefs in lagoons or calm backreef areas, often in turbid water.

Aquarium Care: *Alcyonium* species are quite hardy in captivity and they ship very well, so they have been popular with reef aquarists since the earliest availability of live corals for aquariums. Several very similar species are known by the common name "Colt Coral" or "Cladiella," and they grow very quickly in captivity. An imported colony of just 10 cm height may proliferate into a 35 cm tall bush in about six months. If branches are severed with a scissors, these also grow quickly into large colonies. Placement of the colony is important since the rapid growth may cause it to contact neighboring species. In our experience *Alcyonium* will sting gorgonians. Conversely, mushroom anemones (corallimorpharia) will sting *Alcyonium*. When *Alcyonium* is stung it may succumb to bacterial infection or infection with protozoans such as *Helicostoma* (see volume one) that can rapidly destroy the whole colony. If the colony appears collapsed for two days or more and some branches are rotting while others are not, it best to cut the whole colony out of the aquarium and, in a bucket of seawater, sever the healthy branches with a scissors and discard the remaining rotting tissue. The healthy branches should be placed in a shallow aquarium illuminated with fluorescent light at least, or other light sources. The bottom of the aquarium should have large gravel fragments for the coral to attach to, and circulation should be adequate to prevent the new cuttings from falling on the bottom and suffocating in a spot with no water motion.

Reproduction: The most common form of reproduction is asexual as colonies will often split lengthwise into two or more individuals. Fragmentation of branches, both intentional and unintentional often occurs too. Sexual reproduction in aquaria has been reported and photographed (see chapter one). Most *Alcyonium* studied to date are dioecious broadcast spawners. On the GBR, two species studied, *A. aspiculum* and *A. molle* were found to spawn four to five days after the full moon in November, at 8:30 PM (Alino and Coll, 1989).

Genus: *Parerythropodium*

This genus has been synonymized with *Alcyonium* by Groot & Weinberg, (1982). It is quite a different looking beast from the

Alcyonium (*Parerythropodium*) sp.
J. C. Delbeek

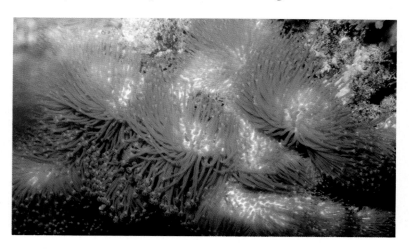

typical *Alcyonium*, however, and it has been our experience that scientists still use the old name, the revision apparently not gaining wide acceptance so far. We realize that by keeping the old name here we are in a way perpetuating the situation, but we felt it was necessary in order to give the most accurate description.

Scientific Name: *Alcyonium (Parerythropodium)* spp.

Common Name: Encrusting leather coral

Colour: Yellow or brown

Distinguishing Characteristics: Encrusting thin sheets with long polyps that resemble those of leather corals (*Sarcophyton* spp.) The sheets are extremely soft and fragile with consistency like *Xenia* and *Anthelia*. Strong pungent odor when lifted out of water.

Natural Habitat: *Alcyonium (Parerythropodium) fulvum fulvum* is common in the Red Sea while *Alcyonium (Parerythropodium) membranaceum* occurs in the Indo-Pacific. Wide ranging, but most abundant in shallow lagoons in turbid water. Encrusts dead coral fragments and gravel.

Aquarium Care: *Alcyonium membranaceum* and *A. fulvum fulvum* are easy to grow and propagate in aquariums. They prefer intense light and strong water motion and will encrust rocks, glass, and anything else in their way very rapidly. They can become a problem species because of this rapid growth. Give plenty of room, as they can harm stony corals and encrust over them. Like *Xenia* spp., *Alcyonium (Parerythropodium)* does not ship well, but once it is established in the aquarium trade it should be widely available as tank raised specimens. It is curious that the branchy forms of *Alcyonium* (i.e.. "Colt Corals") are very durable in shipping, while this encrusting type is not. Also, the smell of the encrusting *Alcyonium (Parerythropodium)* is quite like that of *Xenia* spp., which ship poorly, and quite unlike branchy *Alcyonium*, which have a different, slight odor. They feed well on minute food particles such as brine shrimp nauplii or *Daphnia* (Wilkens, 1986), but do not need to be fed.

Reproduction: Most commonly asexual by growth of the encrusting mat, from which new polyps arise. Sexual reproduction unknown from aquaria. In studies conducted in the wild, colonies of *Alcyonium Parerythropodium fulvum fulvum* begin to repro-

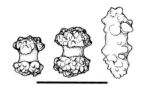

Dumbell shaped sclerites of *Cladiella.* Scale bar is 0.2 mm. *After Williams, 1993.*

duce sexually after three to four years (Benayahu and Loya, 1983). They are dioecious and brood planulae externally (Benayahu and Loya, 1983). Spawning takes place just after dusk between June and August. Eggs take ten to eleven months to develop, while sperm take seven to eight. Fertilization is internal, but development is external in a mucus sheath on the side of the polyp. Within six days the eggs are developed into planulae and are released to drop to the bottom. Presumably currents then carry them away. This was the first soft coral species discovered to employ external brooding of planulae.

Genus: *Cladiella* Gray, 1869

This is a typical *Cladiella* species with short fingers and dark brown polyps. When disturbed the polyps contract and the colony "blanches" white. J. C. Delbeek

Cladiella sp. J. C. Delbeek

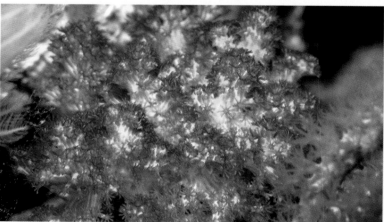

The origin of the name is from the Greek, klados, meaning branch or sprout, referring to the numerous lobe-like branches of the polyparium. There are approximately 40+ species.

Common Name: Finger leather, Colt coral, Cauliflower coral, Blushing coral

Colour: Brown polyps contrasting with strikingly paler tissue. When the polyps are expanded the colony looks bushy and brown. When disturbed the polyps contract and the colony blanches white.

Distinguishing Characteristics: *Cladiella* spp. are slippery, like a wet bar of soap. The blush or blanch from brown to white when the polyps close is typical for the genus, but also occurs in a few unrelated nephtheidae, which could easily be mistaken for *Cladiella* based on their appearance and this blanching characteristic. The nephtheidae are not slippery at all, however, due to the presence of large sclerites in their tissue and less production of mucus. *Cladiella* and *Alcyonium* species may be so similar as to be indistinguishable on gross appearance alone. The name *Cladiella* has been used incorrectly in aquarium literature to identify members of the genus *Alcyonium* commonly imported as "colt coral." The sclerites are distinctively dumbell-shaped in *Cladiella*.

Similar Genera: *Alcyonium, Sinularia*. There are species of *Alcyonium* and *Sinularia* that cannot easily be distinguished by gross morphology from *Cladiella* (and vice versa), requiring examination of the sclerites for positive confirmation. See additional comments under *Alcyonium*.

Natural Habitat: *Cladiella* species occupy several different reef habitats, including rubble zones on the reef flat (where they occur along with *Sarcophyton, Lobophytum,* and *Sinularia*), reef slopes, and back-reef margins or lagoons. The compact forms commonly occur in areas with strong light and high water turbulence.

Aquarium Care: *Cladiella* are hardy and fast growing soft corals that adapt to a wide variety of light intensity and water flow. In general the best conditions for them are moderate to very bright light and strong water motion, at least intermittently. There are so many forms that it is hard to generalize about the whole genus.

Reproduction: Asexual reproduction is most common in aquaria. Some species split transversely, and these clones then tend to move

Without examining the sclerites it is nearly impossible to determine if this soft coral is *Alcyonium* or *Cladiella*. It is also similar to *Sinularia* spp. J. C. Delbeek

This is probably a *Cladiella* species, but it could also be *Alcyonium*. The sclerites must be examined for positive identification. J. C. Delbeek

Most *Cladiella* species are compact with short lobes, but some form more distinct branches. This specimen could be *Cladiella* or *Alcyonium*. J. Sprung.

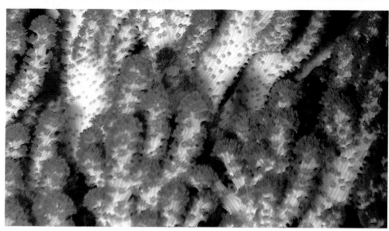

slowly away from each other. On the GBR *C.* (cf.) *prattae* was found to be a dioecious broadcast spawner (see chapter one). Eggs and sperm were released five days after the full moon in November, at 8:30 PM (Alino and Coll, 1989). Eggs did not possess zooxanthellae. Sexual reproduction has not yet been observed in aquaria.

Genus: *Lobophytum*

Typical *Lobophytum* sp., aka "Devil's hand Coral." J. C. Delbeek

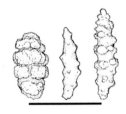

Sclerites of *Lobophytum*. Scale bar is 0.2 mm. *After Williams, 1993.*

Scientific Name: *Lobophytum* spp.

Common Name: Devil's hand, finger leather, "Lobophyton" Please note that the correct spelling of the genus is *Lobophytum*. Aquarists often confuse the spelling, changing the ending "um" to "on" because of the spelling of the closely related *Sarcophyton*.

Colour: Pale brown or gray with white tentacled polyps. Occasionally yellow or greenish.

Distinguishing Characteristics: This genus is very closely related to *Sarcophyton*, and some colonies appear essentially the same as that genus, like large toadstools, except that in *Lobophytum* the crown has finger-like branches or lobes. Like *Sarcophyton*, *Lobophytum* has two types of polyps, autozooids and siphonozooids.

Similar Genera: *Sarcophyton* spp., but *Lobophytum* has branches or distinctly raised lobes. In some cases small colonies of *Lobophytum* may not have developed lobes and so they cannot be

A common variety of *Lobophytum* sp. that has upright lobes arranged like spokes. J. C. Delbeek

A more compact form of *Lobophytum* sp. J. C. Delbeek

distinguished from *Sarcophyton* without examination of the sclerites. In fact, the sclerites are not always dramatically different either, and it seems that these two genera intergrade slightly, while there are many species on opposite extremes of the spectrum of differences. *Sinularia* spp. are also similar to *Lobophytum*, particularly the massive encrusting species, but *Sinularia* spp. do not have two types of polyps and they do have large robust spicules around the base.

Natural Habitat: Wide ranging, but most abundant in shallow lagoons in turbid water. Huge stands of *Lobophytum* along with *Sarcophyton* and *Sinularia* are common in very shallow water close to shore where they receive very bright light. Large encrusting forms are also common on reef flats and at the reef crest.

This species of *Lobophytum* sp. has finger-like lobes that make it appear similar to some *Sinularia* species. J. C. Delbeek

Upon closer inspection one can see that there are two types of polyps: autozooids and siphonozooids. Therefore this "Finger Leather" is a *Lobophytum* species. J. C. Delbeek

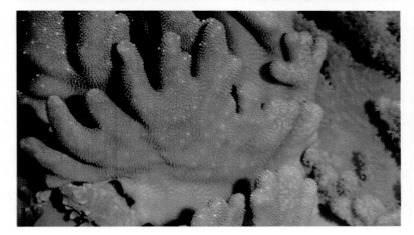

Aquarium Care: Same as *Sarcophyton* spp. Tolerates dim illumination or intense illumination, shows most beautifully under moderate to bright light. Appreciates gentle to strong currents.

Reproduction: Asexual reproduction is most common in aquaria where new colonies can bud off the base. Can be easily propagated, see *Sarcophyton*. *Lobophytum* spp. are dioecious broadcast spawners. On the GBR six species all spawn one week after the full moon in November in the early evening (Alino and Coll, 1989). Populations of *L. crassum* in Okinawa, Japan spawned from June to August (Yamazato *et al.*, 1981). Eggs are fertilized in thirty minutes and planulae develop within two days. Settlement occurs approximately two days later. Eggs take two years to develop and sperm take only one year. As a result, two sets of eggs are usually seen in sexually mature polyps in female colonies; small, light-coloured immature eggs and larger, darker-coloured mature eggs (Yamazato *et al.*, 1981). Sexual reproduction in aquaria not reported, yet.

Genus: *Sarcophyton* Lesson, 1834

Etymology: The name is derived from the Greek words sarkos, which means flesh, and phyton, which means creature. There are at least 36 species (Verseveldt, 1982).

Closeup of the beautiful polyps of *Sarcophyton* sp. J. Macare

Two very beautiful small *Sarcophyton* sp., probably *S. glaucum*, in the aquarium of Bob and Debbie James in Toronto Canada. J. C. Delbeek

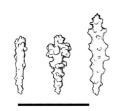

Sclerites of *Sarcophyton*. Scale bar is 0.2 mm. *After Williams, 1993.*

Sarcophyton glaucum.
J. C. Delbeek

Sarcophyton elegans. This species is imported from Tonga and Fiji where it occurs in clear shallow water at the reef crest and in partially exposed backreef areas. In this location it receives intense illumination and strong water motion. It is therefore more demanding in this regard than other *Sarcophyton* species. It often suffers in shipping, developing black necrotic areas similar to shipping injuries in some *Sinularia* species. Strong light encourages the maintenance of the bright yellow colour. J. C. Delbeek

Scientific Name: *Sarcophyton* spp.

Common Name: Leather coral

Colour: Pale brown, yellow, gray, or green with white, yellow, green, or rarely, pale blue tentacled polyps.

Distinguishing Characteristics: *Sarcophyton* species all look like mushrooms or toadstools, with lovely polyps that extend from the upper surface. Their appearance is highly variable, and the same species from slightly different locations can look radically different. The common species available include *S. trochelio- phorum, S. glaucum, S. tenuispiculatum, S. elegans,* and *S. ehren- bergi. Sarcophyton ehrenbergi* is considered the most beautiful

species by hobbyists, but the name is often attributed to any especially well adapted and beautiful *Sarcophyton*. Recently a bright yellow leather coral has been imported from Tonga and Fiji. The common name is "Tonga Yellow Leather." This is *Sarcophyton elegans* Moser, 1919. Not only is the colour distinctive, the polyps are too. They are large but don't extend out on long tubular stems as in other *Sarcophyton* species, appearing more like *Sinularia* polyps. *Sarcophyton elegans* polyps are further distinguished by having a lot of large sclerites.

Natural Habitat: Wide ranging throughout the Indo-Pacific and Red Sea, but most abundant in shallow lagoons in turbid water. Also common on reef slopes and reef flats.

Aquarium Care: *Sarcophyton* species like gentle currents, but are stimulated by occasional "blasts" of surge or strong currents that help them shed the waxy film that develops on their surface. With the exception of *S. elegans*, they are hardy and recommended for the beginner, but they do sometimes fall prey to a variety of parasites. See additional information in the chapter on diseases and parasites.

Reproduction: Easily propagated by cutting with a sharp scissors and tying the cuttings to live rock with monofilament. See chapter on propagating techniques. Leather corals often split spontaneously, or bud off new colonies around the base. At least one species buds off colonies from under the umbrella-like head. Most will also form necrotic areas on the head that cause a "flap" of tissue with polyps to separate, and a new colony may thus be formed. Sexual reproduction in aquariums not yet reported, but is likely to occur. *Sarcophyton* colonies can take several years to reach sexual maturity. For example, *S. glaucum* matures within seven to ten years (see Benayahu and Loya, 1984a). In the wild *Sarcophyton* spp. have been found to be dioecious broadcast spawners (Alino and Coll, 1989). Three species studied on the GBR spawned one week after the full moon in November, in the early evening. Egg and sperm development are as in *Lobophytum*. Development and settlement of planulae are also similar to *Lobophytum*. Zooxanthellae were incorporated into the tissue of young polyps fifteen days after spawning (Alino and Coll, 1989). *Sarcophtyon glaucum* Quoy and Gaimard, 1833 in the Red Sea were found to exhibit similar patterns (Benayahu and Loya, 1986).

Sarcophyton cf. *ehrenbergi* commonly reproduces by forming tears in the polyparium. The partially severed fragments of the crown soon fall off and attach to the rocks to form new colonies.
J. C. Delbeek

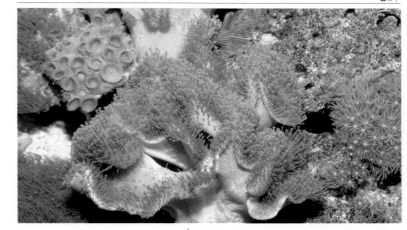

Sarcophyton cf. *ehrenbergi* (probably). This species does not always have such sharply pointed marginal folds. Interestingly, there is a species of *Lobophytum* with thin, elongate polyps virtually identical to those of *S. ehrenbergi*.
J. C. Delbeek

Sarcophyton species can grow very large in a short period of time. These two large specimens photographed in the aquarium of John Burleson have the form typically called *S. trocheliophorum*, but there are many species with this exact appearance and positive identification is not possible without examination of the sclerites.
J. C. Delbeek

Sarcophyton sp., possibly *S. tenuispiculatum*. J. C. Delbeek.

A very large specimen of Sarco-phyton sp. at the Löbbecke Museum in Düsseldorf, Germany. J. Sprung

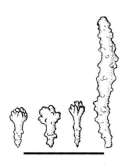

Sclerites of *Sinularia*. Scale bar is 0.2 mm. *After Williams, 1993*.

Genus: *Sinularia*

Scientific Name: *Sinularia* spp.

Common Name: Finger Leather, Soft finger

Colour: Whitish, gray, yellow, brown, green.

Distinguishing Characteristics: The genus *Sinularia* contains many species with very different appearance. Some have fat branches, some have thin branches, some have no branches at all, forming thick encrusting sheets with raised lobes, some appear more like tree fungus (bracken). The characteristic that links them

Sinularia sp. B. Carlson

Sinularia notanda, left, is one of the prettiest species. It resembles *Nephthea*. To the right of it is a gorgonian, probably *Rumphella*. J. Sprung

This encrusting *Sinularia* sp. looks like *Lobophytum,* but lacks the siphonozooids that characterize that genus. J. Sprung

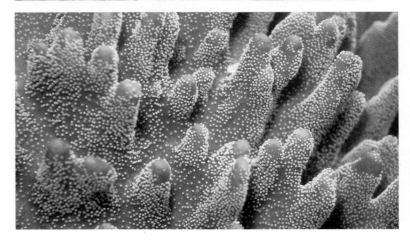

Sinularia and *Lobophytum* both have species with short upright lobes that encrust large areas on exposed reef slopes. Sometimes the two genera grow right next to each other. *Sinularia* is to the left, *Lobophytum* to the right. Upon close inspection one can see the siphonozooids of *Lobophytum*. *Sinularia* does not have siphonozooids, but close inspection of it reveals large white spindle-shaped sclerites. J. Sprung

Sinularia flexibilis, a species with extremely elongate branches. There are numerous species with such fine branches, and positive identification requires examination of the sclerites. J. Sprung

is the presence of long robust spicules of characteristic shape around the base of the colony. There are hundreds of species of *Sinularia* described, exhibiting a wide variety of growth forms. Although many may superficially resemble *Lobophytum* they can be differentiated based on the presence of monomorphic polyps; *Lobophytum* has dimorphic polyps.

Natural Habitat: Wide ranging in the Indo-Pacific, but most abundant in shallow lagoons in turbid water. Thick encrusting species typically occur on reef slopes exposed to strong water motion.

Aquarium Care: Some species require strong water motion, but generally a light turbulent flow is sufficient. Most adapt to a wide range of light intensity, but moderate lighting or indirect but

This very slippery fine-branched *Sinularia* sp. has forms that may be yellow or green. It has large spiny sclerites concentrated in the base where it is attached to rock. This species bears some resemblance to *Lemnalia* spp. It has been propagated in captivity for several years from parent colonies collected in Palau, and tank-raised specimens are being marketed to the aquarium industry. A similar species, *S. mollis* (see Nilsen and Fosså, 1996) is also slippery with lots of long sclerites in the base, but it is usually brownish gray and with thicker branches, though it is a highly variable species. J. Sprung

Sinularia sp. J. Sprung

bright light (as from fluorescent lamps) will produce the most beautiful expansion of polyps and good growth.

Reproduction: *Sinularia* spp. are easily propagated by cutting off branches with a scissors or sharp knife, and planting them on rocks using monofilament line or a plastic toothpick for positioning (see chapter six). Arborescent forms of *Sinularia* regularly drop tips of branches by fission, which then attach to rocks or other stationary objects encrusted with coralline algae. *Sinularia* are dioecious broadcast spawners. On the GBR spawning of six species occurred during the early evening hours of November, approximately three to five days after the full moon (Alino and Coll, 1989). Eggs on the mesenteries appear to be of two stages of development, indicating a two year maturity period as in *Lobo*

Sinularia dura has a form quite unlike typical *Sinularia* spp.
J. C. Delbeek

This *Sinularia* sp.? was common in the Solomon Islands on reef slopes. It superficially resembles *S. dura* but grows much larger, with individual capitula exceeding two feet (60 cm). The polyps are also larger than those of *S. dura*. All specimens observed had fine white sand trapped in their bowl-like surface. It is possible that this is not a *Sinularia* at all, but a closely related genus, *Dampia* (P. Alderslade, pers. comm.).
J. Sprung

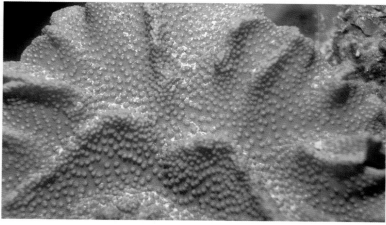

The shape of *S. dura* is highly variable, depending on light and water motion. Here the normally flat platy colony has begun to grow branches. J. C. Delbeek

Colonies with this shape have been given the name *Sinularia brassica*, but some taxonomists consider that genus synonymous with *S. dura*. We believe there are two species, but that they both have forms that look like the other, depending on the lighting and water flow conditions. *Sinularia brassica*, from what we can tell, forms thickened upright branches in the middle of the colony, while *S. dura* tends to extend its margin into branches, with a few thin branches forming upright in the middle. The big question is whether the sclerites are different. That we don't know. J. Sprung

Is this *Sinularia brassica* or *S. dura* that has formed branches? J. C. Delbeek

Morphing in *S. dura* showing how clones of the same colony can have quite different appearance. The camera flash washed out the differences in illumination. Note how branching in this species tends to occur from the periphery as extensions of the jagged lappets. J. Sprung

phytum and *Sarcophyton* (Alino and Coll, 1989; Benayahu and Loya, 1986; Yamazato *et al.* 1981). However, the eggs of *Sinularia* are much larger than those of *Lobophytum* or *Sarcophyton* spp., approximately 800 um compared to 650 um (Alino and Coll, 1989). Development of planula takes forty eight hours, with settlement following within four to fourteen days. Spawning of *Sinularia* in aquaria has not been reported to us but we are sure that it has occurred.

Family Nephtheidae

Corals in this family tend to be arborescent with non-retractile polyps but some genera have retractile polyps (i.e. *Paralemnalia*). Some species may resemble broccoli or cauliflower in shape (Williams, 1993). The polyps are usually supported by bundles of sclerites and are grouped together along or at the end of the branches in bundles called catkins. These sclerites are thought to protect the polyps from predators in species where they are non-retractile. Recent theories have proposed that they play an important role in supporting the polyp in strong current, allowing the polyp to continue to capture food (Fabricius, 1995b).

Genus: *Capnella*

Colonies are arborescent but some species may also be lobed. The lobes tend to be crowded with incurved polyps (Mather and Bennett, 1993). Sclerites on the interior are often globular, while those on the exterior of the branches and stalk tend to be shorter capstans, consisting of two distinct parts. There is an externally projecting, leaf-like part and a more spindle-like basal portion that may or may not have high warts or root-like outgrowths (Verseveldt, 1977). There are currently 17 species described from Africa to the western Pacific. See Verseveldt (1977) for a key to the species.

Scientific Name: *Capnella* spp.

Common Name: Kenya tree, "Nephthya", *Nephthea*

Colour: Gray with brown polyps, sometimes green. Bleached colonies may be yellow.

Distinguishing Characteristics: Forms a thick trunk like a tree with beautiful branches that sometimes hang like weeping willow branches. The polyps are like *Nephthea*, *Lemnalia*, and *Litophyton*, but they are larger. Sometimes (on reef slopes

A delicate looking colony of
Capnella grown in the aquarium in
partial shade. J. Sprung

Capnella sp. J. C. Delbeek

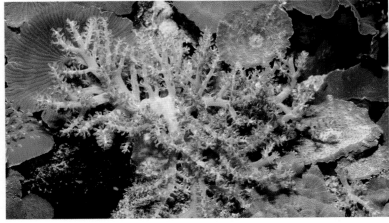

Capnella maintained under strong illumination and water motion becomes quite bushy. J. Sprung

An uncommon *Capnella* sp. with branches that form distinctive catkins. J. Sprung

exposed to strong water motion) forms compact flattened colonies with short branches.

Natural Habitat: Reef slopes in clear water, both shallow and deep, with strong tidal currents. Sometimes in shadier locations. Also found on coral rubble in shallow water very close to shore with bright illumination. *Capnella imbricata* occurs in New Guinea and the Philippines (Gosliner *et al.*, 1996), and the genus is wide-ranging throughout the Indo-Pacific region, from the African coast to the Western Pacific.

Aquarium Care: *Capnella* grows rapidly under bright, indirect light with a gentle current. Strong currents will make the polyps bushy, and cause longer branch extension. Strong direct illumination appears to stunt growth and expansion, so colonies are best placed out in the open on the bottom of the aquarium, or to either side

Reproduction: Sexual reproduction of this species is not reported in aquariums. Asexual reproduction in this genus is very distinctive. Swellings at branch tips will form and the tips will drop off to form new colonies. The severed tips have remarkable capacity to stick to rocks within a day. Tall colonies will bend over and reattach to the substrate, or form new colonies by "creeping" and subsequent division of the base, or by longitudinal fission. Branches may be cut with a scissors, and new colonies can thus be formed artificially. This genus grows so quickly that it can easily be propagated commercially in captivity to supply aquariums. The only report of sexual reproduction is for the temperate Australian species, *C. gaboensis*; a reported surface brooder of planulae (Farrant, 1985). This seems highly unusual and may be a case of misidentification, or surface brooding may be unique to this species.

Genus: *Dendronephthya*

Dendronephthya is a widespread genus, with over 250 described species that occur throughout the Indo-Pacific and Red Sea (Williams, 1993). This genus is badly in need of revision so it is likely that the number of species will decrease. Colonies can be very tree-like in appearance with long slender branches. Some colonies have short branches with clusters of polyps at the ends in umbrella-like shapes while others can be more globular on the ends. These different forms have been described as separate genera (i.e. *Roxasia, Spongodes,* and *Morchellana*). The polyps

A particularly colourful
Dendronephthya (*Spongodes*) sp.
from the Solomon Islands.
J. Sprung

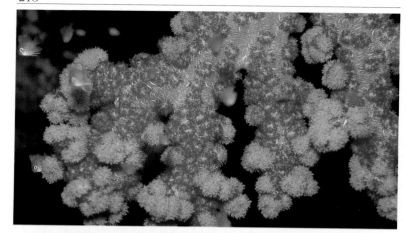

Closeup of the polyps of a
Dendronephthya (*Morchellana*) sp.
A. Storace

Lovely contrast of colour is typical
in *Dendronephthya* (*Roxasia*) spp.
J. Sprung

are non-retractile but are surrounded by sclerite bundles, within which they can retract. These sclerite bundles give the branches a rather spiky appearance and rough texture. Colonies tend to be highly coloured, often the branches, polyp branchlet tips and sclerites contrasting markedly. Branches are usually white or yellow, while the sclerites can be orange, pink, or red.

Scientific Name: *Dendronephthya* spp.

The generic name comes from the Greek, *dendron*, a tree, and *Nephthea*, a related genus that is superficially similar (Williams, 1993).

Common Name: Strawberry corals, Cauliflower coral, Dendrophyta, Dendronephyta. The latter common names are common contraction/mangling of the genus name as accomplished by aquarists.

Colour: Pink, purple, red, yellow, orange; sclerite and branchlet tip colour contrasting sharply with the paler branches and trunk.

Distinguishing Characteristics: Branchy soft corals with brightly colored spicules and polyps. Able to expand tremendously with water or deflate into a sorry-looking blob. Spicules afford a rough texture. Not photosynthetic.

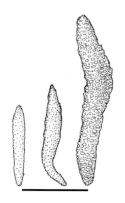

Sclerites of *Dendronephthya*. Scale bar is 0.5 mm. *After Williams, 1993.*

Closeup of the column of a *Dendronephthya* sp. Note the conspicuous sclerites. The small branches bearing polyps are known as "twigs." J. Sprung

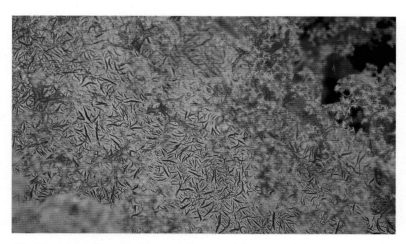

Similar Species: Similar to *Scleronephthya*, *Nephthyigorgia*, and *Stereonephthya*.

Natural Habitat: Lives in areas with strong tidal currents or surge,

It is simply not true that all *Dendronephthya* spp. must be kept in the shade. While some species are found more typically under ledges or in deep water, this *Dendronephthya* (*Spongodes*) sp. is growing in full sunlight on a reef top near Bequa, Fiji. Large multi-coloured stands were common here in areas with strong tidal flow. J. Sprung

If you wish to try the challenge of keeping *Dendronephthya* spp., be sure to choose a colony that is well attached to a rock base that will allow it to be easily epoxied to the tank walls or tied to the reef structure projecting out into strong water flow. J. Sprung

Peter Wilkens stirs the gravel bottom with a glass rod to kick up detritus to feed the soft corals. He uses this technique to feed non-photosynthetic species such as *Scleronephthya* and *Dendronephthya*. J. Sprung

and lots of plankton. May occur out in the light or shaded under a ledge. Often upside down, hanging from the roof of a cave, but also common out in the current stream in full sunlight attached to a projection off the reef.

Aquarium Care: Mysteriously difficult to keep. Not recommended to beginners. It is beneficial to hang colonies upside down from ledges, using monofilament line and epoxy cement. It is possible that these corals feed on the abundant mucus in the water of a coral reef. This food source traps bacteria and phytoplankton, and attracts zooplankton. The spines on *Dendronephthya* could help snare large blobs of mucus, allowing the polyps to feed from more than just minute particles. Fabricius *et al.* (1995a and b) report that *Dendronephthya hemprichi* and *D. sinaiensis* in the Red Sea get their nutrition from phytoplankton, therefore they may need phytoplankton daily to grow and thrive (see chapter one, Nutrition). They also do take some zooplankton. Brine shrimp nauplii, preferably live, make a good zooplankton substitute. May require certain trace elements, in addition. Feed at night. The use of a pipette for feeding the polyps directly is helpful. The authors are experimenting with a food source that duplicates the mucus and trapped bacteria/phytoplankton, which may be the real food "package" that these corals need. In addition, Peter Wilkens showed us that detritus stirred up from the bottom substrate by churning it with a glass rod provides a food source readily accepted by many non-photosynthetic soft corals. This detritus is nutritious and also has bacteria, protozoans, crustaceans, and other microorganisms attached.

Perhaps the most critical parameter in keeping these corals is water flow. Water flow not only carries food to the coral, but the correct type and rate of flow will encourage the coral to open and will improve its feeding efficiency. While most aquarists provide turbulent flows, few really have any idea what the actual flow rates around their corals are. Studies have shown that for *D. hemprichi*, feeding on phytoplankton was most efficient at a water flow rate of 15 to 20 cm/s (approx. 6-8 inches/sec), in the form of a laminar (straight) flow (Fabricius *et al.*, 1995b). Studies on feeding in gorgonians have shown that optimal flow rates are species specific, therefore the figure quoted above should be used as a guideline only i.e. different species of *Dendronephthya* may require different flow rates (see chapter one, Nutrition).

We have seen thriving small colonies of *Dendronephthya* spp. propagated asexually in aquaria. It may be best to try to grow these rather than concentrating on large, wild-caught specimens.
J. C. Delbeek

It is important to look carefully to be sure that all hitchhiking predatory snails are removed. *Dendronephthya* spp. carry many well-camouflaged snails that quickly consume the soft coral's tissue in captivity (see chapter eleven).

Reproduction: *Dendronephthya* regularly reproduce asexually via fission in the wild (in Fabricius *et al.*, 1995b). In aquaria we have seen small specimens of *Dendronephthya* on the substratum, presumably the result of fission of branchlets off of larger parent colonies. Some species (especially *Morchellana* spp.) form stolon-like tendrils at the base of the trunk, and these may produce daughter colonies. *Dendronephthya* are most likely dioecious broadcast spawners and have been observed to release gametes almost daily in the wild (in Fabricius *et al.*, 1995b).

Genus: *Lemnalia*

Lemnalia spp. are all arborescent with non-retractile polyps located on the distal branchlets and twigs. The interior sclerites are long thin needles while the exterior sclerites can be capstans, crescents or brackets (Mather and Bennett, 1993). The polyps are generally smooth, and mostly without supporting bundles of sclerites. This genus is found throughout much of the Indo-Pacific from East Africa to parts of Polynesia (Gosliner *et al.*, 1996).

Scientific Name: *Lemnalia* spp.

Common Name: Spaghetti coral (Wilkens, 1986), Branch Coral, Tree Coral

Lemnalia sp. J. Sprung

Lemnalia sp. Note that the stalks resemble those of *Nephthea* or *Litophyton*, but the polyps are arranged more sparsely. This tall species was typically about 40 cm (16 in.) in height. J. Sprung

A diminutive *Lemnalia* sp. that appears to be "in bondage" with commensal brittle stars. J. Sprung

This *Sinularia* species could easily be confused with *Lemnalia,* which it superficially resembles. However, *Sinularia* has large spindle type sclerites in the base. J. C. Delbeek

In the surface, *Lemnalia* spp. usually have capstans and/or capstan derivatives (curved or boomerang shaped spindles often with knobs that make them look like drawings of flying seagulls). Sometimes they have smooth spindles with a few large knobs near the centre. In the interior normally they have long needle shaped sclerites, often with rough ends. There is a lot of variability to sclerites in this genus, however.

Colour: Light brown, whitish gray.

Distinguishing Characteristics: *Lemnalia* is arborescent but with finer branches than *Nephthea,* polyps generally without supporting sclerite bundles, and, to the naked eye the sclerites are not as obvious in the stalk.

Similar Species: A closely related genus, *Paralemnalia,* is distinguished by forming encrusting mats with digitate branches that bear retractile polyps similar to the other members of this group (*Nephthea, Capnella, Neospongodes...*). There are several species of *Sinularia* that superficially resemble *Lemnalia. Lemnalia* does not have the large spindle shaped sclerites of *Sinularia,* however.

Natural Habitat: Reef slopes with strong illumination and periodically strong water motion.

Aquarium Care: *Lemnalia* species like strong light but can be grown well even in aquariums with just a few fluorescent tubes. Their care is essentially the same as for *Capnella* and *Nephthea*. *Lemnalia* and *Paralemnalia* both are very prone to infections that can wipe out an entire colony. If a portion of the colony appears to be decomposing, sever it with a scissors and remove the decomposing piece from the aquarium. Do not delay because such infections spread quickly and may kill the whole colony. The removed piece can be isolated in an aerated bucket of water with 5 ppm of Streptomycin. Sometimes it is possible to save infected fragments or colonies this way. Do not place an infected fragment or colony into an aquarium with other invertebrates. The fouling could kill them too. *Lemnalia* species are rare imports from Africa, Indonesia, and the Solomon Islands, where they are common. They do not ship well and die easily if mishandled. For this reason *Lemnalia* is unlikely to become common in the aquarium trade unless captive propagation makes it available locally, thus avoiding the trauma of collection and long-distance shipping.

Reproduction: In aquaria *Lemnalia* often drop branchlets as a result of fission. Small cuttings can be taken with a scissors also. No reports of sexual reproduction are known.

Genus: *Neospongodes*

Scientific Name: *Neospongodes* sp.

Formerly *Lemnalia* spp. in aquarium literature (see Wilkens, 1990). *Lemnalia* is a valid genus, but it differs from *Neospongodes* in several ways. See previous description.

Common Name: Broccoli coral, Cauliflower coral, *Lemnalia*

Colour: Whitish, brown, yellow, purplish, yellow with purple or red spicules. Sometimes green.

Distinguishing Characteristics: Spicules are conspicuous on all branches. Colonies seldom larger than 10 inches tall.

Similar Species: Very similar to *Nephthea* and *Capnella*, but smaller in height and less branchy. It is most similar to *Nephthea* and *Stereonephthya*.

Neospongodes spp. come in a variety of colours. J. Sprung

Closeup of *Neospongodes* sp. J. C. Delbeek

Neospongodes sp. inflated and deflated. J. Sprung

Natural Habitat: Shallow lagoons and reef slopes with bright light and tidal currents. Also occurs on coral rubble or gravel in areas with heavy sedimentation, based on the attached pieces in newly imported specimens. This genus also occurs in the Caribbean and South Atlantic, where two species are known. One is from shallow water and is photosynthetic, and the other one is from deep water and is not. The shallow water species, *Neospongodes atlantica*, looks practically identical to the Indo-Pacific varieties. It occurs only off the coast of Brazil. The deep water species, *N. portoricensis*, is more widespread in the Caribbean, though it is not common and generally only occurs below safe diving depths. It is bright orange, yellow or pinkish, like the other wonderful arborescent alcyonacean soft corals from the Indo-Pacific.

It is possible that *Neospongodes atlantica* is actually a species of *Nephthea*. A specimen from Brazil (see photograph) that we sent for identification was determined to be *Nephthea*. It is possible that the specimen was an unidentified photosynthetic *Nephthea* species from Brazil, and not *Neospongodes atlantica*, but based on the photos we have seen in Verseveldt's description of this species (Verseveldt, 1983) we believe it is *N. atlantica*. The distinctions between *Neospongodes* and *Nephthea* are not very compelling and it may be that revision of this group will cause at least some of the species in this genus to be included in the genus *Nephthea*.

Aquarium Care: Not as hardy as most soft corals. Not recommended to beginners. Though *Neospongodes* spp. are photosynthetic, they seem to appreciate supplemental feedings of baby brine shrimp, *Daphnia*, or other plankton substitutes to really thrive, phytoplankton may also play a critical role in feeding as has been shown in *Dendronephthya*. Strong currents stimulate colony and polyp expansion. Lighting should be strong, but not direct! Place colonies on the bottom in the light, or hanging sideways on vertical walls or from the edge or underside (if illuminated) of ledges.

Reproduction: Asexual reproduction in aquaria is as described for *Lemnalia* and *Litophyton*. Nothing is known of sexual reproduction in this genus.

Neospongodes atlantica, a Brazilian species that looks just like its relatives from the Indo-Pacific. It has zooxanthellae too. J. Sprung

Revision of soft coral taxonomy may place *Neospongodes atlantica* together with *Nephthea.* An Indo-Pacific *Neospongodes* sp. with pinkish colour is just above the uniformly cream coloured Brazilian specimen. J. Sprung

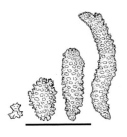

Sclerites of *Nephthea*. Scale bar is 0.5 mm. *After Williams, 1993.*

This finely branched variety of *Nephthea* is frequently called *Litophyton arboreum*. *Litophyton* is probably synonymous with *Nephthea*. Photographed at Jago Aquaristik in Berlin. J. Sprung

Genus: *Nephthea*

Scientific Name: *Nephthea* spp.

Common Name: Broccoli coral, Cauliflower coral, *Litophyton arboreum*, "Lithophyton," "Nephthya," "Nepthya," "Nepthea" Note the common mis-spellings. The correct spelling is *Nephthea*.

Colour: Brown, yellow, whitish, occasionally green

Distinguishing Characteristics: Upright and bushy, arborescent colonies. Non-retractile polyps with supporting bundle of sclerites that do not project much beyond the polyp when closed. As a result they lack the spiky appearance of *Dendronephthya*. Polyps arranged in lobes (catkins). Sclerites irregular, spindle, or caterpillar-like.

Nephthea sp. J. C. Delbeek
There are *Capnella* spp. that are
nearly identical to this one.
However, the sclerites of *Nephthea*
are quite different from those of
Capnella.

Nephthea sp. in an aquarium at the
Oceanographic Museum in
Monaco. J. Sprung

Similar Species: Very similar to *Capnella* spp. *Nephthea* has compact, triangular growth of branches, and the polyps are slightly smaller than in most *Capnella* spp. While the external appearance is very similar, the sclerites of *Nephthea* are quite different from those of *Capnella*. "*Litophyton* " is between *Lemnalia* and *Nephthea* in external appearance, and may simply be slender types of *Nephthea*, the distinction not being very clear. Some soft coral biologists consider *Litophyton* synonymous with *Nephthea*. *Stereonephthya* is also arborescent, but it is stiffer than *Nephthea* and has much more obvious sclerites. When the branches of *Stereonephthya* deflate, the bundles of sclerites around the polyps at the branch tips form distinctive spiny bur-like processes. *Stereonephthya* species may be highly colourful: In Fiji there is a common photosynthetic species that is a magnificent blue-violet (J. Sprung, pers. obs.).

Stereonephthya spp. have very conspicuous sclerites that afford them a rough texture. They are quite stiff. They are delicate in captivity but it is possible to maintain them, particularly those species that have zooxanthellae. J. Sprung

Natural Habitat: Wide ranging from the coast of east Africa, the Red Sea and throughout the Pacific. Most abundant in shallow reefs with clear water and strong tidal water motion. May occur on reef tops that receive very intense illumination and water flow like a river, and may be exposed on extreme low tides. In deeper water it prefers to project out into the current and light. It nearly always grows on horizontal surfaces (as opposed to walls with a high slope). In fact, the occurrence of Indo-Pacific *Nephthea* on reefs can be predicted based on the slope of the bottom (Fabricius, 1996 in press). *Nephthea* species primarily occur in the Indo-Pacific and Red Sea, but there may be one species that occurs off the coast of Brazil, see photo and description under *Neospongodes*.

Aquarium Care: Initially delicate, and a poor shipper, this is a most beautiful coral once established, and it grows very rapidly. Its health and growth may be impeded by the presence of certain stony corals. Allow adequate distance to prevent stinging and use protein skimming to remove defensive chemicals released by corals. A gentle to strong current, and strong illumination are its preference. It should be placed with the branches facing upward rather than sideways. *Nephthea* can be used to make nice "bushes" on the bottom in the foreground of a tall aquarium. *Nephthea* has been shown to be a poor feeder of zooplankton on the GBR, suggesting that phytoplankton may be the prey of choice aside from the nutrition obtained from the photosynthetic products of its symbiotic zooxanthellae (in Fabricius *et al.*, 1995b).

Reproduction: Asexual reproduction can occur as in the other genera in this family via fission of branchlets. Cuttings can also be taken with care. Nothing is known about sexual reproduction in this genus. They are probably dioecious broadcast spawners.

Genus: *Paralemnalia*

Species in this genus generally have a digitate growth form, with numerous finger-like lobes. The polyps are located on the lobes and in some species can be retracted into the surface of the lobes. Interior sclerites of *Paralemnalia* are thin needles, surface sclerites are spindles and crescents (Mather and Bennett, 1993).

Paralemnalia colonies are composed of upright finger-like lobes bearing the polyps. This "thick-finger" species was common in the Solomon Islands. J. Sprung

Another variety of *Paralemnalia* with slightly thinner branches photographed in the Solomon Islands. J. Sprung

Paralemnalia sp. J. Sprung

Paralemnalia growing against the glass in an aquarium. J. Sprung

Scientific Name: *Paralemnalia* sp.

Common Name: Finger Leather

Colour: Gray, brown, sometimes greenish

Distinguishing Characteristics: *Paralemnalia* spp. form encrusting mats with digitate branches that bear retractile *OR* contractile polyps. Two forms are common, one with branches as wide as a finger, the other with much finer branches. There are about five species, with some intermediate in appearance. Gosliner *et al.* (1996) call the thicker branched one *Paralemnalia* cf. *clavata* and the fine branched one *P.* cf. *thyrisoides*, though it is impossible to identify them to species without careful examination of the sclerites.

This is the fine-branched *Paralemnalia* sp. from the Solomon Islands, polyps closed. In this species the polyps are retractile. In the thicker branched species they seem only to be contractile, or partially retractile. This difference suggest that species classified in this genus may belong to more than one genus. (P. Alderslade, pers. comm.) J. Sprung

The fine-branched *Paralemnalia* sp. (*P.* cf. *thyrsoides*) from the Solomon Islands, polyps open. J. Sprung

Similar Species: Mature colonies of the thick branch species resemble *Lobophytum* spp., because they develop a round base from which the lobe-like branches protrude. The polyps have the distinctive appearance of Nephtheidae, however, and are most like those of *Capnella*. The thin-branched species are similar in appearance to some *Sinularia* species, and may especially be confused with small *Lemnalia* species.

Natural Habitat: Abundant on reef slopes and in lagoons in shallow water 3 to 20 metres deep in the Solomon Islands. Best growth in clear water with moderate currents.

Aquarium Care: We first obtained a species of *Paralemnalia*

several years ago from Helmut Schmidt and Peter Findeisen. It had been propagated in several aquariums in the vicinity of Lünen, Germany, and probably originated from Indonesia. The colonies we received had a very strong odor and looked stressed from the transport, even though they had been handled carefully. Within a day or two most of the tissue mass of the colonies was decomposing despite being placed immediately in a strong current stream to keep them well oxygenated. One tiny fragment (about 1 cm) survived out of many severed from the decomposing mass. From this fragment many large colonies have grown. The species is now established in several aquariums and with time will be available in the aquarium trade as a captive propagated species. *Paralemnalia digitiformis* has been shown to be a poor feeder of zooplankton on the GBR, suggesting that phytoplankton may be the prey of choice, aside from the nutrition obtained from the photosynthetic products of its symbiotic zooxanthellae (in Fabricius *et al.*, 1995b).

In aquariums *Paralemnalia* grows best under strong illumination with moderate to very strong water motion. It adapts to lower light levels and reduced water flow, but the growth form becomes altered. In low light it becomes spindly, and in low water flow it is prone to infections that can destroy the whole colony. If some of the lobes turn mushy and begin to "dissolve" an infection has begun that can consume the whole colony or spread to other corals. Cut out the affected area carefully and remove it from the aquarium as soon as this is observed.

Reproduction: Nothing is known about the sexual reproduction of this species. This species is easily propagated by taking cuttings with a scissors. Colonies can also spread easily by horizontal growth over the substrate.

Genus: *Scleronephthya*

Scientific Name: *Scleronephthya* sp.

Common Name: Strawberry corals. Pink/Orange cauliflower

Colour: Pink, orange, yellow, red

Distinguishing Characteristics: Contracted colonies can have a rather fleshy and lobular appearance with short stalks from which the branches extend. When expanded it is obvious that the polyps

Scleronephthya sp. J. Sprung

Scleronephthya sp. J. C. Delbeek

Scleronephthya sp. J. C. Delbeek

Scleronephthya sp. J. C. Delbeek

Scleronephthya sp.
Note the sclerites. A. Storace

do not have supporting bundles of sclerites and they are scattered over the branches and twigs. Often brightly coloured, the stalks, branches and tips tend be varying shades of one colour i.e. orange, pink or yellow-orange (Gosliner, *et al.*, 1996). Often the polyps have contrasting oral disc colour.

Similar Species: Similar to *Dendronephthya* species but not as spiky or branchy and most species are not as tall.

Natural Habitat: This genus is found throughout the Indo-West Pacific, from the Red Sea to New Guinea, Philippines, Solomon Islands and Micronesia (Gosliner *et al.*, 1996). Most species are found growing upside-down from the roofs of caves or underside of ledges in areas with strong water flow, in the shade or partially exposed. There are also spectacular deepwater species that form large erect colonies on reef slopes in strong current. These tall species have much reduced sclerite abundance and are quite soft.

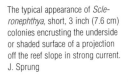

The typical appearance of *Scleronephthya*, short, 3 inch (7.6 cm) colonies encrusting the underside or shaded surface of a projection off the reef slope in strong current. J. Sprung

Aquarium Care: This is one of the few species of colorful, non-photosynthetic soft corals that actually fares well in aquaria. It is easy to keep when provided with strong currents and regular feedings of baby brine shrimp (nauplii), *Daphnia* (water fleas), or wild plankton. These foods can be frozen and fed directly over the colony by means of a long pipette or baster. In really nutrient rich aquaria with heavy growth of algae and associated micro-crustaceans, this species may thrive without supplemental feeding, as long as the algae does not smother it. The common species grow several inches tall and readily attach to new substrates,

The "Orange Thing," an uncommon species of *Scleronephthya* that grows unusually tall and has reduced sclerites. It is found in deep water with strong current on steep reef slopes or walls in the Solomon Islands. A very similar (or the same) species occurs in Bali, but it has much redder colour. J. Macare

A closer view of the Orange Thing expanded. J. Sprung

The Orange Thing, once deflated, looks like a more typical *Scleronephthya* sp. J. Sprung

spreading new colonies onto the glass and adjacent rocks. They also benefit by feeding on detritus stirred into the water column by fish or by the aquarist disturbing the aquarium's bottom sand/gravel substrate. Recent studies have shown that Red Sea specimens feed readily on phytoplankton (Fabricius *et al.*, 1995b).

A new variety recently imported from Bali Indonesia is brilliant red-orange (orange stalk, red polyps) and quite tall, with very few sclerites, mostly concentrated at the base. It is quite similar to an orange and yellow species (yellow stalk, orange polyps) that occurs in the Solomon Islands on steep reef slopes usually in deep water in strong currents (see photos). These are really spectacular soft corals! They survive shipping well and also survive reasonably well in captivity.

The Bali specimens have a habit of falling off of the original rock and then re-attaching to other rocks. This may be preventable if they are suspended upside down or horizontally at least and given strong currents as soon as they are put into the aquarium.

Reproduction: Asexual reproduction is common in aquaria via fission and also by outgrowths from the base that stretch across the bottom, giving rise to new colonies. Nothing is known about sexual reproduction in this genus.

Family Nidaliidae

Scientific Name: *Chironephthya* sp.

Common Name: (among aquarists) *Dendronephthya*

Colour: Pink, purple, red, yellow, orange.

Distinguishing Characteristics: Branchy soft corals with appearance somewhere between gorgonians and *Dendronephthya*, with brightly colored spicules and polyps. In some species drooping branches arise from an upright stalk, in others the entire colony is upright (Gosliner, *et al.*, 1996). The branches tend to be rather stout and end abruptly, there is no tapering off as in other soft corals. The polyps are located in very spiny calyces, with very thick and large sclerites. The polyps are most concentrated at the ends of the branches. Able to expand with water or deflate into small tangle of stiff branches. Sclerites afford a rough texture. Non-photosynthetic.

Natural Habitat: Lives in areas with strong tidal currents or surge. May occur partially out in the light, especially on steep walls, but usually found shaded under a ledge. Often upside down, hanging from the roof of a cave, or out in the current stream attached to a projection off the reef wall. *Chironephthya* are found from east Africa to southern Japan, Philippines, New Guinea, Indonesia, Solomon Islands, Australia, and Micronesia (Gosliner, *et al.*, 1996).

Aquarium Care: Difficult but possible to keep. Not recommended to beginners. *Chironephthya* are somewhat hardier than *Dendronephthya*, but require special care with regard to feeding. Place *Chironephthya* sideways or upside-down in a strong or intermittently strong current flow. Feed zooplankton or substitute, possibly also phytoplankton. Also stir up detritus from the bottom substrate when the polyps are out and feeding.

Chironephthya sp. J. Sprung

Chironephthya sp. J. Sprung

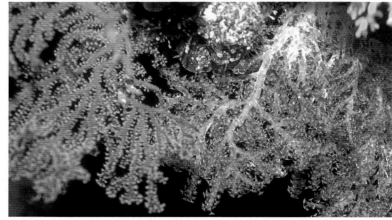

Chironephthya sp. J. Sprung

Reproduction: Unknown, but probably drops branches by fission to reproduce asexually.

Scientific Name: *Siphonogorgia* sp.

Common Name: (among aquarists) *Dendronephthya*

Colour: Red, yellow, orange, pink, purple.

Distinguishing Characteristics: Arborescent soft corals with appearance like gorgonians, with brightly colored sclerites and polyps. Rigid, but able to expand with water or deflate somewhat. No central axis. Branches are formed from packed spindles. These sclerites afford a rough texture, though expanded colonies are somewhat slippery. Polyps are completely retractile into the branches. Non-photosynthetic.

Natural Habitat: Lives along reef slopes and on walls with strong tidal currents or surge. Occurs partially out in the light, especially on steep walls, but usually at least partially shaded or else in relatively deep water. Usually not upside down, but rather out in the current stream attached to a projection off the reef wall.

Aquarium Care: Not known. Possibly difficult to keep. Not recommended to beginners. *Siphonogorgia* require special care with regard to feeding since they are not photosynthetic. Place *Siphonogorgia* sideways or upright in a strong or intermittently strong current flow. Do not expose to strong direct light. Feed zooplankton or substitute, possibly also phytoplankton. Also stir up detritus from the bottom substrate when the polyps are out and feeding.

Siphonogorgia spp. are among the most exquisite soft corals. They have seldom been collected for home aquariums so little is known about their ability to survive in captivity. This is probably *S. godeffroyi*.
J. Sprung

We believe this beautiful soft coral is a *Siphonogorgia*, but it also could be a species of *Nephthyigorgia*. It was on a reef wall in the Solomon Islands. J. Sprung

Reproduction: Sexual reproduction not studied. Asexual reproduction not observed but it is likely that branches that become severed can form new colonies.

This brilliant red sea fan is probably a *Siphonogorgia* sp., but it could also be confused with *Chironephthya*. J. Sprung

Scientific Name: *Nephthyigorgia* sp.

Common Name: Chili Sponge, Red Finger (soft) Coral, Devil's Hand

Colour: Red, orange, purple.

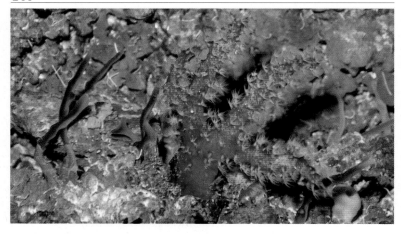

Distinguishing Characteristics: Tough thick tissue with some prominent sclerites. Small colony size, normally not much more than 6 in (15 cm) tall, with finger-like lobes or branches. There may be other species with taller colonies and finer branches.

Similar Species: Most similar to *Siphonogorgia* and *Chironephthya*. Small colonies may also be confused with *Eleutherobia*, *Minabea* or *Scleronephthya*, which occur in the same habitat and have orange forms.

Natural Habitat: Indo-Pacific in shady regions on reef slopes with strong currents. Also in lagoon areas with strong tidal currents in shade attached to hard substrate.

Aquarium Care: This is another one of the few species of colorful, non-photosynthetic soft corals that actually fares well in aquaria. It is easy to keep when provided with strong currents and regular feedings of baby brine shrimp (nauplii), *Daphnia* (water fleas), or wild plankton. These foods can be frozen and fed directly over the colony by means of a long pipette or baster. In really nutrient rich aquaria with heavy growth of algae and associated micro-crustaceans, this species may thrive without supplemental feeding, as long as the algae does not smother it. It grows several inches tall and readily attaches to new substrates, spreading new colonies onto the glass and adjacent rocks. It will also benefit by feeding on detritus stirred into the water column by fish or the aquarist disturbing the aquarium's bottom sand/gravel substrate. May also be a phytoplankton feeder.

Reproduction: Unknown, but probably produces outgrowths from the base asexually.

Family Xeniidae

The name *Xenia* is derived from the Greek word for hospitality. This may be owing to the appearance of the pumping polyps of some members of this group, which give the impression of so many hands waving their greetings. Members of this family have characteristic sclerites; their platelet-like disc shapes are unlike any other soft coral sclerites (Bayer, 1973). Colonies in this family have fleshy polyps and can grow as membranous sheets or stalks.

Genus: *Anthelia*

Scientific Name: *Anthelia* sp.

Common Name: *Anthelia*, waving hand polyp

Colour: White, gray, brown, pale blue

Distinguishing Characteristics: *Anthelia* species have polyps like *Xenia* species, large and with long pinnules that afford a snowflake or tufty appearance. They grow by means of a creeping mat that may form stolon-like fingers. *Anthelia glauca* has large polyps that greatly resemble those of *Clavularia* spp. and *Tubipora musica*. *Anthelia* polyps are not retractable and are monomorphic. They open flat in still water, whereas *Xenia* polyps have tentacles that curve inward toward the center of the polyp.

Sclerites of *Anthelia*. Scale bar is 0.5 mm. *After Williams, 1993.*

Closeup of *Anthelia* cf. *glauca*
J. Yaiullo and F. Greco

Anthelia cf. *philippinensis*
J. Macare

Anthelia cf. *glauca*
J. C. Delbeek

Anthelia cf. *glauca* resembles
Clavularia spp. but the polyps are
not divided into two parts and are
not retractable. J. C. Delbeek

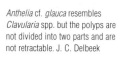

There is probably more than one genus presently grouped under the single genus *Anthelia*, (Phil Alderslade, pers. comm.).

Similar Species: *Xenia* and *Cespitularia* spp. form stalks, while *Anthelia* forms a creeping mat. *Clavularia* has similar polyps, but these are retractable into the club-like anthostele. *Stereosoma* is quite similar but differs by lacking sclerites.

Natural Habitat: *Anthelia* spp. are found from the Red Sea to Hawaii in shallow lagoon and back reef areas, often in high surge or strong tidal currents. The Hawaiian species, *A. edmondsoni*, is found in surge habitats and down slopes to about 20 m (60 ft.).

Aquarium Care: *Anthelia* species are incredibly fast-growing colonizers of rocks, glass, plants, or any substrate with which they come in contact. Strong currents and bright light are key to success with this genus. Trace elements are also important for long term survival. This species is very susceptible to attack by protozoans.

Reproduction: Members of this genus are rapid colonizers of all substrates. Sexual reproduction has been reported in aquaria (Delbeek, 1989), and involves the release of what appeared to be eggs from the tips of tentacles! *Anthelia glauca* is, however, believed to release planulae as it is an internal brooder with separate male and female colonies (Benayahu and Loya, 1984b).

Genus: *Cespitularia*

Scientific Name: *Cespitularia infirmata*

Cespitularia species often have an attractive blue sheen. Strong illumination promotes the maintenance of this colour. J. C. Delbeek

Common Name: *Cespitularia*, Blue *Xenia*

Colour: white, blue, brown, reddish

Similar Species: *Xenia, Anthelia, Efflatournaria, Alcyonium. Cespitularia infirmata* is not the only species, but it may be the common type imported.

Natural Habitat: Like *Xenia*, encrusting dead coral skeletons and among algae, usually in shallow water with good water movement, either surge or tidal currents. Most colonies are imported from Kenya.

Distinguishing Characters: *Cespitularia* has an appearance that is somewhere between *Xenia* and *Alcyonium*. Colonies may be several inches tall and arborescent like *Alcyonium*, and the polyps may pulse like *Xenia*. When branches touch a substrate they attach to it and encrust it. Such branches may then separate from the original colony. The typical colour is bright blue-white, which is unlike any similar soft coral. Polyps are non-retractile.

Aquarium Care: This species ships poorly, and is delicate. We do not recommend it to the beginner. It does grow rapidly, however, once established. *Cespitularia* likes bright light and strong water motion. Trace elements are essential for long-term success with this species.

Reproduction: Aquarists propagate this species by cutting off branches with a scissors and attaching them with cyanoacrylate glue, or allowing it to encrust neighboring rocks and then dividing the colonies with a blade. Little is known about sexual reproduction in this species but they likely exhibit the common Xeniidae traits of internal brooding of planulae and colonies are probably dioecious.

Genus: *Heteroxenia*

Scientific Name: *Heteroxenia* spp.

Common Name: Pulse corals, Pumping *Xenia*, Pump-end *Xenia*, Waving hand Polyps

Colour: White, gray, brown. Rarely green or blue.

Distinguishing Characteristics: The most distinctive feature of this

The *siphonozooids* are what looks like pores between the larger autozooid polyps of *Heteroxenia* spp.
J. Sprung

Heteroxenia sp.
J. Sprung

genus is the fact that it is dimorphic, possessing two types of polyps autozooids and siphonozooids (see chapter one). However, the smaller siphonozooids tend to develop later as the colony grows.

Similar Species: *Xenia*, see next description.

Natural Habitat: *Xenia* and *Heteroxenia* spp. can be found in a variety of reef habitats, from brightly illuminated reef flats where they may be exposed at low tide to reef slopes where the light is bright but more indirect. There are also species that live in lagoon environments. Where they occur they generally are exposed to strong tidal currents for a portion of the day.

Aquarium Care: Same as for *Xenia*, see next description.

Reproduction: Asexual reproduction occurs in aquaria by pedal laceration caused by gradual movement of the colonies across the substrate. Also, budding and fission rapidly occur with growth, forming many new "heads" that divide and creep along over the substrate as they grow. These branches or heads may be cut off with a sharp scissors and planted elsewhere in the aquarium.

Sexual reproduction occurs via internal brooding of planulae. When released planulae are not very buoyant and tend to fall to the bottom within a short distance of the main colony. The planulae appear to be released with zooxanthellae (Alino and Coll, 1989). Some species (e.g. *H. elizabethae, H. fuscescens, H. ghardaqensis*) are hermaphroditic, while others are dioecious (in Benayahu and Loya, 1984a). In *Heteroxenia fuscescens*, the colonies begin life as monomorphic (i.e. one polyp type) and exhibit a size-dependent, sequential hermaphroditism (Achituv and Benayahu, 1990). *Heteroxenia fuscescens* planulates throughout the year in the northern Red Sea (in Zaslow and Benayahu, 1996). When planulae are released they lack zooxanthellae but usually pick them up by the third day. Sexual maturity occurs at a small size, and autozooid polyps only are present. These polyps are capable of producing sperm at an early age. As the colonies grow in size, siphonozooids begin to appear and the autozooids shift their function and eventually produce ripe eggs with relatively few sperm (Achituv and Benayahu, 1990). Mature eggs fill the majority of the gastrovascular cavity, and often share space with fertilized eggs. Developing eggs move into brooding pouches until they are fully developed into planulae (see *Xenia* below). On the GBR, *Heteroxenia* planulation occurs at noon, two to four days after the full moon (Alino and Coll, 1989).In tanks at the Waikiki Aquarium, *Heteroxenia* has become a bit of a plague in some aquaria, covering every available surface and smothering other corals. As mentioned in chapter one, *Heteroxenia* is an excellent candidate for aquaculture due to the fact that each colony can release several thousand planulae!

Genus: *Xenia*

Xenia spp. are rapid colonizers on coral reefs throughout the Indo-Pacific and Red Sea, occurring in a wide variety of habitats and depths. For example, in the Red Sea, *X. macrospiculata* can be found from three to thirty meters and on some reefs they can cover over 70% of the surface area (Benayahu and Loya, 1984a). Many species rhythmically open and close the polyps, hence the common name. Some species do not pump, or do so very slightly.

Scientific Name: *Xenia* spp.

Common Name: Pulse corals, Pumping *Xenia*, Pump-end *Xenia*, Waving hand Polyps

Colour: White, gray, brown. Rarely green or blue.

Distinguishing Characteristics: Encrusting or stalked, the monomorphic polyps are non-retractile. Colonies are usually quite soft, but larger, stalked varieties may be tougher. In some species, the colonies are very slimy (e.g. *X.* cf. *mucosa*) and can produce lots of mucus (Gosliner *et al.*, 1996)! *Xenia umbellata* is an uncommon and very welcome guest to aquariums, with large, pulsing polyps. The color and form of *Xenia* species is highly dependent on environmental conditions, making visual ID difficult. Sclerites are minute platelets (Bayer, 1973).

Similar Species: The closely related genus *Heteroxenia* is distinguished by having dimorphic polyps (two types: siphonozooids between the autozooids, as in *Sarcophyton* and *Lobophytum*), compared to *Xenia*'s monomorphic polyps. Also similar to *Anthelia*, but *Xenia* generally forms stalks while *Anthelia* forms creeping mats. However there are *Anthelia* species in which the mats divide into distinct clumps of polyps (i.e. see photo of *Anthelia* cf *philippinensis*) and there are encrusting *Xenia* spp. that don't have an obvious stalk (see photo). *Anthelia* polyps generally open flat in still water, whereas *Xenia* polyps have tentacles that curve inward toward the center of the polyp, and generally finer pinnules.

Natural Habitat: *Xenia* and *Heteroxenia* spp. can be found in a variety of reef habitats, from brightly illuminated reef flats where they may be exposed at low tide to reef slopes where the light is bright but more indirect. There are also species that live in lagoon environments. Where they occur they generally are exposed to strong tidal currents for a portion of the day.

Aquarium Care: *Xenia* species like bright light and intermittent strong currents, with periods of little current. They also adapt to mild constant flow. They prefer high pH, and some species show rapid growth with the additions of kalkwasser and trace elements,

A colony of *Xenia* sp. with *Anthelia* cf. *glauca* behind it. J. C. Delbeek

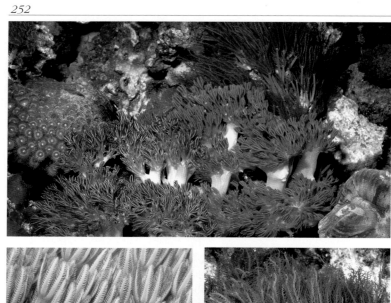

This encrusting *Xenia* sp. has a stalk so low and broad it resembles a creeping mat. J. C. Delbeek

This encrusting *Anthelia* cf *glauca* has very fluid polyps that "blow" in the currents. Compare its appearance to the adjacent *Xenia* sp. and similar *Clavularia* spp. J. C. Delbeek

This "Pom-Pom" *Xenia* sp. has polyps quite similar to *Anthelia*, but the stalk clearly shows it is not *Anthelia*. It may be a juvenile *Heteroxenia* sp. that has not yet developed siphonozooids. J. C. Delbeek

A common and hardy *Xenia* species from Indonesia. It grows very quickly and exhibits very nice rhythmic pumping when healthy. S. W. Michael

particularly iodide and iron. Sometimes colonies will "crash" after many months of vigorous growth and asexual division. It is believed that depletion of trace elements may play a role in such crashes, as is common in marine algae. Sexual reproduction in some species, evidenced by the release of gametes, may be followed by colony death. Protozoans also may attack colonies and rapidly consume them. Beware that fish and crabs may also

This extremely large *Xenia* sp. is one of the most lovely but, unlike the other species, it is most difficult to keep, see comments in the text. J. C. Delbeek

eat *Xenia. Xenia* colonies become flaccid and unhealthy looking when the pH falls below 8.1 for extended periods of time. They are most vigorous at a pH of 8.3 or higher. The pumping becomes less coordinated when the pH is low, and the tentacles curl outward, the tips not touching equally when they are brought together. When the pH increases the tentacles curl inward and the tips touch in a more coordinated central point. *Xenia* are mostly dependent on their symbiotic zooxanthellae for their nutrition. The pumping, often mistakenly interpreted as planktonic prey capture, does not serve this function. *Xenia* do not capture zooplankton, but this does not mean that they don't take food from the passing water. In fact they do. *Xenia* and *Heteroxenia* species take advantage of a special type of food capture: the copious mucus they secrete is a type of "molecular net" that traps dissolved organic compounds (Schlichter, 1982). Though they grow beautifully when activated carbon is used, it is possible that aggressive use of activated carbon and protein skimming could impede the growth of *Xenia*.

Most *Xenia* species thrive under the conditions outlined here, but one species, the giant one occasionally imported from Indonesia (see photo) seems to have special requirements. Although we have heard reports of success with this species, in our experience it generally shrinks and dies after several months and does not grow as prolifically in captivity as other species do. Julian Sprung observed it growing in large fields on a nearly vertical face along a steep reef slope in the Solomon Islands. It was in relatively deep water, about 50 feet (16 m), with bright but indirect light and strong water motion. Perhaps this species needs supplemental food, such as phytoplankton.

Reproduction: Budding and fission rapidly occur with growth, forming many new "heads" that divide and creep along over the substrate as they grow. These branches or heads may be cut off with a sharp scissors and planted elsewhere in the aquarium.

Sexual reproduction in *Xenia* has been observed by many aquarists and has been studied for some Red Sea and Australian species. Most *Xenia* spp. are dioecious though there is a hermaphroditic species (*X. viridis*) and there can be the odd hermaphroditic polyp in a colony. As in *Heteroxenia*, *Xenia* are internal brooders. Eggs or sperm develop along the mesenteries in the portion of the polyp within the capitulum. Fertilization occurs when sperm enters the gastrovascular cavity. As the eggs begin to develop they detach from the mesenteries and migrate into special brooding pouches located at the base of the anthocodium, where they develop into planulae. Red Sea populations of *X. macrospic*

Xenia sp. growing on the glass demonstrates the process of formation of daughter colonies by budding as they "creep" toward the light. J. Sprung

ulata spawn from August to September. Developed zooxanthellate planulae are released from the brooding pouches via temporary openings at the base of each anthocodium. This occurs at dusk near the first and last moon quarters for *X. macrospiculata* in the Red Sea (Benayahu and Loya, 1984b). On the GBR, colonies spawn a day before the full

The Sea Pen *Cavernularia obesa* lives with its base anchored in the sand. J. Sprung

moon in the morning hours (Alino and Coll, 1989; Benayahu and Loya, 1984a). In *X. macrospiculata* from the Red Sea, the planulae were found to swim very little and tended to settle quickly. They can then crawl over the surface until a suitable site is found where the planula can then anchor down via secreted mucus (Benayahu and Loya, 1984a). Development is rapid and within a month the polyp bears eight tentacles and several pairs of pinnules.

As the stalks of *Xenia* grow in length, the length of the gastrovascular cavities increases too, so that older colonies are capable of producing more eggs and sperm. In *X. macrospiculata* maturation occurs within two years (Benayahu and Loya, 1984a).

Order Pennatulacea Verrill, 1865

Family Veretillidae Herklots, 1858

Genus: *Cavernularia*

Scientific Name: *Cavernularia obesa*

Common Name: Sea Pen

Colour: Brown or light tan with white tipped polyps.

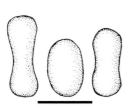

Sclerites of *Cavernularia*. Scale bar is 0.05 mm. *After Williams, 1993.*

Distinguishing Characteristics: Soft clavate (club shaped) colony. Primary polyp forms a muscular peduncle, like the column and foot of a sea anemone, which buries and anchors the coral in the substrate. The upper portion of the primary polyp forms a reduced axis. Secondary polyps are arranged around the entire length of the primary polyp. Sclerites are usually smooth needles or angular plates.

Similar Species: There are several species in the genus

Natural Habitat: Sandy bottoms between reefs in the Indo-Pacific region. Imported from Indonesia and Singapore.

Aquarium Care: Easy to care for when fed regularly. Although this species has brownish pigmentation, there are no zooxanthellae and the polyps feed actively on detritus, zooplankton, and possibly phytoplankton. Feed *Artemia* nauplii, *Daphnia*, pulverized flake food, and detritus stirred up from the bottom of the tank. Be sure to provide a sand layer at least 3 inches (7.6 cm) deep.

Reproduction: Sexual reproduction not reported in captivity. Asexual reproduction also not reported.

This wonderful sea fan photographed in the Solomon Islands had multiple colours within the same colony, prompting Julian to dub it "Fruit-Loops" gorgonian. J. Sprung

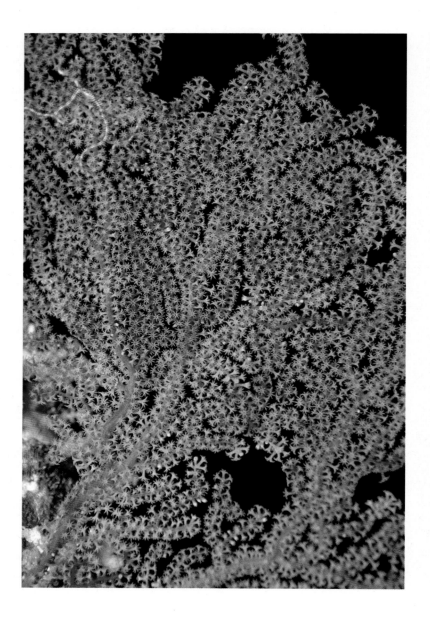

Order Gorgonacea

The order Gorgonacea is comprised of soft coral colonies that are mostly tree-like, with a common colonial coenenchyme supported on an axial skeleton (a specialized part of the coenenchyme) made of a proteinaceous material (gorgonin) that is similar to the substance in animal horns. The axis may be permeated by calcium carbonate, sometimes as sclerites or sometimes not. The order is artificially divided into two groups, Holaxonia and Scleraxonia on the basis of the structure of this axial skeleton. Taxonomists working on soft corals do not completely agree on the boundary between the two groups, but the division remains a convenient way to segregate some of the gorgonians on the basis of their construction.

Suborder Scleraxonia

Family Anthothelidae

Scientific Name: *Diodogorgia nodulifera*

Common Name: Finger Sea Fan. Yellow Finger, Red Finger

Colour: Two colour morphs. One is bright orange-yellow with red calyces and white polyps. The other is deep red with red calyces and white polyps.

Distinguishing Characteristics: Brittle: breaks easily. Does not grow very large, usually about 10 cm (4 in) tall, up to 25 cm (10 in), and generally not more than 25 cm (10 in) across. The sclerites on the interior are reddish. Not photosynthetic.

Similar Species: There are some gorgonians in the Indo—Pacific with the same colour combination, but no other gorgonians in the Caribbean would be mistaken for *Diodogorgia*.

Natural Habitat: Hardbottoms and low profile reefs in deep water 25 metres (75 feet) or more in the Caribbean, attached on the bottom in strong current.

Aquarium Care: Provide strong water motion. Secure base to the rock with underwater epoxy. May be kept in the light or shaded, but always where it receives constant strong water motion, and where it would be easy to feed it. Feed detritus, brine shrimp (nauplii and frozen adults), *Daphnia*, *Cyclops*, or pulverized

The most common form of *Diodogorgia* is yellow with red calyces and white polyps. J. Sprung

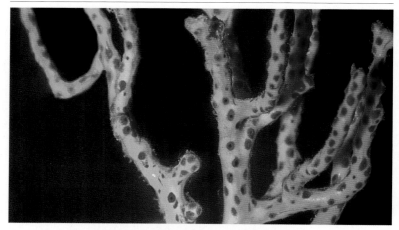

The red form of *Diodogorgia* is less common. S. Michael.

The typical appearance of *Erythropodium* with polyps expanded. J. C. Delbeek

shrimp or clam, or flake food. In general this gorgonian is not recommended for beginners or those who will not take the time to feed it. When it is not offered food weekly it does not survive more than a year, and gradually shrinks and dies. With dedicated feeding it can grow in captivity.

Reproduction: Sexual reproduction not reported. Branches easily fragment and can be re-attached with underwater epoxy.

Scientific Name: *Erythropodium caribaeorum* (Duchassaing & Michelotti), 1860

Common Name: Encrusting Gorgonian, Briareum

Distinguishing Characteristics: *Erythropodium* is very similar in appearance to *Briareum*, and the two are often confused. Some distinguishing visual features include coloring; *Briareum* tends to be purplish gray or brown when the polyps are closed, whereas *Erythropodium* is pale brown like coffee with a lot of cream in it, texture; *Erythropodium* is quite smooth when the polyps are contracted, whereas *Briareum* usually appears bumpy, and finally, polyp appearance; The polyps of *Briareum* tend to open to face the light, whereas *Erythropodium*'s polyps have elongate tentacles that "string-out" in the current, looking like filamentous brown algae. Although they look similar, *Briareum* and *Erythropodium* are not closely related. They have a different internal structure and quite different sclerites.

Similar Species: *Briareum* spp., *Anthelia* spp., *Xenia* spp.

Natural Habitat: *Erythropodium caribaeorum* is a Caribbean species that is common on reefs and coastal hardbottoms in clean water and turbid water. It prefers heavy turbulence and strong currents, though it also occurs in light tidal flow. Typically it encrusts dead coral skeletons and rubble, but it may also encrust and kill other gorgonians. Other *Erythropodium* species from the Indo-Pacific region live in essentially the same habitat. Some range into temperate waters, in Australia for example.

Aquarium Care: *Erythropodium* is extremely hardy and recommended to the beginner. It is a useful decorative species for rapidly coating the rocks, back and sides of the aquarium, and for covering plastic pipes, or the overflow wall. It is an excellent candidate for aquaculture. Its requirements are simple: strong light and current. It survives under dim light or with little current, but then it does not grow as quickly. It does not appear to capture prey, so feeding particulate food is not beneficial. Its stringy sweeper tentacles pack a potent sting that will kill most stony corals on contact (Sebens and Miles, 1988). As this soft coral spreads quickly over the rocks, it must be placed carefully to insure that it will not grow to meet stony corals.

Reproduction: Asexually propagates readily through growth. Small sections of coenenchyma can be torn free and placed on new substrate (see also *Pachyclavularia*). Sexual reproduction not reported in aquaria though like *Briareum asbestinum*, it is likely an external brooder.

Scientific Name: *Swiftia exserta*

Common Name: Orange Sea Fan, Soft Red Sea Fan, Orange Tree

Colour: Orange with red polyps

Distinguishing Characteristics: Bushy large gorgonian, sometimes fan shaped but with loose branches. Large red polyps are distinctive.

Natural Habitat: Caribbean. Medium depth to deep reefs with high profile, deepwater hardbottoms, and on deep shipwrecks. Not usually found shallower than 17 m (50 feet). Occurs in clear or slightly turbid water with strong current.

Aquarium Care: Not very hardy in captivity but definitely possible to keep. For dedicated aquarists only. Since it does not have symbiotic zooxanthellae this species requires regular feeding to survive. Adding food to the water stimulates the polyps to expand. They will take brine shrimp, chopped shrimp, *Mysis*, clam, fish eggs, Daphnia, and flake food. Strong currents also encourage polyp extension. This species sometimes suffers from tissue loss during shipping, exposing part of the skeleton. Under the right conditions this will heal and the exposed skeleton will be covered again with new tissue.

Reproduction: Release of eggs in captivity has been reported (Tyree, S. in Fosså and Nilsen, 1996). Branches easily fragment and can be re-attached with underwater epoxy.

Swiftia exserta is a beautiful gorgonian that requires daily feeding to thrive in captivity. Because of this maintenance requirement we don't recommend it to casual aquarists. J. Sprung

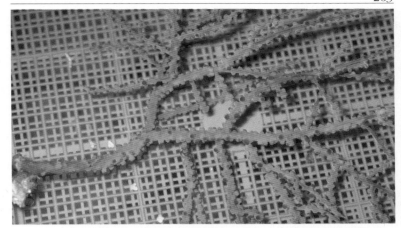

The polyps of *Swiftia exserta* are stunning deep red and create a spectacular sight against the orange rind of the branches. H. Feddern

The natural habitat of *Swiftia exserta*, shown here on hardbottom in deep water. Other gorgonians are also present, including *Diodogorgia nodulifera*. H. Feddern

Photosynthetic Gorgonians

Whereas the leather corals of the genera *Sinularia* and *Sarcophyton* are the dominant photosynthetic soft corals in the Indo-Pacific region, with just a few photosynthetic gorgonians there for good measure, in the Caribbean the photosynthetic gorgonians rule the scene, and there are no leather corals. Caribbean gorgonians are very popular with European hobbyists since they are hardy, beautiful, and include many varied species. In North America they have not been made as readily available as in Europe, but their popularity is gaining steadily. We discuss the most readily available species. Scientists are especially interested in these and other soft corals for the natural products they produce that have anti-inflammatory or anti-tumor capability.

Aquarium Care: The care of virtually all of the photosynthetic gorgonians is the same. Therefore we chose to summarize their care here, and only make additional comments about specific types when necessary. These flexible soft corals all like strong currents. Water motion is critical for assisting with the shedding of the waxy film that most species develop as a protection against fouling algae. The motion also stimulates the polyps to expand. Really well extended polyps can be achieved with surge devices or light turbulent water flow. Good illumination is important as well. They adapt easily to average lighting as from standard output fluorescents, and they may take time to adapt to really bright light as from metal halides, extending polyps on the lower regions only at first. The brighter light does increase their growth, however. Some species do not seem to capture zooplankton, but most will eat small food particles, such as brine shrimp nauplii or water fleas. Others will eat fairly large prey, but it is not necessary to feed them at all. A few species also appear to capture and consume tiny bubbles drifting in the water (J. Sprung, pers obs.). It is possible that gorgonians obtain some nutrition this way since the bubbles would have amino acids and carbohydrates attached to them, and possibly even bacteria and other microorganisms. Propagation of these corals is easy to accomplish. Simply cut off a branch and push the cut end into a rock, using underwater epoxy or monofilament line to secure the piece if necessary (see chapter six). Shipping for some but not all is best done by the "dry" method described in chapter five.

Reproduction: These gorgonians can all be easily reproduced asexually by taking cuttings (see chapter six). It is also common for species to periodically drop small branch tips that then reattach elsewhere. This is a common mechanism of vegetative propagation on reefs. Frequent storms also help to fragment colonies and spread the fragments throughout the reef.

Caribbean photosynthetic gorgonians are dioecious by nature, with separate male and female colonies. The majority of genera are internal brooders with eggs being fertilized internally and planulae released in the evening hours when mature e.g. *Eunicea, Muricea, Pseudoplexaura*. However, at least one genera (e.g. *Plexaura*) is a broadcast spawner and others may also be (Lasker and Kim, 1996).

Scientific Name: *Eunicea* spp.

Common Name: Knobby candelabrum

Colour: Usually pale gray with gray or brown polyps, but may be tan, yellow, or rarely, purple.

Distinguishing Characteristics: Sclerites in the axial sheath are mostly spindles, or blunt spindles and capstans, the latter being more typical of thicker branches and the main stem. These sclerites are often purple, sometimes violet or nearly colourless.

Eunicea species usually have characteristic knobby projections for calyces that afford an *Acropora*-like appearance when the polyps are closed. Colonies are often candelabrum shaped. The most commonly available species are *E. mammosa, E. succinea,* and *E. tourneforti*. There are many species, however, some with strongly projecting calyces, such as *E. laxispica*, and some with relatively smooth branches, such as *E. knighti*.

Similar Species: Smooth forms resemble *Pseudoplexaura* or *Plexaurella*. *Eunicea* is more rigid than the former and the latter genus never has purple sclerites. *Muricea* species are similarly spiny, but have projecting spicules that give them a distinctively prickly texture. They do not have purple sclerites

Natural Habitat: Shallow, brightly illuminated reefs, hardbottoms, and backreef or lagoon environments in the Caribbean. Most abundant where there is prevailing surge.

Aquarium Care: Strong light and water motion. This genus feeds well on fairly large prey. It will take brine shrimp, mysis, or flake foods.

Typical *Eunicea* sp.
J. C. Delbeek

Three varieties of *Eunicea*.
Note projecting calyces.
J. Sprung

Eunicea closeup.
J. Sprung

Scientific Name: *Muricea* spp.

Common Name: Spiny Sea Fan, Spiny gorgonian

Colour: gray, brown, golden brown or orange with brown polyps.

Natural Habitat: Reefs and hardbottom areas especially, but also occasional among seagrass and in bays. Shallow or deep water.

Distinguishing Characteristics: The several common *Muricea* species all have spiny projecting calyces that afford a rough texture when handled. Colonies may grow in one plane or may be bushy. *M. atlantica, M. laxa,* and *M. muricata* are common species in aquaria.

Muricea species are quite spiny.
J. Sprung

Muriceopsis flavida has a pinnate form similar to *Pseudopterogorgia* spp., but has thicker, bumpier branches with a round, not flattened cross section. J. C. Delbeek

Closeup of *Muriceopsis flavida* shows how the branches are rounded and bumpy.
J. Sprung

Muriceopsis sulphurea is a beautiful species, typically yellow, which is occasional in the southern Caribbean and Brazil.
J. Sprung

Similar Species: May be confused with *Eunicea* species, which also have a spiny appearance, but *Muricea* never has purple spicules in the axial sheath.

Aquarium Care: See description for general topic: Caribbean Photosynthetic Gorgonians. *Muricea* is one of the genera that is capable of producing sweeper tentacles to sting neighboring corals. Use caution when placing it near other corals that might be stung by it.

Scientific Name: *Muriceopsis flavida*

Common Name: Feather Gorgonian, Sea Plume, Purple Bush

Colour: purple, gray, brown, yellow

Distinguishing Characteristics: *Muriceopsis flavida* appears at first like a type of *Pseudopterogorgia* because its form is also pinnate (feather-like). Upon closer inspection one can see that the branches are thicker, rounder, and more robust than most *Pseudopterogorgia* species. In addition, the texture is rough, almost as rough as a *Muricea* species, because of projecting spicules around the calyces. A rare and beautiful relative, *Muriceopsis sulphurea* is locally abundant is some localities in the southern Caribbean and Brazil. It forms low bushes of short branches that are usually lemon yellow. It occurs in shallow water, brightly illuminated, exposed to strong water motion and often among algae.

Aquarium Care: See description for general topic: Caribbean Photosynthetic Gorgonians. *Muriceopsis* is one of the genera that is capable of producing sweeper tentacles to sting neighboring corals. Use caution when placing it near other corals that might be stung by it.

Scientific Name: *Plexaura* spp.

Common Name: Sea Rod, Candelabrum

Colour: Dark brown, gray, bright purple

Distinguishing Characteristics: The sclerites in the axial sheath are short capstans with six or eight rays, or belted rods developing into multiradiate spheroidal bodies. These sclerites are reddish purple. *Plexaura homomalla* has tough branches about 1 cm thick that are chocolate brown with contrasting light brown

The Purple Sea Rod, *P. flexuosa*, is an attractive species that, unfortunately, does not ship well. Once acclimated in a well illuminated aquarium, however, it is quite hardy. J. Sprung

Purple Sea Rod, *P. flexuosa* in the natural habitat. opened and closed. H. Feddern

The Brown Sea Rod, *P. homomalla*, is an attractive chocolate colour with lighter brown polyps. J. C. Delbeek

polyps. *Plexaura flexuosa* may be a variety of colours, but the most striking one is bright purple with almost white polyps (photo). Colonies often branch in one plane when small, becoming bushy when large. They grow to at least four feet tall.

Natural Habitat: Caribbean. Reef crest, backreef areas with strong surge.

Aquarium Care: *Plexaura* spp. do not ship well and often disintegrate a day or two after arrival. If they survive, once established in the aquarium they are hardy if provided with very strong currents and very bright light.

Scientific Name: *Plexaurella* spp.

Plexaurella sp. J. C. Delbeek

Young colonies of *Plexaurella* are typically shaped like a "Y."
J. C. Delbeek

Typical colony shape of *Plexaurella*.
J. Sprung

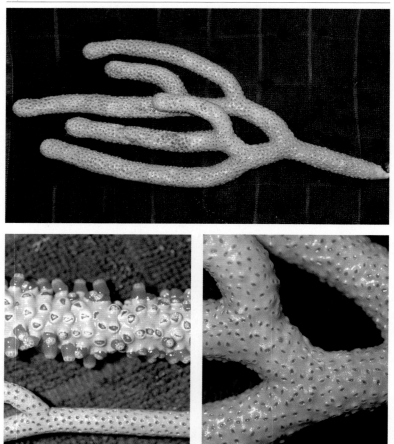

Two quite different species of *Plexaurella*. The lower specimen has round pores like *Pseudoplexaura*, but it does not have purple sclerites inside.
J. Sprung

Closeup of *Plexaurella*, showing the typical slit-pore-like calyces
J. Sprung

Common Name: Corky sea fingers, Slit-pore sea rod

Colour: Light brown, almost yellow, with darker brown polyps.

Distinguishing Characteristics: *Plexaurella* species have a corky appearance when the polyps are retracted. *P. dichotoma, P. natans,* and *P. grisea* are the most common species available. Small colonies are often shaped like a "Y", while large colonies are often bushy. Another species, *P. grandiflora* has huge polyps, about 1 to 1.5 cm in diameter, with the main branch at least 2 to 3 cm in diameter (appearing 5 cm in diameter when the polyps are expanded). *Plexaurella grandiflora* typically grows straight up as a single trunk with at most a few side branches like a sahuaro cactus. Most *Plexaurella* spp. have crescent shaped pores when the polyps are closed, though some have round pores like the similar-looking *Pseudoplexaura* spp.

Similar Species: *Pseudoplexaura* has more slippery texture and round pores when the polyps are closed. It also typically has a purple cortex while *Plexaurella* is uniformly yellowish brown throughout. Some smooth pale brown varieties of *Eunicea* may be confused with *Plexaurella*, though the polyps at the tips of the branches in *Eunicea* nearly always show the characteristic bumpy calyces when the polyps retract, and *Eunicea* usually have dark or purplish sclerites in the cortex. One species of *Plexaurella* is slippery like *Pseudoplexaura*, but it has characteristic crescent-shaped calyces and the cortex is not purple.

Aquarium Care: This genus is especially hardy, ships well, and grows beautifully under a variety of lighting conditions. See description for general topic: Caribbean Photosynthetic Gorgonians.

Scientific Name: *Pseudoplexaura* spp.

Common Name: none

Colour: Gray or lavender branches with yellow or brown polyps. One uncommon species in Florida may have yellow or green branches.

Distinguishing Characteristics: Two *Pseudoplexaura* species are occasionally imported from the Caribbean and Florida. Both are

Typical appearance of a branch of
Pseudoplexaura.
J. Sprung

Pseudoplexaura spp. are among the most stunning of the photosynthetic gorgonians, with big feathery polyps that move beautifully in the current. S. W. Michael

slimy to the touch, and have the most beautiful polyps. They resemble *Plexaurella* spp., but *Pseudoplexaura* spp. are usually very gray instead of pale brown, and *Plexaurella* never has purple sclerites in the axial sheath. Colonies grow absolutely huge, to at least eight feet tall and several feet across. These "trees" have a sturdy base that may be six inches or more in diameter! It is really an impressive site to be in six feet of water and encounter a six foot tall, four foot wide *Pseudoplexaura* tree with resident school of fish. *P. flagellosa* is one of the prettiest gorgonians of all, with large bushy brown polyps that extend very far and sway in the current. It is more slimy than *P. porosa*, and has thicker branches that are more flexible in the current. *P. porosa* stands more erect in the current, and usually has more purplish branch coloration than *P. flagellosa*. There are at least three common species in Florida.

Aquarium Care: One of the best gorgonians for aquariums since they are extremely hardy and grow rapidly (at least one inch per month per branch is not unusual). Exquisite polyps when fully acclimated.

Family Gorgoniidae

Scientific Name: *Gorgonia ventalina, G. flabellum*, and *G. mariae*

Common Name: Sea Fan

Colour: Purple, yellow, gray, brown. Polyps brown.

Distinguishing Characteristics: *Gorgonia ventalina* is the common variety of sea fan, with the branching flattened in the same plane as the fan. It is typically purple, but can also be pale gray or yellow. *G. flabellum* is distinguished by branches flattened perpendicular to the plane of the fan, and it is more rigid. It may be any of the aforementioned colors, but yellow is most typical. A third species, *Gorgonia mariae*, has branches that are rounded instead of flattened.

Natural Habitat: Sea fans grow most profusely where they receive regular surge action that rocks them to and fro. *Gorgonia ventalina* grows both in high surge zones and in zones where the predominant water motion is from tidal currents. It may occur in shallow or deep water. *G. flabellum* only occurs in shallow water, commonly in zones that receive heavy surge.

Aquarium Care: In the aquarium *G. ventalina* and *G. mariae* are very hardy and grow well under intense illumination and strong water motion. *Gorgonia flabellum* is more delicate, though certainly possible to grow when provided with very strong illumination (which will maintain the lemon yellow colour) and strong water motion. *Gorgonia flabellum* does not ship as well as the other two species.

Important note: Because of the curio trade in dead corals, the three Caribbean sea fan species are prohibited to collect in Florida, and prohibited to collect in many Caribbean localities. Please be sure that these wonderful soft corals are obtained legally. Where legal to collect, there is no harm done by harvesting small, four inch colonies since these are only about one year old or less, and clearly renewable. When they are collected, the small fragments of the base or holdfast that remain on the reef grow into new fans.

Gorgonia ventalina may be purple or yellow. The most colourful ones are from shallow water where they receive strong UV illumination. In deeper water the yellow and the purple forms are nearly gray. If gradually acclimated to an increase in UV they will become more colourful as they develop protective pigments. J. C. Delbeek

Gorgonia flabellum is usually yellow and it has branches flattened perpendicular to the plane of the fan. J. Sprung

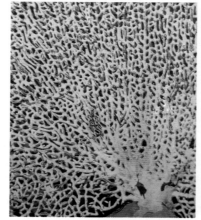 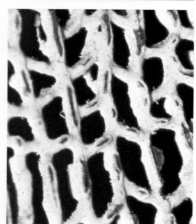

Gorgonia mariae photographed in the Caribbean. G. Schiemer

Scientific Name: *Pacifigorgia* spp.

Common Name: Red Sea Fan, Panamic Sea Fan

Two species of sea fans, probably *Pacifigorgia* spp. from Puerto vallarta, Mexico.
J. Sprung

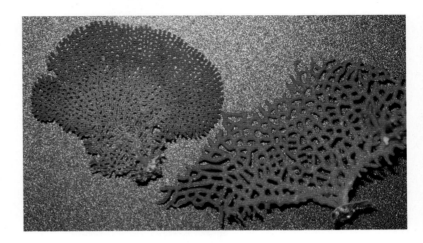

Colour: Red, orange, brown with whitish polyps.

Distinguishing Characteristics: Growth in one plane. Reddish colour, stiff horny skeleton, white or clear polyps. Not photosynthetic. Three species are available occasionally. Two of them are shown here. Described species include *P. adamsii* and *P. irene.*

Similar Species: There are numerous other bright red sea fans in the Indo-Pacific with whitish polyps.

Natural Habitat: Rock walls in areas with surge along the eastern Pacific coast including the Sea of Cortez down to Peru.

Aquarium Care: Secure in place with underwater epoxy. Provide strong water motion and feed daily if possible. Feed plankton substitutes such as *Artemia* nauplii, *Daphnia*, or *Cyclops* (copepods). Also phytoplankton. While they ship very well, *Pacifigorgia* spp. are not hardy and do not thrive in captivity. Not recommended to beginners.

Scientific Name: *Phyllogorgia dilatata*

Common Name: Sea Fan, Brazilian Blade Sea Fan, Elephant's Ear Coral, Palma (in Brazil)

Phyllogorgia dilatata is seldom collected, does not ship very well, and therefore is rarely available to aquarists. It is a hardy and beautiful species when given strong light and water motion. J. Sprung

The typical pinnate form of *Pseudopterogorgia* spp. that gives this genus its common name, "Sea Plume." This is probably *P. acerosa.*
J. C. Delbeek

Colour: Typically brown or gray, but it can also be yellow, and may have violet highlights when strongly illuminated. Polyps brown.

Distinguishing Characteristics: *Phyllogorgia* is a special variety of sea fan that only occurs in Brazil, from the Rocas atoll, Fernando de Noronha, the Isle of Trindade, and along the Brazilian coast from Cera to Rio de Janeiro. The branching is flattened in one plane, and there are two colony forms, depending on water motion. In heavy pounding surf the colony develops thin rounded branches. In more quiet waters the colonies form the leaf-like fans.

Similar Species: There are no similar gorgonians in the Atlantic, but there are several similar looking genera in the Indo-Pacific.

Natural Habitat: *Phyllogorgia* grow most profusely with regular surge action that rocks them to and fro. They may occur in shallow or deep water, but they need light to survive since they have zooxanthellae in their tissues.

Aquarium Care: In the aquarium *Phyllogorgia* is very hardy and grows well under intense illumination and strong water motion. Unfortunately it does not ship well, is seldom collected, and so it is quite rare in the aquarium trade.

Reproduction: Can be propagated by fragmentation but the fragments do not easily re-attach to the substrate. Underwater epoxy must be used to hold the fragmented branches in place. Sexual reproduction not observed in captivity.

Scientific Name: *Pseudopterogorgia* spp.

Common Name: Sea plume, Feather Gorgonian, Purple Frilly

Colour: Gray, brown, purple, yellow

Distinguishing Characteristics: Sea plumes are most often shaped like feathers, or groups of feathers, but there are a few species (seldom available to hobbyists) that do not have this shape. The most common species available to hobbyists are *P. americana*, *P. acerosa*, and *P. elisabethae*. Pale to deep purple with brown polyps is the usual colour. *Pseudopterogorgia elisabethae*, the so-called "Purple Frilly" gorgonian, is nearly always a lovely deep purple with pale brown to almost white polyps. The branching is usually in one plane in this species, a common trait

A tall specimen of
Pseudopterogorgia in an aquarium.
J. C. Delbeek

Pseudopterogorgia elisabethae is a
beautiful species known as "Purple
Frilly," and it is being studied for
its novel chemistry. It produces
useful anti-inflammatory and skin
healing drugs. J. C. Delbeek

of many of the members of this genus. *Pseudopterogorgia bipin-nata* is similar in appearance, but the branches are finer than in *P. elisabethae. Pseudopterogorgia americana* is very slimy, a characteristic that readily identifies it. It does not ship well, unfortunately, but is a beautiful species that grows well once acclimated. It also is probably the largest species, attaining over eight feet (2.6 m) in height and even greater span side to side.

Natural Habitat: Caribbean primarily, but there may be some species in the Indo-Pacific. Most species occur on hardbottoms, rubble zones, and reef tops, oriented upright, while others, such as *P. elisabethae* and *P. bipinnata* are typically attached to the sides of reefs and coral heads, oriented horizontally. All species appreciate surge and strong tidal currents. They range from shallow to deep water.

Aquarium Care: See description for general topic: Caribbean Photosynthetic Gorgonians.

Scientific Name: *Pterogorgia* spp.

Common Names: Sea Blades, Angular Sea Whip, Cactus Gorgonian, Purple Ribbon, Yellow Ribbon.

Colour: Purple, brown, gray, yellow.

Distinguishing Characteristics: flattened branches with polyps extending only from the edges. There are three common species, *P. anceps, P. guadalupensis,* and *P. citrina,* and a possible fourth species.

Natural Habitat: Prefers hardbottoms in back-reef areas, near shore, or among seagrass. *P. anceps* and *P. guadalupensis* are seldom found up on the reef itself.

Aquarium Care: Extremely hardy, care as in the introductory remarks for Caribbean Photosynthetic Gorgonians. *Pterogorgia citrina* is slightly more delicate and requires extremely bright light and strong water motion or surge to really thrive. When it does not receive enough light it stops expanding the polyps, and algae start to cover the surface of the colony. It can shed the algae off with a waxy film, but if the polyps do not expand, eventually the colony just disintegrates. *Pterogorgia anceps, P. citrina,* and a fourth unnamed *Pterogorgia* species all are very brittle and branches readily break off. They reproduce asexually by such

Pterogorgia citrinus is usually yellow with brownish red calyces at the edges of its thin flattened branches. J. Sprung

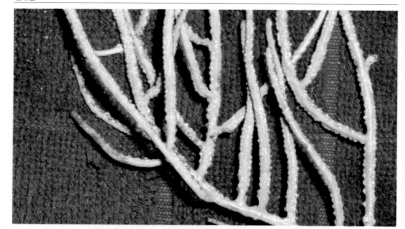

Pterogorgia citrinus
J. C. Delbeek

Pterogorgia anceps is often dark purple, particularly when brightly illuminated in shallow water. J. C. Delbeek

fragmentation in nature and can rapidly colonize large areas of hardbottom. In the aquarium they can also be propagated by fragmentation. *Pterogorgia guadalupensis* is not so brittle as the other three, and must be cut with a scissors to propagate it in captivity.

Reproduction: Fragmentation of branches readily produces new colonies. The fragmented branches grow and attach to rock quickly.

Pterogorgia spp. frequently shed a waxy film to rid their surface of attached algae. This normal process may take several days and is assisted by strong water currents. This is probably *P. guadalupensis*.
J. Sprung

Rumphella, center, with *Sinularia brassica*, upper right and *Sinularia notanda*, left.
J. Sprung

This photosynthetic gorgonian photographed in Berlin is probably a *Rumphella* sp. A pair of Longnose Hawkfish perch on it naturally.
J. Sprung

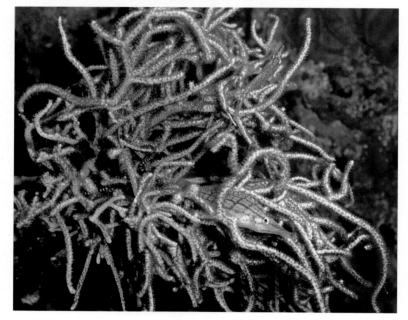

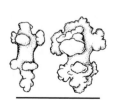

Sclerites of *Rumphella*. Scale bar is 0.1 mm. *After Williams, 1993.*

Scientific Name: *Rumphella* sp.

Common Name: Sea Rod, Sea Whip

Colour: Light tan, pale yellow, brown, gray

Distinguishing Characteristics: Bushy gorgonian with continuous gorgonin axis. Sclerites are symmetrical clubs and spindles.

One of the few photosynthetic Indo-Pacific gorgonians.

Similar Species: This gorgonian is most similar to *Plexaurella* and *Plexaura* species that are also bushy and grayish brown.

Natural Habitat: Widespread through the western Indo-Pacific region. Lagoon environments with moderate to strong illumination and periodic surge. Often in sand adjacent to the reef. Occasionally on reef slopes.

Aquarium Care: Easy to care for. Give strong light and moderate to strong water motion. Feeding is unnecessary as this gorgonian has symbiotic zooxanthellae. It may take small plankton, however, and this may enhance growth.

Reproduction: Fragments of branches can easily be made to create new colonies (see chapter six).

Family Isididae

Subfamily Isidinae

Genus: *Isis*

Scientific Name: *Isis hippuris*

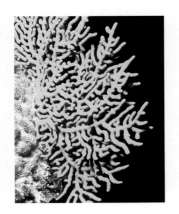

Isis hippuris.
A. J. Nilsen

Common Name: Sea Fan

Colour: Pale gray, brown, or yellow

Distinguishing Characteristics: Axis composed of alternating node-like segments of gorgonin and calcium carbonate (fused sclerites).

Similar Species: Superficially resembles *Plexaura* species from the Caribbean, but the skeleton (axis) is entirely different.

Natural Habitat: Indo-Pacific reefs in shallow water with bright light and surge.

Aquarium Care: Delicate in shipping but hardy in captivity when given strong water motion and strong light. Attach to rock with underwater epoxy.

Reproduction: Fragments of branches can be made to create new colonies.

Chapter Eight　　　　**The Identification and Care of Zoanthids in Aquaria**

Zoanthids are pretty undemanding in their requirements. Zooxanthellate genera require medium to strong lighting and water motion. Azooxanthellate species do not require light but will tolerate it. Good water motion is especially important for *Epizoanthus* and *Parazoanthus* , particularly for the organisms with which they live i.e. sponges and hydroids. We give more specific recommendations for each genus later in this chapter.

Filtration and Water Quality

Zoanthids are fairly tolerant of poor water quality. They are commonly found in turbid, so-called "polluted" areas in canals and harbours, as well as intertidal areas and on the reef. Poor water quality with high levels of nitrate, phosphate and dissolved organics cause other problems that can then indirectly affect zoanthid health. The most obvious of these is excessive algae growth. Cyanobacteria and hair algae can easily overgrow and smother zoanthids. Do not allow massive growths of undesirable algae to invade zoanthid colonies! Please follow the recommendations in volume one for preventing and controlling undesirable algae growth. As with anemones simple systems are best (see chapter ten).

Water Motion

As with most sessile invertebrates, zoanthids rely on water motion to bring food and dissolved substances to them and to rid themselves of wastes. Moderate water motion with the occasional strong burst are appreciated by zoanthids. Good water motion will also encourage faster growth of the colony. Finally, good water motion will prevent the accumulation of detritus between the polyps. If detritus and sand are allowed to accumulate between the polyps, undesirable algae may proliferate in these pockets.

A colony of brillant green
Protopalythoa psammophila from
Hawai'i. J. C. Delbeek

Lighting

Lighting is only of importance to species that have zooxanthellae. Zoanthids can be kept under a wide range of lighting types, but generally the more light the better. If the zoanthids are contracting a great deal and/or show signs of bleaching (lightening) then they may be getting too much light. Symptoms of low light include stretching of the polyps towards the light

A colony of Yellow polyps being over grown with hair algae. Attention to nutrient levels, the use of herbivores and good water motion will help prevent this from occurring. J. Sprung

Zoanthus spp. are easy to maintain with strong illumination.
J. C. Delbeek

source, loss of fluorescent colouring and browning (darkening) of the polyps as the zooxanthellae increase their pigment levels, followed by gradual lightening due to loss of zooxanthellae.

Tankmates

When adding zoanthids to an aquarium or adding tankmates to an aquarium with zoanthids one should be aware of a few things. There are a few fish that will pick at and even eat zoanthids, the most notable being certain species of butterfly fish such as Raccoon butterflyfish (*Chaetodon lunula*). These normally prey on anemones and will often pick at zoanthids enough to prevent them from opening, eventually resulting in their death. Filefish (Monacanthidae) and sharpnose puffers (Tetraodontidae) are also potential zoanthid nippers.

A *Condylactis* anemone stinging a colony of *Zoanthus*. J. Sprung

A colony of *Palythoa* being stung by a neighbouring *Euphyllia divisa*. J. C. Delbeek

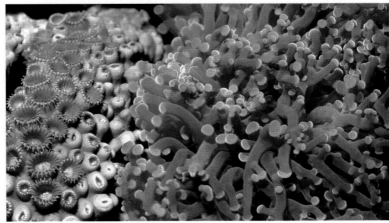

Usually corallimorpharia and zoanthids do not do well next to each other; the zoanthids normally lose such interactions. J. Sprung

When placing organisms near zoanthids keep in mind the potential for rapid growth in zoanthids as we discussed in chapter two. Also be aware that zoanthids can be stung by or sting neighbouring corals and anemones, and allow enough space between colonies to take this into account.

Feeding

As we mentioned in chapter two, zoanthids can be fed but some genera are much less reliant on supplemental feeding than others. We cover each genera in detail in the sections below.

Purchasing Healthy Specimens

When acquiring zoanthids there are a few things one should be on the look-out for. Avoid any colonies that have polyps with brown, jelly-like masses on them. This is a protozoan infection that can rapidly spread throughout an aquarium (see volume one). Zoanthids with this condition have usually been weakened in some way, making them susceptible to infection. The polyps themselves should be open and brightly coloured with no bleaching evident. If the polyps are dark brown in colour and lack bright colours such as green, orange or pink, this is often a symptom of low light levels. These colonies will usually regain their bright colours if gradually acclimated to higher light levels. Finally, inspect the colony closely for any predatory snails (e.g. *Heliacus*). They eat zoanthids and must be removed to avoid losing the colony.

This colony of zoanthids is suffering from a bacterial infection and an infestation of protozoans. Such colonies often become "mushy" and die. J. Sprung

Heliacus sp., these snails are common on newly imported colonies of *Zoanthus* and *Protopalythoa* and should be removed immediately! J. Sprung

Look for white necrotic areas on the rock with the zoanthids. This may indicate a dead or dying sponge that can cause the zoanthids to die-off. Inspect the rock closely to find any fouling sponges and remove them completely. Also check for filamentous algae patches and remove these too.

Species Descriptions

Class Anthozoan
Subclass Zoantharia (Hexacorallia)
Order Zoanthidea
Suborder Brachycnemina

Family Zoanthidae

Genus *Isaurus* Gray, 1828

Zoanthids in this genus are found firmly attached to live rock and coral rubble, in rubble zones and reef crests around the world. Polyps can be found singly or in small colonies connected by a thin stolon. Although it is reported that they possess zooxanthellae in the endo- and ectodermis (Muirhead and Ryland, 1985), the oral end of an *Isaurus* polyp remains closed during the day and the whole polyp tends to bend towards the substratum, often lying completely down. At night the polyps extend themselves upwards and the capitulum opens, revealing the tentacles that capture prey items.

The colour of the tentacles often contrasts with the rest of polyp and can be white, pink or iridescent green. Under actinic lighting the body wall of some species will glow a metallic green or bluish with pale lavender blotches (e.g. *Isaurus tuberculatus*). There is always one side of the polyp which is exposed to the light and it is thicker, often with more pronounced tubercles than on the shaded side, and usually more colourful (irridescent). Although the polyps do not incorporate sand in their column walls, they are often found embedded in sand. Other distinguishing characteristics can be found internally and will only be revealed by dissection and microscopic examination of the sphincter muscle. The mesenteries in the bottom portion of the polyp form a mesh-like network and the sphincter muscle covers at least 75% of the mesogloea (Mather and Bennett, 1993).

There are currently three species recognized: *Isaurus cliftoni, I. maculatus* and *I. tuberculatus*. These three can be differentiated quite easily based on the presence and shape of tubercles (swellings of mesogloea) on the body wall.

Isaurus tuberculatus, typical daytime appearance with the polyps closed. J. Sprung

I. tuberculatus showing the characteristic swellings on the body wall. J. Sprung

Scientific Name: *Isaurus tuberculatus* Gray, 1828

Common Name: Snake Polyps

Colour: Variable; column brown, green or grayish; tubercles cream/white; tentacles white or fluorescent green under actinic lighting; may have a metallic iridescent sheen on the polyp columns.

Distinguishing Features: Large tubercles on upper body wall though some polyps within a colony may lack them; tubercles vary in size and are not arranged in rows; large tubercles also found along the rim of the capitulum (crown) of the polyp; body can be elongated or short depending on location collected (i.e. shallow or deep, from crevices or in the open) (Muirhead and Ryland, 1985). The great variety in body and tubercle shape led to much taxonomic confusion, with several species being described. Recent work has shown that most of these species were in fact morphs of *I. tuberculatus* (see Muirhead and Ryland 1985).

Similar Species: *Isaurus maculatus* (Ryland 1979) and *Isaurus cliftoni* (Gray, 1867). *Isaurus maculatus* also has tubercles but they are much smaller and greater in number than in *I. tuberculatus*, are arranged in both rows and series, and are darkly pigmented (Muirhead and Ryland, 1985). The crown of *I. maculatus* lacks tubercles. *Isaurus cliftoni* is easily distinguished from the other two in that it lacks tubercles, the body is smooth and has an emerald green colour with numerous mauve blotches (Muirhead and Ryland, 1985).

Natural Habitat: *Isaurus tuberculatus* is found in tropical waters throughout the world ranging from Hawaii in the Pacific to Perth, Australia. In the Atlantic it can be found as far north as Bermuda (Muirhead and Ryland, 1985). This species occurs from shallow reef crests to depths as great as 40 m (120 ft). They are often found attached to coral rubble, coralline algae clumps, bivalve shells and worm tubes. Often growing mixed among other zoanthids, especially Zoanthus spp. *Isaurus maculatus* is found on reef the crest and wave break zone in Fiji, while *I. cliftoni* has so far only been reported from Western Australia (Muirhead and Ryland, 1985).

Aquarium Care: *Isaurus* spp. are relatively easy to maintain in aquaria. They require a strong to medium light intensity and should be located in the upper third of the aquarium. Medium to occasionally strong surges of current will best duplicate their natural habitat. Weekly feedings of the polyps can be done in the early evening using frozen mysis shrimp, adult brine shrimp or finely chopped fresh shrimp; sometimes the polyps can be trained to open during daylight hours by adding food or shrimp juice to the aquarium a few minutes before actual feeding.

Reproduction: Asexual propagation of polyps is the most frequently seen means of reproduction in *Isaurus* spp. Small polyps will form on creeping stolons and can eventually separate to form individual colonies. Sexual reproduction in *Isaurus* has not been observed but both hermaphroditic and gonochoristic (separate sex) polyps have been recorded (in Muirhead and Ryland, 1985). It is likely that broadcast spawning with external fertilization occurs in the warmer months of the year. No records of spawning in aquaria are known.

Genus *Palythoa*

Palythoa spp. are easily distinguished from other zoanthids. The polyps are encased by a thick, sand encrusted coenenchyma giving the colony the appearance of a single mass. They grow mat-like over substrates, forming flat, convex, concave or mushroom-like growths. *Palythoa* spp. are golden brown to cream in colour, with the polyps often being darker in colour than the coenenchyma. *Palythoa* are usually found in shallow areas, either on reef crests or reef flat areas just behind the reef crest, on lagoon bottoms or lining tidepools. In Hawaii, *Palythoa tuberculosa* is found along wave-swept shorelines, often subject to heavy wave action during parts of the year (J. C. Delbeek, pers. obs.).

There are several species of *Palythoa* that occur throughout the tropical seas of the world. The most commonly encountered in the aquarium trade are *Palythoa caesia* Dana, 1848, and *P. tuberculosa* from the Pacific, and *P. caribaeorum* Duchassaing and Michelotti, 1866 and *P. mammillosa* (Ellis and Solander, 1786) from the Caribbean. All of them require the same care in aquaria.

Palythoa have one of the most potent marine poisons known to science, palytoxin (Mereish, et al. 1991). Care should be taken when handling these animals; avoid touching them if you have cuts on your hands, and do not touch your mouth after touching a colony. It is always a good idea to wash ones hands thoroughly after working in an aquarium. It is also wise to avoid working in a marine aquarium when one has skin abrasions or open cuts on the hands or arms, to prevent the risk of contracting bacterial infection e.g. *Vibrio* spp.

Colonies of *Palythoa* are sometimes the home of small crabs of the genus *Platypodiella* (den Hartog and Türkay, 1991). These crabs live in small holes under the colony but can also be found in small slits and pits dug into the colony. *Platypodiella spectabilis* is a small reddish crab, with irregular yellow blotches that has been found in Caribbean colonies of *Palythoa* and may appear in aquaria (den Hartog and Türkay, 1991). These crabs do feed on the zoanthid but it is not known if this is their sole food source. *Platypodiella* crabs have been shown to concentrate palytoxin in their tissues (Gliebs et al., 1995).

One of several *Platypodiella* sp. crabs that are found in association with *Palythoa* spp. J. C. den Hartog

Platypodiella spp. concentrate palytoxin in their tissues. J. C. den Hartog

Scientific Name: *Palythoa* spp.

Common Name: Golden Sea Mat

Colour: Golden brown, to cream, polyps often darker, will darken in aquaria with inadequate lighting. Sometimes with fluorescent green or yellow tentacles.

Distinguishing Features: Thick encrusting growth; coenenchyma embedded with sand grains; polyps open during the day and night; zooxanthellate; single sphincter muscle; few mesenteries (15-20); mesenteries not mesh-like (Mather and Bennett, 1993). *Palythoa mammillosa* forms thicker, more cushion-like growths than the other species.

Palythoa sp. Note the polyps embedded in continuous tissue, characteristic of this genus.
J. C. Delbeek

Similar Species: none

Natural Habitat: see above. *Palythoa caribaeorum* and *P. mammillosa* are found in the Caribbean and Atlantic, and *P. caesia* and *P. tuberculosa* in the Pacific and Red Sea.

Aquarium Care: *Palythoa* spp. are amongst the easiest of invertebrates to keep and grow in aquaria. They enjoy high light intensities but will grow (slowly) in shaded areas. They require medium currents with the occasional strong surge to promote rapid growth, but will do well in lower current areas. When given sufficient light no feeding is required but they will capture stray food items fed to the fish in the system, so the occasional direct feeding is not harmful and will in fact promote growth.

Reproduction: Asexual reproduction in *Palythoa* is the most common form seen in aquaria. This is achieved by a spreading growth over the substratum and polyp budding. In the wild, local disturbances can fragment large colonies and facilitate the spreading of colonies over large areas of the reef.

Although sexual reproduction has not been recorded in the wild, Fadlallah *et al.* (1984) found that *P. caribaeorum* was reproductively active from January to June and recorded oocyte densities as high as 723 per polyp. Male, female, and hermaphroditic colonies were found. Fertilization is presumably external, though it is possible that eggs are fertilized internally and brooded larvae are released (based on anecdotal observation in aquarium, J.

Sprung). Yamazoto *et al.* (1973), found that colonies of *P. tuberculosa* in Okinawa became sexually productive in March/April and in October (see also chapter two).

Genus *Protopalythoa*

Protopalythoa spp. are found in tropical seas around the world. At one time referred to as *Palythoa* (even recent references still call them such) or *Gemmaria*, they are now all classified as *Protopalythoa*. They occur as loosely connected polyps or individual polyps in small clumps, in shallow forereef, reef crest and backreef areas (Mather and Bennett, 1993). Colonies can cover over 90% of the substratum in some areas. The body column is sand encrusted, though this may diminish somewhat in aquaria.

Protopalythoa (vestitus?).
J. Sprung

Protopalythoa vestitus.
J. C. Delbeek

The oral disc can be so large in some species that the polyp cannot close completely (e.g. *Protopalythoa* (=*Palythoa*) *grandis*). The tentacles can be either long or short but they always are thin with pointed tips. *Protopalythoa* spp. contain zooxanthellae but they will actively feed on small pieces of shrimp, adult brine shrimp, flake food and mysis shrimp. The species with long tentacles are especially good at prey capture.

This entire genus is currently under revision, therefore no species names can be assigned, even though those formerly classified as *Palythoa* will in all likelihood retain their species names under the new genus.

Scientific Name: *Protopalythoa* spp.

Common Names: Button Polyps, Polyp Rock

Colour: Brown usually, often with an iridescent green oral disc; sometimes mostly green; sometimes with white marbling or white stripes; the shade of brown ranges from straw coloured to chocolate.

Distinguishing Features: Body wall sand encrusted; tentacles thin and pointed; polyps of uniform colour in most cases; numerous mesenteries (>60); occur as solitary polyps or connected by a thin coenenchyma (Mather and Bennett, 1993).

Similar Species: *Zoanthus* spp. are often confused with *Protopalythoa*, but when viewed side-by-side there are several readily apparent external differences. *Zoanthus* do not have sand encrusted body columns; *Zoanthus* grow via a stolon or a continuous sheet of coenenchyma; the tentacles of *Zoanthus* tend to be shorter relative to the oral disc, with blunt tips; the oral disc and/or tentacles are often brightly coloured in *Zoanthus*, and usually contrast with the body column or oral disc, respectively. Internally, the sphincter muscle in *Zoanthus* consists of two parts while in *Protopalythoa* it is continuous (Mather and Bennett, 1993).

Natural Habitat: see above

Aquarium Care: Although no species names can be assigned at present, most of the *Protopalythoa* in the trade today require much the same care. They should be placed in the upper 2/3 of the aquarium and will benefit from medium to strong lighting, though they will survive in lower light areas. Weekly feedings are beneficial but not necessary for success. Water currents should be low to medium, with the occasional strong burst to prevent the settling of detritus between the polyps, otherwise detritus accumulation could favour the growth of hair algae there.

Reproduction: In aquaria *Protopalythoa* can quickly spread asexually, covering most of the substratum, via growth of the coenenchyma and polyp budding. Though little is known about their sexual means of reproduction, it is likely that they are very similar to *Palythoa* and *Zoanthus*.

Scientific Name: *Protopalythoa grandis*

Common Name: Button Polyps, Polyp Rock, Cinnamon Polyp

Protopalythoa grandis.
J. Sprung

Protopalythoa grandis.
J. C. Delbeek

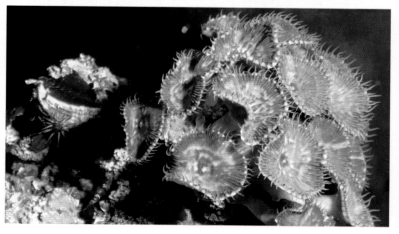

Colour: Brown usually, often with green oral disc. Sometimes mostly green, sometimes with white marbling or white stripes. The shade of brown ranges from straw colored to chocolate, often with slight reddish hue like cinnamon.

Distinguishing Features: Gigantic polyps compared to other members of the genus. Polyps to at least 5 cm (2 in.) diameter. Otherwise quite like other members of the genus.

Similar Species: *Protopalythoa variabilis* from the Caribbean when found in deep water may resemble this species, but the polyps are not nearly as large. *Protopalythoa grandis* may be circumtropical or there may be a closely related species found in the Indo-Pacific (Colin and Arneson, 1995).

Natural Habitat: Deep water reefs and hardbottoms in the Caribbean. Found covering large areas of hardbottom in some localities at about 100 feet or more depth. Found in the Northern Gulf of Mexico and off the central east coast of Florida. Tolerates relatively cold water, and therefore may range as far north as the Carolinas, though we have not seen that range reported.

Aquarium Care: Very easy to care for. Does not tolerate very bright direct illumination, and will bleach and remain closed in response. Provide medium intensity light. Blue fluorescent light will enhance fluorescent green or cinnamon colour. Feed often with flake food, chopped fish, or chopped clam meat.

Reproduction: Asexual reproduction by budding of daughter polyps as is typical for other members of this genus. Sexual reproduction not studied.

Genus *Sphenopus*

Sphenopus is a genus that is seldom encountered by aquarists. It is distinguished by its solitary polyp existence as opposed to the colonial nature of other members of the order Zoantharia. Found in sandy or muddy areas, the base of the polyp extends into the sand and the capitulum is extended at night to feed. They do not contain zooxanthellae. The reader is directed to Colin and Arneson (1995) for a photo.

Genus *Zoanthus* Lamarck, 1801

Zoanthus sociatus.
J. Sprung

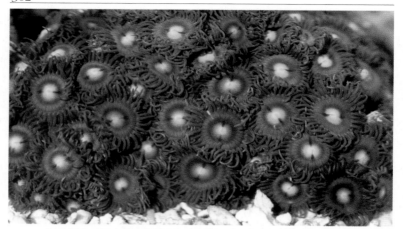

Zoanthus sp.
J. C. Delbeek

Zoanthus sp. Despite their large
size these are clearly *Zoanthus*.
Note their blunt tentacles, multi-
coloured oral discs and lack of
sand on the column.
J. C. Delbeek

Found throughout the world's tropical oceans, *Zoanthus* spp. are most commonly found in shallow waters along reef crests and in backreef areas. In sandy areas often only the tops of the polyps are visible (Mather and Bennett, 1993; Delbeek, 1997 pers. obs.).

Scientific Name: *Zoanthus* spp.

Common Names: Button Polyps, Sand Polyps, zoanthids, *Zoanthus sociatus*

Colour: Often "two-toned". Come in virtually all colours, including red, pink, orange, and blue, but the most typical combinations are brown and green, or green and yellow. Different colour varieties and species may be placed adjacent to one another, creating a pansy-patch effect!

Distinguishing Characteristics: Body wall not sand encrusted; tentacles short and blunt; sphincter muscle split in two; oral disc and tentacles often contrasting colours; grow from mats of coenenchyma or stolons.

Similar Species: *Protopalythoa*; see *Protopalythoa* for differences.

Natural Habitat: *Zoanthus* spp. occupy several different niches on and near coral reefs. The most typical location for many species is the intertidal zone on rocky shores, particularly along channels where there is a swift tidal current. Intertidal species are often exposed at low tide. In some areas they may also extend into tide pools. Some species live in shallow backreef, lagoon, or

Zoanthus sociatus is commonly exposed at low tide. J. Sprung

These *Zoanthus sociatus* are fully exposed to the sun at low tide. They slowly release water to keep their surface from drying out completely. Some of them are also emitting zooxanthellae (dark brown blobs) from their mouths.
J. Sprung

seagrass areas, on coral fragments or rocks in the sand. Other species occur only on reefs and hardbottoms to considerable depths, though their need for light limits them generally to depths less than 30 metres (100 ft.).

Aquarium Care: Place *Zoanthus* high in the tank where they will receive the most light. Strong currents are not required, but intermittent blasts help to prevent detritus from collecting between the polyps, which could promote the development of filamentous algae.

Reproduction: *Zoanthus* spp. spread readily through aquaria via

coenenchyma or stolon extension, and polyp budding. Taking advantage of this, *Zoanthus* spp. can be easily propagated and are now being offered by aquaculture facilities in the Pacific. Fadlallah *et al.* (1984) found that colonies of *Zoanthus sociatus* and *Z. solanderi* off the coast of Panama were either hermaphroditic with separate male and female (dioecious) polyps, or hermaphroditic with monoecious polyps. Gametogenesis occurred between December and June (see chapter two for more information). Sexual reproduction has not been reported in aquaria

Suborder Macrocnemina

Family Epizoanthidae

Genus *Epizoanthus*

This bright red *Epizoanthus* sp. is common in the Eastern Pacific, from the Sea of Cortez southward. A blenny admires their beauty from his encrusted barnacle hollow.
S. W. Michael

Herberts (1972, in Fosså and Nilsen, 1995) states that there are probably 53 nominal species of *Epizoanthus*. Very little work has been done on this genus and it is likely that this number will change in the coming years.

Scientific Name: *Epizoanthus* spp.

Common Name: none

Colour: Gray, yellow, beige, brown, occasionally red, sometimes colourless, depending on colour of host.

Distinguishing Characteristics: Azooxanthellate; body column may be encrusted with sand particles in some species; mesogloeal sphincter; canals and lacunae in the mesogloea (Mather and Bennett, 1993).

Similar Species: *Parazoanthus* spp.

Natural Habitat: *Epizoanthus* spp. are found in close association with sponges, hydroids and pagurid crabs. Several species are found growing within the body wall of hexactinellid sponges, encrusting hydroids and covering the carapace of deep water pagurid crabs. The zoanthids cover the carapace of the crab, eventually dissolving it away, completely enclosing the crab, a condition known as carcinoecium (Hyman, 1940). Not all species are exclusively associated with a host sponge or other organism. Some simply encrust rocks.

Acrozoanthus sp. growing on a worm tube. J. Sprung

Aquarium Care: Given that the host organisms such as sponges and hydroids do not do particularly well in closed systems, aquarium care for this genus is poorly known. Feeding would be required given the lack of zooxanthellae.

Reproduction: Asexual reproduction is presumably accomplished by growth of the coenenchyma over the and through the host. To the best of our knowledge sexual reproduction has not been studied in this genus.

Family Parazoanthidae

Genus *Acrozoanthus**

This genus has recently been resurrected and may remain in this family or be placed in the Zoanthidae (Ryland, 1997).

Scientific Name: *Acrozoanthus* spp.

Common Name: Stick Polyp

Colour: Oral disk and tentacles gray-brown, column light fawn Gray, paler towards the base. Some specimens have blue or green highlights (possibly more than one species).

Distinguishing Characteristics: Grow on the worm tube of *Eunice tibiana*; have mesogloeal sphincter muscle; tentacles possess zooxanthellae.

*Acrozoanthus belongs to the family Zoanthidae, despite its external similarity to *Parazoanthus* spp. and the fact that it is associated commensally with another organism. Its internal anatomy is like members of the family Zoanthidae, and it is a distinct, valid genus (J. S. Ryland, pers. comm.). We have incorrectly placed *Acrozoanthus* in Parazoanthidae but were unable to change this layout of the book before printing. It is likely that the following species, "Yellow polyp" also belongs to the family Zoanthidae, possibly also to the genus *Acrozoanthus*, but possibly to a new genus.

Similar Species: Similar to *Zoanthus* spp. internally but reproductive method is distinct.

Natural Habitat: Found growing on the parchment-like tubes of worms in muddy habitats.

Aquarium Care: Require good strong lighting and regular feeding. Eventually the tubes disintegrate and the polyps sometimes do not seem to survive much beyond that point. Sometimes the polyps readily encrust rock and the walls of the aquarium and continue to thrive despite the absence of the normal worm-tube substrate. Strong light and water motion combined with feeding several times per week encourages rapid asexual propagation in this species. It is possible that the association between this zoanthid and worms of the genus *Eunice* could be duplicated in the aquarium. These worms are common in the intertidal zone along muddy or sandy shores just inside of seagrass meadows. A shovel is needed to dig up the entire worm tube intact. If this is planted carefully in an aquarium with a deep sand substrate it might be possible to encourage the *Acrozoanthus* to encrust on the tubes of numerous species of *Eunice*. One could then observe them to learn about how these creatures may interact, if they do at all.

Reproduction: Asexual reproduction is accomplished by budding of polyps from the base of the parent colony. Ryland (1995) found no gonads in dissected specimens so very little is known about sexual methods of reproduction in this genus.

Scientific Name: Undescribed, possibly new genus or *Parazoanthus* or *Acrozoanthus* sp.?

Common Name: Yellow Polyps, Yellow Encrusting Anemones, Bali-polyp, *Parazoanthus gracilis**

*This name has been in common use in the aquarium literature but is not the correct scientific name for this species (Fosså and Nilsen, 1995). Therefore we have listed it as one of the common names.

Colour: Yellow, brownish yellow

Distinguishing Features: Polyps with zooxanthellae. Overall quite similar to those of *Acrozoanthus* and *Parazoanthus*. They are slightly smaller than *Acrozoanthus* and are not associated with the tubes of *Eunice* worms. Similar in appearance to *Parazoan-*

Close-up of Yellow polyps.
J. Yaiullo and F. Greco

A field of Yellow polyps in the
aquarium. Give them plenty of
room to grow since they proliferate
quickly and sting their neighbors.
J. Sprung

Yellow polyps growing on the glass
in Julian's 15 gallon aquarium.
Note the method of growth by
budding. In this species, clumps of
several polyps remain together
temporarily. Eventually they become
separated into individual polyps or
smaller groups. A. J. Nilsen

thus axinellae from the Mediterranean (see photo), but that species does not contain zooxanthellae and has a tougher column. *Parazoanthus axinellae* is associated with sponges, gorgonians, and tunicates. The undescribed "Yellow polyps" zoanthid from Indonesia encrusts rocks in shallow reef flats and is not strongly associated with a particular organism, though it is reported to be found on tunicates (Colin and Arneson, 1995). Daughter polyps bud off from the pedal disc and remain attached to the mother polyp temporarily. The colony consists mostly of individual polyps adjacent to each other but not attached by tissue, with some clumps of three or four polyps still attached together.

Similar Species: *Parazoanthus axinellae, Acrozoanthus.* See comments above.

Natural Habitat: Indonesia on sandy reef flats, backreef areas and seagrass meadows, growing on loose coral rubble in the sand, in shallow water with strong illumination.

Aquarium Care: Very easy to care for. Give strong light and moderate to strong water motion. Tolerates low light levels which may make the yellow pigmentation seem more intense. Brightly illuminated specimens that have healthy zooxanthellae populations appear browner or greener. This species feeds readily. If it is not fed the colony will not grow rapidly and may slowly decline. Feed brine shrimp (*Artemia*), chopped worms, flake food, mysis. Do not place this species next to *Discosoma* spp. or other corallimorpharia. They do not tolerate each other. This species will sting and injure stony corals. The polyps slowly migrate across solid surfaces (including aquarium glass) leaving a trail of daughter polyps.

Reproduction: Sexual reproduction not reported. Asexual reproduction occurs via budding from the base of the parent polyp and extension of tissue as polyps "creep" over solid surfaces, seagrass, and algae. Transverse fission is also common in this species (J. Sprung, pers. obs.).

Genus *Parazoanthus*

Herberts (1972, in Fosså and Nilsen, 1995) states that there are probably 25 nominal species of *Parazoanthus*. Very little work has been done on this genus and it is likely that this number will change in the coming years. Studies have indicated that *Para-*

zoanthus spp. render the host distasteful to predators; their contrasting colour acting as a warning (aposematic colouration) (Colin and Arneson, 1995).

Scientific Name: *Parazoanthus* spp.

Common Name: none

Colour: Yellow, brown, colourless, pink, red, the colour often contrasts sharply with that of the host.

Distinguishing Characteristics: Azooxanthellate; body column not encrusted; endodermal sphincter; common membranous mat covers other animal; well-developed canal system, including a ring canal (Mather and Bennett, 1993; Gosliner et al., 1996).

Similar Species: *Epizoanthus* spp.

Natural Habitat: Found encrusting other organisms such as sponges, hydroids and gorgonians.

Aquarium Care: Must be fed a diet of zooplankton, or a plankton substitute such as powdered flake food, baby brine shrimp, *Daphnia*, pureed shrimp, crab, or fish meat.

Reproduction: Presumably asexual reproduction is by extension of the membranous sheath and budding. Little is known about sexual reproduction in this genus.

Parazoanthus sp. growing on a hydroid. J. Sprung

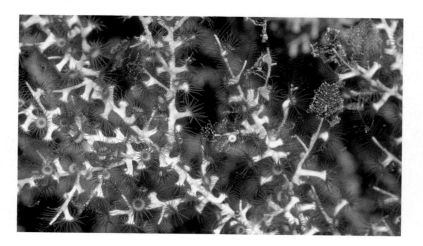

Parazoanthus sp. growing on a
sponge. J. Sprung

Parazoanthus axinelliae from the
Mediterranean Sea. One of the few
Parazoanthus that can grow freely.
J. Sprung

Parazoanthus sp. growing on a
hydroid. J. Sprung

Chapter Nine

The Identification and Care of Corallimorpharians

Aquariums for Corallimorpharia

Corallimorphs are not very demanding regarding water quality or water motion. Therefore they may be maintained in the simplest possible aquaria. This combined with their attractive appearance makes them an excellent choice for novice aquarists.

While they may be maintained in more sophisticated reef aquaria, corallimorphs can be grown quite well in old-style undergravel-filtered aquaria or in the "modern" natural systems employing live sand, rock, and little more than an airstone or water pump for circulation. They can be maintained with fishes in aquaria in which the nitrate level climbs to very high concentration, though they do not appreciate chronic low pH. They seem to expand most beautifully when the pH is 8.2 or higher.

Chemical Filtration

It is entirely possible to grow corallimorpharia in aquariums without the use of protein skimming or activated carbon to filter the water. They are hardy, tolerate the buildup of organic compounds, and may even utilize organic compounds as food. However, they do have better appearance and their colours are better appreciated in water that is clear and free of water tinting organic compounds.

Lighting

Most corallimorphs prefer indirect light or shade, so creating an aquarium for them does not entail the installation of a high intensity light source. The brightly fluorescent coloured blue, red and green disc anemones commonly called elephant ears do not tolerate bright light. They shrivel up and become pale when over illuminated. The few types which live in bright sunny areas also tolerate and thrive in less intense light. When properly placed in the aquarium with respect to light intensity they thrive with either metal halide or fluorescent light (or combinations of both), but the best appearance in colourful disc anemones is achieved under fluorescent lighting, with emphasis on the blue spectrum.

Multicoloured mushroom anemones, *Rhodactis* cf. *inchoata*. J. Sprung

Strong illumination, particularly if it has a high quantity of UV wavelengths, stimulates the production (via photosynthesis by zooxanthellae) of toxic high levels of oxygen in the tissues of the host anemone, corallimorpharian, or coral. We should clarify that

Combining different colour morphs
of *Discosoma* spp. in an aquarium
can create an amazing garden in
which the blossoms never fade, but
multiply. Corallimorpharia are
among the most beautiful cnidarians, and they are also among the
easiest to maintain in captivity.
J. C. Delbeek

the molecular oxygen produced is not so problematic. When the
anemone is illuminated by high intensity light, the energetic UV wavelengths in the presence of photosensitizing agents such as chlorophyll
and flavins act synergistically to produce singlet oxygen and the superoxide radical (0_2^-), which is very reactive and readily forms hydrogen
peroxide H_2O_2 (Shick, 1991). If you've ever poured hydrogen peroxide
on a cut or put it in your hair you know it is also very reactive, and not
something you want accumulating in your tissues! Dykens and Shick
(1982) describe the enzymatic defenses utilized to counter the effects
of the superoxide. In one strategy the enzyme superoxide dismutase
keeps cellular levels of superoxide low while other enzymes, catalase
and peroxidase, convert the hydrogen peroxide produced into water
and oxygen. Other biochemical antioxidants may also be used instead
of enzymes (Tapley, Shick and Smith, 1988). Dykens (1984) showed
that zooxanthellae have high levels of superoxide dismutase activity,
and the enzyme used is a form with copper and zinc ions, a form not
known from other unicellular eukaryotic algae.

What is mysterious is the effect of trace elements on this condition. Iodine (as potassium iodide) seems to help prevent this

Discosoma (*Rhodactis*) sp. showing brightly coloured "bubbles" that we believe may be a response to excess U.V. light. J. Sprung

In response to strong illumination and UV wavelengths *Discosoma* and *Rhodactis* spp. develop swollen, often brightly coloured discal tentacles. We found this unusual *Discosoma* sp. at the Baltimore Aquarium. It had developed bubble shaped swellings at the pale striping zones on the oral disc. J. Sprung

problem, and it is possible that other trace elements help also. Perhaps the trace quantities of copper and zinc from added weekly supplements assist in the formation of the zooxanthellae's special enzymes. Perhaps there is an antioxidant effect achieved by the iodide being converted to iodate, as suggested by Buddemeier in Delbeek and Sprung (1994). With all the talk about antioxidants and health lately, it's no wonder this has application to the subject of reef corals, anemones, etc.

Insufficient light is also a problem, however, corallimorphs will readily indicate this. When light levels are too low, corallimorphs take on a typical trumpet-like shape, stretching upwards to capture the light (see Delbeek and Sprung, 1994).

For most photosynthetic cnidarians adaptation to the artificial light is just a matter of time, and it involves changes in pigment density and quantity of zooxanthellae. For some the adaptation is difficult, and if they are daily stressed by light intensity that produces toxic oxygen radicals beyond their physiological capacity to detoxify them, they may never adapt. The light in nature is pulsed because of the passage of clouds. The periods of rest provided do actually assist in preventing the accumulation of superoxide by limiting its production. It is not essential to duplicate this pulsing of the light, but it is possible to do it (Gutierrez,1991), see our next book, *Techniques* for information about electronic ballasts and dimmable lamps.

Algae

The presence of rapidly growing filamentous algae or species of *Caulerpa*, which grow with root-like stolons, can sufficiently irritate corallimorphs so that they do not thrive. The effect is not one produced in the water but an irritation only upon contact with the algae. Be sure to avoid growing *Caulerpa* species among corallimorphs.

Tankmates

Corallimorphs are compatible with many types of fish and invertebrates. *Amplexidiscus fenestrafer* is an exception since it traps and eats fish. *Pseudocorynactis* from the Indo-Pacific are also quite capable of snaring small fish with their sticky tentacles. Angelfish and butterflyfish may nip at or eat certain corallimorphs. Bristle worms also will eat corallimorphs, usually at night. Most corallimorphs will sting and injure or kill stony corals. Some are killed by stony corals, however (see chapter three). It is best to avoid placing them close together, leaving plenty of room for tissue expansion.

Selecting Healthy Mushroom Anemones

Of course it is best to choose colonies which are acclimated and expanding. We want to offer a few important things to look for to avoid selecting a colony that might not survive or which might introduce parasites or disease to the aquarium. These symptoms also describe conditions that may develop later on even in a healthy aquarium, due to injury of the corallimorph.

Flatworms

Commensal acoel flatworms are common hitchhikers on *Disco soma* spp. from Indonesia and elsewhere in the Indo-Pacific region. The genus *Waminoa* is the most common representative (see Winsor, 1990, for a review of tropical Australian species).

Acoel flatworms, *Waminoa* sp., covering *Discosoma* sp.
J. C. Delbeek

These flatworms are not especially harmful to their host, but they do effectively block light when they occur in numbers over the surface of the oral disc. They are not exclusively commensal on the corallimorphs and readily jump (OK, not literally, they crawl) to stony corals and soft corals. They can be controlled by removing the colony from the aquarium and shaking it in a bucket of saltwater. The agitation will knock them loose. If freshwater is used instead of saltwater in the bucket they will fall off more readily, but there is a risk of injury to the corallimorphs. Corallimorphs generally tolerate dips of up to one minute in freshwater. Natural predators of these flatworms are not well known, but they may include certain fishes or specialized nudibranchs* (see volume one, also chapter eleven in this volume).

*Nudibranchs of the genus *Chelidonura* are effective natural predators of *Waminoa* and other acoel flatworms. See chapter eleven for more details about them.

Brown Jelly

When injured *Discosoma* and *Rhodactis* species sometimes appear to "melt" into a mass of what appears like chocolate left too long in the sun on the dashboard of your car. This is the brown jelly infection caused by *Helicostoma nonatum* (see volume one). The condition can spread to adjacent polyps and to other colonies or corals. Avoid purchasing a colony with this condition. If the condition develops, immediately siphon out the "melted" polyps, leaving healthy ones alone, and check to be sure that the cause is not stinging by something next to the colony.

Mesenterial Filaments

The appearance of what looks like tangled white strings being emitted from the mouth or side of the polyp is actually digestive filaments that are part of the mesenteries. These are emitted as a defense mechanism when the corallimorph is disturbed by something in its environment (see chapter three). Physical disturbance as when a fish nips at the polyp or when something falls on it will cause this condition. Rough handling will also cause it, as will sudden change in temperature, water motion, or water chemistry. The condition is a sign of displeasure only and is harmless. Observe to see if it persists, indicating the irritation is chronic. Usually the condition goes away within a few hours.

The Identification and Care of Corallimorphs in Aquariums

Order Corallimorpharia Carlgren, 1940

Members of this order are intermediate between the Actiniaria and the Scleractinia; and share many of their features. Corallimorphs have a cnidom similar to stony corals but lack a skeleton. The aboral end is usually flat and adheres to the substratum as in sea anemones, but lacks basilar muscles, making movement difficult. The column is smooth, and some species have weak longitudinal muscles. The tentacles are retractile or not; they can be simple (capitate or not), or branched; typically they are radially arranged, particularly over the endocoels. The mesenterial filaments lack cilia, and gonads are at the same level as the filaments. Siphonoglyphs are either weak or absent altogether (den Hartog, 1980; Dunn, 1982). See chapter three for more detailed descriptions of this order.

Family Corallimorphidae R. Hertwig, 1882

Corynactis californica photographed at the Monterey Bay Aquarium. The tentacles on some of the polyps are pigmented brown but this is pigment only, *Corynactis* does not have zooxanthellae. J. Sprung

Members of this family can be found at great depth or in shallow waters and are not known to have zooxanthellae. The tentacles are simple with well-developed acrospheres, and numerous, large nematocysts (den Hartog, 1980). The body tends to be rather firm to extremely rigid. There are three genera: *Corallimorphus*, *Corynactis* and *Pseudocorynactis*. However, den Hartog (1987) has proposed that the Sideractidae genera *Nectactis* and *Sideractis* be moved to this family. The genus *Corallimorphus* is known primarily from deep dwelling cold water species (see photos of specimens from the Monterey Bay Aquarium). Corynactis species occur most abundantly in temperate water but there are tropical species as well. Pseudocorynactis is both tropical and temperate.

Genus Corynactis Allman, 1846

Corynactis spp. are found in all the world's oceans. Their polyps tend to be somewhat smaller than the other genera but can cover wide areas of substratum due to their gregarious growth habit. They have numerous well-formed tentacles, the tips of which have well-developed acrospheres. Due to the presence of well-developed sphincter muscle *Corynactis* can easily withdraw its oral disc and tentacles enclosing itself within its body wall (den Hartog, 1980). Temperate species are the most common but there are a few tropical species that aquarists may acquire as by-catch on live rock, or from mariculture facilities.

Scientific Name: *Corynactis californica* Carlgren, 1936

Common Name: Strawberry Anemone

Colour: Orange, red, pink, yellow, gray. Sometimes with brown pigment in tentacles.

Distinguishing Characteristics: Colonial, small disc diameter normally not more than 2.5 cm (1 in.). Tentacles with ball-shaped tips.

Similar Species: Similar to *Pseudocorynactis* and *Corallimorphus*. *Corynactis* forms dense colonies of clones that encrust large areas of rock surface, while the others do not.

Natural Habitat: Intertidal and subtidal on rocky coastlines. Most species are temperate. Beautiful *Corynactis* species occur in California, the Mediterranean, South Africa, and southern Australia. In the tropics *Corynactis parvula* Duchassaing and Michelotti, 1860 are often less colourful and form less conspicuous colonies under coral rubble in shallow waters. They are not as prolific or as ubiquitous (in their natural habitat) as *C. californica*.

Aquarium Care: Provide strong water motion at least intermittently. Feed often with foods such as chopped shrimp, mysis, worms, pulverized flake food, mussel flesh, fish roe, or plankton substitutes such as brine shrimp and *Daphnia*. Temperate species must be kept in chilled water, not warmer than 68° F (20°C).

Reproduction: Asexual reproduction in these prolific anemones occurs by longitudinal fission and pedal laceration. Sexual reproduction not reported in aquaria but probably occurs (see chapter three for information on sexual reproduction in the wild).

Genus: *Pseudocorynactis* den Hartog, 1980

Pseudocorynactis spp. are very beautiful, fairly large, corallimorphs that are the favourite of underwater photographers the world over. The large, conspicuous, often brightly coloured acrospheres of *Pseudocorynactis caribbeorum* are, unfortunately, only visible when the tentacles are extended at night. During the day the polyps are completely closed and retracted. The polyp base can be up to 4 cm in diameter. When fully expanded they are trumpet-shaped with the column differentiated into a scapus and scapulus. Their well-developed sphincter muscles allow them to fully retract the oral disc and tentacles presenting a mammiform shape (den Hartog, 1980).

Scientific Name: *Pseudocorynactis caribbeorum* den Hartog, 1980

Common Name: Orange Ball Anemone

Colour: Column brown, orange, or red, often mottled. Tentacles clear and nearly colorless except for the ball-like tips which are typically orange, sometimes white. Oral disc often spotted with white markings.

Distinguishing Characteristics: Inconspicuous during the daytime because it remains closed. At night this corallimorph opens to become an exquisite starburst of colour, with bright orange balls held erect out from the oral disc.

Similar Species: Most similar to some species of *Corallimorphus*.

Pseudocorynactis caribbeorum.
J. Sprung

Pseudocorynactis caribbeorum with
tentacles contracted. J. Sprung

The most distinct differences between these genera are the presence
(in *Pseudocorynactis*) or absence (in *Corallimorphus*) of a marginal
sphincter, and the arrangement of the endocoelic tentacles in radial
rows (*Pseudocorynactis*), or just one discal and one marginal tentacle
communicating with each endocoel (*Corallimorphus*). In relation to
the presence of a marginal sphincter, species of *Pseudocorynactis*
can close, by withdrawing oral disc and tentacles, whereas species
of *Corallimorphus* are not known to be capable of doing so.
Species of *Corallimorphus* as a rule are much more rigid and apt
to loose their ectoderm, whereas the ectoderm is always well-
developed in *Pseudocorynactis*. Also, the tentacles in *Pseudocorynactis* are always well-developed and motile, whereas they are
often strongly reduced in *Corallimorphus*, though there are

exceptions, as seen in *Corallimorphus profundus* from Monterey. The spirocysts of the acrospheres of *Pseudocorynactis* are at least twice as long as in *Corallimorphus*. Species of *Pseudocorynactis* are restricted in their distribution to tropical and subtropical shallow waters, whereas *Corallimorphus* is a cold water genus, mainly restricted to water below 500 m depth. The shallowest record is from about 30 m in the Antarctic (den Hartog, pers. comm.).

Natural Habitat: Cryptic. Found on reef slopes or sometimes along limestone shores in clear water in the Caribbean. Usually partially shaded. Only open at night unless well shaded. Only found as solitary individuals.

Aquarium Care: Provide a shady location where it is easy to feed the polyp. To thrive *Pseudocorynactis* must be fed small pieces of shrimp and fish several times per week. Do not place where it may sting or be stung.

Reproduction: Pedal laceration and longitudinal fission are common. Sexual reproduction in aquaria not reported. Since this species is both uncommon and cryptic (during the day) in its natural habitat, it is unlikely to be collected in any significant quantity for the aquarium trade. However, its capacity for asexual reproduction makes it an excellent candidate for aquaculture. Its beauty could justify a high price.

Scientific Name: *Pseudocorynactis* sp.

Common Name: White Ball Anemone, Orange Ball Anemone, Fiji Corallimorph

Colour: Column red orange, maroon, or brown, having clear slightly pigmented tentacles with white tips or orange tips.

Distinguishing Characteristics: Largest of the family Corallimorphidae. Pedal disc to at least 10 cm. Oral disc to at least 10 cm with tentacle span to at least 20 cm. Tentacles numerous with ball tips. Tentacles expanded both day and night. Column thick but soft. Tentacles EXTREMELY sticky.

Similar Species: Most similar to *Corallimorphus profundus* from Monterey. *Pseudocorynactis caribbeorum* differs from the Fiji *Pseudocorynactis* in several ways. That species expands its tentacles

Pseudocorynactis collected in Fiji.
J. Sprung

Corallimorphus profundus from
Monterey looks a lot like the Fiji
Pseudocorynactis sp.
J. Sprung

at night only, has fewer tentacles, the column is thick and quite hard, and the tentacles retract into the column which closes up like a cinched purse, turning the animal into a well camouflaged mottled button. The corallimorph from Fiji does not close up this way, and in fact resists contracting the tentacles even when heavily disturbed. It does close up at times, forming an irregular conical shape rather than a flattened button.

Natural Habitat: This tropical corallimorph was collected for us by Tony Nahacky in Fiji. It occurs in crevices and caves in shallow water on the reef front, upper reef slope, and down the slope into deep water. Unless one is looking specifically for them, or for cave-dwelling creatures, one is unlikely to see them even though they are fairly common. They are frequently upside-down. They are tricky to collect intact because of their habitat. Collecting them along with a bit of the substrate by using a geological hammer could help, if it fits in the crevice. They are difficult to handle, as their sticky tentacles do not retract quickly when the anemone is disturbed, and they readily stick to fingers, gloves, nets, plastic bags and anything else with which they come into contact!

Aquarium Care: The specimen in the photograph had been damaged severely, with a large torn hole in the former position of part of the pedal disc. During transport from Fiji to Miami it turned itself inside out, a remarkable acrobatic feat that leaves mesenterial filaments on the outside and tentacles on the inside. We acclimated it to new water and it slowly reversed itself, though it remained hollow for a couple of weeks. Just before it had the chance to become firmly attached to a rock, it managed to get sucked into the intake strainer of a water pump, which successfully destroyed half of its crown of tentacles. Within a few days, however, it was firmly attached to a rock and taking food. The tentacles grew back and the specimen is growing and thriving. These are very hardy animals! Unfortunately, they are virtually non-existent in the aquarium trade as of this writing. No doubt that will change, as collections are made and captive propagation begins to supply them. The above account about this anemone is a good indication that this corallimorph can be propagated asexually by making divisions of the polyp. The remarkable regeneration abilities of this specimen is also reminiscent of that described for *Pseudocory-nactis caribbeorum* (den Hartog, 1980).

The Fiji corallimorph adapts well to captivity, tolerating a wide range of conditions. Ideally it should be placed in a slightly shaded position where it receives intermittently strong water motion. Shade is not an absolute requirement, however. One should avoid positioning the anemone in a place where feeding it would be difficult, since it thrives best when fed regularly. Feed it at least once per week. For rapid growth and reproduction feed it once per day. Because it has sticky tentacles we must caution that it may not be safe to house this corallimorph with small fishes that could be snared and eaten.

Reproduction: As mentioned above, this anemone can be asexually propagated by making divisions of the polyp (longitudinal fission). This genus may also spontaneously produce daughter polyps by pedal laceration (see chapter three), though this is not recorded in the literature. We suspect that the sticky tentacle tips torn off by fish that contact them may be able to drop off and form complete polyps. This mode of asexual reproduction is known for the stony coral *Euphyllia glabrescens*.

Family Ricordeidae Watzl, 1922

Body rather firm and flat, tentacles simple and short, with rounded, clavate or capitate tips, never with distinctly differentiated acrospheres (den Hartog, 1980). Tentacles arranged radially from the mouth, with up to twenty tentacles in each row (den Hartog, 1980). The oral disc and tentacles cannot be completely withdrawn, just as in the Discosomatidae, but "trumpeting" is possible when light levels are inadequate.

Genus: *Ricordea* Duchassaing and Michelotti, 1860
Due to their wide range of colours this genus is one of the most

A collection of *Ricordea florida* showing three colour morphs, green, orange and blue.
J. C. Delbeek

Blue colour morph of *R. florida*.
J. C. Delbeek

Yellow colour morph of *R. florida*.
J. C. Delbeek

popular corallimorphs in the aquarium industry. However, because it occurs mainly on solid reef or hardbottom, it is usually necessary to chip away pieces of reef substratum to collect *Ricordea florida*. As a result, their collection in U.S. waters was banned in the early 1990's. Today most specimens come from Caribbean countries. There is also at least one species from the Indo-Pacific. It is hoped that mariculture will offer a greater supply to the industry in the coming years.

Ricordea are taxonomically intermediate between the Corallimorphidae and the Discosomatidae. The cnidom is similar to the Corallimorphidae in that they possess spirocysts, unlike Discosomatidae, but the spirocysts are rather small and less numerous (den Hartog, 1980). Their tentacles are simple as in the Corallimorphidae but they are small, devoid of acrospheres (in R. florida) and non-retractile, as in the Discosomatidae. *Ricordea* rely to a great deal on zooxanthellae for nutrition but they will feed when offered food.

Scientific Name: *Ricordea florida* Duchassaing and Michelotti, 1860

Common Name: *Ricordea*, Florida False Coral

Colour: Green, blue, brown, gray, fluorescent orange, pink, copper, yellow, and combinations of these colours.

Distinguishing Characteristics: Tentacles with rounded or clavate tips look like small berries arranged in a radial pattern over the surface of the oral disc. Tentacles never have distinctly differentiated acrospheres at tips nor pimple-like projections off of the tentacles. Marginal tentacles often more elongate than discal tentacles. Firm flattened body. Column develops only under shade conditions as polyp stretches to receive light. Oral disc and tentacles do not close up or withdraw, merely deflate and shrink when disturbed. Temporary partial closure of the polyp may occur when feeding.

Natural Habitat: *Ricordea florida* prefers slightly turbid water but also occurs on reefs in clear water. It grows on hard substrate, usually on the sides of old coral heads, so that it is oriented perpendicular to the water surface. This orientation reduces the light intensity, even in shallow water. In deeper water, *R. florida* can be found growing over horizontal substrates, often in small groupings or solitarily (den Hartog, 1980). It can be found occasionally in shallow water on a horizontal substrate (flat hardbottom), and in this situation it is typical for it to be very pale

brown or slightly bleached, pale yellow in color. On occasion the wonderful pink and orange varieties occur in shallow water on reefs with a high profile and with strong illumination. These color varieties of *R. florida* can take (and appreciate) bright light.

Aquarium Care: *Ricordea florida* thrives in the natural environment with summer temperatures of at least 30 $^{\circ}$C (85 $^{\circ}$F), but success in captivity is better when the water is cooler, about 24 $^{\circ}$C (75 $^{\circ}$F). Many corallimorpharia prefer indirect light, and *Ricordea* is no exception, though it does occur at times in places where it receives fairly strong illumination. Placement is best midway in the tank, not 5-6 inches from the light. Place them at least 12 inches away. *Ricordea florida* requires a bit more light than the smooth disc anemones from the Indo-Pacific. Under dim light *R. florida* may initially expand greatly, but the polyps will become pale and gradually shrink. Under just sufficient light it will continue to grow, but slowly, and it may lose some of its color. Under ideal light *R. florida* retains its bright color and grows more rapidly, particularly if the polyps are fed. Blackworms and mysis shrimp are readily accepted if the fish or serpent stars don't steal them first! If the light is too intense the polyps will shrink, for the reasons we explained earlier regarding the development of superoxide radicals in the tissues. If trace element additions do not make them recover and adapt to the light, then they must be shaded, moved lower, or the orientation to the light should be at an angle or placed perpendicularly, not horizontally. It is common to find a commensal *Periclimenes* spp. shrimp in association with *Ricordea* colonies in the Caribbean. This association would make an interesting aquarium display. Two copepods have also been found associated with *Ricordea*; *Asteropontius longipalpus* and *Paramolgus antillianus* (den Hartog, 1980).

Reproduction: Longitudinal fission is the principal means of reproduction in *Ricordea florida*. Pedal laceration is occasional, while transverse fission is rare, but possible. *Ricordea* polyps typically develop numerous mouths on the oral disc and then divide into separate polyps. Sexual reproduction has not been reported in aquaria nor in nature. During a study in Curacao, den Hartog (1980) found that as depth increased the number of individuals of *R. florida* in a colony decreased until at a depth of 10 -15 m, mostly solitary specimens were encountered. These specimens usually had only a single mouth and grew much larger than their shallow water counterparts. He speculated that rates of asexual reproduction probably decreased with depth and that perhaps sexual reproduction took on greater importance. This reminds us of the differences between *Entacmaea quadricolor* from deep versus shallow water. He also noted the presence of several larvae in the tentacles, which means they may be brooders. These preliminary observations provide a tantalizing glimpse at the reproductive behaviour of this species and invite further investigation!

Scientific Name: *Ricordea yuma* Carlgren, 1900

Common Name: Hairy Mushroom, *Ricordea, Rhodactis*

Colour: Usually brown or green. Some localities (such as Tonga) have fluorescent orange or red hue.

Distinguishing Features: Tentacles with rounded or clavate tips look like small berries arranged in a radial pattern over the surface of the oral disc. Tentacles never have distinctly differentiated acrospheres at tips nor pimple-like projections off of the tentacles. Marginal tentacles often more elongate than discal tentacles, though sometimes a few discal tentacles become elongate in well acclimated specimens that are fully expanded. Firm flattened body, not as firm as *R.. florida*, however. Column develops only under shade conditions as polyp stretches to receive light. Oral disc and tentacles do not close up or withdraw, merely deflate and shrink when disturbed. Temporary partial closure of the polyp may occur when fed food particles.

Ricordea yuma. Note the raised oral cone with tentacles, characterisitc of this species. J. Sprung

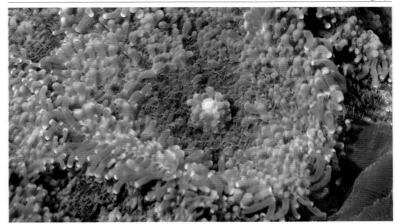

Ricordea cf. *yuma.* In the Coral Sea, Fiji, and Tonga, *Ricordea* cf. *yuma* typically has tentacles that are more berry-like, and sometimes the oral cone flattens out so that the tentacles are not clearly surrounding it as they do in specimens from Indonesia and Singapore. The polyps also grow slightly larger in this region, and they may be more colourful. We have seen bright orange, purple, and dark green specimens from Tonga This specimen was photographed in Fiji. S. W. Michael

Similar Species: This species is a common import from Indonesia and Singapore. It is quite similar to *R. florida* from the Caribbean, but can be distinguished by noting the tentacles on the upraised cone of the mouth. *Ricordea yuma* has them (usually) while *R. florida* does not. Also, *R. yuma* is seldom as colourful as *R. florida. Ricordea florida* commonly forms polyps with two or (often many) more mouths and the multiple mouthed polyps subsequently divide into several daughter polyps. By contrast, *R. yuma* polyps typically only have one or at most two mouths, which may indicate more rapid division of the polyps before multiple mouths develop. *Ricordea yuma* does grow and spread more rapidly than *R. florida.* An unidentified *Rhodactis?* sp. (see photo) is similar to *R. yuma*, but the tentacles taper and can become branched in the former. den Hartog (1980) mentions that *Discosoma fungiforme* may be a *Ricordea* sp. and that he also found what he believed to be a *Ricordea* sp. in Singapore, possibly *R. yuma*.

Natural Habitat: In the Solomon Islands we found *R. yuma* in a calm, clear, green-water lagoon at about 15 metres (45 ft.) growing on intact *Pavona cactus* skeletons; part of a reef slope built almost entirely by *Pavona*. This species is most commonly imported from Indonesia and Singapore.

Aquarium Care: Moderate to bright light. Slight water currents or calm. It will lose its dark pigment (bleach) and shrink if the light is too dim, or shrivel up and emit mesenterial filaments if the light is too strong (or if it is stung). Feed occasionally with blackworms.

Reproduction: Longitudinal fission and pedal laceration are common. Transverse fission is rare but possible. Sexual reproduction has not been reported in aquaria nor in nature.

Family Discosomatidae Duchassaing and Michelotti, 1864

As mentioned in chapter three, den Hartog (1980) proposed that all remaining genera of corallimorphs be included in this one family. Due to the lack of reliable taxonomic characters to differentiate between the genera, he further proposed that they all be classified as *Discosoma* (except for *Amplexidiscus*). To aid in identification of the various species we have opted to retain the four main genera: *Amplexidiscus*, *Discosoma*, *Rhodactis*, and *Metarhodactis*.

Metarhodactis was erected by Carlgren (1943) to describe a special corallimorph, *M. boninensis*. Photographs of this species in the original description look like *Discosoma* or especially like small *Amplexidiscus*. The description notes that this corallimorph has no sphincter and no marginal tentacles, though the margin is crenelate (like *Amplexidiscus*). It has tentacles on the oral disc, branched at the inner part of the disc and simple toward the margin. The presence of a special type of nematocyst distinguishes it: it has long hoplotelic p-mastigophors, similar to those of Corallimorphidae, otherwise not known in Discosomatidae.

Members of the Discosomatidae possess the following traits: the body tends to be soft (*Discosoma*) to very rigid (*Rhodactis* cf. *mussoides*); tentacles range from inconspicuous protuberances (*Discosoma*) to well developed and branched outgrowths (*Rhodactis*); both marginal and discal tentacles may be present and are non-retractile; marginal tentacles, when present, are tiny, acute or finger-shaped appendages, often with acrospheres (sometimes well-developed, see chapter three); mesogloea usually thick to very thick; sphincter very weak to absent; spirocysts are absent with the exception of *Amplexidiscus* which has minimal amounts; nematocyst batteries mainly containing homotrichs, can develop in marginal tentacles if present, or in acrospheres when present (see chapter 3); and the ectoderm has very few nematocysts (den Hartog, 1980). Finally, all the species within this family possess zooxanthellae but benefit from occasional feeding.

Amplexidiscus fenestrafer.
J. C. Delbeek

A. fenestrafer showing the characteristic naked band near the margin.
J. Sprung

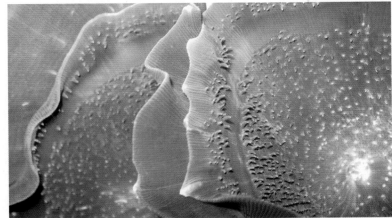

Genus: *Amplexidiscus* Dunn and Hamner, 1980

Scientific Name: *Amplexidiscus fenestrafer* Dunn and Hamner, 1980

Common Name: Giant Elephant Ear mushroom anemone,
Elephant Ear, Giant Mushroom

Amplexidiscus fenestrafer is an animal version of the Venus
flytrap. It is speculated that their resemblance to some (clownfish)
host sea anemones may serve to lure anemonefish larvae to settle
in them (Hamner and Dunn, 1980; Fautin and Allen, 1992). Other
fishes are mysteriously attracted to these anemones as well, and

regularly take refuge in the oral disc, which does not sting them. The oral disc slowly closes like a drawstring purse around a fish, which seems to remain unfrightened by the closure. After the fish is completely enveloped and unable to escape, the mouth opens and the prey is swallowed and digested. The remarkable thing about this whole process is the lack of struggle by the fish. It is our opinion that there may be more to the lure of this coral-limorph than mere looks. We think that they emit chemical attractants and that the fish may become "intoxicated" once in the folds of the oral disc (see oral mucus discussion in chapter three). We have seen quite a diverse group of species disappear into these deadly beauties, including among others Mandarinfish, Royal grammas, and Clownfish.

Colour: Pale cream or whitish gray. Occasionally with fluorescent green sheen.

Distinguishing Characteristics: Soft body reaching enormous size up to 45 cm, but usually 20 to 25 cm (Dunn and Hamner, 1980). A tentacle-free "naked" ring occurs on the disc just before the margin which has pointed lobes. Lacking a sphincter but with endodermal musculature in the upper body column; simple tentacles; discal tentacles short, conical, arrayed in radial rows over endocoels, single or lacking over exocoels; marginal tentacles few, appearing as short lobular projections of the oral disc when the animal is expanded; no siphonoglyphs; has spirocysts, but few in number (Dunn and Hamner, 1980).

Similar Species: May resemble other *Discosoma* spp. at first glance but is much larger, and has the tentacle-free zone between the discal and marginal tentacles. A second, much smaller species that has been identified by rDNA sequencing and morphological examination will be described soon (Chen, unpubl. in Chen *et al.* 1995a).

Natural Habitat: Fore-reef slopes, vertical walls and protected grottoes on fringing reefs on shaded, hard surfaces that receive direct light only briefly but indirect light most of the day. Usually occurs in groups of about four large polyps with a few small daughter polyps around the bases. Sometimes forms colonies of twenty or more large polyps on vertical walls. Often found in relatively shallow, quiet, often turbid areas on the lagoon side of coral reefs (Dunn and Hamner, 1980).

Aquarium Care: Fluorescent light preferred but adapts well to all lighting types, provided the light is not too strong. Feed regularly shrimp or fish meat. Later on as the polyp grows one can offer "pinkies", hamsters, and finally kittens and Chihuahua's. (please note: that was just a joke, not to be taken seriously and certainly not to be tried!)

Reproduction: *Amplexidiscus fenestrafer* readily divides by longitudinal fission and pedal laceration. Transverse fission is occasional under strong water motion. Budding of daughter polyps from the column is occasional. Sexual reproduction is not reported in aquaria nor in nature though individuals with functional male gonads have been found (Dunn and Hamner, 1980).

Genus: *Discosoma* (=*Actinodiscus*) Ruppell and Leuckart, 1828

Scientific Name: *Discosoma* spp.

Common Name: Mushroom Anemone, Elephant Ear, Metallic Mushroom

Colour: Highly variable. Blue, Orange, Brown, Red, Green. With stripes of varying thickness or spots of varying diameter.

Distinguishing Characteristics: Smooth surface, occasionally with numerous round papilla-like tentacles.

Similar Species: The most common types available to aquarists (i.e. blue, red, and green pinwheel-striped types) are colour morphs of the same species which we have seen called *D. nummiforme*, but we hesitate to say that this is the correct name. *Discosoma neglecta* from the Caribbean is similar, but has more pronounced tongue-like projections at the margin of the disc and thicker tissue. Young *D. carlgreni* look like Indo-Pacific *Discosoma* spp., while older *D. carlgreni* look like *Rhodactis* spp.

Natural Habitat: *Discosoma* occur over a wide range of habitats. They may be found among the dead branches of *Porites* and *Acropora* in shallow reef flats, on the sides of coral bommies in shallow lagoons, and in deep reef environments, particularly on dead coral rubble on soft muddy substrates, or on the dead coral base of reefs in deep lagoons.

Aquarium Care: Provide indirect light and very little water motion. Fluorescent light is ideal. With metal halide light place *Discosoma* in a shady location, below a ledge, or far to either side

Discosoma sp. with wagon-wheel
colour pattern S. W. Michael

Spotted variety of Discosoma sp.
J. C. Delbeek

Green Striped Discosoma sp.
J. C. Delbeek

White margined and blue
Discosoma sp. J. C. Delbeek

of the tank. In our experience, most *Discosoma* do not take food when offered. Some species do, such as *D. neglecta* and *D. (Rhodactis) sanctithomae*.

Reproduction: *Discosoma* spp. readily divide by pedal laceration. Transverse fission is occasional under strong water motion. Longitudinal fission is possible, but uncommon for most species, except *D. (Rhodactis) sanctithomae*. Budding of daughter polyps from the column is also common, particularly for the red morph of Indo-Pacific *Discosoma*. To the best of our knowledge, sexual reproduction has not been reported in aquaria nor in nature.

Scientific Name: *Discosoma* (=*Paradiscosoma*) *carlgreni* (Watzl, 1922)

Common Name: Neon-Disc Anemone

Colour: Turquoise, Green, Blue, Purple, and (rarely) fluorescent orange

Distinguishing Characteristics: Small pimply tentacles on oral disc, small tongue-like projections at edge of disc. Average size disc is 5 cm, but this species attains 10 cm diameter. Large specimens have well developed branched discal tentacles.

Similar Species: There are some Indo-Pacific species that resemble *D. carlgreni*. *Discosoma neglecta* is easily confused with this species since both have the "tongues" at the edge of the oral disc. Those in *D. neglecta* are fewer in number but much larger and *D. neglecta* does not have quite as pronounced tentacles on the surface of the disc. *Discosoma* (=*Rhodactis*) *sanctithomae* is similar to *D. carlgreni*, but the tissue of *D.* (=*Rhodactis*) *sanctithomae* is much softer, and it has a bare, tentacle-free ring at the outer edge of the oral disc that is greatly expanded at night (see chapter three).

Natural Habitat: Uncommon inhabitant of Caribbean reefs and hardbottoms. Occurs on coral reefs on the underside of ledges growing on coralline algae or sponge. Also occasionally on coral rubble (dead coralline encrusted *Acropora* or *Porites* branches) on reef slopes or in brightly illuminated shallow back-reef areas. Sometimes occurs in very shallow water, growing on undercut vertical walls or overhangs of eroded ancient limestone reefs and beachrock found on shore along many Caribbean island coasts. Usually occurs as groups of 5 to 20 polyps, clones of an original polyp. Seldom forms the large "colonies" typical of many other members of the genus, but can be locally abundant over large but patchy areas as

A large specimen of *Discosoma carlgreni*. with well developed tentacles on the oral disc.
J. Sprung

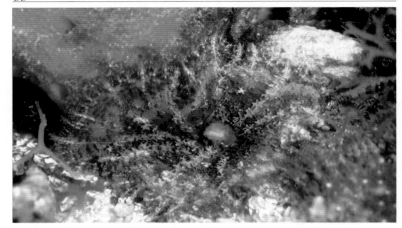

Grouping of the uncommon orange morph of *D. carlgreni*.
J. C. Delbeek

The marginal tentacles of *D. carlgreni* are smaller, more numerous, and not as elongated as in *D. neglecta*. J. Sprung

"colonies" of two or three polyps per piece of dead finger coral rubble. *Discosoma carlgreni* normally lays very flat against the substrate it grows on. Tolerates strong water motion.

Aquarium Care: Very easy to care for. Adapts to virtually all lighting and water flow regimes. Displays best under moderate light with slight water currents.

Reproduction: Asexual means. Pedal laceration and transverse fission most typical, longitudinal fission possible. Sexual reproduction not reported in aquaria nor in nature.

Scientific Name: *Discosoma* (=*Paradiscosoma*) *neglecta* (Duchassaing and Michelotti, 1860)

Common Name: Umbrella Corallimorph

Colour: Green or brown with darker and lighter mottling

Distinguishing Characteristics: Large projecting "tongues" at edge of oral disc. Small papillae on oral disc. Disc diameter to 11 cm. Disc may lay flat against rock or "cup up" by folding up the edge of the oral disc.

Similar Species: Most similar to *D. carlgreni,* but differs from it primarily on the basis of *D. carlgreni* having larger tentacles on the oral disc while *D. neglecta* has larger "tongues" projecting from the margin of the disc. *Discosoma neglecta* grows larger than *D. carlgreni,* to at least 6 in. (15 cm).

Discosoma (=*Paradiscosoma*) *neglecta.* Note the extremely elongate marginal tentacles. This is the largest Caribbean species, and it is a voracious feeder. J. Sprung

Natural Habitat: Rare cryptic inhabitant of Caribbean reefs. Found on the underside of ledges, growing on coralline algae or sponges. Usually occurs as a solitary polyp or at most just a few polyps. A large group of clonemates colonizing a surface of several square feet or metres seldom occurs with this species, though sometimes they can be abundant in shallow seagrass beds.

Aquarium Care: Easy to care for, as with most *Discosoma*. Adapts to strong illumination but prefers moderate illumination. Tolerates strong water motion but does best under low water velocity conditions. Feeding is not necessary, but *D. neglecta* does capture prey. Not all food items offered will be taken, but in our experience worms (such as blackworm or chopped earthworm) placed on the oral disc will elicit a feeding response. Shrimp is also taken voraciously. Feeding promotes growth and asexual reproduction. The oral disc will cup up and close over the food like a purse. The response time is fast, as in *Amplexidiscus*. We haven't seen it happen, but this species may also trap and eat fish.

Reproduction: *Discosoma neglecta* readily divides by pedal laceration. Transverse fission is occasional under strong water motion. Longitudinal fission is possible, but uncommon. Sexual reproduction is not reported in aquaria.

Scientific Name: *Discosoma* (=*Rhodactis*) *sanctithomae* (Duchassaing and Michelotti, 1860)

At present, this species can be classified either as *Discosoma* or *Rhodactis*, given the ambiguity of some its taxonomic characters (den Hartog, pers. comm.)

Common Name: Bubble corallimorph

Colour: Turquoise, brown, green, blue.

Distinguishing Characteristics: Encrusting colonies of many polyps crowded next to each other with the edges of the oral disc curved upward. Disc diameter to 14 cm. The outer margin of the disc is smooth and naked (free of tentacles) while the inner part is full of tentacles that come in a variety of forms. Most typical is small tentacles with several hair-thin filaments of tissue, giving the disc a hairy appearance. Another form has more swollen tentacles, and the filaments are reduced to mere pimples on their surface. Still another (rare) form has completely smooth, rounded tentacles

Discosoma (=Rhodactis) sanctithomae. Note the smooth margin on the oral disc. This margin greatly extends at night to trap prey. Polyps with round tentacles like the specimen on the left were at one time classified as *Orinia torpida*, but are simply a variant of *D. sanctithomae.* The specimen on the right is the more common form. J. Sprung

that resemble those of *Ricordea florida.* These round bubbles may swell quite large, and the contrast with the smooth outer edge of the oral disc is stunning. This form was formerly described as *Orinia torpida* Duchassaing & Michelotti (see den Hartog, 1980).

Similar Species: Similar to Indo-Pacific *Rhodactis* species that also have a distinctive naked margin.

Natural Habitat: Common inhabitant of Caribbean reefs and hardbottom areas with vertical relief. Forms huge colonies of clonemates encrusting coral skeletons and limestone walls in shallow water. Generally brightly illuminated, but vertical orientation provides indirect light exposure.

Aquarium Care: Prefers moderate to strong light and moderate to strong water motion. Orient the polyps vertically so that their pedal discs are perpendicular to the water surface (light source). Excess illumination, particularly with UV wavelengths, can cause build-up of photosynthetically generated superoxides (see Sprung, 1989, 1995). This seems to be remedied by the addition of trace elements, or via shading. *Discosoma (=Rhodactis) sanctithomae* is predatory and should be fed regularly to stimulate growth and reproduction. Feed at night by reducing water flow and placing food into the expanded polyps (see chapter three). A little disturbance will speed the rate at which the polyps close, like a purse drawn by strings, to surround the prey. Prey items may include small pieces of shrimp, crab, squid, live blackworms, or flake food.

Reproduction: *Discosoma* (=*Rhodactis*) *sanctithomae* readily divides by longitudinal fission and also produces daughter polyps by pedal laceration and budding. Transverse fission is occasional under strong water motion. Sexual reproduction is not reported in aquaria nor in nature.

Genus: *Rhodactis* Carlgen, 1943

Little is known about the taxonomy of this particular genus. Chen and Miller (1996) have found that *Discosoma* (=*Rhodactis*) *sanctithomae* is genetically more distinct from *R. indosinensis* and *R. rhodostoma*, than the latter two Indo-Pacific/Red Sea species are from each other. This is presumably due to the separation of the Atlantic and Pacific oceans in the geologic past. There are several other species of *Rhodactis* that we do not cover here, most notably *R. howesii* Saville-Kent, 1893, but their care most likely parallels that of those mentioned here.

Scientific Name: *Rhodactis* cf. *inchoata* Carlgren, 1943 .

Common Name: Hairy Mushroom Anemone, Tonga Blue Mushroom

Colour: Blue, turquoise, purple, rusty red-orange.

Distinguishing Characteristics: In large polyps the tentacles on the oral disc are highly branched and look like stony coral polyps. A distinct type of tentacle at the disc margin forms a row of "toes" This species does not have a naked margin, but it sometimes curls the margin underneath the oral disc so that the tentacles are not apparent.

Similar Species: There are several related species in the Indo-Pacific, all having the row of numerous, fine, toe-like tentacles at the disc margin In some species the discal tentacles form what look like complete scleractinian polyps. This may offer a form of camouflage.

Natural Habitat: Reef slopes and backreef margins on walls or on coral rubble, particularly dead branches of *Acropora*. In strong sunlight (partially shaded by the branches they grow on or by slope of the reef). Exposed to intermittently strong water motion (surge or currents). Imported most often from Tonga.

Aquarium Care: Easy to care for when provided with strong, but indirect light; either fluorescent or metal halide. Grows quickly. Feeding not necessary, but may accept food offered.

Rhodactis cf. *inchoata* , Blue Tonga mushroom. J. C. Delbeek

Close-up of *R.* cf. *inchoata.* J.C. Delbeek

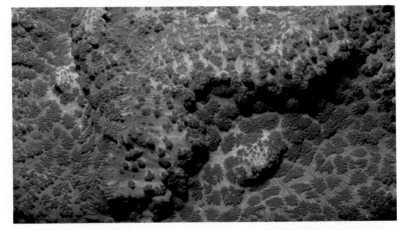

Red morph of *R.* cf. *inchoata.* J. Sprung

Unidentified *Discosoma* (*Rhodactis*) sp. This species is closely related to *R. inchoata* but grows much larger and has better developed tentacles on the oral disc. It has the same toe-like margin tentacles as *R.* cf. *inchoata*. It does not have a naked margin. J. Sprung

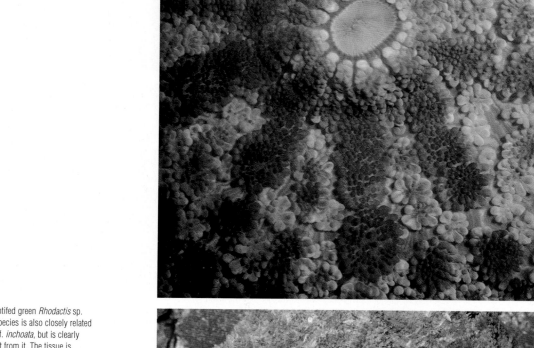

Unidentifed green *Rhodactis* sp. This species is also closely related to *R.* cf. *inchoata*, but is clearly distinct from it. The tissue is thinner and the polyps grow larger. Note the toe-like margin tentacles. J. Sprung

Reproduction: Longitudinal fission primarily, but probably also by pedal laceration. Sexual reproduction not reported in aquaria nor from nature.

Scientific Name: *Rhodactis* cf. *indosinensis* Carlgren, 1943

Common Name: Hairy mushroom anemone

Colour: Pale green or brown

Distinguishing Characteristics: Majority of the surface of the oral disc covered with robust (but soft, thin-walled), branched tentacles some shaped like gloves. Tentacles at the center of the disc are usually smaller, less branched and more thinly set. Tissue of the oral disc is

While not always very obvious, the naked margin is clearly evident in these *Rhodactis* cf. *indosinensis*. Otherwise they are nearly identical to the undescribed? species called Giant Green Metallic Mushroom. They are also quite similar to *Discosoma* (=*Rhodactis*) *sanctithomae*. J. Sprung

This species resembles both *R. indosinensis*. and *Ricordea*! Close inspection of the tentacles reveals many of them are branched, unlike those of *Ricordea*. There is no naked zone at the margin. Fosså and Nilsen, (1995 page 287 top photo) call this species *R*. cf. *indosinensis*, based on the advice of Chen. If you look at the photo here and in their book it is clear that this species does not have a distinct naked margin. It therefore cannot be *R. indosinensis*. What it is we can't know for certain. J. C. Delbeek

relatively thin and soft, like that of *D. (Rhodactis) sanctithomae*. A naked zone between the discal tentacles and marginal tentacles exists, but it is not especially broad, and sometimes it is not very obvious. Colonies are prolific and cover large areas of rock substrate.

Similar Species: Similar to *Discosoma (=Rhodactis) sanctithomae*, especially because of the smooth naked margin on the edge of the disc. The discal tentacles are identical in shape and colour to the undescribed species called Giant Green Metallic Mushroom, but that species lacks a naked margin. There are several similar species described, including *Rhodactis howesii* and *R. rhodostoma*.

Natural Habitat: Lagoons, reef flats and backreef margins in strong sunlight, growing on dead coral heads. Found throughout most of the Indo-Pacific region. Forms extensive beds.

Aquarium Care: Strong light as from metal halide stimulates most rapid growth in this species, though they adapt well to lower light intensity. Provide strong but intermittent water motion. Polyps show preference for certain foods. Reduce water flow when feeding. Try a small quantity of food (blackworm, mysis, fish roe, chopped clam) on a few polyps to see if it elicits a positive response (polyp folds to retain it).

Reproduction: Longitudinal fission primarily, but probably also by pedal laceration. Chen *et al.* (1995a) report three forms of asexual reproduction observed in wild populations; longitudinal fission, inverse budding and two-mouth fission. Sexual reproduction in aquaria: release of eggs or egg-sperm bundles reported (Fosså and Nilsen, 1995). Recently sexual reproduction in nature described by Chen *et al.* (1995a). See chapter three for a complete description.

Scientific Name: *Rhodactis (Platyzoanthus)* cf. *mussoides*

Common Name: Elephant ear, metallic mushroom, Leaf mushroom, Leather coral

Colour: Brown, green, gray

Distinguishing Characteristics: Very thick tissue with a tough leathery texture. Polyps often lobed or convoluted, with many mouths, but may also be with just one mouth. The polyps are typically about 15 cm across when expanded, but may grow to more than twice that size.

This is a copy of the drawing of *Platyzoanthus mussoides* by Saville-Kent from his 1893 description. Was *Platyzoanthus mussoides* the species shown in the photographs below? If so, the original description and drawing are bad.

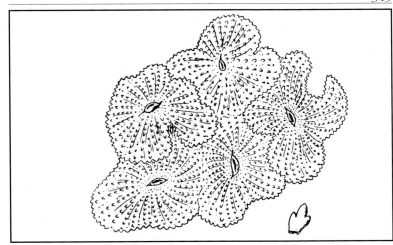

Rhodactis (Platyzoanthus) mussoides?
J. C. Delbeek

Colonies encrust over large areas of substrate. The appearance and texture of this corallimorph is remarkably similar to stony corals of the family Mussidae. Saville-Kent described *Platyzoanthus* as follows: "This species is remarkable for the fact that it coincides in structure with what might be termed a skeletonless replica of the compound coral, hereafter referred to under the generic title of *Mussa.* The polyps in this type are flat, exceedingly irregular in

outline, coalescing with one another in such a manner that two or three oral centres are frequently included in the same tentacular system. The tentacles are exceedingly short, in most instances minutely lobate, and developed over the greater portion of the area of the expanded disc. The life colours of the disc are light greenish brown..." So far this sounds like a perfect match for the very distinctive species shown in the photographs here.

But then the description diverges from this perfection: "...the tentacles redder brown and white-tipped, while the slightly-exposed inner lining of the oral opening is rose pink...The individual polyps in this species, where enclosing only a single oral system, bear a considerable resemblance to those of Klunzinger's *Cryptodendrum adhaesivum,* but with the shorter-branched tentacles of *Rhodactis rhodostoma....*"

Furthermore, in the drawing the saw-toothed disc margin, the tentacles on the disc, (one removed tentacle is shown) do not seem to match the very distinctive species shown in the photographs. Therefore we suspect it is possible that What Saville-Kent described in 1893 was something else. For what it's worth, everyone who sees this distinctive species agrees it is quite different from other *Rhodactis* and *Discosoma* spp. It seems that it should belong to a different genus, which is something Saville-Kent said about his specimen: "It seems imperative here again to employ both a new generic and a new specific title for its distinction..."

Similar Species: Most similar to mussid corals. Single polyps with one mouth basically look like *Discosoma* spp., but they are much more rigid, and when they develop multiple mouths the polyps become very oblong or even meandroid in shape, something that does not occur in other *Discosoma* spp, though it does occur in *Ricordea florida*, which also develops multiple mouths within the same tentacular system.

Natural Habitat: Reef walls and deep reef environments in the Indo-Pacific. Usually on solid reef, not loose rubble. May be exposed periodically to strong water motion. Generally grows on vertical substrate and therefore receives indirect light.

Aquarium Care: Easy to care for. Does not take food, but subsists on light and probably ingests bacteria trapped on its mucus. Green specimens will grow large and become stunningly fluorescent under low intensity blue light.

Reproduction: Asexual reproduction by longitudinal fission is the principle means of spreading. Polyps typically have multiple mouths and divisions occur between these. Budding and pedal laceration also occur, but infrequently. Sexual reproduction not reported in captivity nor in nature.

Scientific Name: Unkown (*Rhodactis* sp.)

Here again we have another puzzle, and it cannot easily be worked out. Perhaps after viewing the original preserved specimens, if they still exist, we can draw a conclusion about what is what. More likely, however, the mess is not possible to solve by simply looking backwards. This is a common problem with the discosomatidae. Fosså and Nilsen, (1995) call this species *Rhodactis cf. rhodostoma*. Ehrenberg, (1834) described that

Just before this book went to press J. Sprung observed a special form of budding in this species in the show aquarium of Jan and Joe Genero at Fish World in Richmond, Virginia. Only a few days earlier Julian had seen this type of budding in *Ricordea florida*. A ball of tissue on the oral disc becomes swollen and differentiated. It rocks in the current until it becomes severed. Where it settles it develops into a complete polyp. Though never before reported, it was not such a surprising fact. However, Julian was very surprized when Joe Genero told him that this species also develops similar buds internally and spits them out of the mouth!

species from the Red Sea. While *R. rhodostoma* probably also occurs in the Indo-Pacific region, we do not believe that the species in the photograph below is *R. rhodostoma*.

Common Name: Giant Green Metallic Mushroom Anemone

Colour: Green, often with purplish tentacles forming radiating lines. Sometimes with white or pinkish tentacles forming radiating lines. Sometimes whole disc is bluish gray or brown. Mouth is whitish, never pink or red.

Distinguishing Characteristics: Branched or "pimply" tentacles on the oral disc, tentacles usually of contrasting colour. Disc usually fluorescent green, tentacles brown, maroon, pink, or pale gray. No naked zone near the margin. Tentacles at margin of disc are fat and similar to disc tentacles. Polyps grow to at least 30 cm (12 in.) in captivity, but usually are only about 10 cm (4 in.) in the natural habitat.

Similar Species: Nearly identical to *Rhodactis indosinensis*, but grows larger and does not have a naked margin on the oral disc.

Natural Habitat: Commonly occurs in lagoon reefs on vertical walls and on the sides of coral bommies, usually forming colonies of 10 to 50 polyps, but sometimes forming larger colonies. Specimens for the aquarium trade are collected from Indonesia and Singapore.

Aquarium Care: Very easy to care for. Thrives under fluorescent or indirect metal halide light. Grows to enormous size in aquaria,

Rhodactis sp. Giant Green Metallic Mushroom. J. Sprung

Rhodactis cf. *rhodostoma?* These *Rhodactis* sp. seem very similar to *R. indosinensis*, but they don't seem to have much of a naked margin at all. Also note that they have a pink mouth. This character suggests they may be the true *R. rhodostoma*, but colouration could be variable, so the pink mouths do not confirm their identity. J. C. Delbeek

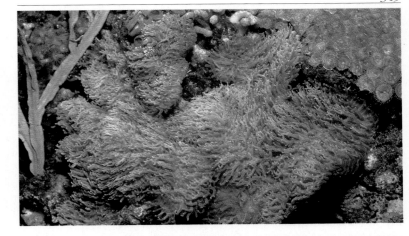

The tentacles on this species are quite similar to those of the unidentified species on the opposite page. However, that species never has a pink mouth and it grows to much larger size. J. C. Delbeek

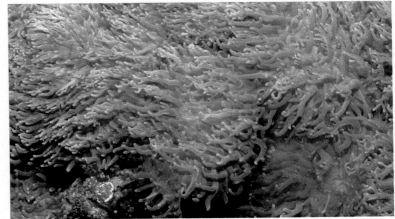

to at least 30 cm (12 in.). Feeds readily on most foods offered, including flake food, worms, shrimp, or mussel meat (a photo of this species feeding is in chapter three on the top of page 84).

Reproduction: Longitudinal fission is most typical, pedal laceration occasional. Transverse fission possible but does not often occur. Longitudinal fission often produces three or more daughter polyps at the same time. The polyp appears to be unhealthy for a few weeks during the process of division (see photo in chapter 3, page 80). Sexual reproduction not observed.

Chapter Ten

Identification and Care of Anemones

As we described in Chapter 4, the class Anthozoa contains the anemones, corals, and other anemone-like creatures. We have separate chapters for the identification and care of zoanthids and corallimorpharians, but have included Ceriantharia here in this chapter with the true anemones, Actiniaria, though they are only distantly related. In addition, we felt it was necessary to include a special section describing aquarium set ups for the care of the true sea anemones since it is clear that their special requirements are not widely known among aquarists or scientists.

Aquarium Design for Anemones

"Tropical sea anemones, including those with which clownfishes live, generally do not survive well under artificial conditions for reasons that are not entirely understood, but that probably have to do with nutrition. Most anemones lose their zooxanthellae after a short time in captivity. This phenomenon may be related to light, but the appropriate wavelengths and intensity are unknown, so the problem is difficult to remedy. It may also be related to the level of nitrogenous and other compounds in the water."

——— Fautin and Allen, 1992.

The physical conditions required by the tropical sea anemones commonly imported for aquariums essentially mirror those of the reef corals presently being grown and propagated so successfully by marine aquarists. Why, then, is it a fact that success with these anemones in the same aquaria is sometimes elusive? There are numerous possible reasons for the lack of success with anemones, including substrate, predators, stinging neighbors, infections, trace elements, water flow, and light, among other things. Having a little background information about the habitat where a particular species of anemone commonly occurs helps a great deal and is the first step in preparing the aquarium to house it.

The skunk clownfish *Amphiprion perideraion* at home in its host anemone *Heteractis magnifica*. J. Sprung

One of the important requirements for an aquarium environment designed to house anemones is the absence of intakes for pumps or powerheads inside the aquarium. Anemones tend to wander and the marriage of anemone and powerhead is a potentially fatal situation both for the anemone and the aquarium's other inhabitants. If a pump intake or a submersible pump must be located in the same aquarium as an anemone, it must be completely covered by a large cartridge or foam material that will diffuse the suction of water over a large enough surface area to prevent the anemone from getting sucked in. A simple strainer will not suffice! Anemones are easily pulled though strainers and thus made into thin strips before they get pureed by the impeller. Another option might be the use of a separate chamber for pumps and power-heads within the aquarium, such as those created by a false back overflow or a backdrop.

Macrodactyla doreensis normally lives with its pedal disc attached to an object deep in the sand. When it is first placed in an aquarium, if it wanders near a powerhead it may be drawn into the uptake screen and killed or severely injured. J. Sprung

It is also possible for anemones to wander over the wall of an over-flow drain, plug up the drain or sufficiently block the flow of water to cause an overfilling of the aquarium and a small flood on the floor. This is less likely than the powerhead accident, but it is possible. One can prevent this occurrence by either avoiding an overflow altogether in the design or by having the overflow located someplace where the anemone can't possibly wander (a real challenge!). One can also create a baffle from mesh material (black DLS for example) such that the anemone cannot completely cover the overflow. In large aquaria if the overflow screen is broad enough the risk of the anemone blocking it is minimized.

Another potential obstacle for sea anemones is submersible heaters. If an anemone attaches its pedal disc to the heater, it cannot quickly let go when the heating element comes on. The resulting burn, aside from being painful no doubt, is likely also fatal. Heaters should be located in the sump, in external heater

Figure 10.1
Natural Systems for Maintaining Anemones

Top: In the Jaubert System a perforated plenum isolates a body of water within the deep gravel bottom substrate. A screen located about one and a half inches (4 cm) above the plenum prevents burrowing organisms from digging deep enough to expose the plenum. Strong light, live rock, and water circulation via air stones or pumps are used. See volume one for additional information.

Middle: In this variation the same plenum system is used, but water drains off the surface into a sump below the aquarium. A pump returns the water. Activated carbon may be located conveniently in the sump. Although we do not show a protein skimmer in these diagrams, one could be used. In the top and bottom examples the skimmer could be an internal model, or an external one with a water pump. In the middle design an external skimmer would best be installed so that the surface skimmed water drains through it on the way to the sump. See volume one for diagrams of skimmer installations.

Bottom: The "old fashioned" undergravel system also works well for maintaining anemones. In this system airlift sends water up through a pipe connected to the perforated plate. This effects a water circulation within the tank and through the gravel. For the health of the anemones strong light and water motion are also used. Live rock, though optional, helps to establish a diverse community of microorganisms, providing a more stable environment.

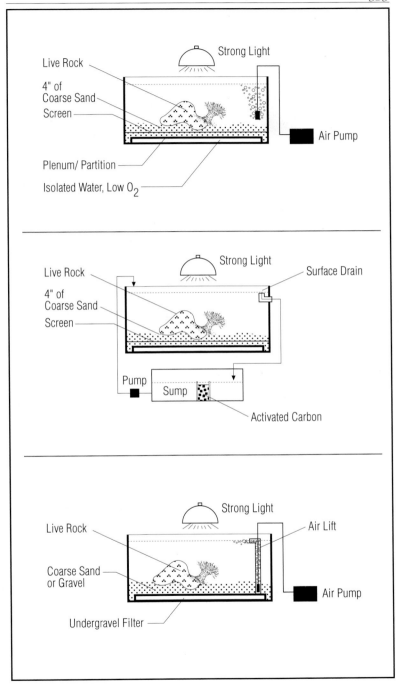

modules, or if they must be inside the aquarium they can be inserted inside an outer sleeve that prevents contact with anemones but still allows sufficient flow of water over the element to properly heat the aquarium.

Of the systems we have tried for maintaining clownfish host anemones, the simplest ones provide the best results. These systems include the "Jaubert System" and Lee Chin Eng's natural system, and the old Undergravel system. One word of caution about these systems with anemones concerns the use of rising air bubbles to move the water. Two problems may arise from this for some anemones. First, popping air bubbles may produce salt crystals, so-called "salt creep," around the rim of the aquarium. As the salt creep increases by layers it may suddenly break off and drop into the aquarium right onto the anemone. Such an event may go unnoticed by the aquarist since the salt dissolves in minutes. However, the damage done to the anemone may be severe. Another potential problem with aeration can occur when an anemone wanders close to the rising airstream and manages to swallow air bubbles. This is a problem mostly for *Stichodactyla gigantea* and *Heteractis magnifica*. The aquarist is usually alerted to the problem when the anemone floats! The anemone can expel the air if isolated from the source of the bubbles.

Temperature

The metabolic functions of sea anemones work within a range of temperatures. Exposure to temperatures beyond this range will injure or kill the anemone in a very short period of time. In this book we describe the tropical sea anemones commonly kept in aquaria, but we have also included a couple of subtropical/temperate species because they sometimes end up for sale to aquarists keeping tropical aquariums. In general, tropical species suffer if the temperature falls below 20°C (68 °F) or rises above 31 °C (87 °F), although there can be exceptions. Ideal temperature (in aquariums) for most tropical species is about 24 °C (75 °F). Temperate species can also survive at 24 °C (75 °F), but are healthier at 20 °C (68 °F), just outside the range for tropical species. Temperature affects the function of enzymes that are involved in metabolic processes such as digestion of food, tissue maintenance, and detoxification of superoxide radicals produced during photosynthesis. The symbiosis with zooxanthellae operates within a temperature range, but is abandoned when the temperature range is exceeded. The resulting expulsion of zooxanthellae is known as "bleaching." Temperature also affects metabolic rates, the consumption of oxygen, and its solubility. As temperature rises, the demand for oxygen by the anemone generally also increases, while the solubility of oxygen in the water decreases. During the daytime when the anemone is bathed in light and its zooxanthellae are producing oxygen by photosynthesis the decrease in oxygen solubility from high temperature is not a problem. At night it is, when the zooxanthellae consume oxygen instead of produce it. This can become particularly problematic for anemones that live with their column buried in the sand, where low oxygen levels can produce anoxic conditions. High temperatures are not always bad. Temperature increase and photoperiod changes may also be the keys to getting anemones to spawn. Furthermore, we have had success maintaining *Stichodactyla haddoni*, *S. gigantea*, and *Macrodactyla doreensis* in outdoor aquaria utilizing natural sunlight, in which the temperature sometimes exceeded 20 °C (95 °F) for part of the day (though it cooled by about 10 °F by nightfall).

Macrodactyla doreensis lives with its pedal disc buried in the sand. At night this specimen would stand up tall to bathe its tentacles in the stream of air bubbles from an airstone. This was an indication of insufficient water circulation and resulting low oxygen level.
J. Sprung

Lighting

Anemones with symbiotic zooxanthellae depend on light to stimulate the production of their food. The zooxanthellae function best within certain parameters of light intensity and spectrum, and these parameters differ for different species of anemone, and for different forms of the same species, depending on the depth where they were collected. Combinations of fluorescent and/or metal halide lamps can be used to provide sufficient light intensity. The spectrum of the bulbs used should approximate daylight, about 5000 to 6500 Kelvin, and supplemental blue lighting with much higher Kelvin colour temperature is beneficial. For more information about illumination for reef aquariums, refer to *The Reef Aquarium* volume one and *The Modern Coral Reef Aquarium* volume 1. It is also possible to set up an anemone aquarium that utilizes natural sunlight for illumination. As long as the water temperature is maintained by means of a chiller/heater or air-conditioning, this method works very well. The aquarium may be located outside, in a greenhouse, below a skylight, or next to a window with good sun exposure.

This outdoor aquarium for anemones was created by Jose Mendez, Aquarius Inc., of Miami Florida. It uses the Jaubert system, with live sand and a plenum, and is illuminated by natural sunlight. J. Mendez

One of the problematic features of aquarium lighting is that it is constant, that is to say there are no clouds to provide the non-static equilibrium (peaks and valleys in intensity) of natural illumination. A recent development employing electronic ballasts offers the possibility of dimming the lamps. This system offers a big advantage in the care of tropical photosynthetic sea anemones. In captivity the anemones often suffer from the buildup of toxic superoxide radicals in the tissues as a result of photosynthesis during constant strong illumination (Lesser and Shick, 1989 a & b, Lesser and Shick, 1990, Shick, Lesser, and Stochaj, 1990).

Dr. Fautin's statement about anemones mysteriously losing their zooxanthellae no longer applies as an ultimate fate. While temporary bleaching (loss of some of the zooxanthellae) is common, especially when the anemones are first imported, the now commonplace use of high intensity full spectrum light sources provides a means of supporting the health of the zooxanthellae, and of the anemones as a consequence.

Water Motion

The motion of water affects anemones in several ways. Water brings food and oxygen to the anemone. It also carries away wastes, including respired carbon dioxide. The movement of the tentacles affects the rate of photosynthesis by the zooxanthellae contained there, alternately exposing them to the light and shading them from it, depending on the tentacles' changing position because of the water flow.

Anemone species have quite different requirements regarding water motion. For example, *Heteractis magnifica*, *Heteractis crispa*, and *Stichodactyla mertensii* all frequently occur on outer reef slopes where they generally receive fairly strong surge water motion, at least intermittently. By contrast, *Stichodactyla gigantea* commonly occurs in less exposed backreef environments. Although *S. gigantea* lives in quiet backreef environments, it is often exposed to strong tidal currents, and in our experience it needs strong water motion to thrive in captivity. Those anemones that live on sand bottoms can withdraw to avoid water motion that is too strong, but they are also dependent on sufficient water motion to provide oxygen since their habitat (in the sand or mud) easily becomes anaerobic.

Trace Elements

The importance of trace elements to the health of sea anemones is recognized but far from well-understood. The function of the different elements can be related to pigment formation and the metabolism of the symbiotic zooxanthellae, but it can also be important for growth and tissue repair of the host anemone. Aquarists have noted positive effects from the addition of trace quantities of iodide, bromide, copper, and zinc, for example, which are included in the ingredients of many commercially available trace element supplements for aquariums. There are certainly other elements that are important, and there are differences in this regard depending on species, but the discovery of the roles of trace elements in different anemones is not likely to see much progress until the care and mass propagation of anemones in captivity becomes more commonplace. Overdose of trace elements is more harmful than shortage, so one should not haphazardly dump them into the aquarium.

Tankmates

When all the requirements are met regarding water quality, temperature, light, water motion, and nutrition, it is still possible to be unable to maintain anemones in an aquarium because of unsuitable tank mates. Certain fishes and invertebrates eat anemones, while others may sting them. Butterflyfish and angelfish will destroy many anemone species, and so they should not be included in an aquarium in which anemones are the focus of the display. An exception to this can be achieved with sufficient numbers of clownfish to protect the anemone from the butterfly and angelfish. In the natural environment when clownfish are removed from the sea anemone, butterflyfish quickly move in to eat the anemone (Fautin and Allen, 1992).

Certain invertebrates are also unsuitable tankmates with anemones, and clownfish may not be able to protect their host from them. Crabs that come into the aquarium with live rock may subsist for years on food scraps, algae and detritus, but when large enough they may one day attack and devour part or all of a sea anemone. For this reason it is best to be sure that all rocks introduced into the aquarium for anemones are free of crabs (easier said than done!) Similarly, bristle worms that come in with live rock may grow to enormous size before they are detected and they can severely injure or completely consume an anemone overnight. There are traps available from your pet dealer for catching worms and crabs, and we discussed techniques for eliminating them in volume one of *The Reef Aquarium*.

While anemones occur on coral reefs and in areas where stony corals grow, their exact location may or may not be among stony corals. Some anemones are easily stung by many types of stony coral, and some may also sting and kill corals. For this reason one should carefully plan the anemone tank either to be without corals, or if the tank is large enough, segregate it into zones. Bottom dwelling anemones such as *H. aurora*, *M. doreensis* and *S. haddoni* are easily kept away from corals. *S. gigantea* can also be kept on the bottom, but it often wanders upward onto the rocks to receive more light and water motion. The bottom dwelling species must be provided with very strong light and water motion to help keep them from wandering. *Entacmaea quadricolor* lives among coral branches with its base shaded but with the tentacles up in the light. *Heteractis magnifica* and *S. mertensii* live attached to solid reef in prominent positions where they receive strong light and water motion. In an aquarium they should be given their own tall, isolated "coral bommie" on which they will sit slightly to the edge of the top.

Other Unsuitable Tankmates

We want to also mention that slow swimming fishes are also not very suitable tankmates with large clownfish host anemones, unless the aquarium is quite large, which would minimize potential contact with the anemone. In small aquaria, fish such as dragonettes (Mandarinfish, Scooter Blenny), seahorses, pipefish, boxfish, pufferfish, and others are likely to be severely stung or eaten by the anemone. Also, if a fish is rare and a treasured pet, do not place an anemone in the same aquarium!

Use of Antibiotics

Anemones often succumb rapidly to infections, particularly when they are first imported. The use of streptomycin or neomycin at a dosage of 5 to 10 ppm may prevent or cure such infections, although our experience has shown poor success with these antibiotics. The bacteria that attack and kill anemones are probably *Vibrio* spp. Success in treating *Vibrio* infections in stony corals has been achieved with the antibiotic Chloramphenicol (Bingman, in press). We have not tried Chloramphenicol to treat anemones, but suspect it may be helpful. The problem with Chloramphenicol is that it is considered extremely toxic to humans and it is therefore difficult to obtain. The treatment of pathogenic bacteria in marine aquaria is a field in need of research and it has good potential for rewarding the researcher with important discoveries. If we knew what antibiotics to use, anemones could be shipped with prophylactic antibiotic treatments. Newly received specimens of *S. gigantea*, *H. magnifica*, and *E. quadricolor* might benefit from treatment for a day or two. Antibiotics should be used in separate treatment tanks, never in display aquariums.

Symptoms of Illness in Anemones

Bleaching

This newly imported *Stichodactyla gigantea* bleached (lost zooxanthellae) overnight, turning from brown to pale yellow in the process. It took 3 weeks for it to regain its original colour afterwards. J. Sprung

Loss of pigment in anemones is a common and often unrecognized problem. Dealers often sell "white" anemones as rare (=expensive) colour forms! In fact, truly white photosynthetic anemones have merely lost most of their symbiotic zooxanthellae, which they need to survive. Under good conditions the zooxanthellae can repopulate their host. The formerly white creature turns light tan or brown, leaving the naive aquarist dismayed, or worried that the healthy brown colour in this formerly white creature is a sign of illness. Sometimes anemones "bleach" in response to over-illumination, often as a result of the development of toxic superoxide radicals from photosynthesis under strong illumination, particularly with U.V. wavelengths. The use of cloud simulation (light dimming) helps prevent this. Also reduction in light intensity and the addition of trace elements has a positive effect. In most cases, however, the loss of pigment occurs from the anemone not receiving enough light in captivity. If the anemone becomes pale and shrinks while climbing as close to the light as possible it is not getting enough light and the intensity should be increased. If the anemone becomes bleached and retreats into the rocks as if it were afraid to come out, chances are the light intensity is too strong or the UV wavelengths (from a high intensity light source) are not sufficiently filtered out. On this subject, the aggressive use of activated carbon can rapidly remove yellowing substances from the water that filter out UV wavelengths. Once the water is clear the light intensity reaching the bottom of the aquarium, UV wavelengths in particular, increases dramatically (Bingmann, 1995). A sudden change from yellow to colourless water as achieved by activated carbon filtration may temporarily and severely disturb anemones due to the sudden increase in the penetration of UV wavelengths into the aquarium. We encourage the use of activated carbon and consider it beneficial, but it should not be used too agressively, or the water should not be allowed to become too yellow before changing the old for fresh activated carbon.

Dyes or Artificial Colours in Anemones

Aquarists see carpet anemones with vibrant blue, pink, or green bases or tentacles and wonder whether these colours are natural or produced by the injection of dyes or artificial colouring. Considering the tacky painted freshwater fishes it is easy to understand the concern, even more so because exceptionally coloured marine invertebrates command a very high price. In general most of the brilliantly coloured anemones are not dyed. Incredible, aren't they? The colours are pigments that develop under specific lighting regimes in nature, and there is a genetic component as well. A green anemone, for example, does not become a red or a blue one when the lighting is changed, though a bleached anemone that is initially white, or a brown one may develop genetically determined coloured pigments when exposed to bright light. The brilliant blue or green carpet anemones (usually *Stichodactyla gigantea* but sometimes *S. haddoni*) are accustomed to very bright light and they will fade in captivity when not provided with light of sufficient intensity.

Bright yellow *Heteractis* spp. are commonly offered for sale to aquarists. The colour is not natural, but caused by a dye or yellow food colouring! The anemones are kept in dyed water temporarily and as they respire they take in the pigmented water, which stains their tissues. The stain lasts for several weeks. This novelty is not healthy for the anemone! It alters the light they can use and the anemone does not regain health until after the dye fades. Usually these anemones die before that happens. We hope to encourage importers to refuse to buy these dyed anemones to end this pointless practice. J. Sprung

The presence of these brilliant pigmented anemones notwith-standing, there are such things as artificially coloured anemones, we regret to say. The most common type is *Heteractis malu,* but we have also seen *Heteractis crispa* and *Condylactis gigantea* dyed with a yellow pigment that lasts several weeks. After the pigment fades the anemones are usually white. If they survive, they will regain zooxanthellae and become brown again when given a suitable environment with good illumination. Note: natu-rally green pigmented anemones that have "bleached" (lost pigment) often are bright yellow. They regain the green pigment under strong illumination. See topic "bleaching."

Shrinking

Anemones that do not receive adequate light to maintain their popula-tions of symbiotic zooxanthellae that provide them with much of their nutrition usually shrink gradually. The shrinking involves consumption of tissues as a means of making up for the deficit in energy from the zooxanthellae. If an anemone is shrinking, increase the light intensity and feed the anemone at least once per week to promote growth. Try a variety of foods. If the anemone refuses food do not try to force feed it. Just insure that it is getting strong light.

Loss of Stickiness

This is an interesting observation made by aquarists: unhealthy anemones are less sticky than healthy ones. The stickiness is a product of the firing of cnidae or nematocysts secreted by stinging cells (cnidocytes). Healthy anemones have the energy reserves to secrete dense numbers of cnidae. Unhealthy ones do not, directing their use of energy in the repair of damaged tissue, defense against pathogens, or just maintenance of metabolic func-tion. It is a sad fact that an anemone starved for food may not have the energy to feed. Loss of stickiness often occurs when the anemone is not receiving enough light. The aquarist should not attempt to force feed the anemone to make it recuperate. The food will be rejected. Instead, one should concentrate on providing proper illumination, to encourage the development of healthy zooxanthellae in the anemone's tissues.

Refusal of Food

Anemones do not need to be fed often when they receive enough light. They should be fed at least occasionally, however (see recom-mendations under the individual species descriptions). If the anemone refuses all varieties of food offered do not try to force food into the mouth. Just insure that it is getting adequate light.

Mouth Open or Everted

When first placed in the aquarium, particularly after a long time in the shipping bag, it is common for anemones to open the mouth wide and partially evert the actinopharynx. This can be a symptom of the need for more oxygen, as the anemone may have been suffocating in the bag. It can also be a result of the anemone doing a water change in its body column. In any case, when an anemone has a wide open mouth it should NOT be placed in a quiet spot in the aquarium with no water motion. On the contrary, it should be provided with strong water motion that makes the tentacles sway and lifts the folds of the oral disc, aiding ventilation of the coelenteron.

This *Stichodactyla gigantea* is dying. It is succumbing to a ravaging bacterial infection that literally dissolves the tissue. Once this type of infection sets in it is nearly impossible to save the anemone. The use of Chloramphenicol to treat the anemone in a separate holding tank may stop the infection if caught early enough. Anemones with this condition must be removed from the display tank immediately as the rotting tissue can foul the aquarium or spread the infection to other anemones or corals. J. Sprung

This symptom is also common in newly imported anemones that are suffering from local or systemic bacterial infection. Lightly flap up the edges of the oral disc to see below it and check the pedal disc and column for sloughing necrotic tissue. If there is none present, then provide strong water flow and simply observe the anemone to see if the condition persists or worsens. Normally, if there is no necrosis the direction of strong water motion over the anemone will reverse the condition. If there is necrosis, the anemone must be treated in a hospital tank with antibiotics (see previous description of their use and see chapter eleven).

Deflated Flaccid Anemone

Anemones normally deflate on a rhythmic cycle of expansion and contraction, and this may send the aquarist into throws of alarm. Long term contraction is often but not always a sign of a problem, such as infection or predation by a bristle worm or fish. In *Entacmaea quadricolor* the process of asexual reproduction via longitudinal fission is preceded by several days of deflation followed by tearing of the oral disc through the mouth and then through the column. It is easy to appreciate why such an appearance could lead the aquarist to assume the anemone is dying!

The Identification and Care of Anemones Kept in Aquariums

Phylum Cnidaria, Class Anthozoa
Subclass Hexacorallia

Order Ceriantharia

Genera: *Arachnanthus, Anthoactis, Cerianthus*, and *Pachycerianthus* are tropical genera

Common Name: Tube anemone, Cerianthus anemone

Colour: Brown, purple, green, pink, blue

Distinguishing Characteristics: Lives in soft grayish tube partially buried in the sand or mud bottom. The tube is made from fired nematocysts. Short tentacles around the mouth. Long tapering tentacles on rest of oral disc. Often has commensal phoronid worms on tube. Column ends in a burrowing pointed foot with an anal pore.

These healthy *cerianthid* anemones at the Shedd Aquarium are being fed brine shrimp nauplii. J. Sprung

Similar Species: Although cerianthids are only distantly related to true sea anemones, they could be confused with some anemones that have long tapering tentacles, such as *Bartholomea annulata*, the curleycue anemone.

Natural Habitat: In mud or sand in seagrass beds, lagoons, bays, sandy areas between reefs.

Aquarium Care: Do not keep cerianthids with fish. They snare fish, especially at night. Provide thick bottom substrate and periodic

currents. Feed daily or weekly brine shrimp nauplii or *Daphnia*.
Some species also take chopped fish, shrimp, and mussels.

Reproduction: Asexual reproduction generally does not occur in
cerianthids, though it is possible (Tifton, 1987). Loeb (1905)
demonstrated that an oral end (ring of tentacles) regenerated from
a cut in the column (see Hyman, 1940). Sexual reproduction
produces a swimming larva called an arachnanthid. Ceriantharians
are all hermaphrodites (Tifton, 1987).

Order Actiniaria
Suborder Nyantheae

Tribe Boloceroidaria

Family Aliciidae

Scientific Name: *Lebrunia danae*

Common Names: Antler Anemone, Branch Anemone

Colour: Pseudotentacles brown with white spots. Sometimes with blue
highlights. Smaller true tentacles of different colour, usually grayish.

Distinguishing Characteristics: Two types of tentacles. The
most obvious ones, called pseudotentacles, are extended during
the day to capture light. Secondary ones are for food capture, and
they expand at night, when the pseudotentacles are contracted.
The cnidae of the pseudotentacles are restricted to ball-like vesi-

The psuedotentacles of the
Caribbean Antler Anemone,
Lebrunia danae, are extended
during the daytime to capture light.
The pale spots are defensive
stinging vessicles. P. Humann

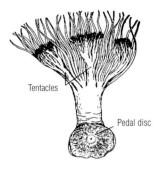

This drawing of *Lebrunia danae* shows the two types of tentacles and the column, which is normally hidden in a crevice. *After Hyman, 1940*

Tentacles

Pedal disc

This anemone photographed in Indonesia seems quite similar to *Lebrunia* from the Caribbean. It also resembles *Thalassianthus aster.* It is probably the anemone *Triactis producta*, another night-active anemone that extends pseudotentacles with zooxanthellae during the day to capture light. At night it extends the oral disc with white tentacles that snare zooplankton and other prey. S. W. Michael

cles scattered on the branches, and they are not for prey capture. They serve a defensive function only, protecting the large pseudo-tentacles that are vulnerable to predation while expanded to capture light. These cnidae are so potent that the nettling sensation penetrates human skin and may cause intense pain. The cnidae on the food capturing tentacles are not so powerful.

Similar Species: *Lebrunia coralligens* also has two types of tentacles, but the branching is less pronounced, the pseudotentacles end in bulbs, and the habit of living inside live rocks is different. The extended branched tentacles of *L. danae* greatly resemble the tentacles of the Indo-pacific corals *Euphyllia paradivisa* and *Euphyllia cristata*. They are also similar to *Capnea lucida*, and small specimens of the latter could be confused with *L. danae* in the field.

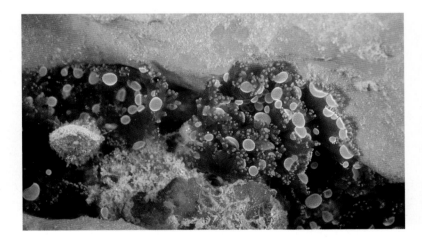

Natural Habitat: Occurs most regularly in two distinct types of environments, on reefs and seagrass beds of the Caribbean, including Florida. On reefs it is found under ledges that provide a gap only a few inches over sand or in crevices between rocks. On grass beds it is found among *Thalassia* turtle grass and *Halimeda opuntia* algae, or attached to rocks in the grass. Generally it only occurs in grassy areas with clean water and strong currents. Several symbiotic or commensal shrimp species may be found among the tentacles, including *Periclimenes* spp., *Thor amboinensis* and other *Thor* species.

Aquarium Care: Easy to care for. Prefers moderate to bright light but adapts to low light. Specimens collected under ledges are adapted to indirect light and will retract from intense direct illumination. This anemone has a potent sting that aquarists should be wary of. It also may wander and injure corals in an aquarium, so we do not recommend it for a reef aquarium with prized specimens that could be injued or lost. It is not entirely out of the question to include it in a reef aquarium, but use caution!

Reproduction: Pedal laceration and longitudinal fission suspected. Sexual reproduction not observed in captivity.

Scientific Name: *Lebrunia coralligens*

Common Name: Antler anemone, branch anemone

Colour: Blue, brown and white

Lebrunia coralligens in its typical habitat imbedded in coral
P. Humann

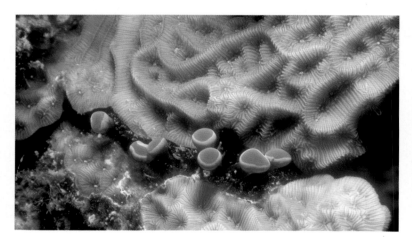

Distinguishing Characteristics: Two types of tentacles. The most obvious ones are berry-like and extend during the day to capture light. Secondary ones are for food capture.

Similar Species: *Lebrunia danae*

Natural Habitat: Coral reefs in the Caribbean, including Florida, in coral rock in shallow water.

Aquarium Care: This anemone is unlikely to be collected without the rock it is imbedded in. Give strong illumination and strong water motion.

Reproduction: Not well observed because the anemone is located within rock, but probably occurs by asexual means. Adults release planulae that already contain zooxanthellae (Lewis, 1984).

Scientific Name: *Phyllodiscus semoni* Kwietniewski, 1897

Common Name: Night Anemone

Colour: Mottled brown green and lavender with white column and tentacles. The overall colour of the anemone is dark greenish brown because of the mass of finely branched vessicles.

One of the most bizarre looking anemones, *Phyllodiscus semoni*, photographed in Indonesia.
S. W. Michael

Distinguishing Characteristics: Looks like a clump of dark seaweed. White tentacles and column are hidden by a distinctive mass of dark, highly branched vesicles containing symbiotic algae. True tentacles emerge at night when the anemone feeds.

Similar Species: Resembles *Actinodendron*. The night vs. day extension of pseudotentacles and true tentacles is like *Lebrunia*.

Natural Habitat: Cryptic on Indo-Pacific reefs attached to live rock or in sand in shallow water. Often associated with numerous commensal shrimps.

Aquarium Care: Hardy. Provide strong illumination, intermittently strong water motion. Feed chopped fish, clam, or shrimp meat at night.

Reproduction: Sexual reproduction method unknown. Asexual reproduction method also unknown.

Tribe Mesomyaria

Family Aiptasiidae

Genus *Aiptasia*

Species Names: *Aiptasia pallida* and *A. pulchella*

Common Name: *Aiptasia*, Glass Anemone, Glassrose Anemone

Colour: Brown, sometimes with blue highlights.

Distinguishing Characteristics: *Aiptasia* are relatively small anemones, generally up to about 4 inches (6 cm) tall with an oral disc about 1 inch (2.5 cm) diameter, though most specimens are much smaller. They have elongated tapering tentacles. They reproduce prolifically by asexual means, mostly by pedal laceration. Any small fragment of tissue, however physically mangled and mutilated, can become a new anemone. This is the lesson learned by aquarists who have tried to eliminate them by chopping them up or crushing them with the turn of a screwdriver. Try it and you make more anemones!

Similar Species: none

Natural Habitat: Intertidal along rocky or mangrove lined shore-lines, in bays and protected oceanic coasts. Also on reefs on live rock. Occurs even in deep water. Usually occurs where there is good tidal exchange.

Aquarium Care: Ignore, Inject with boiling water, copper sulfate, potassium hydroxide, calcium hydroxide, or sprinkle calcium chloride crystals over it, cuss and shout, add copperband butter-flyfish to eat it. This anemone will thrive anyway. But seriously, this anemone has zooxanthellae, so it thrives under bright illumi-nation. It also feeds well on all types of food. Aquariums to which brine shrimp nauplii are added as a plankton substitute often develop disastrous blooms of *Aiptasia*. The best natural control of this anemone is the sea slug *Berghia*, see chapter 11. See also volume one for various techniques of removal.

Reproduction: Reproduces usually (and prolifically) by pedal laceration. Any portion of the tissue is capable of regeneration; becoming a complete anemone. Sexual reproduction not observed in captivity, but *Aiptasia diaphana* is dioecious and oviparous (Shick, 1991).

Scientific Name: *Bartholomea annulata*

Common Names: Curley-cue anemone

Colour: Clear brown, gray, or pale blue with white bands on tentacles.

Bartholomea annulata resembles *Aiptasia* with numerous swollen bands on the tentacles.
J. Sprung

Distinguishing Characteristics: Long stringy, often curly tentacles with pale bands on them.

Similar Species: Similar to *Aiptasia* but grows larger and has distinctively longer tentacles with numerous swollen bands. Also could be confused with *Capnea lucida*, which has bead-like vessicles on the tentacles.

Natural Habitat: Lives in mud, sand or gravel in shallow water, often in large numbers. Also found attached to the underside of rocks in shallow water, particularly in seagrass beds. Sometimes abundant in *Thalassia testudinum* seagrass, with the base attached to the roots of the grass below the sand, or in thick pillows of the green macroalgae, *Halimeda opuntia*, growing among the grass. Occasional on coral reefs in holes with sand. Several symbiotic or commensal shrimp species may be found among the tentacles, including *Periclimenes* spp., *Thor amboinensis* and other *Thor* spp., and pistol shrimp, *Alpheus* spp.. The most typical arrangement found with this anemone is a pair of pistol shrimp at the base and several *Periclimenes pedersoni* at the periphery of the tentacles. The red and white striped antennae of the pistol shrimp can be seen sticking out at the base and a gentle touch will trigger a twenty-one gun salute.

Reproduction: Simultaneous hermaphrodite. Also asexual reproduction (proliferation) via pedal laceration, and budding (J. Sprung, pers. obs.). In budding a new pedal disc with its own small column forms like a branch on the column of the parent and presumably develops internal structures before severing.

Scientific Name: *Capnea* (=*Heteractis*) *lucida*

Common Name: Atlantic Beaded Anemone

Colour: Transparent brown or gray with conspicuous white beads on tentacles.

Distinguishing Characteristics: Long tentacles with pale bead-like vessicles on them. These tentacles typically emerge from a hole in a rock or a crevice where the rock meets sand on coral reefs.

Similar Species: From a distance this anemone seems like *Bartholomea* upon closer inspection it is obviously distinct. Instead of bands on the tentacles it has beads. The beads on the

The vessicles on the tentacles of *Capnea lucida* are distinctive.
D. Perrine

tentacles are similar in appearance to the vessicles on the pseudo-tentacles of *Lebrunia danae,* and small *C. lucida* may be confused with *Lebrunia.*

Natural Habitat: On Caribbean reefs. May be found expanding from a hole in solid reef or from a hole in sand or gravel at the base of the reef, with the pedal disk attached to the reef or a large solid rock. Difficult to collect because the pedal disk is most often deeply buried in the rock or sand. Several symbiotic or commensal shrimp species may be found among the tentacles, including *Periclimenes* spp., *Thor amboinensis* and other *Thor* spp. There is also an associated red mysid shrimp that schools among the tentacles. A display of these in an aquarium would be spectacular!

Tribe Endomyaria

Family Actiniidae

Scientific Name: *Anemonia* cf. *majano*

Common Name: *Aiptasia, Anemonia*

Colour: Brown or green

Distinguishing Characteristics: Numerous tentacles often with swollen "bulb" tips. We do not know if the genus assigned to this species is correct. This anemone seems quite distinct from *Anemonia viridis* (=*sulcata*) from the Mediterranean.

"Anemonia" cf. *majano* commonly arrives as a hitchhiker on live rock from Fiji or Indonesia. J. Sprung

"Anemonia" cf. *majano*
J. C. Delbeek

"Anemonia" cf. *majano*
J. C. Delbeek

Similar Species: *Aiptasia*. Large specimens, which form bulbous tips at the ends of their tentacles, could be confused with small *Entacmaea quadricolor*.

Natural Habitat: Reef flats and rubble zones in the Indo Pacific.

Aquarium Care: same as for *Aiptasia*. This anemone is a pest that can quickly overrun and ruin a reef aquarium. It stings and kills stony corals and multiplies rapidly, spreading over the killed corals' skeletons. No established control has been reported, but we suspect that the anemone-eating nudibranch *Spurilla neapolitana* would provide a means of control.

Reproduction: Prolific asexual reproduction via longitudinal fission and possibly pedal laceration.

Scientific Name: *Anemonia viridis* (=*sulcata*)

Common Name: Snake Locks Anemone

Colour: Gray, purple, bluish.

Anemonia viridis (=*sulcata*) photographed at the Oceanographic Museum in Monaco.
J. Sprung

Distinguishing Characteristics: Numerous long tentacles of mostly uniform colour, with brightly coloured tips. Achieves substantial size, to at least 30 cm (12 in) diameter.

Similar Species: Similar to *Condylactis* and *Heteractis crispa*. Do not confuse this anemone with them! This anemone rarely enters the trade in North America, though it is not uncommon in Europe. It comes from the Mediterranean.

Natural Habitat: In sand or among rock rubble in seagrass beds, sometimes in crevices in rock on reefs in the Mediterranean.

Aquarium Care: Easy to care for when given sufficient bottom substrate and medium to strong illumination. Should be maintained at slightly cooler than tropical water temperature. About 24 °C (72 °F) is ideal. Feed chopped shrimp, worms, snail, or clam meat.

Reproduction: Not reported in captivity.

Scientific Name: *Condylactis gigantea*

Common Name: "Condy" Anemone, Atlantic Anemone, Haitian Anemone, (often called *C. passiflora* in aquarium literature)

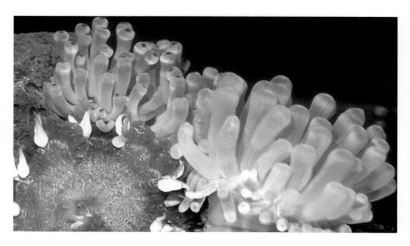

Condylactis may develop "bubble-tipped" tentacles like *Entacmaea*. *Epicystis crucifer* is at bottom left. J. Sprung

Colour: White, brown, green, or purple, often with contrasting magenta, purple, or green tips on the tentacles. The column may be orange, yellow, or the same predominant colour as the rest of the anemone

Distinguishing Characteristics: Tentacles may develop "bubble tips" like *Entacmaea quadricolor*. Juveniles have bands on the tentacles that may even be swollen.

Juvenile *Condylactis gigantea* have beaded tentacles like *Heteractis aurora* or *Bartholomea annulata*. Two commensal shrimp, *Periclimenes pedersoni*, have made a home in this young anemone in Julian Sprung's aquarium. J. Sprung

As the anemone grows the beads gradually disappear. J. Sprung

Similar Species: *Condylactis* develop bubble tipped tentacles and so may be confused with *Entacmaea quadricolor*. Young specimens with beaded tentacles look like *H. aurora* or *B. annulata*.

Natural Habitat: Common among *Halimeda opuntia* algae in shallow seagrass (*Thalassia testudinum*) beds in Florida and the Caribbean. Also found along rocky shores imbedded in rock crevices and on reefs in sand or on rock.

Aquarium Care: Easily cared for when given sufficient light. Can be maintained with a few fluorescent tubes or with stronger illumination. Feed twice per month with shrimp, crab or fish meat. The clownfish *Amphiprion clarki* and *A. frenatus* will adapt to this anemone.

Reproduction: Transverse fission is possible when artificially performed (J. Sprung, pers. obs.). Sexual reproduction is the only known means of reproduction in the wild. Spawning is most pronounced in spring but occurs throughout the year. Separate sexes typical, though hermaphrodites are known (Jennison, 1981). Not reported to reproduce in captivity.

Scientific Name: *Entacmaea quadricolor* (Rüppell and Leuckart, 1828)

Common Name: Bubble-Tip Anemone, Bulb-tip anemone, Bulb-Tentacle Sea Anemone, Maroon Anemone

Colour: Brown, green, fluorescent reddish orange

Entacmaea quadricolor with a yellow morph of *Amphiprion clarkii* that resembles *A. bicinctus*. Note the well-developed bubble tips. Photographed in the Solomon Islands. J. Sprung

A green *E. quadricolor* with a resident *Amphiprion ocellaris*. This aquarium photo demonstrates a partnership that normally does not occur in nature. *A. ocellaris* normally lives in *Stichodactyla mertensii*, *S. gigantea*, or *Heteractis magnifica*. J. Sprung

This form of *E. quadricolor* has fluorescent red or orange pigment. It is commonly called "Rose Anemone." J. C. Delbeek

A red *E. quadricolor* in the natural habitat in the Red Sea. This photograph provides a beautiful scene to consider recreating in a home aquarium with soft corals and anemones. A. Storace

Distinguishing Characteristics: Column without verrucae. The swellings at the tentacle tips are the characteristic for which this anemone is named, though the presence of the "bubble tips" is transient. Fautin and Allen (1992) observe that the presence of anemonefish among the tentacles can cause a non-bubble tipped *E. quadricolor* to develop the swollen tips within minutes. This is a curious observation! We agree with them that the reason why this occurs is an enigma, but we do not agree that the bubble tips develop "only in the presence of (anemone)fish." We have seen adjacent clonemates of *Entacmaea* with resident clownfish swishing from anemone to anemone, and one anemone has the swollen tips while its neighbor does not. In general, we have seen a correlation between illumination and the development of the bubble tips: those tentacles receiving the most intense illumination are shorter and often bubble tipped. Those receiving less illumination are longer and stringy. Some aquarists report that "hungry" *Entacmaea* display stringy tentacles (presumably sweeping for food) and that the tentacles shorten and the bubble tips return after the anemone is fed. Perhaps a similar "hunger vs. satisfied" effect is achieved with the presence of fish and their excreted wastes, or via photosynthetically produced food under intense illumination.

Similar Species: Under low illumination when *E. quadricolor* develops stringy tentacles it resembles *Macrodactyla doreensis*. *Condylactis gigantea* may develop bubble tips and therefore resembles *Entacmaea*.

Adjacent *E. quadricolor*, one with and one without bubble tips despite the presence of clownfish.
J. Sprung

Adjacent *E. quadricolor* with and without bubble tips in an aquarium. The difference seemed to be related to light in this case. The specimens with bubble tips were more brightly illuminated. J. Sprung

Natural Habitat: Imbedded in coral bommies or in solid reef with the pedal disc attached deep within the dead coral, so that much of the column is shaded while the tentacles are expanded upward to the light. Clones in same coral head expand together so that they appear to be one giant anemone. This is the condition at the top of the reef or coral bommie. In deeper water *E. quadricolor*

This anemone living in the sand near a shipwreck in the Solomon Islands looked at first like *Macrodactyla doreensis*. It is *Entacmaea quadricolor*, however. Note the smaller specimen to the right with bubble tips. The anemone's column in this case is not buried in the sand, but attached to the underside of this piece of the wreck.
J. Sprung

tends to grow large and does not often reproduce by division. It is possible that the difference (cloning vs. non-cloning forms) is merely an artifact of location: deepwater specimens receive less light and therefore don't grow as quickly. The rapid proliferation by vegetative propagation can be viewed simply as a form of growth. There is no doubt, however, that anemones living in deep water are adapted to the light they recieve, so they could be considered distinct ecomorphs. Interestingly, the shallow water smaller clone variety usually is host for *Amphiprion frenatus* and *A. melanopus* while the deeper water, large non-cloning variety is usually host to *Premnas biaculeatus* (D. Fautin, pers. comm.). *Premnas* may also be found living with *A. melanopus* in the clone variety in shallow water (J. Sprung, pers obs.).

Aquarium Care: With small specimens assume it is the clone variety and provide strong illumination and branchy coral rock or live rock with deep holes and crevices. With large specimens assume it is the deeper water variety and provide moderate to strong illumination and tall rocks with deep crevices. May be delicate for a brief period after shipping, when it is prone to infection; otherwise quite hardy and easy to keep. Should be kept with clownfish for best success. *Premnas biaculeatus*, *A. frenatus*, and *A. melanopus* are best. Feed chopped fish, shrimp, or worms once per week. If clownfish are present, supplemental feeding is not necessary beyond the food given to the clownfish.

Reproduction: Longitudinal fission is common in aquarium specimens. Aquarists have reported the production of very small offspring from *Entacmaea quadricolor*, these offspring not resulting from the usual longitudinal fission. It is possible that such offspring are produced by pedal laceration, but they may also be the product of parthenogenesis or vegetative (somatic) embryogenesis, or sexual reproduction. Separate sexes are common in reproducing colonies. At the Waikiki Aquarium, the colonies there spawn each April at 7 AM, two days after the full moon. Planulae develop within 24 hours after fertilization, and settle out on a variety of substrata. These newly settled anemones are already self-sufficient as they are packed with zooxanthellae.

Scientific Name: *Macrodactyla doreensis* (Quoy And Gaimard, 1833)

Common Name: Corkscrew Anemone, Sebae Anemone, Sand Anemone, Long Tentacle Anemone (L.T.A), Red Base Anemone, Long Tentacle Red Based Anemone, Purple Long Tentacle Anemone

Colour: Many colours and patterns. Brown, green, gray, blue, or Purple. Often with radiating stripes on oral disc extending onto tentacles. Column is usually reddish orange with distinctive white verrucae.

Distinguishing Characteristics: Tentacles sparse, more concentrated toward the periphery so that oral disc is clearly visible. Uniformly long tentacles tapered to a point. Tentacle ends may form corkscrew shape. Oral disc widely flared, up to 50 cm (20 in.) in diameter, often with pale radial lines that may extend onto tentacles. Column buries in sediment. Lower part of column and pedal disc orange or red. Upper part of column pale brown or white. Verrucae in longitudinal rows, usually white but sometimes magenta.

Phil Shane of Quality Marine, Los Angeles, California (pers. comm.) noticed an interesting attribute of this anemone. It apparently contains some anti-viral compound(s). Shane noticed that fishes suffering from *Lymphocystis*, a viral disease that produces

A tank full of *Macrodactyla doreensis* at an importer's holding facility. Note the variety of colours and patterns. This species survives transportation well and is very hardy. J. Sprung

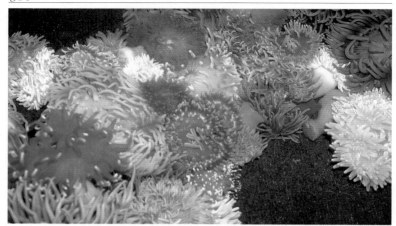

The prized purple morph of this species is particularly attractive. It is hardy and most anemonefishes will accept it as a host. J. Sprung

cauliflower-like growths on the fins and mouth, spontaneously healed quite rapidly when placed in aquaria containing *Macrodactyla doreensis*. His observation is based on hundreds of fish in many aquariums and has been corroborated by other aquarists and importers. *Lymphocystis* is a condition quite similar to *Herpes*, and it is possible that the beneficial compounds produced by this anemone could be used to treat or control conditions caused by herpes type viruses including chicken pox, shingles, genital herpes and cold sores in humans. Antiviral compounds such as this are sought by natural products chemists for the pharmaceutical industry in the search for new drugs to treat AIDS and other viral diseases.

Similar Species: May be confused with *Heteractis crispa*, but *M.*

doreensis has fewer tentacles, and the column of *H. crispa* is tougher. Most similar to *H. malu*, which lives in the same habitat, but *M. doreensis* has longer tentacles and grows to larger size.

Natural Habitat: *Macrodactyla* lives on sandy bottoms with its pedal disc and column deeply burrowed into the sand and attached to some buried object. Sometimes it occurs on reefs, particularly on rubble slopes, but it is most common in sand or mud. It usually occurs in shallow water and so is accustomed to bright illumination. It has a restricted range, from Southern Japan southward through the Philippines, Eastern Indonesia, New Guinea, the Solomon Islands, and Northern Australia. Most specimens in the aquarium trade come from the Philippines, where they are apparently very common.

Aquarium Care: Very hardy and easy to keep. This is a beginner's anemone. Must have thick sand or gravel substrate with small rocks. Give strong to moderate light. Feed snails, clam meat, chopped worms, shrimp at least once per month. Keep with *A. clarki* and *Dascyllus trimaculatus*. Strong water motion is required to maintain high oxyen levels with deep sand substrates. At night the anemone may stand up or "walk" to take in more oxygen if the water flow is not sufficient. Although this species has a limited range, which might suggest that collection of it could risk its survival, it is common in its natural habitat and apparently not at any risk of overharvesting.

Reproduction: Not observed in captivity. Longitudinal fission is suspected based on anecdotal reports (Jean Chua, All Seas Fisheries, Miami FL, Pers. Comm.).

Family Phymanthidae

Genus *Phymanthus*

Common Name: Rock anemone

Colour: Gray and green, brown.

Distinguishing Characteristics: Beaded tentacles or tentacles with ornate side branchlets. Tentacles concentrated at margin of oral disc. Flattened shape, with bare (tentacle-free) central oral disc. *P. buitendijkii* is one species from the Indo-Pacific region.

Similar Species: *Heteractis aurora*

Natural Habitat: Lives in shallow water with its tentacles brightly illuminated and its column shaded, with pedal disc attached to a rock in sand or gravel. Common on reef flats among rubble and sand.

Aquarium Care: *Phymanthus* spp. are among the most beautiful anemones and very easy to care for. They adapt to low light and intense light. Feed at least once per month. Feeding several times per week will enhance growth. This anemone is ideal in a reef aquarium too. It tends not to wander, and it is not a particularly bad stinger. Place it on a gravel bottom next to a rock in strong illumination.

Reproduction: This anemone may reproduce like the closely related *Epicystis* from the Caribbean, which releases gametes into the water. Sperm are ejected from the mouth and eggs exit from the tentacles.

Scientific Name: *Epicystis* (=*Phymanthus*) *crucifer*

Common Name: Rock anemone

Colour: A whole palette of colour possibilities exists for this species, and in nature differently coloured forms can be found adjacent to one another giving a pansy-patch effect. The colours include green, brown, orange, and gray and white stripe patterns. The oral disc may be striped or solid. The tentacles may be ringed with pale stripes or solid in colour. The mouth may be a different shade than the oral disc, often a strongly contrasting bright magenta, green, or orange, or it may be the same colour as the oral disc. The column often has contrasting round spots of colour

(verrucae) that may be orange or pink or green. Sometimes they are of the same colour as the column.

Distinguishing Characteristics: Pink or orange veruccae on the column, Tentacle free oral disc that is often very colorful or patterned. Tentacles are often, but not always beaded.

Similar Species: other rock anemones, *Tealia, Actinia*, also similar to *Phymanthus* and *Heteractis aurora*.

Natural Habitat: Lives in sand or gravel over hardbottom in shallow water throughout the Caribbean, including Florida, often in large numbers. Also found attached to the underside of rocks in shallow water, particularly in seagrass beds. Sometimes abundant in *Thalassia testudinum* seagrass, with the base attached to the roots of the grass below the sand, or in thick pillows of *Halimeda opuntia* algae growing among the grass. Sometimes has *Periclimenes* spp.shrimps associated with it. Often has *Thor* spp., but seldom *Thor amboinensis*. Despite the colourful oral disc this anemone is cryptic.

Reproduction: Viviparous, larviparous in some populations (Jennison, 1981). Males may be seen shedding sperm into the water. Females may release eggs (or larvae?) from the tentacles! (J. Sprung, pers. obs.) Although this species is supposed to be live-bearing, we know of no reports of offspring being released in aquaria. Spawning has been seen, however, as noted above.

Family Stichodactylidae

Scientific Name: *Heteractis aurora*

Common Name: Sand Anemone, Beaded Sea Anemone, Mat Anemone, Aurora Anemone, Button Anemone

Colour: Usually grayish white with white banding on the central part of the oral disc around the mouth. Sometimes greenish, rarely purple.

Heteractis aurora has a very distinctive appearance. Here it is in the natural habitat in the Solomon Islands. J. Sprung

Distinguishing Characteristics: Beaded tentacles. *Heteractis aurora* seldom contains large adult clownfish or sexually mature pairs. It is thus termed a "nursery anemone" (Fautin and Allen, 1992).

Similar Species: Quite similar to *Phymanthus* species, which also have beaded tentacles. There is also a range of appearance of specimens that seem to be midway between *H. aurora* and *H. malu* that suggests possible hybridization between them.

Natural Habitat: Sand or gravel bottoms on outer reef slopes, reef flats, and clear lagoons.

Aquarium Care: Usually easy to care for when given a deep sand or gravel substrate and strong illumination. Sometimes delicate. *Amphiprion clarkii* is the best clownfish for this anemone. Feed a few times per month with chopped mussel, snails, earthworm or shrimp.

Reproduction: Not reported in captivity.

Scientific Name: *Heteractis crispa*

Common Name: Sebae anemone, Leather Anemone, Formerly *Radianthus keukenthali*

Colour: Usually pale brown or straw coloured, sometimes purple or green. Sometimes available coloured with artificial yellow dye.

Although *Heteractis crispa* normally lives on the reef among corals, sometimes it occurs in gravel or rubble zones between reefs.
J. Sprung

Distinguishing Characteristics: Dull coloured (usually) column is tough and leathery, with prominent adhesive verrucae. Numerous long tapering tentacles

Similar Species: *Heteractis crispa* is similar to *Macrodactyla doreensis*, but the latter has much fewer tentacles on the oral disc. When in captivity with improper lighting *H. crispa* may contract the tentacles so that they appear short and stubby like those of *H. malu*.

Natural Habitat: Clear water outer reef slopes on coral rock and among (dead) branchy corals with column and pedal disc deep inside a crevice; also in sand or gravel. Backreef lagoon environments among coral rubble or gravel.

Aquarium Care: Delicate. Difficult to keep. Provide very strong light and moderate water motion. Give porous live rock and gravel bottom for attachment substrates. Feed chopped clam, worms, shrimp or fish once per week or more. Most clownfish will adapt to this anemone. Success is improved by keeping

Two colour morphs of *H. crispa* living next to each other. J. Sprung

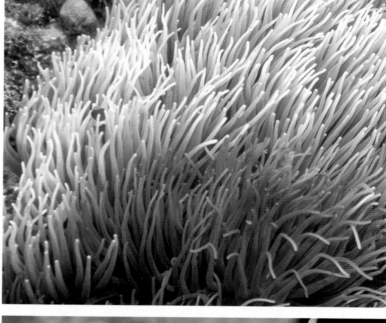

The column of *H. crispa* has a thick leathery texture. Sometimes, however, it is difficult to distinguish *H. crispa* from *H. malu*. J. Sprung

This is the typical anemone species that is dyed with yellow food colouring. It is probably *H. crispa*, but often the tentacles are short and sparse, so the anemones seem to be *H. malu*. J. Sprung

This *H. crispa* is stinging its neighbor, *Entacmaea quadricolor*. Not all anemones can safely be in contact with other anemones. Keep this in mind when planning an aquarium for anemones. J. Sprung.

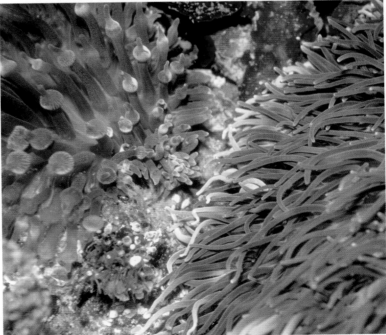

A lovely pale green *H. magnifica* with *Amphiprion perideraion*.
J. Sprung

clownfish such as *A. chrysopterus* with it. The anemone requires less food when clownfish are present. With inadequate lighting this anemone shrinks and eventually dies.

Reproduction: Asexual reproduction is occasional in the natural environment (J. Sprung, pers. obs.) and probably occurs by longitudinal fission. Sexual reproduction not reported in captivity.

Scientific Name: *Heteractis magnifica* (Quoy and Gaimard, 1833)

Common Name: Magnificent Sea Anemone, Ritteri Anemone, *Radianthus* anemone, *Radianthus ritteri*, Bulb-tip anemone, Maroon Anemone, Yellow-Tipped Long Tentacle Anemone

Colour: very colourful column (base) with contrasting coloured tentacles. Column may be red, purple, pink, with brown, green, blue, or purple tentacles.

Distinguishing Characteristics: Very large anemone, growing up to just over one meter in diameter. The tentacles are of uniform thickness and do not taper at the tip. Sometimes the

Heteractis magnifica typically has a brightly coloured column.
J. Sprung

tentacle tips are slightly swollen. The contrasting column colour is distinctive. When disturbed the anemone "balls up," showing just the colourful column with a few protruding tentacles at the top. Verrucae present but not distinctive. They are the same colour as the column or slightly darker.

Similar Species: Small maroon-coloured individuals with white-tipped tentacles may be confused with the corallimorph *Pseudo-corynactis* sp. The latter has distinctive ball shaped white tips on the tentacles. Although they are quite different anemones, the fact that *Entacmea quadricolor* and *Heteractis magnifica* share the common name "Maroon Anemone" suggest confusion about them. In the former the name most probably refers to the association between this anemone and the Maroon Clownfish. In the

The tentacles may also be brightly coloured in *Heteractis magnifica*.
J. Sprung

Heteractis magnifica often fares poorly in aquaria. It needs very strong light and water motion to thrive. Lacking a suitable perch, it will climb up on the glass to reach a position with the strongest light and water motion.
J. C. Delbeek

latter the name may refer to specimens of *H. magnifica* which have a maroon coloured base.

Natural Habitat: On reef slopes *H. magnifica* occurs on projecting prominent solid structures, with the entire column and pedal disc clearly visible. Sometimes occurs on the skeletons of densely branched corals. Occurs in regions that periodically receive strong water currents.

Aquarium Care: Delicate. Difficult to keep. May wander all over the tank. Should be placed on a prominent, isolated tall rock (as if on a pedestal) so that the anemone is positioned in strong light and water motion. Presence of clownfish improves success. *Amphiprion perideraion* is a very good partner. Once acclimated and settled on a prominent rock *H. magnifica* can be hardy and can thrive in captivity, but most aquarists fail to provide the right habitat with sufficient light and water motion. May be a suspension feeder (Barnes, 1980) that captures plankton via nematocysts and mucus on the surface of its oral disc, passing the trapped food via cilia and tentacle movement to the mouth. Also takes chopped fish or shrimp but sometimes refuses food.

Reproduction: *Heteractis magnifica* employs asexual reproduction by longitudinal fission, but varies in this capacity depending on origin. In the central part of its distribution it most typically occurs as single, large individuals. In the periphery of its distribution it commonly forms large clusters of clonemates (Fautin and Allen, 1992). In Fiji we saw large anemones that had divided into two or three clones, each also quite large. In the Solomon Islands we only saw large individual anemones, some of which were in excess of one meter in diameter. In Fiji we also saw evidence of pedal laceration forming new anemones (see chapter four).

Scientific Name: *Heteractis malu* (Haddon And Shackleton, 1893)

Common Name: Sebae Anemone, Hawaiian Anemone, Delicate Anemone

Colour: Pale cream, brown, gray, green, or purple. Tentacles often magenta tipped, sometimes with white rings. Sometimes available coloured with artificial yellow dye.

Distinguishing Characteristics: Oral disc with sparse tentacles that are relatively short and stubby, often swollen in middle.

Heteractis malu in the natural habitat in the Solomon Islands. This large specimen has an appearance quite like *H. aurora*, and may be a hybrid. J. Sprung

This is the natural habitat, embedded in a sandy coral rubble bottom in shallow water with bright light. Note how this specimen has some beads on the tentacles. Is this *Heteractis malu* or *H. aurora?* This appearance suggests a close relationship with *H. aurora* or possible hybridization. J. Sprung

Tentacle colour variable, often magenta tipped but sometimes green tipped or with pale white rings at the tips. Oral disc reported up to 20 cm (8 in.) in diameter (Fautin and Allen, 1992), but may reach more than 25 cm (10 in.) (J. Sprung, pers. obs.). Tentacles expansion beyond disc may yield a total diameter of about 30 cm (12 in.). Oral disc commonly creamy brown, sometimes green or gray, sometimes with white radial lines. The different colour forms of *H. malu* resemble other similar sand dwelling species. For example, white radial lines on the oral disc are also found in *Macrodactyla*. In rare instances when the normally shortened tentacles of *H. malu* are extended to unusual length the anemone is strikingly similar to *Macrodactyla doreensis*. The white rings on the tentacles of *H. malu*, when

A purple aquarium specimen with white bands on the tentacles that form beads like those of *H. aurora*. J. Sprung

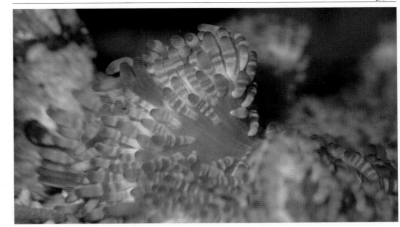

This large *H. malu* photographed on a reef slope in the Solomon Islands has elongate tentacles with corkscrew shape, which makes it really look a lot like *Macrodactyla doreensis*. J. Sprung

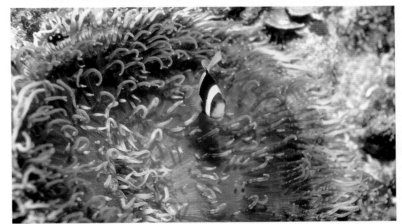

Another *H. malu* with long tentacles that make it closely resemble *Macrodactyla doreensis*. J. Sprung

present, are reminiscent of the swellings on the tentacles of *H. aurora*. In fact, sometimes the rings may occur with slight swelling, forming beads as in H. aurora, though not as prominently. *Heteractis malu* seldom contains large adult clownfish or sexually mature pairs. It is thus termed a "nursery anemone" (Fautin and Allen, 1992).

Similar Species: *Heteractis malu* is similar to and often confused with *H. crispa*. *Heteractis malu* has fewer tentacles and they are usually shorter in length. *Heteractis crispa* has a tougher column. *Heteractis malu* may also be confused with *H. aurora*, which has similar tentacle number and size, but which has the distinction of the swollen beads on the tentacles. This distinction can be blurry when *H. aurora* has cross-striping rings on the tentacles, some of which form swollen beads (see photos) or when the beads are not fully inflated in *H. aurora*. *Heteractis aurora* normally has distinctive radial stripes on the oral disc around the mouth. It is possible that *H. malu* hybridizes with *H. auroroa*. Another possibility is that in some localities *H. crispa* and *H. aurora* may hybridize, producing anemones that look like *H. malu*.

Natural Habitat: Sandy or gravel bottoms in shallow water on the reef flat and back-reef margin. Sometimes on reef slopes on rock. Widespread in the Indo-Pacific. Also in Hawaii.

Aquarium Care: May be delicate initially, but usually easy to keep. Give thick sand or gravel bottom with small rocks. Strong light. Do not place this anemone up on the rocks. Place it on the sand or gravel adjacent to rock. *Amphiprion clarki* is the best tenant. Hawaiian specimens, sold as "White Sand Anemone" are especially hardy.

Reproduction: Asexual reproduction not reported but the authors suspect it is possible. Sexual reproduction not studied.

Scientific Name: *Stichodactyla gigantea* (Forsskål, 1775)

Common Name: Giant Carpet Anemone, Formerly *Stoichactis kenti* in aquarium literature

Colour: Brown, Green, Purple, Pink, Blue, and (rarely) fluorescent reddish pink. Yellow specimens are green ones that have lost most of their zooxanthellae.

Three color morphs of
Stichodactyla gigantea.
These "Colored Carpet" anemones
command a high price. Their
colouration is natural. Strong
illumination is required to keep
these pigments.
J. Sprung

A nice healthy green *S. gigantea*
photographed in an aquarium.
J. Sprung

An all too common occurrence:
Stichodactyla gigantea dying of a
bacterial infection. This species is
prone to rapid tissue necrosis from
pathogenic bacteria. J. Sprung

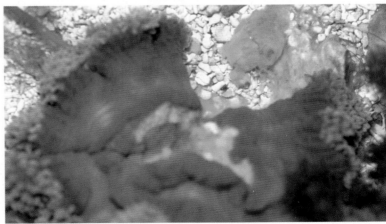

This green carpet anemone is *Stichodactyla haddoni*. This form shows twitching tentacle movement like that of *S. gigantea*, and may be a hybrid. *S. haddoni* are much easier to maintain in captivity than *S. gigantea*. J. C. Delbeek

Distinguishing Characteristics: Oral disc highly folded. Tentacles constantly moving like squirming worms. Despite the name, this is not the largest carpet anemone, that distinction belonging to *S. mertensii*.

Similar Species: *Stichodactyla mertensii* is most similar, but it is larger with a less distinct column, and has less folds in the oral disc, which is usually held flat against limestone rock on the reef. *Stichodactyla haddoni* has shorter tentacles, except at the margin of the disc, and usually has a more folded disc shape, though that is highly variable depending on illumination. The tentacles of some specimens of *S. haddoni* do move like those of *S. gigantea* when illuminated strongly. It is possible that *S. gigantea* hybridizes with *S. haddoni.*

Natural Habitat: In shallow lagoon environments on rock or in sand or mud, with strong illumination. Sometimes abundant on intertidal mudflats. At low tide they experience stagnant conditions and may even be partly emersed, though they can withdraw into the wet mud/sand. At these times they may experience very strong illumination during the day or reduced salinity during rainstorms. When the tide comes in they are exposed to strong currents that carry numerous food items directly in their path. At high tide they may be in water 10 feet (3 meters) or more deep, though they were nearly exposed at low tide. This means that the light field varies a lot. The temperature also varies with the tide cycle.

Aquarium Care: Delicate. Difficult to keep, but can be hardy once established under the right conditions. This anemone suffers in shipping and often contracts fatal systemic bacterial infections as a result. Treat newly imported anemones with Neomycin at ca. 10 ppm and provide adequate water circulation. Chloramphenicol may be a more effective alternative drug, though it is difficult to obtain and toxic to humans, see chapter eleven. Ideally each anemone should be given a clownfish immediately. The fish seem to stimulate the flaccid anemone back to health. Give very strong light and moderate to strong water motion (at least intermittently). The aquarium should have a sand bottom with some small and some large rocks, since these anemones can occur in the sand or up on rocks over the sand. Must have clownfish partner for best success. *Amphiprion percula* and *A. ocellaris* are best choice. The clownfish will "feed" the anemone, but healthy anemones are very sticky and will take some food items including worms and small pieces of chopped fish or crab. May also be a suspension feeder (Barnes, 1980) that captures plankton via nematocysts and mucus on the surface of its oral disc, passing the trapped food via cilia and tentacle movement to the mouth. When placing the anemone in the tank it is best to put it on rock, not sand, in strong water motion. It will immediately stick to the rock and begin to "walk" to a suitable site, usually staying where the water motion is fairly strong, sometimes digging its column into the sand, sometimes not. If *S. gigantea* is initially placed on sand with little water motion the base and column are prone to contracting a lethal rotting bacterial infection. However, if the anemone crawls (not just falls) to a sandy bottom and plants itself it will usually thrive.

Reproduction: Separate sexes expected. Asexual reproduction not reported in the scientific literature, but we report here (in chapter four) that this anemone can reproduce by longitudinal fission and budding. Collectors who know where to look report finding small anemones downstream of beds where the large ones occur. This suggests sexually produced offspring. It is possible that after fertilization by male gametes released into the water, the resulting larvae or small anemones are brooded by the female and then released. However, no one has seen such larvae or small anemones released in captivity from newly imported specimens, suggesting that fertilization may be external. It is also possible that some of the small anemones are the product of budding.

Scientific Name: *Stichodactyla haddoni* (Saville-Kent, 1893)

Common Name: Saddle Anemone, Carpet Anemone

Colour: Green, gray, brown, blue, purple, pink, fluorescent orange. There are often pale stripes on the oral disk, and some tentacles with different colours and length from the rest.

Distinguishing Characteristics: Very sticky. Oral disc up to 80 cm maximum, usually about 40 cm if spread flat, but the typical habit is with folded margins, hence the name saddle anemone*. Has small non-adhesive verrucae on the upper part of the column, usually the same colour as the column but occasionally pink or purplish. Tentacles bulbous usually, with blunt swollen tips. When the tentacles are uniformly swollen *S. haddoni* appears much smoother than the other carpet anemones.

*The name saddle anemone also refers to the fact that the Saddle anemonefish, *Amphiprion polymnus*, prefers it.

Similar Species: *Stichodactyla haddoni* is most similar to *S. mertensii*, particularly when it occurs on rock but it can also be confused with *S. gigantea*. *Stichodactyla haddoni* usually occurs in sand, like *S. gigantea*. *Stichodactyla haddoni* has a more strongly folded oral disc, and shorter tentacles usually (except those around the mouth and the margin of the oral disc). *Stichodactyla gigantea* has distinctively "vibrating" tentacles. Although it is not reported to do so, *S. haddoni* may occasionally vibrate its tentacles, particularly under strong illumination. It is possible that *S. gigantea* and *S. haddoni* hybridize.

Natural Habitat: Most common in sand, gravel or mud in shallow water. Occasionally on reef slopes to considerable depth. J. Sprung photographed a large *S. haddoni* found by Ann Fielding on a reef slope attached to coral rock at over 110 foot depth. In sand the typical anemonefish is *A. polymnus*, which vigorously defends it's host by getting in the diver's face and barking. On the reef *S. haddoni* is usually populated by *A. clarkii*. Other anemonefishes known to associate with this anemone are *A. akindynos*, *A. chrysogaster*, *A. chrysopterus*, and *A. sebae* (Fautin and Allen, 1992).

Aquarium Care: *Stichodactyla haddoni* is the easiest of the carpet anemones to care for. The aquarium should have a sand or gravel bottom with some rocks. Lighting should be strong. The velocity of water motion is not critical, though it should not be very strong except intermittently. Feed chopped fish, worms, clam, snails, or shrimp at least a few times per month. May also be a suspension feeder (Barnes, 1980) that captures plankton via nematocysts and mucus on the surface of its oral disc, passing the trapped food via cilia and tentacle movement to the mouth. When these anemones are available quite a variety of colours and patterns can be found. A whole display of them would make a spectacular aquarium! The clownfishes best suited to this anemone are *A. polymnus*, *A clarkii*, and *A. sebae*, though a few other clownfish do naturally occur with it and more will adapt to *S. haddoni* in captivity. *Amphiprion polymnus* should never be kept without this anemone! The two are practically inseparable. *Dascyllus trimaculatus* also associates with this anemone. The stunning and uncommon blue and purple colour morphs require especially intense light, and are likely to fade unless maintained under strong metal halide or VHO fluorescent light. The rare fluorescent orange variety may prefer light with emphasis of blue and green wavelengths.

Stichodactyla helianthus in the natural habitat. H. Feddern.

Reproduction: Separate sexes expected. Asexual reproduction not reported in nature, but it is likely that this anemone can reproduce by longitudinal fission. Dr. Ron Shimek reported to us that a specimen spawning in his aquarium may have been a simultaneous hermaphrodite. He found huge numbers of eggs, milky water but could not find active sperm. It is possible that only eggs were released.

Scientific Name: *Stichodactyla helianthus*

Common Name: Sun Anemone, Atlantic Carpet Anemone

Colour: golden brown, green, yellow

Distinguishing Characteristics: Very sticky. Disc diameter usually about 14 cm, up to about 30 cm. Forms large stands of clonemates by transverse fission, and it can be hard to distinguish where one anemone ends and the next begins.

Similar Species: Similar to *S. haddoni* from the Indo-Pacific, but *S. helianthus* has larger, less numerous tentacles. The large round tentacles make this anemone look like a giant polyp of the corallimorpharian *Ricordea florida*.

Natural Habitat: Reefs and hardbottom backreef areas in Florida and the Caribbean, usually in shallow water with strong illumination and occasional surge or strong tidal currents. Sometimes in seagrass beds. Often associated with the shrimp *Periclimenes yucatanicus* and other *Periclimenes* spp.

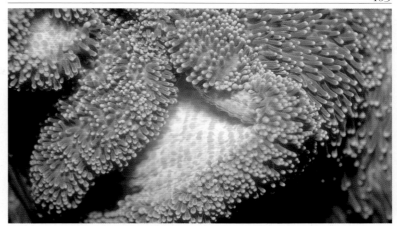

Stichodactyla mertensii often has colourful verrucae. J. Sprung

Aquarium Care: Give strong light and water motion. Feed pieces of shrimp or fish about once or twice per week. *Amphiprion percula* will sometimes accept this anemone as a host, though sometimes the anemone will accept clownfish as a meal! We don't recommend this anemone for reef aquaria since it regularly wanders and will sting neighbors.

Reproduction: Separate sexes expected. Asexual reproduction for this anemone is common in nature, most often by longitudinal fission. Asexual reproduction in this anemone allows it to form stands of clones covering large areas of rock.

Scientific Name: *Stichodactyla mertensii* Brandt, 1835

Common Name: Carpet Anemone, Saddle Anemone, Merten's Carpet Anemone, Sri Lanka Carpet

Colour: Green, brown, with orange or pink verrucae.

Distinguishing Characteristics: Very large oral disc, up to more than one meter across. Verrucae on underside often orange or pink, longest tentacles close to the mouth.

Similar Species: Most similar to *S. haddoni* and *S. gigantea. Stichodactyla mertensii* grows larger than either and does not usually occur in sand. *Stichodactyla gigantea* has tentacles that constantly move by muscular contractions. *Stichodactyla haddoni* has shorter tentacles on the majority of the disc and occurs usually in sand. *Stichodactyla mertensii* is not so sticky as *S. gigantea* and *S. haddoni.*

Sometimes the verrucae are not colourful. J. Sprung

This Bluestripe clownfish is "snug as a bug" in his rug, a *Stichodactyla mertensii.* J. Sprung

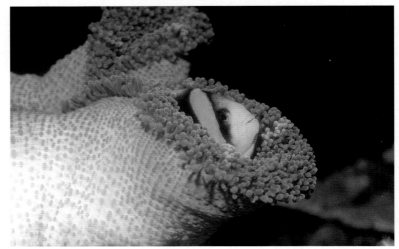

Natural Habitat: On upper reef slopes, exposed on the tops and sides of coral bommies or walls, with strong light and water motion.

Aquarium Care: Of the three Indo-Pacific clownfish host *Stichodactyla* species, this one is least commonly imported, so our experience with it is limited. We consider it a delicate species, like *S. gigantea.* It needs strong illumination and strong water motion, and should be placed up high on live rock. *Amphiprion chrysopterus* is an ideal partner. Feed small pieces of chopped fish or shrimp. May also be a suspension feeder (Barnes, 1980) that captures plankton via nematocysts and mucus on the surface of its oral disc, passing the trapped food via cilia and tentacle movement to the mouth.

Reproduction: Separate sexes. Probably the eggs are fertilized internally and brooded. We witnessed a male *S. mertensii* releasing sperm into the water in the Solomon Islands, a few days after the full moon at the end of November. Asexual reproduction is not reported. It seems likely that large individuals could divide in half, but we have never seen it nor is it reported to occur naturally. We saw a small, uplifted (partially separating?) tuft of tentacles on the oral disc of one large individual in the Solomon islands, but could not determine whether this was caused by an injury or if it was a type of asexual reproduction (budding). See chapter four for a photograph.

Family Thalassianthidae

Scientific Name: *Cryptodendrum adhaesivum*

Common Name: Pizza anemone. The differently coloured outer "rolled" ring of tentacles look like a crust. The common name is further developed in that the commensal shrimp that lives on the oral disc of this anemone (*Periclimenes brevicarpalis*) is called "pepperoni shrimp."

Colour: Often very colourful. Gray, green, brown, yellow, pink, blue. The outer ring of tentacles are usually strongly contrasting in colour or shade. The mouth is often bright pink, yellow, or green. Sometimes patches of tentacles are differently coloured than the rest on the disc, or tentacle stalks and tips differ in colour.

Distinguishing Characteristics: Two forms of tentacles: those on the main central part of the oral disc and those on a ring

Cryptodendrum adhaesivum, the "Pizza Anemone" with its peperoni shrimp, *Periclimenes brevicarpalis*. J. Sprung

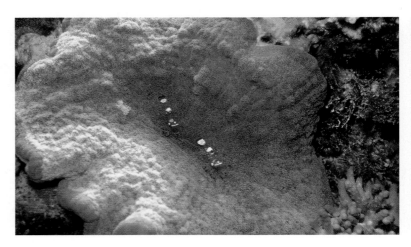

Cryptodendrum adhaesivum often has a brightly coloured mouth.
J. Sprung

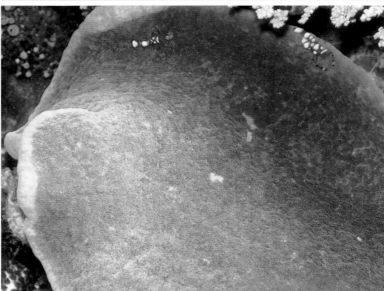

Cryptodendrum adhaesivum next to *Stichodactyla mertensii* in the natural environment. Apparently there is no harm to either from their proximity. Note the typically elongated tentacles around the mouth in *Stichodactyla mertensii*.
J. Sprung

around the edge of the disc. The tentacles of the central part of the disc are branched while those on the outer ring are short bulbs about 1 mm in diameter. At the extreme edge of the disc (often rolled underneath and so not always visible) is another row of branched tentacles, not as branched as those on the central part of the disc. Tentacles very sticky.

Similar Species: Can be confused with members of the genera *Stichodactyla*, *Heterodactyla*, and *Actineria*, which also have a carpet-like appearance. The rolled outer margin with tentacles different from those on the rest of the disc is distinctive. The tentacles of *C. adhaesivum* are very sticky but do not readily tear off as do the tentacles of *Stichodactyla* species.

Natural Habitat: Reef slopes and backreef margins or lagoons on coral rock with pedal disc attached deep between rocks and oral disc expanded flat over rock surface. Does not grow on top of coral bommies, but occurs instead usually partly shaded around the base of the coral bommies, though still receiving strong indirect light.

Aquarium Care: Easy to care for, but a powerful stinger that can catch fish and injure corals. Provide strong light and intermittently strong water motion. Feed chopped fish or shrimp a few times per month. The commensal shrimp *Periclimenes brevicarpalis* lives very well among the tentacles of this anemone. *Amphiprion clarki* lives with this anemone, despite its potent sting.

Reproduction: Not reported in captivity. Asexual reproduction via longitudinal fission is likely.

Scientific Name: *Heterodactyla hemprichii*

Common Name: None

Colour: Green, Yellow, Red, Purple. Grape-like nematospheres are usually purplish with green spots.

Distinguishing Characteristics: Nearly the whole surface of the oral disc is covered with tentacles. Grape-like clusters of nematospheres are located on the disc margins.

Similar Species: *Actineria* has different tentacles from *Heterodactyla hemprichi*, but otherwise is quite similar. Both have grape-like nematospheres. From a distance these anemones could

Heterodactyla hemprichii.
J. Sprung

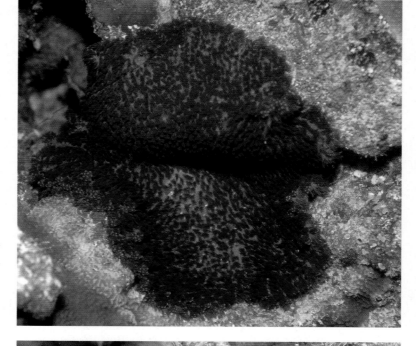

Heterodactyla hemprichii showing
the column with colourful verrucae.
J. Sprung

The distinctive nematospheres of
Heterodactyla hemprichii. J. Sprung

This odd specimen was
similar to but quite distinct from
Heterodactyla hemprichii. It may be
an *Actineria* sp. J. Sprung

Actinodendron plumosum is an anemone with a powerful sting.
J. Sprung

This anemone looks like a species of *Actinodendron*, but it is probably the related *Megalactis hemprichii.*
J. Sprung

be confused with carpet anemones of the genus *Stichodactyla*, or *Cryptodendrum adhaesivum*, but up close the distinct appearance of the tentacles is obvious.

Natural Habitat: Upper reef slopes in the Indo-Pacific. Sometimes in shallow seagrass beds. Usually attached in crevices between rocks with oral disc expanded up toward the light.

Aquarium Care: Not frequently imported. No record of its care in aquaria. It should be easy to keep, but one must take care since it may sting neighboring corals or anemones.

Reproduction: Not reported in captivity.

Family Actinodendridae

Species Names: *Actinodendron plumosum, Actinodendron arboreum*

Common Name: Tree Anemone, Hell's Fire Anemone

Colour: Brown, green, whitish, sometimes with pink.

Distinguishing Characteristics: Looks like a soft coral of the family Nephtheidae. Potent stinger.

Similar Species: *Megalactis hemprichii*

Natural Habitat: Backreef margins and lagoons among rock rubble in sand or in seagrass beds.

Aquarium Care: Easy to care for and fascinating to observe. Give strong light and a deep sandy substrate.

Caution: potential fish killer. May be kept with corals in a deep aquarium if sufficient distance is allowed, but these anemones will expand to very large size. Place on sandy bottom adjacent to a large rock, in strong illumination. Use extreme caution when handling this anemone as its sting is among the most powerful of all anemones. Wear protective gloves.

Reproduction: Not reported in captivity.

Thalassianthus aster
A. J. Nilsen.

Thalassianthus aster proliferates
rapidly in aquaria and stings other
invertebrates. Though quite beautiful, it is a pest. Note how much
the tentacles resemble those of soft
corals such as *Anthelia* or *Clavularia.* A. J. Nilsen.

Scientific Name: *Thalassianthus aster*

Common Name: None

Colour: Grayish white

Distinguishing Characteristics: Looks like a cluster of soft coral polyps, like *Anthelia, Xenia* or *Clavularia.*

Similar Species: None

Natural Habitat: Reef flats or backreef margins among rock rubble.

Aquarium Care: Strong light and water motion. This is a pest species that can be difficult to eradicate. It stings and kills many coral species. Nevertheless it is a beautiful anemone, worthy of a small display by itself.

Reproduction: Asexual reproduction is typical, via longitudinal fission and possibly pedal laceration. Sexual reproduction in this species has not been studied.

Chapter Eleven

Predators, Pests, Commensals And Good Guys

Aquarists often wonder whether a new creature they observe is a beneficial organism or a potential trouble maker. In this chapter we want to provide a broad overview of some of the creatures that make reef keeping difficult, some that make it easy, and some that just make reef keeping interesting.

Polychaetes

Reef aquarists know that certain types of polychaete worms can wreak havoc on other invertebrates. We discuss two particularly nasty worms here, and refer the reader to volume one for additional information about them.

The "Fire Worm" or "Bristle Worm," *Hermodice carunculata* is a voracious predator of gorgonians and anemones. They can also feed on other soft and stony corals. Search the aquarium with a flashlight late at night to spot them during their midnight eating binges, when they are easiest to catch. Don't touch this worm with bare hands! They bear an armor of fiberglass-like bristles that not only imbed in and irritate the skin but also convey a searing pain-inflicting poison.

Another bad worm is *Oenone fulgida*, a long orange guy that is active mostly at night feeding on mollusks. It eats snails by first covering them with a mucus blob that suffocates them. The worm then pops off the snail's operculum and eats the meat. As we described in volume one, this worm also bores holes in the shells of tridacnid clams, feeding on their tissues while they are still alive, and often killing them as a result.

Mollusks

Nudibranchs

While some nudibranchs do not survive in aquaria because of their specialized diets, other species can become pests because they eat corals and multiply in the aquarium.

Phyllodesmium longicirra
A. Storace

The polychaete *Hermodice carunculata* eating a gorgonian in an aquarium. The photograph was taken at night. Immediately afterwards Julian netted the worm. J. Sprung

This *Epicystis crucifer* bears the evidence of a recent encounter with *Hermodice carunculata*. Note the worm's shed bristles on its surface. The worm can consume an entire anemone overnight! The aquarist saved this anemone when he saw it being attacked. J. Sprung

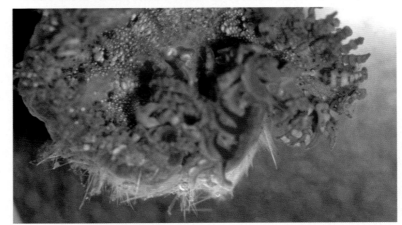

The polychaete *Oenone fulgida* was first mentioned in Volume One. There we described how it can suffocate a snail by exuding a mucus blob over it. It also bores holes into clam shells and can be devastating to tridacnid clams. This photo shows the worm preparing to eat a snail it has suffocated with mucus. J. Sprung

Top and middle
Cuthona poritophages feeding on
Porites cylindrica. Inspect newly
collected or imported colonies
closely for this nudibranch and its
egg masses. If this species is introduced into the aquarium it may be
difficult to eradicate. Freshwater
dips effectively kill the adults but
may not be as effective for killing
the eggs they lay on the coral.
J. Sprung

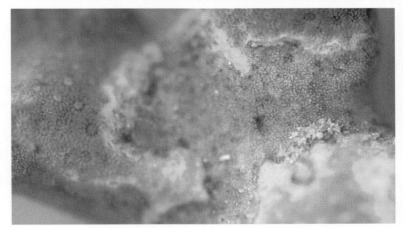

Phestilla melanobrachia, feeds on
the polyps of *Tubastraea* spp. stony
corals. They exhibit a range of
colours (e.g. orange, black or
yellow) that mimics the colour
morphs of *Tubastraea.* Inspect
newly collected or imported
colonies for this nudibranch. Also
look closely for white egg masses
at the base of the colony. If left
unattended, these nudibranchs can
strip the tissue off of a colony in a
few days. Photo taken at the Waikiki
Aquarium. J. C. Delbeek

Phyllodesmium longicirra
This nudibranch is "solar powered."
It feeds on *Sarcophyton* spp. and
retains and farms the zooxanthellae
within its own tissues. Its cerata are
solar panels, providing a high
surface area for capturing light. We
don't know whether this nudibranch
does any harm to *Sarcophyton*. It
may be that it harmlessly sucks out
some zooxanthellae once in a while
to recharge its supply. A. Storace

Another species, *Phyllodesmium
briareus*, feeds on Star Polyps
(*Pachyclavularia* (*Briareum*)
violacea) and is occasionally
imported with colonies. We have
maintained them together and
found that they were not particularly
harmful to the star polyps as long
as there were not too many nudibranchs, which tended to cause the
star polyps to remain closed.
A. J. Nilsen

These eggs are from the soft coral
eating nudibranch *Tritonia* (see
volume one). Members of that
genus can be devastating to many
different soft coral species. Be sure
to closely inspect all new acquisi-
tions for egg masses! J. Sprung

Snails

There are some snails that can quickly consume coral and anemone tissue as well. In volume one we discussed snails that are parasites on tridacnid clams, and the subject was also covered thoroughly by Knop (1996). We show here another possible parasite on tridacnids, but we haven't been able to identify it or even prove that it is harmful. It may be simply a herbivore, but we suspect it is harmful to tridacnid clams, based on the large numbers we have seen on the shells of newly imported clams sometimes.

Drupella cornus is a coral predator. These photos show the destruction it can cause, something like the effect of the Crown of Thorns Sea Star. These photos were taken at the Ningaloo reefs off Western Australia, where these snails have had population explosions that devastated Acroporid corals in some areas. P. Baker

Drupella cornus P. Baker

This *Epitonium* sp. a type of wentletrap snail, feeds exclusively on *Tubastraea*. Check newly imported or collected colonies for this snail and its similarly coloured egg masses. J. Sprung

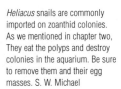

Heliacus snails are commonly imported on zoanthid colonies. As we mentioned in chapter two, They eat the polyps and destroy colonies in the aquarium. Be sure to remove them and their egg masses. S. W. Michael

These unidentified snails were found on newly imported Red Sea *Tridacna maxima* clams. Whether these are parasitic is unknown, but when faced with the possibility of damage to a precious specimen it is always best to err on the side of caution and remove the questionable hitchhikers! J. C. Delbeek

Cyphoma spp. snails are predators of Caribbean photosynthetic gorgonians. The rarer species on top, *C. signatum*, feeds preferentially on *Plexaurella* spp. In the natural habitat it causes more damage than the common *C. gibbosum*, by actually stripping away the coenenchyme, exposing the gorgonin; *Cyphoma gibbosum* below, only eats the polyps (Ruesink and Harvell, 1990). In aquaria both species strip away and eat the coenenchyme, and they will feed on more species than they normally do in the wild, so they cannot be maintained safely with gorgonians, unless the aquarium houses an enormous number of gorgonians or they are replaced periodically. J . Sprung

Chances are when these eggs hatch they will release *Sarcophyton* eatin' varmints, probably the snail *Calpurnus verrucosus.* J. Sprung

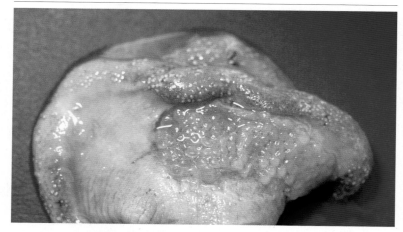

The ovulid snail, *Diminovula* (*alabaster?*), feeds on *Dendronephthya* and is occasionally found on newly imported colonies. In the natural environment how destructive these are is not known. Left in the aquarium, they typically consume the tissue of *Dendronephthya* very rapidly. J. C. Delbeek

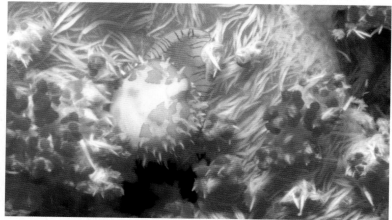

Vermetid snails

Often mistaken for worms, the sessile vermetid snails are common in reef aquaria. Large species such as the one pictured, erect long calcareous tubes from which they extrude filaments of mucus.

These long strands entrap detritus and plankton on which the snail feeds. Smaller species are found in large numbers on live rock and in filter systems. They can become problematic when they reach large numbers in pipes and filters, where they can significantly impede water flow. Otherwise they are harmless, and their proliferation indicates the aquarium is healthy.

Vermetid snails are harmless suspension feeders that cast out a mucus net to trap particulate and dissolved organic matter.
J. C. Delbeek

Anemones

We have some encouraging new information about the control of prolific stinging anemones such as *Aiptasia* spp. We hope that it won't be long before biological controls for these anemones are readily available and effective.

Anemonia sp. anemones can divide and gradually spread throughout the aquarium; they are also quite mobile. They are common on live rock imported from Fiji and Indonesia, and they sting corals.
J. C. Delbeek

These small anemones multiply prolifically by pedal laceration in aquaria. We were not able to get a positive identification for them but we believe they are the Turtle Grass anemone, *Viatrix globulifera*. Anemone-eating fish and specialized anemone-eating nudibranchs are probably the best control for them. J. Sprung

Berghia verrucicornis and its circular egg mass.
Photo by D. Sheehy and G. Moss courtesy of Jack Jewell, Marine World Africa USA

Aiptasia

Aquarists are always asking us how to get rid of the glassrose anemone, *Aiptasia*. A number of products have been marketed to help eradicate these pest anemones, but lately advanced aquarists have been investigating the use of nudibranchs that feed on *Aiptasia*.

Recently there has been some excited discussion among advanced aquarists regarding a nudibranch, *Berghia verrucicornis*, that eats *Aiptasia* anemones. While other *Aiptasia*-eating nudibranchs have been reported (see *The Reef Aquarium* Vol. One), this species is now being cultured so that in time it should be widely available as a biological control for this prolific reef-wrecking anemone. That is quite a breakthrough for the reef aquarium hobby! (For additional information about culturing this nudibranch, see Carroll and Kempf, 1990)

Other nudibranchs which may be useful for control of *Aiptasia* include *Baeolidia nodosa* and *Spurilla neapolitana*.

We mentioned using certain fishes to control *Aiptasia* in Volume One. The Copperband butterflyfish, *Chelmon rostratus* is a popular choice. More recently hobbyists have reported that brackish water Scats (Scatophagidae), which can be acclimated to full strength seawater, can also be employed for *Aiptasia* control, as can the related batfishes *Platax teira* and *P. orbicularis*. We must remind aquarists that any fish that eats *Aiptasia* may also eat corals.

Flatworms

In volume one we discussed ways to control the populations of acoel flatworms that proliferate vegetatively in reef aquaria. The most common species is the reddish *Convolutriloba retrogemma*. We offered the possibility that certain wrasses such as *Macropharyngodon* spp. and some gobies and dragonettes may eat them. Now we have found another predator that eats them.

Since the publication of Volume One we've discovered that certain nudibranchs may be the best natural predators for control of these flatworm plagues. In the book *Coral Reef Animals of the Indo-Pacific*, by Gosliner, Behrens, and Williams we read that nudibranchs of the genus *Chelidonura* feed exclusively on acoel flatworms, which lead us to believe there may be certain species that feed upon the flatworms that proliferate in aquaria, including *Convolutriloba retrogemma* and *Waminoa* spp. In a peculiar manifestation of the saying, "you are what you eat," *Chelidonura*

The red acoel flatworm *Convolutriloba retrogemma*. J. Sprung

Acoel flatworms commonly proliferate (vegetatively by fission) in blooms in which they cover corals and aquarium decorations. These blooms also occur in the natural environment, in lagoons in the Indo Pacific region. Here flatworms are coating the surface of a soft coral in the Solomon Islands. J. Macare

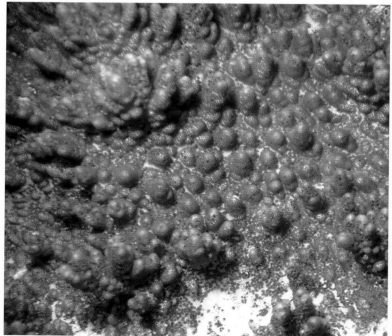

spp. nudibranchs have a shape that is quite similar to the shape of *Convolutriloba retrogemma*. The flatworm and the nudibranch both have "tails" and the shape of the "head" and overall silhouette is the same. A possible origin of this evolution of similar shape we will discuss shortly. Good candidates to try for flatworm control include *Chelidonura electra, C. inornata, C. amoena, C. castanea, C. flavolobata, C. fulvipunctata, C. livida, C. hirundinina, C punctata, C. sandrana, C. tsurugensis, C. pallida,* and the exquisite *C. varians,* which is black with electric blue lines. We have not had the opportunity to try all of these species, but are happy to report that one of the most beautiful ones, *C. varians,* quite readily eats the red flatworm *Convolutriloba*. It is fascinating to watch this slug eat the flatworms. It appears as if a little "tongue" is quickly everted to snatch the worms as they are sucked in. Upon closer inspection it can be seen that this "tongue" is actually a tube-like proboscis composed of two flaps curled together, and it is used like a straw. A hungry *C. varians* may slurp up nearly a hundred *C. retrogemma* per hour before it is satiated. It will later defecate large red fecal pellets.

The flatworms avoid predation by most fishes and other potential predators by accumulating in their tissues nasty pungent and probably toxic substances. They smell like a combination of iodine and putrid vegetables, not unlike *Acropora* spp. corals, and the red colour can leave stains on ones fingers. We suspect that the nudibranchs that eat these flatworms may further concentrate the chemicals from their prey, thus gaining the benefit of becoming distasteful or inedible. The stunning colour pattern of *Chelidonura varians* is no doubt aposematic, a warning to potential predators. In this regard, perhaps the shape of the nudibranch has evolved to protect the young of the species from predation. They may be mimics of the toxic flatworms they eat. Another species in the genus, *Chelidonura castanea*, is coloured exactly like the red flatworm (see the book *Nudibranchs and Sea Snails Indo-Pacific Field Guide* by Helmut Debelius).

Chelidonura varians is an exquisite sea slug that will certainly become popular among reef aquarists as they recognize that it eats the flatworm *Convolutriloba retrogemma* that proliferates to plague proportions in well illuminated reef aquaria. The slug is an excellent candidate for aquaculture.
J. Sprung

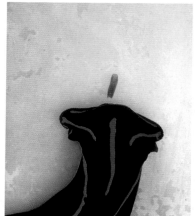

Chelidonura varians approaching the flatworm *Convolutriloba*.
J. Sprung

In the blink of an eye *Chelidonura varians* slurps up the flatworm.
J. Sprung

We regret to report that *Chelidonura varians* are not very long lived. We have seen them lay nests of eggs, which they spin like a cocoon, but we have not been able to raise any young. It is possible that one or more of the numerous species in this genus would exhibit better survival in captivity, or that a captive culture effort could be made to provide these nudibranchs in substantial numbers to the aquarium industry.

Some aquarists have devised treatments based on antihelminthic drugs to rid the aquarium of flatworms. These methods can be effective, but we must emphasize the need for extreme caution with such treatments! It is essential to siphon out the majority of the flatworm population before treating the tank. When the red flatworm *Convolutriloba retrogemma* dies, it releases highly toxic substances into the water. As we mentioned in volume one, the sudden death of a large population of flatworms in the tank will turn the water reddish brown, kill all of the fish and severely stress or kill the invertebrates.

Hydroids

There are several species of photosynthetic hydroids that sometimes proliferate in reef aquariums. These creatures are actually quite beautiful, and they are sometimes confused with soft corals because of their feathery polyps, brown colour and growth on stolon-like structures. Despite their beauty, many aquarists hate them! The reason is that these hydroids have a powerful sting that

Photosynthetic stinging hydroids that can grow like algae.
J. C. Delbeek

These look like hydroids but are probably the polyp stage of *Nausithoe* sp., a jellyfish. They are generally harmless and do not spread as rapidly as hydroid colonies do.
J. C. Delbeek

These beautiful hydroids can sting
and kill corals.
G. Recchia

After publication of the first edition
of this book we learned from Greg
Schiemer that a nudibranch,
Pteraeolidia ianthina, voraciously
consumes these hydroids and is by
far the most effective solution to
controlling them. The nudibranch
does not consume the entire
colony, however, it merely eats the
crowns, which are richly populated
by zooxanthellae. The nudibranch
incorporates the consumed zooxanthellae into its cerrata, where it
"farms" them to supply itself with
additional nutrition. The crowns
will grow back if there are no nudibranchs present. There are
numerous genera of nudibranchs,
primarily the Aeolids, that feed on
hydroids, but some other types of
nudibranchs also do, including
Facelina spp. and *Learchis* spp.
The presence of this food source
(the hydroids), generally considered a nuisance, opens a new
opportunity for cultivating several
types of nudibranchs in the
aquarium, something formerly
considered an impossibility.

affects or kills neighboring stony and soft corals, and tridacnid
clams. The sting of some species is strong enough to be felt by the
aquarist who accidentally touches them. To make matters worse,
the strong illumination we provide for the cultivation of healthy
corals, anemones, and tridacnid clams creates an environment
where these hydroids also proliferate, and some species grow

about as quickly as algae. So far no one has positively established a good control for these creatures. Most aquarists who have trouble with them resort to brushing them periodically with a toothbrush to halt their progress across the rock. This is only temporarily effective. Still, some tanks have trouble with them and some tanks don't. It is possible that certain limpets will eat them, and they may be the best natural control, but the limpets may also periodically eat soft or stony corals. If we discover a fish or invertebrate that is especially good at eating them we will report that in the next volume. In the meantime we offer keyhole limpets as a possible solution.

Sea Stars

There are several species of very tiny sea stars (*Asterina* spp.?) that proliferate vegetatively in reef aquaria. They divide spontaneously and the severed parts regenerate the missing legs quickly. In our experience these sea stars are generally harmless, but we have seen one species eat small polyped stony corals, while another species seems to eat coralline algae. Most species are scavengers that eat detritus. Because of the possibility that some species eat corals we view these sea stars with suspicion. It is wise to hold them in a separate tank with coral fragments to observe if they are well-behaved or not. We don't want to encourage aquarists to annihilate any creature they think might cause a problem. On the contrary, we hope aquarists will become interested in all of the little creatures that make a reef aquarium (and coral reef) a complex, diverse ecosystem.

These small sea stars (*Asterina* sp.?) are sometimes found in reef aquaria. What they are and what they do is unknown. They reproduce vegetatively by fission and can become quite numerous. They are probably harmless algal and detrital feeders, but some species do graze on small polyped stony corals. Photo taken at the Waikiki Aquarium. J. C. Delbeek

Brittle Stars

In live sand and from live rock we obtain many species of small brittle stars that are wonderful complements to the healthy community of a reef aquarium. They sort through the gravel and sand, picking out morsels of detritus as their food. They are important in aerating the sand layers and preventing the formation of dead zones beneath the rocks.

Brittle stars living in the gravel are excellent scavengers, sifters and detrital feeders. They are a beneficial part of the "live sand" community. J. Sprung

Coeloplana extends its nearly invisible long delicate tentacles to trap food from the passing water. J. C. Delbeek

Ctenophores

Often aquarists notice what appear to be long feather-like "hairs" floating in the aquarium. The "hairs" appear to retract and elongate sporadically. They collapse into a tangled ball and then unfurl into perfect order in mere seconds. These belong to the platyctene comb-jellyfish genus *Coeloplana*. These odd, flattened jellyfish resemble flatworms to the untrained eye. Some species are mottled in colour while others are almost transparent. Some species live attached to the bottom or on algae, while others live in association with soft corals and sea stars. The pictured *Coeloplana* is the one most often encountered by aquarists and it is often imported along with *Sarcophyton* spp.

Forams

Foraminiferans are primitive creatures closely related to amoeba. Unlike amoeba they build a calcareous home. Some forams are unattached and capable of crawling over the rocks, plants or sand. Many are sessile, attached to the rocks by the calcium carbonate they deposit. One common species on live rock is bright red, and it is often mistaken for a small colony of *Tubipora*, the pipe organ coral which has a skeleton with the same colour (see chapter 1). *Homotrema* forms small red burs and crusts on the underside of rocks. In living specimens one can see the tiny thread-like pseudopods extending from pores in the surface of the calcareous test. This harmless creature feeds on bacteria and fine detritus which it catches on the pseudopods. The occurrence and proliferation of little creatures like these in a reef aquarium are good signs that the ecological system is diverse and healthy.

Homotrema is a beautiful little sessile foraminiferan.
J. C. Delbeek

Biological Algae Control

The control of problematic species of algae is probably the most troublesome hurdle for new and veteran reef aquarists alike. We covered the topic quite thoroughly in Volume One, but we have some additional information to offer here, some in the captions and some in the text.

Dinoflagellates have coated the surface of this gorgonian, *Pseudopterogorgia elisabethae*, preventing it from opening. Such blooms can smother and kill gorgonians and other soft corals. These blooms can persist for several weeks but usually die back spontaneously. It is a good idea to swish the algae off of gorgonians to prevent it from injuring them. As we mentioned in volume one, the use of kalkwasser and protein skimming is effective in curbing the growth of dinoflagellates. J. Sprung

Black band disease is caused by a cyanobacteria, *Phormidium corallyticum*. It smothers the coral tissue as it grows. This gorgonian, *Pseudopterogorgia* sp. is unable to ward off the growth of *Phormidium*, and is losing tissue as a result. Without intervention the gorgonian will be completely consumed within a few weeks. Stopping the progress of this disease is quite simple: Siphon the algae off with a small diameter hose and lightly brush the exposed area to remove the remaining filaments of *Phormidium*. A brief dip in freshwater of about 30 seconds duration is also effective in killing the remaining filaments. After replacing the specimen in the aquarium, direct a billowing water current over it to encourage the tissue to grow back over the exposed skeleton.

The green alga *Bryopsis* is a chronic nuisance in many reef aquaria, though normally it only appears during the first six months after the aquarium is set up and gradually disappears. We discussed this problem alga in volume one, and offered some recommendations for controlling it, including the use of a sea slug, *Tridachia crispata*.

Another sea slug, *Elysia ornata* (Ophistobranchia, Elysidae) feeds on *Bryopsis* only, and other species in the genus are likely to also eat *Bryopsis*. The Mexican lettuce slug, *Elysia diomedea*, which looks like *Tridachia crispata*, is another possibility for the control of *Bryopsis*. In our experience the slugs do eat *Bryopsis*, but they are not very effective at controlling it when the algae is blooming throughout

Elysia sp. J. Sprung

Elysia sp. feeding on a clump of *Bryopsis*. J. Sprung

the tank. The slugs do not graze the algae like other herbivores do. They actually suck the juices out of the plant, leaving it mostly intact. One would probably need many of them to effect any significant control through this form of herbivory. Other genera of sea slugs worth investigating for their ability to eat green algae, possibly *Bryopsis*, include *Berthelinia, Polybranchia, Stiliger,* and *Cyerce.* The beautiful black and yellow species, *Cyerce nigricans* would certainly be a welcome addition to any aquarium, and it feeds on turf algae. To offer another alternative, we have seen long spine sea urchins, *Diadema* spp. graze *Bryopsis*, but usually they avoid it. The Pacific collector urchin, *Tripneustes gratilla,* also removes *Bryopsis*, but strips off coralline algae too, and it cannot remove *Bryopsis* from crevices or the interstices within dead coral heads.

The mystery of the sudden appearance and disappearance of *Bryopsis* seems worth noting to solve the problem of its existence in an aquarium. What we have noticed is that the availability of nitrite in the water seems to be an important limiting factor. When there is some available nitrite (sometimes below the level that common test kits can measure) this alga blooms. When the nitrite level is reduced, one can observe a marked decline in the presence of *Bryopsis*.

Hermit Crabs

Small hermit crabs of the genus *Paguritta* are sometimes encountered in newly imported *Porites* colonies. Occupying old worm tubes, they use their large feathery antennae to strain the passing water for planktonic food. Photo taken at the New York Aquarium for Wildlife Conservation. Such creatures are a real treasure to have in the aquarium as they offer a rare glimpse of the diversity of life on a coral reef. J. C. Delbeek

Probably the best herbivores for controlling algae in the reef aquarium are hermit crabs (see Shiemer, 1994). There are numerous small species that can be "put to work" in your aquarium to keep it free from problems with fast-growing algae. In order to maintain your hermit crab population be sure to provide a selection of empty shells for them to move into as they grow in size. Although we mention that these are herbivorous hermit crabs, they do eat other foods and will act as scavengers of uneaten fish food in the system. It is also important to note that the small (one inch, 2.5 cm) farm-raised tridacnid clams that are more frequently available to aquarists lately may be injured and killed by the otherwise harmless hermit crabs. The hermits first congregate on the clams' shells, eating attached filamentous algae. The presence of the hermit crabs on their shells stresses the clams, causing them to shut frequently. In time this weakens the clam to the point that it emits a stress-related strong smelling mucus, which really attracts the hermit crabs, and makes the situation much worse for the clam! When the clam emits this scented mucus the hermit crabs then begin to feed on its mantle tissue, and in a few hours there is no clam left, just a clean shell. It is safer to keep larger tridacnids with the hermit crabs, and small ones can also be kept with hermit crabs if they are fully acclimated and attached to a rock. Newly added, unattached small clams are the most vulnerable to attack.

From the Caribbean, tropical Atlantic, Eastern Pacific and Hawai'i we have several excellent species for use in the control of algae:

Paguristes cadenati.
J. Sprung

Red-Leg (Scarlet) Hermit Crab *Paguristes cadenati*
This bright red hermit crab has yellow eye stalks. It is found in the Caribbean almost exclusively on coral reefs. Rarely along rocky shores where other hermit crabs are common. It is most active at night. It usually stays on the rocks, but will sift through the substrate. This species is fond of red turf algae but will also feed on green hair algae. It grows to about one inch.

Red-Leg Hermit *Calcinus tibicen*
Bolder than the Red Hermit, as it will be active during the day. Grows to nearly two inches. It is found both on coral reefs and rocky shores in the Caribbean, sometimes in large numbers. Tends to stay on the rocks. Eats turf algae, but also actively scavenges for uneaten food.

Polka-dotted Hermit *Phimochirus operculatus*
This species has a distinctive polka-dot red and white, greatly enlarged claw, and blue eyes. The legs are orange and the enlarged white claw looks like a snail's operculum when it draws

into the shell. This species is also good at eating micro-algae in addition to turf algae. It will also eat coralline algae plates. Found on Caribbean coral reefs and occasionally along rocky shores. Never in large numbers. This is probably the most aggressive and active of the small hermits. They can literally run across the tank. Two specimens placed in the same aquarium may fight. Also sifts through the substrate. Grows to about one and a half inches.

Red-Stripe Hermit *Phimochirus holthuisi*
Quite similar to the Polka-dotted Hermit in shape and behaviour. Found on coral reefs. Eats algae and actively seeks out all dropped food particles, but is safe with corals. Found on Caribbean reefs, uncommon. Grows to about one inch.

Clibanarius tricolor, the "blue-leg" hermit crab is one of the best algae eaters for a reef aquarium. They stay small and move in packs to pick out filamentous algae from all of the nooks and crannies where snails can't reach. J. Sprung

Blue-Leg Hermit *Clibanarius tricolor*
Blue legs with red and white spots and black claws with white spots. Found in large aggregations in the sand or on rocks near shore in the Caribbean. Grows to about three-quarters of an inch. This is probably the best species for control of filamentous green "hair algae" and it is also effective for keeping the bottom substrate free of red slime algae (cyanobacteria).

Red-Leg Hermit *Calcinus californiensis*
This species with orange legs and a dark green body is found on rocky shores on the Pacific coast of Mexico, often in large aggregations. Grows to about one inch (2.5 cm).

Blue-Eye Hermit *Paguristes sanguinimanus*
This hermit has an orange body and bright blue eyes. Occurs on sand flats and patch reefs in aggregations. Eastern Pacific. Good micro-algae eater. Grows to about half an inch.

Blue-Spotted Hermit *Clibanarius digueti*
Reddish-brown legs with bluish spots. Found on rocky inshore substrates in the Eastern Pacific where it feeds on algae. Grows to only one-half inch.

The Left-handed hermit crab *Calcinus laevimanus*
This is a common crab along the shorelines of Hawai'i. It has an enlarged left claw, blue-eyes with orange eyestalks, brown legs

Calcinus laevimanus is a common intertidal hermit crab from Hawaii. It readily feeds on filamentous algae but should also be fed regular fish food. Photo taken at the Waikiki Aquarium. J. C. Delbeek

with white tips and orange antennae. The are commonly found along intertidal shorelines and often use turban shells. They feed on filamentous algae and reach about one inch in length.

The Banded-Leg hermit crab *Calcinus seurati*
Another common hermit crab along intertidal shorelines of Hawaii, it has blue eyes with bluish eyestalks, orange antennae and legs with white and black diagonal bands. Feeding of filamentous algae it grows to one-half and inch, and usually uses *Nerite* shells (pipipi in Hawaiian).

Coral Diseases

We want to discuss some types of coral disease that we did not cover in volume one. One is rapid tissue necrosis, which is actually a group of similar diseases, and the other is "gaping," for lack of a better word, a disease that affects large polyped corals.

Gaping is manifest by the wide opening of the mouth in large polyped corals. The mouth stays open while the coral tissue is deflated. Looking into the mouth one can see the mesenteries and the septa. As the condition worsens, the mouth expands wider and may even tear, and the skeleton often becomes exposed as the tissues within the gastric cavity disintegrate. We believe this disease is of bacterial origin, and that it is akin to the types of infections that quickly kill the sea anemones *Stichodactyla gigantea* and *Heteractis crispa*. The disease progresses more rapidly in the anemones, killing them in about a day, while corals may suffer with the condition for several days or even weeks before either succumbing or recovering.

Euphyllia divisa exhibiting the gaping condition which is probably caused by a bacterial infection. The white region is exposed septa and mesenteries within the gastric cavity. J. Sprung

For treatment we have not yet worked out a protocol, but we suspect that the chloramphenicol treatment proposed by Craig Bingman (see description under RTN, next) is effective in curing this condition.

Rapid Tissue Necrosis (RTN)

Recently as more and more aquarists are growing stony corals, particularly the small polyped stonies (SPS) there have been reports of rapidly progressing diseases that cause the coral tissue to disintegrate. Some hobbyists observing this for the first time confuse the condition with "bleaching," which is just a loss of pigment or photosynthetic zooxanthellae, a less serious ailment. The rapid loss of tissue leaving behind white skeleton is not bleaching, it is death of the coral due to a pathogen. It is contagious and can sweep through and kill the corals in an aquarium in hours or days. Hobbyists discussing this condition in forums via the Internet have been calling it rapid tissue necrosis or RTN.

In nature a condition of this sort called "white band disease" has been known for many years. More recently as scientists have become more aware of coral diseases, the white band condition has been subdivided into several distinct conditions. Although it is not yet proven, it seems apparent that the diseases affecting captive corals are the same as those in the wild.

The clear brown gelatinous blobs on this *Acropora* are destroyed coral tissue teaming with protozoans that eat zooxanthellae. The principal pathogen in this case has been identified tentatively as *Helicostoma nonatum* (see volume one page 328). J. Sprung

After the "brown jelly" is siphoned off, the exposed bare skeleton is flushed with a strong jet of water or brushed with a toothbrush, and then underwater epoxy can be applied as a bandage of sorts. The epoxy should be applied partly onto the living tissue to be sure to cover the exposed area. J. Sprung

One type of tissue necrosis that has been common in reef aquaria for years is caused by a protozoan, *Helicostoma*. It causes "brown jelly" infections in which the tissue is destroyed along a rapidly progressing front of gelatinous mass teeming with the protozoans, which consume zooxanthellae. It can affect small polyp stony corals, other stony corals, soft corals, zoanthids and corallimorpharia. It is a common cause of rapid death in *Euphyllia* species.

Other forms of tissue necrosis have more mysterious causes. It is a general opinion (ours included) that most are caused by bacterial infections, but little is known about this. Dr. Craig Bingman (pers. comm.) recently halted the progress of a particularly virulent tissue necrosis event in one of his aquariums by administering a dose of Chloramphenicol to the water. This antibiotic, while difficult to obtain because of its recognized hazards to human health, is quite effective in the treatment of pathogenic bacteria that live in saltwater.

One type of RTN essentially is identical to the white band disease in nature. White skeleton is exposed along a front of rapidly disappearing coral tissue. In front of the skeleton the tissue appears healthy, behind it the tissue is gone. Another type affects whole branches at once, and causes the tissue to drip off the skeleton. Often the tissue appears perforated before it falls off. This latter condition usually spreads very rapidly, and may wipe out all *Acropora* in the aquarium in a short period.

This is the perforated tissue variety of RTN, here affecting a colony of *Acropora microphthalma* grown in captivity. J. Sprung

In these closeup photos one can see that the loose tissue becomes quite like a network strung over the bare skeleton. J. Sprung

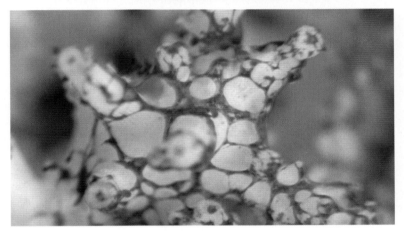

Dr. Bingman's recommended method for treating this condition with Chloramphenicol is outlined as follows:

The safest way to treat affected colonies is to put them in an isolation tank, such as a 5 gallon polyethylene bucket. Use a powerhead for water circulation and gas exchange in the bucket. A heater can be included as well, if necessary. Do not use an airstone, in order to avoid producing an aerosol of bacteria and antibiotic.

Before placing the coral in the Chloramphenicol bath, give it a 30 minute dip with 5-10 drops of full-strength Lugol's solution per liter of seawater. This harsh treatment is designed to allow as few bacteria as possible to experience selection for resistance factors against Chloramphenicol in the following treatment.

Therapeutic doses for isolation tanks are 10-50 mg of Chloramphenicol per litre. Corals survive 2-3 days at the higher doses, but they are not happy. Bingman does not recommend treating the aquarium since it is dangerous, and it is quite possible to crash the tank because the decomposition of dying bacteria from a sand bed can rapidly consume all the dissolved oxygen. Furthermore it is unrealistic to attempt to eliminate such bacteria from aquaria...they are ubiquitous. Nevertheless treatment of the colonies when an RTN event occurs can be effective.

A 100% water exchange with fresh antibiotic should be prepared daily on the isolation tank used to treat the corals.

The old antibiotic treatment water should be treated as follows before discarding it: Put 1/4 cup of bleach per five gallons of antibiotic laden water. Mix. Hold for several hours before you discard the solution down the sanitary sewer. The bleach will destroy the remaining antibiotic and any resistant bacteria present.

When you remove the coral from treatment, give it a 30 minute Lugol's dip at 10 drops of Lugol's per liter. This will surface-sanitize the coral and hopefully kill as many antibiotic-resistant bacteria as possible. Place the coral back in the aquarium.

Bleach the treatment bucket and the dip solution, following the dose-time schedule above.

Important Note: Chloramphenicol is not approved for ANY aquaculture application in the United States.

Failing to destroy the used antibiotic with bleach will result in an increase in Chloramphenicol resistant bacteria in the environment. The protocol above is not EPA approved. It will, however, destroy the chloramphenicol and any other residual organics in the water. Failing to bleach-treat the used water is extremely irresponsible.

An important factor in the occurrence of this condition is the growth of established colonies such that the water flow in the aquarium is reduced by drag on the branches. Overshading by these branches also reduces light to the lower portions of the colony, which often are the first to get white-band type symptoms. When there is such reduced water flow and light, the condition spreads most rapidly. The presence of strong water flow seems to help prevent the spread of the disease to healthy colonies that are bathed in strong currents. On the subject of preventing the spread of this condition, ultraviolet (UV) sterilizers do effectively kill water-borne bacteria, so we suspect that they may be very useful in controlling the spread of this condition, or even limiting its incidence, though they cannot be relied on to effect a cure in colonies already affected within an aquarium.

From this we gather a few important tips: 1.) Keep the corals well pruned to prevent overshading and flow reduction and add more water flow if necessary; 2.) Quarantine new colonies 3.) Always break off several branches from a new as well as old colonies to establish them in as many aquariums as possible to minimize the potential of losing the species should any of the branches become affected. 4.) A UV sterilizer may offer a safer environment for the small polyped stony corals that are so susceptible to RTN infection.

When the disease occurs, remove all affected colonies if possible. Healthy branches far away from the necrosis should be severed and maintained in aquaria separate from unhealthy branches. Underwater epoxy can be used as a band-aid at the progressing front of tissue necrosis, and this may halt the progression of the disease. This does not always work on corals with porous skeletons such as *Acropora* since the bacteria can move within the corals as well as along its surface. Direct an evenly distributed (not a jet-stream), increased water flow over affected colonies if they cannot be removed from the aquarium, but break and remove as many affected branches as possible to avoid spreading the pathogen through the aquarium in large amounts.

Dr. Bingman and Terry Siegel have correctly recognized that this condition has serious implications for the reef keeping hobby as a whole: aquarists who have invested a fortune acquiring rare and colorful *Acropora, Seriatopora, Pocillopora,* and other small polyped species risk losing everything, and this can easily result in many hobbyists getting out of the hobby. We can't stress enough how important it is to maintain these species in several aquariums to be able to re-establish species that can easily be lost to disease when maintained in just one aquarium.

We are reminded of Martin Moe's assertion, "Now that serious marine aquarists have a better understanding of what is required..., and access to the equipment that can provide good marine environments for many invertebrates, a lot of the more mysterious problems that we encounter are probably caused by bacteria." This statement precedes a series of fascinating accounts that Martin noticed "popped out at (him) over the years," all cleverly juxtaposed in his revised edition of *The Marine Aquarium Handbook* (Moe, 1992). The accounts relate his own experience and that of other aquaculturists and aquarium hobbyists in the management, with antibiotic treatments, of mysterious rapid mortalities in fishes and invertebrates, some caused by bacteria in the genus *Vibrio*. This section is one of many gems in this book. If Martin makes any further revisions to it he should include the experience of RTN as another example of bacteria causing devastatingly rapid mortality.

An article by Mike Paletta in the Fall 1996 issue of SeaScope and in the May 1997 issue of Aquarium Fish Magazine discusses the occurrence of "bleaching" in small-polyped stony corals and proposes a pathogen, *Vibrio* spp. bacteria. Lo and behold the same bad guys Moe discussed. Paletta's article was particularly interesting because it highlights an important error of detail that exists in both the scientific and aquarium hobbyist communities. This error surrounds the use of the term "bleaching." It is unfortunate that this word was chosen since it does not precisely convey the meaning of the several maladies that affect corals, causing them to become pale. What is causing the whitening? Are the corals losing tissue or just pigment? The question of the difference between the two options can be more basically asked: are the corals dead or just faded? Quite a difference! In large polyp fleshy corals there is no confusion since the tissue is very obvious. In the small polyped corals there is considerable confusion since the tissue is rather thinly covering the skeleton. In these so-called "bleaching" events the corals are dying fast from tissue destruction, not from losing pigment. The title of Paletta's first article should not have been "Bleaching of Small Polyp Stony Corals in Aquaria." It should have been "Rapid tissue loss and death in Small-Polyped Stony Corals in Aquaria."

In general, scientific articles describing "bleaching" refer to the loss of pigment, not tissue. This malady is quite different from RTN, is seldom fatal, and has numerous causes. However, it is likely that even scientists could make the same error in judgment that aquarists make about small polyped stony corals, especially when compiling statistics about "coral bleaching" based on the observations of other people around the world. When divers report bleaching events do they really know how to distinguish loss of pigment from loss of tissue?

Could anoxic sites promote the development of pathogenic strains of bacteria such as *Vibrio* spp.? We can't say for sure but there could be a connection. Elevated temperature (associated with both bleaching and tissue loss events in the wild) reduces oxygen solubility in the water and therefore increases the possibility of anoxic conditions in the substrate. In nature the warm season is usually also the calm season, which further increases the chance of anoxia in the substrate in the natural environment, or brings the anoxic condition closer to the substrate surface. If an anoxic environment is a breeding ground for pathogenic bacteria, then hot and calm water are dangerous conditions for corals sensitive to bacterial diseases. Coincidentally (?) coral diseases in the natural environment seem to be most prevalent in the warmer months.

Lately there has been a lot of publicity in the news about tissue necrosis diseases in corals, including the long recognized "white band" disease and more recently discovered similar conditions such as "white pox" described by Dr. Jim Porter based on affected colonies of *Acropora palmata* off Key West. The news media has reported these conditions, usually associated with the need for conservation and protection from human influences (which probably have absolutely nothing to do with these diseases). At the same time avid aquarists have been writing their experience and hypotheses in E-mail communications. Mike Paletta, Terry Siegel, Stanley Brown, Bruce Carlson, Craig Bingman, Bob Stark, Larry Jackson, Greg Schiemer, and Greg Cook among others have offered interesting perspectives and described their personal experiences, losses and successes, sharing with us their views about this condition. The combined pool of experience of these people and other aquarists is an invaluable resource for scientists studying these diseases. At the moment scientists haven't got a clue about the causes of tissue necrosis diseases, if the newspaper articles are reporting their opinions accurately.

Although we have attempted to provide an especially informative text in this volume (and we know we've succeeded with that goal), it became apparent as we did the research for this book that we were only scratching the surface. So little is really known about these creatures. We know that as aquarists continue to share their ideas and publish their observations about reef aquariums, the understanding of a great many of the mysteries of coral reefs and the way their inhabitants live will be revealed.

Chapter Twelve

Spectacular Reef Aquariums from Around the World

In Volume One we featured some photographs of reef aquariums from around the world. This was a popular section of the book, so we decided to do it again in Volume Two. We were amused to discover that the appearance of reef tanks has markedly transformed in the few years since our first book was published. The trend lately is to have a reef aquarium full of small-polyped stony corals. Volume Two is about soft corals and anemones, so the aquarium photographs here tend to emphasize the wrong creatures for this book!

While the small-polyped stony corals are certainly challenging to grow and colourful, they lack the fluid motion provided by swaying soft corals or anemones, which can be more interesting to observe. We hope that the information provided in this book stimulates a renewed interest in the great variety of soft corals, anemones, and anemone-like creatures that really provide interesting movement and diversity of shape to a reef aquarium community.

With this tour of beautiful reef tanks we hope to inspire the reader to develop new ideas about reef aquarium construction and the communities established within a reef aquarium.

This 180 gallon reef aquarium owned by Tom Robinson features a nice mix of soft corals, stony corals, zoanthids, and coral-limorphs. Tom's daughter Kathleen has learned a lot about coral reefs by studying the tank. J. Sprung

Greg Schiemer's reef aquarium with many very colourful small polyped stony (SPS) corals and a few soft corals. J. C. Delbeek

A reef aquarium by Joe Yaiullo. J. C. Delbeek

Overview of a section of the reef aquarium of Tony Vargas. J. C. Delbeek

A closeup of a section of the reef tank of Tony Vargas. J. Sprung

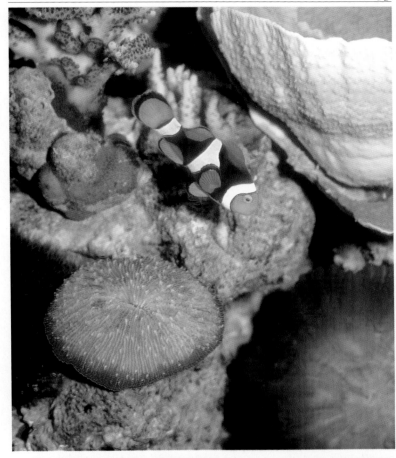

One of Terry Siegel's reef aquariums. G. Schiemer

One of Larry Jackson's reef
aquariums with a nice diversity of
life. L. Jackson

A section of the reef aquarium of
Daniel Ramirez. J. Sprung

Part of one of the show aquariums
at Biotope Aquaristik, near Cologne
Germany. The aquarium features
nice colonies of soft corals and
corallimorphs and rare fish such as
this *Bodianus* sp. J. Sprung

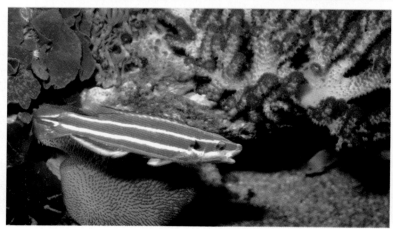

Julian Sprung's 60 gallon reef aquarium with Caribbean photosynthetic gorgonians.
J. Sprung

More information about the next group of tanks can be obtained by visiting the Waikiki Aquarium homepage on the world wide web: www.mic.hawaii.edu/aquarium.

The 1900 L (500 gal) surge coral display is the newest live coral display at the Waikiki Aquarium. Established in September 1996, it replaced a smaller (950 L/250 gal) surge coral tank. Many of the corals from the previous display were placed in this tank. Several of these had grown substantially such as the *Platygyra* and *Lobophyllia* spp. visible in the picture. Some of these corals are 5 or more years old. This is a completely closed system using a downdraft skimmer, a chiller, two surge towers for water movement, a calcium reactor and two 400 W 20000K metal halides plus natural sunlight for lighting. J. C. Delbeek

This 950 L (250 gal) tank contains some of the oldest corals on display at a public aquarium. The large *Goniopora* sp. that dominates the left side of the tank was collected in Palau in 1980 and has grown into several separate heads. In the center of the tank is a 17 year old *Euphyllia ancora* from Palau. The 5 *Heliofungia* on the bottom of the tank are over 9 years old and the green *Sandalolitha* are (female) 15 and (male) 7 years old. The large specimens of *Sarcophyton* on the right are offspring of the original collected over fifteen years ago. The gorgonian, *Rumphella*, collected in 1988 from Palau. The tank has live rock and a crushed coral substrate over an airlift driven undergravel filter. There is a slow trickle of seawater from a saltwater-well, a small external pump and an additional powerhead for creating good current within the tank. Lighting: two 400 W 20000K metal halide lamps and direct natural sunlight in the afternoon. J. C. Delbeek

This 950 L (250 gal) tank at the Waikiki Aquarium features the oldest aquacultured *Tridacna* clams in captivity. The *T. gigas* in the center is 20 years old, obtained from the MMDC in 1982. The two specimens on either side were obtained as juveniles also in 1982. Two *Goniopora* sp. in the tank are over 7 years old. The tank consists of several pieces of live rock and crushed coral gravel over an airlift undergravel filter. It has a slow trickle of seawater from a saltwater-well and an external pump for creating mild current within the tank. Lighting: two 400W 20000K metal halide lamps and direct natural sunlight in the afternoon J. C. Delbeek

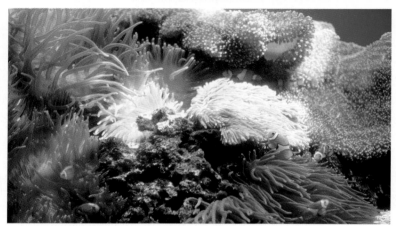

This 950L (250 gal) 5 year old exhibit houses 13 sea anemones. Nine *Entacmaea quadricolor* arose via fission from a specimen collected in 1980 in Palau. They spawn every April (see chapter four). Other specimens include a thirteen year old *Stichodactyla mertensii* collected in Fiji in 1984, two *Macrodactyla doreensis* and two *Heteractis magnifica*. The tank has several pieces of live rock and crushed coral over an airlift driven undergravel filter, with a slow trickle of seawater from a saltwater-well. An external pump creates good current within the tank. Lighting: two 250 W 5500 K metal halides and natural sunlight in the morning. J. C. Delbeek

The Edge of the Reef is a 26600 L (7000 gal) outdoor exhibit that reconstructs a typical Hawaiian shoreline. Established in 1987, it contains many of the original fish and corals. Large heads of *Montipora verrucosa* and *Porites lobata* have grown. The *Montipora* spawns each June a few days after the new moon. Filtration: 3 rapid sand filters and 3- 2HP pumps. Water jets in the walls of the exhibit provide circulation and a 950 L (250 gal.) surge tower empties every five minutes. Natural seawater enters the filtration system at the rate of 2280 L/h (600 g/h) and the exhibit overflows to the ocean as well as recirculating through the sand filters. J. C. Delbeek.

A small portion of Bob and Debbie James' magnificent reef aquarium in Toronto, Canada. J. C. Delbeek

Middle and bottom, This very colourful reef aquarium full of healthy growing stony and soft corals is the pride and joy of a very enthusiastic aquarist, Ricardo Miozzo, who lives in Brazil. A. Povoa

Top view of Julian Sprung's 15 gallon reef aquarium with a mangrove tree growing out of it. J. Sprung

One wing of the enormous U-shaped reef aquarium of David Saxby in London, England. The base rock in this aquarium was installed dry with cement to form a magnificent open and sturdy structure. The work was made much simpler because this rock structure was constructed before the front glass plates were siliconed in place. D. Saxby

Jose Mendez's outdoor aquarium for anemones. *Macrodactyla doreensis* and *Stichodactyla haddoni* thrive in this aquarium with *Amphiprion polymnus*, *Dascyllus* spp., *Protopalythoa,* and hermit crabs. The mangroves provide some shade. This aquarium uses the technique described on page 353, middle diagram. It has a large sump located in the shade (with a heater when necessary) to effect some temperature control. J. Sprung

Glossary

acontium (**pl. acontia**) - the middle lobe of the mesenteries in some anemones continues at the base of the mesentery as a thread-like structure which projects into the gastrovascular cavity. These filaments, which contain digestive enzymes, may be everted through the column wall or even the oral disc as a defensive or aggressive mechanism.

acrosphere - swollen tip of a tentacle, packed with nematocysts.

actinopharynx - the anemone's "throat," a sleeve-like structure that acts as a valve to retain water in the coelenteron.

alcyonacean - octocorals including stolonifera, soft corals, and gorgonians, but not including sea pens.

anastomosis - The fusion of lateral branchlets forming bridges between adjacent branches.

anthocodia (pl. anthocodiae) - The distal portion of a polyp, including the mouth and the eight tentacles. The anthocodia may be retracted into a calyx, the polyparium, cortex, or rachis.

anthostele - the thick, often sclerite stiffened lower part of the polyp into which the anthocodia may be withdrawn; calyx.

arborescent - tree-like octocorals that have a definite stalk (Nephthea) or stem (gorgonians).

asulcal - the side of the gastrovascular cavity opposite the siphonoglyph (sulcus).

autozooid - a polyp with eight well-developed tentacles that functions in feeding and defense. In monomorphic species it is the only type of polyp, in dimorphic species it is the larger, more conspicuous type of polyp.

axis - the internal skeletal support structure found in gorgonians and sea pens, composed of gorgonin, calcium carbonate, or both.

axis epithelium - the cell layer derived from ectoderm, which produces the horny skeleton (axis) of Holaxonia gorgonians.

biogenic - produced by once-living organisms.

One of the most beautiful of all the "mushroom anemones," the *Orinia torpida* form of *Discosoma* (*Rhodactis*) *sanctithomae* from Florida. J. Sprung

biomass - the amount of living matter in a volume or area of habitat.

biota - the living organisms in a habitat.

bur - rough prickly case around the seeds of certain plants. Deflated *Stereonephthya* spp. may appear to have clusters of burs on their branches. What someone says when it is cold outside.

calyx (pl. calyces) - a hard or stiff protuberance forming a tube or cup into which the soft distal part of the polyp retracts in some soft coral species. The calyx does not contract into the coenenchyme or stolon, though it may press flat when the colony is disturbed and fully contacted. A wart-like projecting anthostele.

capitate - unbranched colonies having a head or broad upper portion situated on a basal stalk.

capitulum - the broad rounded polyp-bearing "head" arising from the basal stalk. Also polyparium.

capstan - rod-like sclerite with two whorls of radially arranged tubercles plus clusters of protuberances at both ends.

catkin - a cluster of polyps forming a branch tip that, when contracted, has the appearance of the catkin of a willow tree. Characteristic of many members of the family Nephtheidae.

cf. - an abbreviation of "conferre," the Latin word meaning to compare. This is used with tentative species identifications, suggesting they should be compared with the formal description of the named species.

clavate - shaped like a club.

cnida (pl. cnidae) - capsular organelles ranging in size from about 10 to 100 μm long and containing a slender eversible tube. There are different types including spirocysts, homotrichs (=holotrichs), ptychocysts, and nematocysts.

cnidocyte - a cnida-secreting cell.

cnidome - portion of the tentacle containing the complement of cnidae.

coenenchyma - the tissue of a zoanthid that surrounds the polyps and consists of mesoglea that may have sand imbedded in it.

coenenchyme - the tissue of an octocoral that surrounds the polyps and consists of mesogloea with sclerites imbedded in it.

collar - a circular fold at the junction of the column and oral disc that covers the oral surface of the anemone when it contracts.

column - the cylindrical body of the anemone.

coelenteron - the hollow cavity inside of an anemone or polyp.

contractile - the polyps are capable of shrinking in size and folding the tentacles over the mouth, but unable to pull into the calyx or polyparium. Compare to retractile.

cortex - coenenchyme surrounding the medulla and containing the polyps in some gorgonian species.

dichotomous - as in the letter y, the point of division produces two branches.

digitate - having finger-like lobes.

digitiform - a colony that is unbranched but finger-like in shape.

dimorphic - having two different kinds of polyps, autozooids and siphonozooids.

dioecious - having separate sexes, individuals are male or female.

divaricate - branching.

ectoderm - tissue exposed to the external environment.

endocoel - if the septa (mesenteries) are paired (and in many anthozans, particularly those that clone they are not), the gut space between the two members of a pair is the endocoel.

endoderm - tissue exposed to the internal environment

exocoel - if the septa are paired (and in many anthozans, particularly those that clone they are not), the gut space between the pairs is the exocoel.

gastrodermal tubes (solenia) - gastrodermis-lined tubes that connect the gastrovascular tubes of all polyps in a colony. These are found throughout the coenenchyme and can initiate the formation of new polyps when they reach the surface just below the epidermis.

gastrovascular cavity - the cavity inside the lower part of the column, partitioned by longitudinal radiating mesenteries. This is the "stomach" area.

gastrovascular tubes - the portion of the polyp that extends within the coenenchyma of a colony.

glomerate - sphere-shaped.

glutinant - sticky.

gorgonian - an octocoral that attaches to the substrate by means of a basal holdfast, and having an internal axis or medulla.

gorgonin - the internal axis of many gorgonians is composed of this black or brown tough fibrous horn-like protein. Also secreted as part of the gorgonian's holdfast.

holdfast - the basal portion of a soft coral or gorgonian that attaches it to a hard substrate. May contain consolidated sclerites or, as in most gorgonians, be a sheet of gorgonin.

homotrichs - nematocyst type, commonly found internally on mesenterial filaments and externally in acrospheres.

hydrostatic skeleton - a structural support against which the muscular system can act, provided by control of water pressure.

littoral - the area between high and low tides on rocks, reefs, sand, mangrove roots, etc.

lobate - consisting of several stout lobes.

medulla - in some gorgonians, the inner support structure composed of consolidated sclerites; as opposed to an axis of gorgonin or solid calcium carbonate not from spicules. May occur as a layer around a central axis of gorgonin.

medusa - a bell-shaped swimming stage of some types of

cnidaria, i.e. jellyfish and hydrozoans. Anemones and corals do not have a medusa stage.

mesentery - one of many partitions arranged like spokes in the gastrovascular cavity, each consisting of two layers of gastro-dermis separated by a layer of mesoglea. The free edge is tri-lobed, and is called a mesenterial filament.

mesenterial filament - see mesentery. Often contain numerous cnidae and digestive enzymes.

mesogloea - tissue region that lies between the inner and outer tissue layer.

monomorphic - soft coral colonies possessing just one type of polyp. The polyps are called autozooids.

monotypic - a genus containing only one species.

needles - a type of needle-shaped sclerite.

nematocyst - a microscopic stinging body consisting of a capsule with an ejectable harpoon-like structure. Made by all Cnidaria for defense and prey capture, also for attaching to substrate.

nematosphere - a raspberry-like bundle of stinging tentacles located at the edge of the oral disc in some members of the family Thalassianthidae.

non-retractile - opposite of retractile.

octocoral - a member of the phylum Coelenterata (Cnidaria), class Anthozoa characterized by normally having eight pinnate tentacles surrounding the mouth of each polyp.

oral disc - the flat or convoluted tentacle-bearing surface of the anemone, with a central "mouth" (pharynx).

oviparous - egg laying. The eggs may be released or brooded.

parthenogenesis - development of an egg without fertilization.

pedal disc - the flat base or "foot" of the anemone, with which it attaches to the substrate.

peristome - mouth, region around the mouth.

phagocytosis - intake of small particles of food via invagination of the surface of the cell. See pinocytosis.

pharynx - see actinopharynx.

pinocytosis - intake of dissolved matter by cells via formation of invaginations on their surface that seal off to become liquid-filled bubble-like vesicles called vacuoles within the cell. The vacuole membrane then disintegrates, releasing the engulfed material in the cytoplasm (cytosol) of the cell. When this process involves the intake of solid food via invagination of the surface of the cell it is called phagocytosis.

pinnules - lateral branches on the tentacles of a polyp that give it a feather-like appearance.

polyparium - see capitulum.

protandry (**protandric**) - a type of hermaphroditism in which the individual is a functional male first, then develops into a functional female.

rachis - the upper polyp-bearing region of a pennatulacean (sea pen).

retractile - the state in which a polyp can be withdrawn into a calyx, the polyparium, the cortex or the rachis.

scapus - the body column of a corallimorpharian.

scapulus - the upper part of a corallimorpharian including the oral disc.

sclerite - spicule made of calcium carbonate imbedded in the tissue of most soft corals (octocorallia). Part of the skeletal/structural support element in soft corals.

septum - a section of tissue separating two spaces.

siphonoglyph (**sulcus**) - a ciliated longitudinal groove at one or both ends of the slit-shaped mouth of a sea anemone. The function of the siphonoglyph is to provide circulation of water into the gastrovascular cavity. This assists gas exchange and maintains the internal fluid volume, which helps, along with the muscular system, to maintain the hydrostatic skeleton.

siphonozooid - the smaller less conspicuous polyp in dimorphic octocorals; responsible for driving water currents through large, fleshy octocorals.

solenia - see gastrodermal tube

sphincter - circular muscle that can be used to open or close the mouth.

spicule - skeletal element in soft corals composed of calcium carbonate. In sponges similar skeletal elements may be composed of silicon dioxide.

spirocyst - stinging cells or cnidae that have the distinction of being non-penetrating and glutinant.

stolon - ribbon or root-like growth extensions that adhere to the substrate and link the polyps in Stoloniferan soft corals such as *Clavularia* spp.

stoloniferous - octocorals that have the polyps linked on root-like growth extensions that adhere to the substrate.

sulcal - the side of the gastrovascular cavity closest to the siphonoglyph (sulcus) (see also asulcus).

supporting bundle - what appears to be a shield, cup or sheath below an individual anthocodia, composed of one or a few large sclerites. Typical of nephtheidae and also of Muricea spp. gorgonians.

terpene - Organic compound found in the volatile essential oils, having a strong odor. Manufactured by soft corals to discourage predation.

tubercles - wart-like projections on sclerites.

umbellate - shaped like an umbrella.

vegetative (**somatic**) embryogenesis - formation of embryos internally from pieces of somatic tissue.

viviparous - fertilization and development takes place inside female, nutrition of the larvae provided by the parent, and the developed offspring are released.

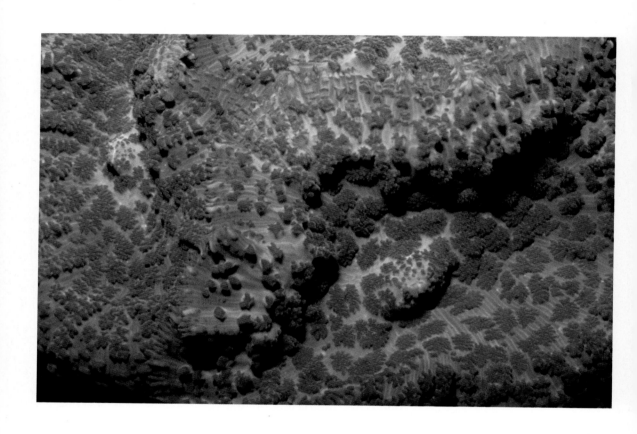

Bibliography

Abel, E. F. (1954) Ein Beitrag zur Giftwirkung der Aktinien und Funktion der Rand-seckchen. *Zool. Anz.*, 153, 259-268.

Abel, E. F. (1960) Liaison facultative d'un poisson (*Gobius bucchichii* Steindachner) et d'une anemone (*Anemonia sulcata* Penn.) en Mediterrane Vie et Milieu, 11, 517-531.

Abeloos-Parize, M. and Abeloos-Parize, R. (1926) Sur l'origine alimentaire du pigment carotinoide d'*Actinia equina*. *C.R. Soc. Biol.*, Paris, 94, 560-562.

Aceret, T.L., Sammarco, P.W. and J.C. Coll. 1995a. Toxic effects of alcyonacean diter-penes on scleractinian corals. *J. Exp. Mar. Biol. Ecol. 188:63-78.*

--------------, -------------------- and ------------. 1995b. Effects of diterpenes derived from the soft corals *Sinularia flexibilis* on the eggs, sperm and embryos of the scleractinian corals *Montipora digitata* and *Acropora tenuis*. *Mar. Biol. 122:317-323.*

Achituv, Y. and Y. Benayahu. 1990. Polyp dimorphism and functional, sequential hermaphroditism in the soft coral *Heteroxenia fuscescens* (Octocorallia). *Mar. Ecol. Progr. Ser. 64:263-269.*

Albrecht, H. (1977) Einige Beobachtungen an Anemonefischen in der karibischen See. *Bijdr. Dierkunde*, 47, 109-119.

Alino, P.M. and J.C. Coll. 1989. Observations of the synchronized mass spawning and post-settlement activity of octocorals on the Great Barrier Reef, Australia: Biological aspects. *Bull. Mar. Sci. 45:697-707.*

Allee, W. C. (1923) Studies in marine ecology: IV. The effect of temperature in limiting the geographical range of invertebrates of the Woods Hole littoral. *Ecology*, 4, 341-354.

Allen, G. R. (1975) *The Anemonefishes. Their Classification and Biology*, 2nd ed., T. F. H. Publications, Neptune City, New Jersey, 352 pp.

Amerongen, H. M. and Peteya, D. J. (1976) The ultrastructure of the muscle system of *Stomphia coccinea*. In G. O. Mackie (ed.), *Coelenterate Ecology and Behavior*, Plenum, New York, pp. 541-547.

Anderson, P. A. V. (1980) Epithelial conduction: its properties and functions. *Prog. Neurobiol.*, 15, 161-203.

Anderson, P. A. V. and Schwab, W. E. (1982) Recent advances and model systems in coelenterate neurobiology. *Prog. Neurobiol.*, 19, 591-600.

Anderson, S. L. and Burris, J. E. (1987) Role of glutamine synthetase in ammonia assimila-tion by symbiotic marine dinoflagellates (zooxanthellae). *Mar. Biol.*, 94, 451-458.

Annett, C. and Pierotti, R. (1984) Foraging behavior and prey selection of the leather seastar *Dermasterias imbricata*. *Mar. Ecol. Prog.* Ser., 14, 197-206.

Ansell, A. D. and Trueman, E. R. (1968) The mechanism of burrowing in the anemone, *Peachia hastata* Gosse. *J. Exp. Mar. Biol. Ecol.*, 2, 124-134.

Arai, M. N. (1972) The muscular system of *Pachycerianthus fimbriatus*. *Can. J. Zool.*, 50, 311-317.

Rhodactis cf. *inchoata* The Tonga blue mushroom. J. C. Delbeek

Arai, M. N. and Walder, G. L. (1973) The feeding response of *Pachycerianthus fimbriatus* (Ceriantharia). Comp. *Biochem. Physiol.*, 44A, 1085-1092.

Asada, K. and Takahashi, M. (1987) Production and scavenging of active oxygen in photosynthesis. In D.J. Kyle, C.B. Osmond and C.J. Arntzen (eds.), Photoinhibition, Elsevier Science Publishers, Amsterdam, pp. 227-287.

Ates, R. M. L. (1989) Fishes that eat sea anemones, a review. *J. Nat. Hist.*, 23, 71-79.

Atoda, K. (1974) Postlarval development of the sea anemone, *Anthopleura* sp. Sci. Rept. T=F4hoku Univ., 4th Ser., Biology, 20, 274-286 + 2 plates.

Atoda, K. (1976) Development of the sea anemone, *Haliplanella luciae*. V. Longitudinal fission and the origin of mono-, di- and tri-glyphic individuals. *Bull. Mar. Biol. Sta. Asamushi*, 15, 133-146.

Atrigenio, M.P. and P.M. Alino. 1996. Effects of the soft coral *Xenia puertogalerae* on the recruitment of scleractinian corals. *J. Exp. Ecol. Biol. 203:179-189.*

Ayre, D. J. (1982) Inter-genotype aggression in the solitary sea anemone *Actinia tenebrosa*. *Mar. Biol.*, 68, 199-205.

Ayre, D. J. (1983) The effects of asexual reproduction and inter-genotypic aggression on the genotypic structure of populations of the sea anemone *Actinia tenebrosa*. *Oecologia*, 57, 158-165.

Ayre, D. J. (1984a) The sea anemone *Actinia tenebrosa*: an opportunistic insectivore. *Ophelia*, 23, 149-153.

Ayre, D. J. (1984b) The effects of sexual and asexual reproduction on geographic variation in the sea anemone *Actinia tenebrosa*. *Oecologia*, 62, 222-229.

Ayre, D. J. (1984c) Effects of environment and population density on the sea anemone *Actinia tenebrosa*. *Aust. J. Mar. Freshw. Res.*, 35, 735-746.

Ayre, D. J. (1985) Localized adaptation of clones of the sea anemone *Actinia tenebrosa*. *Evolution*, 39, 1250-1260.

Ayre, D. J. (1987) The formation of clonal territories in experimental populations of the sea anemone *Actinia tenebrosa*. *Biol. Bull.*, 172, 178-186.

Ayre, D. J. (1988) Evidence for genetic determination of sex in *Actinia tenebrosa*. *J. Exp. Mar. Biol. Ecol.*, 116, 23-34.

Babcock, R. 1990. Reproduction and development of the blue coral *Heliopora coerulea* (Alcyonaria: Coenothocalia). *Mar. Biol. 104:475-481.*

Bach, C. E. and Herrnkind, W. F. (1980) Effects of predation pressure on the mutualistic interaction between the hermit crab, *Pagurus pollicaris* Say, 1817, and the sea anemone, *Calliactis tricolor* (Lesueur, 1817). *Crustaceana*, 38, 104-108.

Bak, R. P. M. and Borsboom, J. L. A. (1984) Allelopathic interaction between a reef coelenterate and benthic algae. *Oecologia*, 63, 194-198.

Balasch, J. and Mengual, V. (1974) The behaviour of *Dardanaus arrosor* in association with *Calliactis parasitica* in artificial habitat. *Mar. Behav. Physiol.*, 2, 251-260.

Batchelder, H. P. and Gonor, J. J. (1981) Population characteristics of the intertidal green sea anemone, *Anthopleura xanthogrammica*, on the Oregon coast. *Est., Coast. Shelf Sci.*, 13, 235-245.

Batham, E. J. (1965) The neural architecture of the sea anemone *Mimetridium cryptum. Amer. Zool.*, 5, 395-402.

Batham, E. J. and Pantin, C. F. A. (1950a) Inherent activity in the sea-anemone, *Metridium senile* (L.). *J. Exp. Biol.*, 27, 290-301.

Batham, E. J. and Pantin, C. F. A. (1950b) Phases of activity in the sea-anemone, *Metridium senile* (L.), and their relation to external stimuli. *J. Exp. Biol.*, 27, 377-399.

Batham, E. J. and Pantin, C. F. A. (1950c) Muscular and hydrostatic action in the sea anemone *Metridium senile* (L.). *J. Exp. Biol.*, 27, 264-289.
Batham, E. J. and Pantin, C. F. A. (1951) The organization of the muscular system of *Metridium senile. Quart. J. Microsc. Sci.*, 92, 27-54 + 2 plates.

Batham, E. J. and Pantin, C. F. A. (1954) Slow contraction and its relation to spontaneous activity in the sea-anemone *Metridium senile* (L.). *J. Exp. Biol.*, 31, 84-103.

Batham, E. J., Pantin, C. F. A. and Robson, E. A. (1960) The nerve-net of the sea anemone, *Metridium senile* (L.): the mesenteries and the column. *Quart. J. Microsc. Sci.*, 101, 487-510.

Battey, J. F. and Patton, J. S. (1984) A reevaluation of the role of glycerol in carbon translocation in zooxanthellae-coelenterate symbiosis. *Mar. Biol.*, 79, 27-38.

Battey, J. F. and Patton, J. S. (1987) Glycerol translocation in *Condylactis gigantea. Mar. Biol.*, 95, 37-46.

Bayer, F. 1973. Colonial Organization in Octocorals. *In:* Boardman R. S., Cheetham, A. H. and W. A. Oliver (eds.): *Animal Colonies: Development and Function Through Time* (pp 69-93). Dowden, Hutchinson & Ross, Inc. Stroudsburg, Pa., USA

------------ 1981. Key to the genera of Octocorallia exclusive of Pennatulacea (Coelenterata: Anthozoa) with diagnoses of new taxa. *Proc. Biol. Soc. Wash. 94:902-947.*

----------, Grasshoff, M. and J. Verseveldt (eds.). 1983. Illustrated trilingual glossary of morphological terms applied to Octocorallia. E.J. Brill and W. Blackhuys, Leiden, The Netherlands.

Bayne, B. L. and Scullard, C. (1977) An apparent specific dynamic action in *Mytilus edulis* L. *J. Mar. Biol. Ass. UK,* 57, 371-378.

Beattie, C. W. (1971) Respiratory adjustments of an estuarine coelenterate to abnormal levels of environmental phosphate and oxygen. *Comp. Biochem. Physiol.*, 40B, 907-916.

Bell, G. (1982) *The Masterpiece of Nature: The Evolution and Genetics of Sexuality,* University of California Press, Berkeley, 600 pp.

Benayahu, Y. and Y. Loya. 1983. Surface brooding in the Red Sea soft coral *Parerythropodium fulvum fulvum* (Forksål, 1775). *Biol. Bull. 165:353-369.*

-------------- and --------------. 1984a. Life history studies on the Red Sea soft coral

Xenia macrospiculata Gohar, 1940. I. Annual dynamics of gonadal development. *Bio. Bull. 166:32-43.*

-------------- and --------------. 1984b. Life history studies on the Red Sea soft coral *Xenia macrospiculata* Gohar, 1940. II. Planulae shedding and post larval development. *Bio. Bull. 166:44-53.*

---------------- and -----------. 1986. Sexual reproduction of a soft coral: synchronous and brief annual spawning of *Sarcophyton glaucum* (Quoy and Gaimard, 1833). *Biol. Bull. 170:32-42.*

--------------. 1995. Species composition of soft corals (Octocorallia, Alcyonacea) on the coral reefs of Sesoko Island, Ryukyu archipelago, Japan. *Galaxea 12:103-124.*

Bennett, L. W. and Stroud, E. (1981) Occurrence and possible functions of g-glutamyl transpeptidase in external epithelia of *Metridium senile. Trans. Amer. Microsc. Soc.,* 100, 316-321.

Benson-Rodenbough, B. and Ellington, W. R. (1982) Responses of the euryhaline sea anemone *Bunodosoma cavernata* (Bosc) (Anthozoa, Actiniaria, Actiniidae) to osmotic stress. *Comp. Biochem. Physiol.,* 72A, 731-735.

Beress, L. (1982) Biologically active compounds from coelenterates. *Pure Appl. Chem.,* 54, 1981-1994.

Beress, L., Beress, R. and Wunderer, G. (1975) Isolation and characterisation of three polypeptides with neurotoxic activity from *Anemonia sulcata.* FEBS Lett., 50, 311-314.

Bergmann, W., Creighton, S. M. and Stokes, W. M. (1956) Contributions to the study of marine products. XL. Waxes and triglycerides of sea anemones. *J. Org. Chem.,* 21, 721-728.

Bernheimer, A. W. and Avigad, L. S. (1976) Properties of a toxin from the sea anemone *Stoichactis helianthus,* including specific binding to sphingomyelin. *Proc. Nat. Acad. Sci.* USA, 73, 467-471.

Best, B.A. 1988. Passive suspension feeding in a sea pen: effects of ambient flow on volume flow rate and filtering efficiency. *Biol. Bull. 175:332-342.*

Bigger, C. H. (1976) The acrorhagial response in *Anthopleura krebsi:* intraspecific and interspecific recognition. In G. O. Mackie (ed.), *Coelenterate Ecology and Behavior,* Plenum, New York, pp. 127-136.

Bigger, C. H. (1980) Interspecific and intraspecific acrorhagial aggressive behavior among sea anemones: a recognition of self and not-self. *Biol. Bull.,* 159, 117-134.

Bigger, C. H. (1982) The cellular basis of the aggressive acrorhagial response of sea anemones. *J. Morphol.,* 173, 259-278.

Bigger, C. H. andHildemann, W. H. (1982) Cellular defense systems of the Coelenterata. In N. Cohen and M. M. Sigel (eds.), *The Reticuloendothelial System,* Vol. 3, Plenum, New York, pp. 59-87.

Bikfalvi, A., Binder, A., Beress, L. and Wassermann, O. (1988) Isolation and blood coagulation inhibition of a new proteinase inhibitor from the sea anemone *Anemonia sulcata. Comp. Biochem. Physiol.,* 89B, 305-308.

Bingman, C. (1995). The Effect of Activated Carbon Treatment on the Transmission of Visible and UV Light Through Aquarium Water. Part 1: Time-course of Activated Carbon Treatment and Biological Effects. *Aquarium Frontiers*.2:3. p 4.

Birkeland, C. 1969. Consequences of differing reproductive and feeding strategies for the dynamics of an association based on the single prey species, *Ptilosarcus gurneyi* (Gray). *PhD. Dissertation, Univ. of Washington, Seattle, WA.*

Bishop, S. H., Barnes, L. B. and Kirkpatrick, D. S. (1972) Adenosine deaminase from *Metridium senile* (L.), a sea anemone. *Comp. Biochem. Physiol.*, 43B, 949-963.

Bishop, S. H., Ellis, L. L. and Burcham, J. M. (1983) Amino acid metabolism in molluscs. In P. W. Hochachka (ed.), The *Mollusca. Vol. 1. Metabolic Biochemistry and Molecular Biomechanics*, Academic Press, New York, pp. 243-327.

Bishop, S. H., Klotz, A., Drolet, L. L., Smullin, D. H. and Hoffmann, R. J. (1978) NADP-specific glutamate dehydrogenase in *Metridium senile* (L.). *Comp. Biochem. Physiol.*, 61B, 185-187.

Black, R. and Johnson, M. S. (1979) Asexual viviparity and population genetics of *Actinia tenebrosa*. *Mar. Biol.*, 53, 27-31.

Blank, R. J. and Trench, R. K. (1985) Speciation and symbiotic dinoflagellates. *Science*, 229, 656-658.

Blank, R. J. and Trench, R. K. (1986) Nomenclature of endosymbiotic dinoflagellates. *Taxon*, 35, 286-294.

Blanquet, R. (1970) Ionic effects on discharge of the isolated and in situ nematocysts of the sea anemone, *Aiptasia pallida*: a possible role of calcium. Comp. *Biochem. Physiol.*, 35, 451-461.

Blanquet, R. S., Emanuel, D. and Murphy, T. A. (1988) Suppression of exogenous alanine uptake in isolated zooxanthellae by cnidarian host homogenate fractions: species and symbiosis specificity. *J. Exp. Mar. Biol. Ecol.*, 117, 1-8.

Blanquet, R. S., Nevenzel, J. C. and Benson, A. A. (1979) Acetate incorporation into the lipids of the anemone *Anthopleura elegantissima* and its associated zooxanthellae. *Mar. Biol.*, 54, 185-194.

Bodansky, M. (1923) Comparative studies of digestion III. Further observations on digestion in coelenterates. *Amer. J. Physiol.*, 67, 547-550.

Bohn, G. (1906a) Sur les courbures dues ela lumiere. *C.R. Soc. Biol., Paris*, 61, 420-421.

Bohn, G. (1906b) La persistance du rhythme des marees chez l'*Actinia equina*. *C.R. Soc. Biol., Paris*, 61, 661-663.

Bohn, G. (1908) L'epanouissement des actinies dans les milieux asphyxiques. *C.R. Soc. Biol., Paris*, 65, 317-320.

Bonnin, J.-P. (1964) Recherches sur la 'reaction d'agression' et sur le functionnement des acrorrhages d'*Actinia equina* L. *Bull. Biol. Fr. Belg.*, 98, 225-250.

Boothby, K. M. and McFarlane, I. D. (1986) Chemoreception in sea anemones: betaine stimulates the pre-feeding response in *Urticina eques* and *U. felina*. *J. Exp. Biol.*, 125, 385-389.

Boschma, H. (1925) The nature of the association between Anthozoa and zooxanthellae. *Proc. Nat. Acad. Sci.* USA, 11, 65-67.

Boury-Esnault, N. and Doumenc, D. A. (1979) Glycogen storage and transfer in primitive invertebrates: Demospongea and Actiniaria. In C. Levi and N. Boury-Esnault (eds.), *Biologie des Spongiaires, Colloques Internationaux du CNRS* No. 291, Centre National de la Recherche Scientifique, Paris, pp. 181-192.

Braams, W. G. and Geelen, H. F. M. (1953) The preference of some nudibranchs for certain coelenterates. *Arch. Neerland. de Zoologie*, 10, 241-264.

Braber, L. and Borghouts, C. H. (1977) Distribution and ecology of Anthozoa in the estuarine region of the rivers Rhine, Meuse and Scheldt. *Hydrobiologia*, 52, 15-21.

Brace, R. C. (1981) Intraspecific aggression in the colour morphs of the anemone *Phymactis clematis* from Chile. Mar. Biol., 64, 85-93.

Brace, R. C. and Pavey, J. (1978) Size-dependent dominance hierarchy in the anemone *Actinia equina. Nature*, 273, 752-753.

Brace, R. C., Pavey, J. and Quicke, D. L. J. (1979) Intraspecific aggression in the colour morphs of the anemone *Actinia equina*: the 'convention' governing dominance ranking. *Anim. Behav.*, 27, 553-561.

Brace, R. C. and Quicke, D. L. J. (1985) Further analysis of individual spacing within aggregations of the anemone, *Actinia equina. J. Mar. Biol. Ass. UK*, 65, 35-53.

Brace, R. C. and Quicke, D. L. J. (1986) Dynamics of colonization by the beadlet anemone, *Actinia equina. J. Mar. Biol. Ass. UK*, 66, 21-47.

Brace, R.C. and Reynolds, H.A. (1989) Relative intraspecific aggressiveness of pedal disc colour phenotypes of the beadlet anemone, *Actinia equina. J. Mar. Biol. Ass. UK*, 69, 273-278.

Brafield, A. E. (1980) Oxygen consumption by the sea anemone *Calliactis parasitica* (Couch). *J. Exp. Biol.*, 88, 367-374.

Brafield, A. E. and Chapman, G. (1965) The oxygen consumption of *Pennatula rubra* Ellis and some other anthozoans. *Z. vergl. Physiol.*, 50, 363-370.

Brafield, A. E. and Chapman, G. (1983) Diffusion of oxygen through the mesogloea of the sea anemone *Calliactis parasitica. J. Exp. Biol.*, 107, 181-187.

Brafield, A. E. and Llewellyn, M. J. (1982) *Animal Energetics*, Blackie & Son, Glasgow and London, 168 pp.

Brasier, M. D. (1979) The Cambrian radiation event. In M. R. House (ed.), *The Origin of Major Invertebrate Groups. Systematics Association Special Vol. No. 12*, Academic Press, London, pp. 103-159.

Brazeau, D.A. and H.R. Lasker. 1989. The reproductive cycle and spawning in a Caribbean gorgonian. *Biol. Bull. 176:1-7.*

Brooks, W. R. (1988) The influence of the location and abundance of the sea anemone *Calliactis tricolor* (Le Sueur) in protecting hermit crabs from octopus predators. *J. Exp. Mar. Biol. Ecol.*, 116, 15-21.

Brooks, W. R. (1989a) Hermit crabs alter sea anemone placement patterns for shell balance and reduced predation. *J. Exp. Mar. Biol. Ecol.*, 132, 109-122.

Brooks, W. R. (1989b) Hermit crabs protect their symbiotic cnidarians-true cases of mutualism. *Amer. Zool.*, 29, 36A (abstract).

Brooks, W. R. and Mariscal, R. N. (1984) The acclimation of anemone fishes to sea anemones: protection by changes in the fish's mucous coat. *J. Exp. Mar. Biol. Ecol.*, 81, 277-285.

Brooks, W. R. and Mariscal, R. N. (1986a) Interspecific competition for space by hydroids and a sea anemone living on gastropod shells inhabited by hermit crabs. *Mar. Ecol. Prog. Ser.*, 28, 241-244.

Brooks, W. R. and Mariscal, R. N. (1986b) Population variation and behavioral changes in two pagurids in association with the sea anemone *Calliactis tricolor* (Leseur). *J. Exp. Mar. Biol. Ecol.*, 103, 275-289.

Buck, M. and Schlichter, D. (1987) Driving forces for the uphill transport of amino acids into epidermal brush border membrane vesicles of the sea anemone, *Anemonia sulcata* (Cnidaria, Anthozoa). *Comp. Biochem. Physiol.*, 88A, 273-279.

Bucklin, A. (1982) The annual cycle of sexual reproduction in the sea anemone *Metridium senile. Can. J. Zool.*, 60, 3241-3248.

Bucklin, A. (1985) Biochemical genetic variation, growth and regeneration of the sea anemone, *Metridium*, of British shores. *J. Mar. Biol. Ass. U.K.*, 65, 141-157.

Bucklin, A. (1987a) Growth and asexual reproduction of the sea anemone *Metridium*: Comparative laboratory studies of three species. *J. Exp. Mar. Biol. Ecol.*, 110, 41-52.

Bucklin, A. (1987b) Adaptive advantages of patterns of growth and asexual reproduction of the sea anemone *Metridium senile* (L.) in intertidal and submerged populations. *J. Exp. Mar. Biol. Ecol.*, 110, 225-243.

Bucklin, A. and Hedgecock, D. (1982) Biochemical genetic evidence for a third species of *Metridium* (Coelenterata, Actiniaria). Mar. Biol., 66, 1-7.

Bucklin, A., Hedgecock, D. and Hand, C. (1984) Genetic evidence of self-fertilization in the sea anemone *Epiactis prolifera. Mar. Biol.*, 84, 175-182.

Bullock, T. H. (1955) Compensation for temperature in the metabolism and activity of poikilotherms. *Biol. Rev.*, 30, 311-342.

Bullock, T. H. and Horridge, G. A. (1965) Coelenterata and Ctenophora. In T.H. Bullock and G.A. Horridge, *Structure and Function in the Nervous Systems of Invertebrates, Vol. I*, W.H. Freeman, San Francisco, pp. 459-534.

Bunde, T. A., Dearlove, G. E. and Bishop, S. H. (1978) Aminoethylphosphonic acid-containing glycoproteins: the acid mucopolysaccharide-like components in mucus from *Metridium senile* (L.). *J. Exp. Zool.*, 206, 215-222.

Bursey, C. R. and Guanciale, J. M. (1977) Feeding behavior of the sea anemone *Condylactis gigantea*. *Comp. Biochem. Physiol.*, 57A, 115-117.

Bursey, C. R. and Harmer, J. A. (1979) Induced changes in the osmotic concentration of the coelenteron fluid of the sea anemone *Condylactis gigantea*. *Comp. Biochem. Physiol.*, 64A, 73-76.

Burton, R. S. and Feldman, M. W. (1982) Changes in free amino acid concentrations during osmotic response in the intertidal copepod *Tigriopus californicus*. *Comp. Biochem. Physiol.*, 73A, 441-445.

Buss, L. W. (1987) *The Evolution of Individuality*, Princeton University Press, Princeton, New Jersey, 202 pp.

Buss, L. W., McFadden, C. S. and Keene, D. R. (1984) Biology of hydractiniid hydroids. 2. Histocompatibility effector system/competitive mechanism mediated by nematocyst discharge. *Biol. Bull.*, 167, 139-158.

Cain, A. J. (1974) Breeding system of a sessile animal. *Nature*, 247, 289-290.

Cairns, S., Hartog, J. D. den and Arneson, C. (1986) Class Anthozoa (Corals, anemones). In W. Sterrer (ed.), Marine *Fauna and Flora of Bermuda. A Systematic Guide to the Identification of Marine Organisms*, John Wiley & Sons, New York, pp. 159-194.

Calow, P. (1977a) Conversion efficiencies in heterotrophic organisms. *Biol. Rev.*, 52, 385-409.

Calow, P. (1977b) Ecology, evolution and energetics: a study in metabolic adaptation. In A. Macfayden (ed.), *Advances in Ecological Research, Vol. 10*, Academic Press, New York, pp. 1-62.

Calow, P. (1978) *Life Cycles: An Evolutionary Approach to the Physiology of Reproduction, Development and Ageing*, Chapman and Hall, London, 164 pp.

Calow, P. (1979) The cost of reproduction-a physiological approach. *Biol. Rev.*, 54, 23-40.

Calow, P. (1981) Growth in lower invertebrates. In M. Rechcigl (ed.), *Physiology of Growth and Nutrition*, S. Karger, Basel, pp. 53-76.

Calow, P. and Sibly, R. M. (1987) Conflicting predictions concerning clonal reproduction? *Functional Ecol.*, 1, 161-163.

Calow, P. and Townsend, C. R. (1981) Resource utilization in growth. In C. R. Townsend and P. Calow (eds.), *Physiological Ecology. An Evolutionary Approach to Resource Use*, Sinauer Associates, Sunderland, Massachusetts, pp. 220-244.

Campbell, R. D. (1974) Development. In L. Muscatine and H. M. Lenhoff (eds.), *Coelenterate Biology: Reviews and New Perspectives*, Academic Press, New York, pp. 179-210.

Carlgren, O. (1900) Zur Kenntnis der stichodactylinen Actiniaren. ibidem, N: r2.

Carlgren, O. (1905) U ber die Bedeutung der Flimmerbewegung fu r den Nahrungstransport bei den Actiniarien und Madreporarien. *Biol. Zentralbl.*, 25, 308-322.

Carlgren, O. (1929) U ber eine Actiniariengattung mit besondern Fangtentakeln. *Zool. Anz.*, 81, 109-113.

Carlgren, O. (1949) A survey of the Ptychodactiaria, Corallimorpharia and Actiniaria. *Kungl. Sven. Vetenskapsakad. Handlingar, Fjerde Ser.*, 1, 1-121 + 4 plates.

Carlson, B. (1986) The *Amphiprion leucokranos* Mystery. *Aquarium Frontiers.*, 3, 34-37.

Carlyle, R.F. (1969a) The occurrence of catecholamines in the sea anemone Actinia equina. *Brit. J. Pharm.*, 36, 182P.

Carlyle, R. F. (1969b) The occurrence of pharmacologically active substances in, and the actions of drugs on, preparations of the sea anemone *Actinia equina. Brit. J. Pharm.*, 37, 532P.

Carlyle, R. F. (1974) The occurrence in and actions of amino acids on isolated supra oral sphincter preparations of the sea anemone *Actinia equina. J. Physiol.*, 236, 635-652.

Carroll, D. J. and Kempf, S. C. (1990) Laboratory Culture of the Aeolid Nudibranch *Berghia verrucicornis* (Mollusca, Opisthobranchia): Some Aspects of Its development and Life History. *Biol. Bull.*, 179, 243-253.

Carter, M. A. and Funnell, M. (1980) Reproduction and brooding in *Actinia*. In P. Tardent and R. Tardent (eds.), *Developmental and Cellular Biology of Coelenterates*, North-Holland Biomedical Press, Amsterdam, pp. 17-22.

Carter, M. A. and Miles, J. (1989) Gametogenic cycles and reproduction in the beadlet sea anemone *Actinia equina* (Cnidaria: Anthozoa). *Biol. J. Linn. Soc.*, 36, 129-155.

Carter, M. A. and Thorp, C. H. (1979) The reproduction of *Actinia equina* L. var. *mesembryanthemum. J. Mar. Biol. Ass. UK*, 59, 989-1001.

Carter, M. A. and Thorpe, J. P. (1981) Reproductive, genetic and ecological evidence that *Actinia equina* var. *mesembryanthemum* and var. *fragacea* are not conspecific. *J. Mar. Biol. Ass. UK*, 61, 71-93.

Cates, N. and McLaughlin, J.J.A. (1976) Differences of ammonia metabolism in symbiotic and aposymbiotic *Condylactis* and *Cassiopea* spp. *J., Exp. Mar. Biol. Ecol.*, 21, 1-5.

Cates, N. and McLaughlin, J. J. A. (1979) Nutrient availability for zooxanthellae derived from physiological activities of *Condylactis* spp. *J. Exp. Mar. Biol. Ecol.*, 37, 31-41.

Chadwick, N.E. 1987. Interspecific aggressive behaviour of the corallimorpharian *Corynactis californica* (Cnidaria: Anthozoa): Effects on sympatric corals and sea anemones. *Biol. Bull. 173:110-125.*

---------------------- 1991. Spatial distribution and the effects of competition on some temperate scleractinia and corallimorpharia. *Mar. Ecol. Progr. Ser. 70(1):39-48.*

--------------------- and C. Adams. 1991. Locomotion, asexual reproduction, and killing of corals by the corallimorpharian, *Corynactis californica. Hydrobiologia 216/217:263-269.*

Chang, S. S., Prezelin, B. B. and Trench, R. K. (1983) Mechanisms of photoadaptation in three strains of the symbiotic dinoflagellate *Symbiodinium microadriaticum. Mar. Biol.*, 76, 219-229.

Chapman, D. M. (1974) Cnidarian histology. In L. Muscatine and H. M. Lenhoff (eds.), *Coelenterate Biology. Reviews and New Perspectives*, Academic Press, New York, pp. 1-92.

Chapman, G. (1949) The mechanism of opening and closing of *Calliactis parasitica*. *J. Mar. Biol. Ass. UK*, 28, 641-649.

Chapman, G. (1953) Studies of the mesogloea of coelenterates. II. Physical properties. *J. Exp. Biol.*, 30, 440-451.

Chapman, G. and Pardy, R. L. (1972) The movement of glucose and glycine through the tissues of *Corymorpha palma* Torrey (Coelenterata, Hydrozoa). *J. Exp. Biol.*, 56, 639-645.

Charnov, E. L. (1982) *The Theory of Sex Allocation*, Princeton University Press, Princeton, New Jersey, 355 pp.

Chen, C.A., Chen, C., and I. Chen. 1995a. Sexual and asexual reproduction of the tropical corallimorpharian *Rhodactis* (=*Discosoma*) *indosinensis* (Cnidaria: Corallimorpharia) in Taiwan. *Zool. Studies: 34:29-40*.
-- 1995b. Spatial variability of size and sex in the tropical corallimorpharian *Rhodactis* (=*Discosoma*) *indosinensis* (Cnidaria: Corallimorpharia) in Taiwan. *Zool. Studies 34(2):82-87*.

-------------, Odorico, D.M., Ten, L.M., Veron, J.E.N. and D.J. Miller. 1995c. Systematic relationships within the anthozoa (Cnidaria:Anthozoa) using the 5'-end of the 28S rRNA. *Mol. Phyl. Evol. 4(2):175-183*.

-------------, Willis, B.L. and D.J. Miller. 1996. Systematic relationships between tropical corallimorpharians (Cnidaria: Anthozoa: Corallimorpharia): Utility of the 5.8S and internal transcribed spacer (ITS) regions of the rRNA transcription unit. *Bull. Mar. Sci. 59(1):196-208*.

------------- and D.J. Miller. 1996. Analysis of ribosomal ITS1 sequences indicates a deep divergence between Rhodactis (Cnidaria: Anthozoa: Corallimorpharia) species from the Caribbean and the Indo-Pacific/Red Sea. *Mar. Biol. 126:423-432*.

Chia, F.-S. (1972) Note on the assimilation of glucose and glycine from seawater by the embryos of a sea anemone, *Actinia equina. Can. J. Zool.*, 50, 1333-1334.

Chia, F.-S. (1974) Classification and adaptive significance of developmental patterns in marine invertebrates. *Thalassia Jugosl.*, 10, 121-130.

Chia, F.-S. (1976) Sea anemone reproduction: patterns and adaptive radiations. In G. O. Mackie (ed.), *Coelenterate Ecology and Behavior*, Plenum, New York, pp. 261-270.

Chia, F.-S. and Koss, R. (1979) Fine structural studies on the nervous system and the apical organ in the planula larva of the sea anemone *Anthopleura elegantissima. J. Morph.*, 160, 275-298.

Chia, F.-S., Lu tzen, J. and Svane, I. (1989) Sexual reproduction and larval morphology of the primitive anthozoan *Gonactinia prolifera M. Sars. J. Exp. Mar. Biol. Ecol., 127, 13-24*.

Chia, F.-S. and Rostron, M. A. (1970) Some aspects of the reproductive biology of *Actinia equina* (Cnidaria: Anthozoa). *J. Mar. Biol. Ass. UK*, 50, 253-264.

Chia, F.-S. and Spaulding, J. G. (1972) Development and juvenile growth of the sea anemone, *Tealia crassicornis. Biol. Bull.*, 142, 206-218.

Ciereszko, L.S. and R.P.L. Guillard. 1989. The influence of some cembranolides from gorgonian corals on motility of marine flagellates. *J. Exp. Mar. Biol. Ecol. 127:205-210.*

Clark, E. D. and Kimeldorf, D. J. (1971) Behavioral reactions of the sea anemone, *Anthopleura xanthogrammica*, to ultraviolet and visible radiations. *Rad. Res.*, 45, 166-175.

Clark, K. B. and Jensen, K. R. (1982) Effects of temperature on carbon fixation and carbon budget partitioning in the zooxanthellal symbiosis of *Aiptasia pallida* (Verrill). *J. Exp. Mar. Biol. Ecol.*, 64, 215-230.

Clark, R. B. (1964) *Dynamics in Metazoan Evolution. The Origin of the Coelom and Segments*, Clarendon Press, Oxford, UK, 313 pp.

Clark, W. H., Jr. and Dewel, W. C. (1974) The structure of the gonads, gametogenesis, and sperm-egg interactions in the Anthozoa. *Amer. Zool.*, 14, 495-510.

Clarke, A. (1983) Life in cold water: the physiological ecology of polar marine ectotherms. *Oceanogr. Mar. Biol. Ann. Rev.*, 21, 341-453.

Clayton, R. K. (1977) *Light and Living Matter. Vol. 2, The Biological Part,* Robert E. Krieger, Huntington, New York, 243 pp.

Clayton, W. S., Jr. (1985) Pedal laceration by the anemone *Aiptasia pallida. Mar. Ecol. Prog. Ser.*, 21, 75-80.

Clayton, W. S., Jr. and Lasker, H. R. (1984) Host feeding regime and zooxanthellal photosynthesis in the anemone, *Aiptasia pallida* (Verrill). *Biol. Bull.*, 167, 590-600.

Clayton, W. S., Jr. and Lasker, H. R. (1985) Individual and population growth in the asexually reproducing anemone *Aiptasia pallida* Verrill. *J. Exp. Mar. Biol. Ecol.*, 90, 249-258.

Coates, A. G. and Jackson, J. B. C. (1985) Morphological themes in the evolution of clonal and aclonal marine invertebrates. In J. B. C. Jackson, L. W. Buss, and R. E. Cook (eds.), *Population Biology and Evolution of Clonal Organisms,* Yale University Press, New Haven, pp. 67-106.

Colin, P.L. and C. Arneson. 1995. *Tropical Marine Invertebrates. A Field Guide to the Marine Invertebrates Occurring on Tropical Pacific Coral Reefs, Seagrass Beds and Mangroves.* Coral Reef Press, Beverly Hills, CA.

Coll, J.C., S. Barre, P.W. Sammarco, W.T. Williams & G. Bakus. (1982)

Coll, J.C. and P.W. Sammarco. 1986. Soft corals: chemistry and ecology. *Oceanus 29:33-37.*

------------, Bowden, B.F., Tapiolas, D.M. and W.C. Dunlap. 1982. In situ isolation of allelochemicals released from soft corals (Coelenterata: Octocorallia): a totally submersible sampling apparatus. *J. Exp. Mar. Biol. Ecol. 60:293-299.*

Conklin, E.J., Bigger, C. H. and Mariscal, R. N. (1977) The formation and taxonomic status of the microbasic q-mastigophore nematocyst of sea anemones. *Biol. Bull.,* 152, 159-168.

Conklin, E. J. and Mariscal, R. N. (1976) Increase in nematocyst and spirocyst discharge in a sea anemone in response to mechanical stimulation. In G. O. Mackie (ed.), *Coelenterate Ecology and Behavior,* Plenum, New York, pp. 549-558.

Conklin, E. J. and Mariscal, R. N. (1977) Feeding behavior, ceras structure, and nematocyst storage in the aeolid nudibranch, Spurilla neapolitana (Mollusca). *Bull. Mar. Sci.,* 27, 658-667.

Conover, R. J. (1978) Transformation of organic matter. In O. Kinne (ed.), *Marine Ecology, Vol. 4, Dynamics,* John Wiley & Sons, New York, pp. 221-499.

Cook, C. B. (1971) Transfer of 35S-labeled material from food ingested by Aiptasia sp. to its endosymbiotic zooxanthellae. In H. M. Lenhoff, L. Muscatine and L. V. Davis (eds.), *Experimental Coelenterate Biology,* University of Hawaii Press, Honolulu, pp. 218-224.

Cook, C. B. (1983) Metabolic interchange in algae-invertebrate symbiosis. *Int. Rev. Cytol., Suppl.* 14, 177-210.

Cook, C. B., D'Elia, C. F. and Muller-Parker, G. (1988) Host feeding and nutrient sufficiency for zooxanthellae in the sea anemone *Aiptasia pallida. Mar. Biol.,* 98, 253-262.

Cook, C. B. and Kelty, M. O. (1982) Glycogen, protein, and lipid content of green, aposymbiotic, and nonsymbiotic hydra during starvation. *J. Exp. Zool.,* 222, 1-9.Cook, P. A., Gabbott, P. A. and Youngson, A. (1972) Seasonal changes in the free amino acid composition of the adult barnacle, *Balanus balanoides. Comp. Biochem. Physiol.,* 42B, 409-421.

Cooke, W.J. 1976. Reproduction, growth and some tolerances of *Zoanthus pacificus* and *Palythoa vestitus* in Kaneohe Bay, Hawaii. G.O. Mackie Ed. *Coelenterate Ecology and Behavior* Plenum Press, New York, 744 pp.

Corner, E. D. S., Leon, Y. A. and Bulbrook, R. D. (1960) Steroid sulphatase, arylsulphatase and b-glucuronidase in marine invertebrates. *J. Mar. Biol. Ass. UK,* 39, 51-61.

Crisp, D. J. (ed.) (1964) The effects of the severe winter of 1962-63 on marine life in Britain. *J. Anim. Ecol.,* 33, 165-210.

Crowell, S. and Oates, S. (1980) Metamorphosis and reproduction by transverse fission in an edwardsiid anemone. In P. Tardent and R. Tardent (eds.), *Developmental and Cellular Biology of Coelenterates,* Elsevier/North-Holland Biomedical Press, Amsterdam, pp. 139-142.

Crozier, R. H. (1986) Genetic clonal recognition abilities in marine invertebrates must be maintained by selection for something else. *Evolution,* 40, 1100-1101.

Cutress, C. E. (1979) Bunodeopsis medusoides Fowler and Actinodiscus neglectus Fowler, two Tahitian sea anemones: redescription and biological notes. *Bull. Mar. Sci.,* 29, 96-109.

Dahl, E., Falck, B., von Mecklenburg, C. and Myhrberg, H. (1963) An adrenergic nervous system in sea anemones. Quart. *J. Microsc. Sci.,* 104, 531-534.

Dai, C.D and M.C. Lin. 1993. The effects of flow on feeding of three gorgonians from southern Taiwan. *J. Exp. Mar. Biol. Ecol. 173:57-69.*

Dalby, J. E., Jr., Elliott, J. K. and Ross, D. M. (1988) The swim response of the actinian *Stomphia didemon* to certain asteroids: distributional and phylogenetic implications. *Can. J. Zool.*, 66, 2484-2491.

Dalyell, J. G. (1848) *Rare and Remarkable Animals of Scotland, Represented from Living Subjects: with Practical Observations on Their Nature, Vol.2,* Van Voorst, London, 322 pp. + 56 colour plates.

Davenport, D. and Norris, K. S. (1958) Observations on the symbiosis of the sea anemone *Stoichactis* and the pomacentrid fish, *Amphiprion percula. Biol. Bull.*, 115, 397-410.

Davenport, D., Ross, D. M. and Sutton, L. (1961) The remote control of nematocyst-discharge in the attachment of *Calliactis parasitica* to shells of hermit crabs. Vie et Milieu, 12, 197-209.

Day, R. M. and Harris, L. G. (1978) Selection and turnover of coelenterate nematocysts in some aeolid nudibranchs. *The Veliger*, 21, 104-109.

Dayton, P. K. (1971) Competition and community organization: the provision and subsequent utilization of space in a rocky intertidal community. *Ecol. Monogr.*, 41, 351-389.

Dayton, P. K. (1973) Two cases of resource partitioning in an intertidal community: making the right prediction for the wrong reason. *Amer. Nat.*, 107, 662-670.

Dayton, P. K., Robilliard, G. A., Paine, R. T. and Dayton, L. B. (1974) Biological accommodation in the benthic community at McMurdo Sound, Antarctica. *Ecol. Monogr.*, 44, 105-128.

Deaton, L. E. and Hoffmann, R. J. (1988) Hypoosmotic volume regulation in the sea anemone *Metridium senile. Comp. Biochem. Physiol.*, 91C, 187-191.

D'Elia, C. F. and Cook, C. B. (1988) Methylamine uptake by zooxanthellae/ invertebrate symbioses: insights into host ammonium environment and nutrition. *Limnol. Oceanogr.*, 33, 1153-1165.

Delbeek, J. C. 1989. Soft corals spawn in the aquarium. *Freshwater and Marine Aquarium Magazine 12(3):128-129.*

den Hartog, J. C. 1977. The marginal tentacles of *Rhodactis sanctithomae* (Corallimorpharia) and the sweeper tentacles of *Montastrea cavernosa* (Scleractinia); their cnidom and possible function. In: *Proc. 3rd Int. Coral Reef Symp. 1977.*

--------------------- 1980. Caribbean shallow water corallimorpharia. *Zoologische Verhandelingen. (176): 1-83.*

--------------------- 1987. Corallimorpharia collected during the CANCAP expeditions (1976-1986) in the south-eastern part of the North Atlantic. *Zoologische Verhandelingen 282:1-76.*

-------------------- and M. Türkay. 1991. *Platypodiella georgi* spec. Nov. (Brachyura: Xanthidae), a new crab from the island of St. Helena, South Atlantic Ocean, with notes on the genus *Platypodiella* Guinot, 1967. *Zool. Mededel. 65:209-220.*

Denny, M. W., Daniel, T. L. and Koehl, M. A. R. (1985) Mechanical limits to size in wave-swept organisms. *Ecol. Monogr.*, 55, 69-102.

Dicquemare, L'Abbe (1773) An essay, towards elucidating the history of the sea-anemonies. *Phil. Trans. R. Soc. Lond.*, 63, 361-403.

Donoghue, A. M., Quicke, D. L. J. and Brace, R. C. (1986) Turnstones apparently preying on sea anemones. *Brit. Birds*, 79, 91.

Dorsett, D. A. (1984) Oxygen production in the intertidal anemone *Anemonia sulcata.* Comp. Biochem. Physiol., 78A, 225-228.

Doumenc, D. A. (1979) Structure et origine des systemes squelettiques et neuromusculaires au cours de l'organogenese des stades postlarvaires de l'actinie *Cereus pedunculatus. Arch. Zool. Exp.* Gen., 120, 431-476.

Doumenc, D. A. and Van-Praet, M. (1987) Ordre des actiniaires. Ordre des ptychodactiniaires. Ordre des corallimorphaires. In P.-P. Grasse (ed.), Traite de Zoologie. Anatomie, Systematique, Biologie. Tome III. Cnidaires Anthozoaires, Masson, Paris, pp. 257-401.

Doumenc, D. and Foubert, A. (1984) Microinformatique et taxonomie des actinies: cle mondiale des genres. Ann. Inst. Oceanogr., Paris, 60, 43-86.

Dromgoole, F. I. (1978) The effects of oxygen on dark respiration and apparent photosynthesis of marine macro-algae. *Aq. Bot.*, 4, 281-297.

Dudler, N., Yellowlees, D. and Miller, D. J. (1987) Localization of two L-glutamate dehydrogenases in the coral *Acropora latistella. Arch. Biochem. Biophys.*, 254, 368-371.

Dunlap, W. C. and Chalker, B. E. (1986) Identification and quantitation of near-UV absorbing compounds (S-320) in a hermatypic scleractinian. *Coral Reefs*, 5, 155-159.

Dunlap, W.C., Chalker, B.E. and J.K. Oliver. 1986. Bathymetric adaptations of reef-building corals at Davies Reef, Great Barrier Reef, Australia. 3: UV-B absorbing compounds. *J. Expo. Mar. Biol. Ecol. 104:239-248.*

Dunlap, W.C. and Y. Yamamoto. 1995. Small-molecule antioxidants in marine organisms: antioxidant activity of mycosporine-glycine. *Comp. Biochem. Physiol. B 112(1):105-114.*

Dunn, D. F. (1975a) Reproduction of the externally brooding sea anemone *Epiactis prolifera* Verrill, 1869. *Biol. Bull.*, 148, 199-218.

Dunn, D. F. (1975b) Gynodioecy in an animal. *Nature*, 253, 528-529.

Dunn, D. F. (1977a) Dynamics of external brooding in the sea anemone *Epiactis prolifera. Mar. Biol.*, 39, 41-49.

Dunn, D. F. (1977b) Variability of *Epiactis prolifera* (Coelenterata: Actiniaria) in the intertidal zone near Bodega Bay, California. *J. Nat. Hist.*, 11, 457-463.

Dunn, D. F. (1978) *Anthopleura handi* n. sp. (Coelenterata, Actiniaria), an internally brooding, intertidal sea anemone from Malaysia. Wasmann *J. Biol.*, 35, 54-64.

Dunn, D. F. (1981) The clownfish sea anemones: Stichodactylidae (Coelenterata: Actiniaria) and other sea anemones symbiotic with pomacentrid fishes. Tran

Dunn, D. F. (1982) Sexual reproduction of two intertidal sea anemones (Coelenterata: Actiniaria) in Malaysia. *Biotropica*, 14, 262-271.

Dunn, D.F. 1982. Cnidaria (Corallimorpharia, pp. 669-705 (700) In: Parker, S.P. (ed), *Synopsis and classification of living organisms 1:i-xviii*, 1-1166, pls. 1-87. New York, NY.

Dunn, D. F. (1983) Some Antarctic and sub-Antarctic sea anemones (Coelenterata: Ptychodactiaria and Actiniaria). In L. S. Kornicker (ed.), *Biology of the Antarctic Seas XIV, Antarctic Research Series Volume 39*, Amer. Geophysical Union, Washington, D. C., pp. 1-67.

Dunn, D. F. (1984) More Antarctic and Subantarctic sea anemones (Coelenterata: Corallimorpharia and Actiniaria). In L. S. Kornicker (ed.), *Biology of the Antarctic Seas XVI, Antarctic Research Series Volume 41*, Amer. Geophysical Union, Washington, D. C., pp. 1-42.

Dunn, D. F., Chia, F.-S. and Levine, R. (1980) Nomenclature of Aulactinia (=3DBunodactis), with description of *Aulactinia incubans* n.sp. (Coelenterata: Actiniaria), an internally brooding sea anemone from Puget Sound. *Can. J. Zool.*, 58, 2071-2080.

Dunn, D. F., Devaney, D. M. and Roth, B. (1980) *Stylobates*: a shell-forming sea anemone (Coelenterata, Anthozoa, Actiniidae). *Pacific Sci.*, 34, 379-388.

Dunn, D. F. and Hamner, W. M. (1980) *Amplexidiscus fenestrafer* n. gen, n. sp. (Coelenterata: Anthozoa), a tropical Indo-Pacific corallimorpharian. *Micronesica*, 16, 29-36.

Dunn, D. F. and Liberman, M. H. (1983) Chitin in sea anemone shells. *Science*, 221, 157-159.

Dykens, J. A. (1984) Enzymic defenses against oxygen toxicity in marine cnidarians containing endosymbiotic algae. *Mar. Biol. Lett.*, 5, 291-301.

Dykens, J. A. and Shick, J. M. (1982) Oxygen production by endosymbiotic algae controls superoxide dismutase activity in their animal host. *Nature*, 297, 579-580.

Dykens, J. A. and Shick, J. M. (1984) Photobiology of the symbiotic sea anemone, *Anthopleura elegantissima*: defenses against photodynamic effects, and seasonal photoacclimatization. *Biol. Bull.*, 167, 683-697.

Dykens, J. A. and Shick, J. M. (1988) Relevance of purine catabolism to hypoxia and recovery in euryoxic and stenoxic marine invertebrates, particularly bivalve molluscs. *Comp. Biochem. Physiol.*, 91C, 35-41.

Edmunds, M. (1966) Protective mechanisms in the Eolidacea (Mollusca Nudibranchia). *J. Linn. Soc.* (Zool.), 46, 27-71.

Edmunds, M., Potts, G. W., Swinfen, R. C. and Waters, V. L. (1974) The feeding preferences of *Aeolidia papillosa* (L.) (Mollusca, Nudibranchia). *J. Mar. Biol. Ass. UK*, 54, 939-947.

Edmunds, M., Potts, G. W., Swinfen, R. C. and Waters, V. L. (1976) Defensive behaviour of sea anemones in response to predation by the opisthobranch mollusc *Aeolidia papillosa* (L.). *J. Mar. Biol. Ass. UK*, 56, 65-83.

Edmunds, P. J. and Davies, P. S. (1986) An energy budget for *Porites porites* (Scleractinia). *Mar. Biol.*, 92, 339-347.

Eibl-Eibesfeldt, I. (1960) Beobachtungen und Versuche an Anemonenfischen (*Amphiprion*) des Malediven und der Nicobaren. *Z. Tierpsychol.*, 17, 1-10.

El Ayeb, M., Bahraoui, E. M., Granier, C., Beress, L. and Rochat, H. (1986) Immunochemistry of sea anemone toxins: structure-antigenicity relationships and toxin-receptor interactions probed by antibodies specific for one antigenic region. *Biochemistry*, 25, 6755-6761.

Ellington, W. R. (1977) Aerobic and anaerobic degradation of glucose by the estuarine sea anemone, *Diadumene leucolena. Comp. Biochem. Physiol.*, 58B, 173-175.

Ellington, W. R. (1979a) Octopine dehydrogenase in the basilar muscle of the sea anemone, *Metridium senile. Comp. Biochem. Physiol.*, 63B, 349-354.

Ellington, W. R. (1979b) Evidence for a broadly-specific, amino acid requiring dehydrogenase at the pyruvate branchpoint in sea anemones. *J. Exp. Zool.*, 209, 151-159.

Ellington, W. R. (1980a) Some aspects of the metabolism of the sea anemone *Haliplanella luciae* (Verrill) during air exposure and hypoxia. *Mar. Biol. Lett.*, 1, 255-262.

Ellington, W. R. (1980b) Partial purification and characterization of a broadly-specific octopine dehydrogenase from the tissues of the sea anemone, *Bunodosoma cavernata* (Bosc). *Comp. Biochem. Physiol.*, 67B, 625-631.

Ellington, W. R. (1981) Effect of anoxia on the adenylates and the energy charge in the sea anemone, *Bunodosoma cavernata* (Bosc). *Physiol. Zool.*, 54, 415-422.

Ellington, W. R. (1982) Metabolic responses of the sea anemone *Bunodosoma cavernata* (Bosc) to declining oxygen tensions and anoxia. *Physiol. Zool.*, 55, 240-249.

Elliott, J. and Cook, C. B. (1989) Diel Variation in Prey Capture Behavior by the Corallimorpharian *Discosoma sanctithomae*: Mechanical and Chemical Activation of Feeding. *Biol. Bull.*, 176, 218-228.

Elliott, J., Dalby, J. Jr., Cohen, R. and Ross, D. M. (1985) Behavioral interactions between the actinian *Tealia piscivora* (Anthozoa: Actiniaria) and the asteroid *Dermasterias imbricata. Can. J. Zool.*, 63, 1921-1929.

Elliott, J. K., Ross, D. M., Pathirana, C., Miao, S., Andersen, R. J., Singer, P., Kokke, W. C. M. C. and Ayer, W. A. (1989) Induction of swimming in Stomphia (Anthozoa: Actiniaria) by imbricatine, a metabolite of the asteroid *Dermasterias imbricata. Biol. Bull.*, 176, 73-78.

Ellis, V. L., Ross, D. M. and Sutton, L. (1969) The pedal disk of the swimming sea anemone *Stomphia coccinea* during detachment, swimming and resettlement. *Can. J. Zool.*, 47, 333-342.

Elmhirst, R. and Sharpe, J. S. (1920) On the colours of two sea anemones, *Actinia equina* and *Anemonia sulcata*. Part I. Environmental. Part II. *Chemical. Biochem. J.,* 14, 48-57.

Elmhirst, R. and Sharpe, J. S. (1923) On the colours of the sea anemone, *Tealia crassicornis. Ann. Mag. Nat. Hist.,* 11, 615-621.

Elyakova, L. A. (1972) Distribution of cellulases and chitinases in marine invertebrates. *Comp. Biochem. Physiol.,* 43B, 67-70.

Elyakova, L. A., Shevchenko, N. M. and Avaeva, S. M. (1981) A comparative study of carbohydrase activities in marine invertebrates. *Comp. Biochem. Physiol.,* 69B, 905-908.

Ewer, D. W. (1960) Inhibition and rhythmic activity of the circular muscles of *Calliactis parasitica* (Couch). *J. Exp. Biol.,* 37, 812-831.

Fabricius, K.E. 1995. Slow population turnover in the soft coral genera *Sinularia* and *Sarcophyton* on mid- and outer-shelf reefs of the Great Barrier Reef. *Mar. Ecol. Progr. Ser. 126:145-152.*

-------------------- and D.W. Klumpp. 1995. Wide-spread mixotrophy in reef-inhabiting soft corals: The influence of depth, and colony expansion and contraction on photosynthesis. *Mar. Ecol. Progr. Ser. 126:145-152.*

-------------------, Benayahu, Y. and A. Genin. 1995a. Herbivory in asymbiotic soft corals. *Science 268:90-92.*

-------------------, Genin, A. and Y. Benayahu. 1995b. Flow-dependent herbivory and growth in zooxanthellae- free soft corals. *Limnol. Oceanogr. 40:1290-1301.*

Fabricius, 1996 In Press. Proceedings of the 8th International Coral Reef Symposium.

Fadlallah, Y.H., Karlson, R. And K.P. Sebens. 1984. A comparative study of sexual reproduction in three species of Panamanian zoanthids (Coelenterata: Anthozoa). *Bull. Mar. Sci. 35(1):80-89.*

Farrant, P.A. 1985. Reproduction in the temperate Australian soft coral Capnella gaboensis. Proc. 5th Int. Coral Reef Congr. Tahiti, French Polynesia 4:319-324.

Faulkner, D.J. 1992. Biomedical uses for natural marine chemicals. *Oceanus 35(1):29-35.*

Fautin, D. G. (1986) Why do anemonefishes inhabit only some host actinians? *Envir. Biol. Fishes,* 15, 171-180.

Fautin, D. G. (1987) Effects of symbionts on anthozoan body form. *Amer. Zool.,* 27, 14A (abstract).

Fautin, D. G. (1988) Importance of nematocysts to actinian taxonomy. In D. A. Hessinger and H. M. Lenhoff (eds.), *The Biology of Nematocysts,* Academic Press, San Diego, California, pp. 487-500.

Fautin, D. G. (1990) Sexual differentiation and behaviour in Phylum Cnidaria. In K. G. Adiyodi and R. G. Adiyodi (eds.), *Reproductive Biology of Invertebrates,* Vol. V, Oxford and IBH Publishing Co., New Delhi (in press).

Fautin, D. G., Bucklin, A. and Hand, C. (1990) Systematics of sea anemones belonging to genus *Metridium* (Coelenterata: Actiniaria), with a description of *M. giganteum* new species. *Wasmann J. Biol.*, 47, 77-85.

Fautin, D. G. and Chia, F.-S. (1986) Revision of the sea anemone genus *Epiactis* (Coelenterata: Actiniaria) on the Pacific coast of North America, with descriptions of two new brooding species. *Can. J. Zool.*, 64, 1665-1674.

Fautin, D. G. and Lowenstein, J. M. (1992) Phylogenetic relationships among scleractinians, actinians, and corallimorpharians (Coelenterata: Anthozoa). *7th Int. Coral Reefs Sym. Guam*, In press.

Fautin, D. G. and Mariscal, R. N. (1990) Cnidaria (Coelenterata), Anthozoa. In F. W. Harrison (ed.), *Microscopic Anatomy of Invertebrates*, pp. ?? Alan R. Liss, Inc., New York (in press).

Fautin, D. G., Spaulding, J. G. and Chia, F.-S. (1989) Cnidaria. In K. G. Adiyodi and R. G. Adiyodi (eds.), *Reproductive Biology of Invertebrates, Vol. IV, Fertilization, Development, and Parental Care*, Oxford and IBH Publishing Co., New Delhi, pp. 43-62.

Feral, J. P., Fusey, P., Gaill, F., Lopez, E., Martelly, E., Oudot, J.and Van-Praet, M. (1979) evolution des teneurs en hydrocarbures chez quelque s organismes marins du Nord Finisterre, depuis l'echouage de L'Amoco Cadiz e t comparaison des methodes de dosage en infrarouge et spectrofluorimetrie. C.R. *Acad. Sci. Paris*, 288, 713-716.

Fishelson, L. 1970. Littoral fauna of the Red Sea: the population of non-scleractinian anthozoans of shallow waters of the Red Sea (Eilat). *Mar. Biol. 6:106-116.*

Fisher, R. A. (1930) *The Genetical Theory of Natural Selection*, Oxford University Press, London, 272 pp.

Fitt, W. K. (1984) The role of chemosensory behavior of Symbiodinium microadriaticum, intermediate hosts, and host behavior in the infection of coelenterates and molluscs with zooxanthellae. *Mar. Biol.*, 81, 9-17.

Fitt, W. K. and Pardy, R. L. (1981) Effects of starvation, and light and dark on the energy metabolism of symbiotic and aposymbiotic sea anemones, *Anthopleura elegantissima. Mar. Biol.*, 61, 199-205.

Fitt, W. K., Pardy, R. L. and Littler, M. M. (1982) Photosynthesis, respiration, and contribution to community productivity of the symbiotic sea anemone *Anthopleura elegantissima* (Brandt, 1835). *J. Exp. Mar. Biol. Ecol.*, 61, 213-232.

Fleure, H. J. and Walton, C. L. (1907) Notes on the habits of some Sea Anemones. *Zool. Anz.*, 31, 212-220.

Ford, C. E., Jr. (1964) Reproduction in the aggregating sea anemone, *Anthopleura elegantissima. Pacific Sci.*, 18, 138-145.

Ford, T. D. (1979) Precambrian fossils and the origin of the Phanerozoic phyla. In M. R. House (ed.), *The Origin of Major Invertebrate Groups. Systematics Association Special Vol. No. 12*, Academic Press, London, pp. 7-21.

Fosså, S., and A. J. Nilsen. 1992. *Korallenriff-Aquarium Band 1.* Birgit Schmettkamp Verlag, Bornheim, Germany, 158 pp.

----------------------. 1992. *Korallenriff-Aquarium Band 2.* Birgit Schmettkamp Verlag, Bornheim, Germany, 203 pp.

----------------------. 1993. *Korallenriff-Aquarium Band 3.* Birgit Schmettkamp Verlag, Bornheim, Germany, 333 pp.

----------------------. 1995. *Korallenriff-Aquarium Band 4.* Birgit Schmettkamp Verlag, Bornheim, Germany, 447 pp.

----------------------. 1996. *Korallenriff-Aquarium Band 5.* Birgit Schmettkamp Verlag, Bornheim, Germany, 352 pp.

----------------------. 1996. *The Modern Coral Reef Aquarium Vol 1.* Birgit Schmettkamp Verlag, Bornheim, Germany, 447 pp.

Fox, D. L. (1953) *Animal Biochromes and Structural Colours,* Cambridge University Press, Cambridge, UK, 379 pp.

Fox, D. L. and Pantin, C. F. A. (1941) The colours of the plumose anemone *Metridium senile* (L.). Phil. Trans. R. Soc. London, B, 230, 415-450.

Fox, D. L., Wilkie, D. W. and Haxo, F. T. (1978) Carotenoid fractionation in the plumose anemone *Metridium*-II. Search for dietary sources of ovarian astaxanthin. *Comp. Biochem Physiol.,* 59B, 289-294.

Fox, H. M. (1965) Confirmation of old observations on the behaviour of a hermit crab and its commensal sea anemone. *Ann. Mag. Nat. Hist.,* 13th Ser., 8, 173-175.

Francis, L. (1973a) Clone specific segregation in the sea anemone *Anthopleura elegantissima. Biol. Bull.,* 144, 64-72.

Francis, L. (1973b) Intraspecific aggression and its effect on the distribution of *Anthopleura elegantissima* and some related sea anemones. *Biol. Bull.,* 144, 73-92.

Francis, L. (1976) Social organization within clones of the sea anemone *Anthopleura elegantissima. Biol. Bull.,* 150, 361-376.

Francis, L. (1979) Contrast between solitary and clonal lifestyles in the sea anemone *Anthopleura elegantissima. Amer. Zool.,* 19, 669-681.

Francis, L. (1988) Cloning and aggression among sea anemones (Coelenterata: Actiniaria) of the rocky shore. *Biol. Bull.,* 174, 241-253.

Frank, P. G. and Bleakney, J. S. (1978) Asexual reproduction, diet, and anomalies of the anemone *Nematostella vectensis* in Nova Scotia. *Can. Field-Nat.,* 92, 259-263.

Fredericks, C. A. (1976) Oxygen as a limiting factor in phototaxis and in intraclonal spacing of the sea anemone *Anthopleura elegantissima. Mar. Biol.,* 38, 25-28.

Frelin, C., Vigne, P., Schweitz, H. and Lazdunski, M. (1984) The interaction of sea anemone and scorpion neurotoxins with tetrodotoxin-resistant Na+ channels in rat myoblasts. A comparison with Na+ channels in other excitable and non-excitable cells. *Mol. Pharm.,* 26, 70-74.

Fricke, H. W. (1975) Selektives Feinderkennen bei dem Anemonenfisch *Amphiprion bicinctus* (Rüppell). *J. Exp. Mar. Biol. Ecol.,* 19, 1-7.

Fricke, H. W. (1979) Mating system, resource defence and sex change in the anemonefish *Amphiprion akallopisos*. *Z. Tierpsychol.*, 50, 313-326.

Friese, U. E. (1972) *Sea Anemones*, T.F.H. Publications, Neptune City, New Jersey, 128 pp.

Fujii, H. (1987) The predominance of clones in populations of the sea anemone *Anthopleura asiatica* (Uchida). *Biol. Bull.*, 172, 202-211.

Fukui, Y. (1986) Catch tentacles in the sea anemone *Haliplanella luciae*. Role as organs of social behavior. *Mar. Biol.*, 91, 245-252.

Gashout, S. E. and Ormond, R. F. G. (1979) Evidence for parthenogenetic reproduction in the sea anemone *Actinia equina* L. *J. Mar. Biol. Ass. UK*, 59, 975-987.

Geddes, P. (1882) *On the nature and functions of the 'yellow cells' of radiolarians and coelenterates.* Proc. R. Soc. Edinburgh, 11, 377-396.

Gemmill, J. F. (1920) The development of the sea-anemones *Metridium dianthus* (Ellis) and *Adamsia palliata* (Bohad). *Phil. Trans. R. Soc. Lond.*, B, 209, 351-375.

Gemmill, J. F. (1921) The development of the sea anemone *Bolocera tuediae* (Johnst.). *Quart. J. Microsc. Sci.*, 65, 577-587 + 1 plate.

George, R. Y. (1981) Functional adaptations of deep-sea organisms. In F. J. Vernberg and W. B. Vernberg (eds), *Functional Adaptations of Marine Organisms*, Academic Press, New York, pp. 279-332.

Gerhart, D.J. 1984. Prostaglandin A_2: an agent of chemical defense in the Caribbean gorgonian *Plexaura homomalla*. *Mar. Ecol. Progr. Ser. 19:181-187.*

Ghiselin, M. (1969) The evolution of hermaphroditism among animals. *Q. Rev. Biol.*, 44, 189-208.

Gibson, D. and Dixon, G. H. (1969) Chymotrypsin-like proteases from the sea anemone, *Metridium senile*. *Nature*, 222, 753-756.

Giese, A. C. (1966) Lipids in the economy of marine invertebrates. *Physiol. Rev.*, 46, 244-298.

Gilles, R. (1975) Mechanisms of ion and osmoregulation. In O. Kinne (ed.), *Marine Ecology, Vol. II, Physiological Mechanisms, Part 1*, John Wiley & Sons, London, pp. 259-347.

Gladfelter, W. B. (1975) Sea anemone with zooxanthellae: simultaneous contraction and expansion in response to changing light intensity. *Science*, 189, 570-571.

Glaessner, M. (1984) *The Dawn of Animal Life. A Biohistorical Study*, Cambridge University Press, Cambridge, UK, 241 pp.

Gliebs, S., Mebs, D. and B. Werding. 1995. Studies on the origin and distribution of palytoxin in a Caribbean coral reef. *Toxicon 33(11):1531-1537.*

Glider, W. V., Phipps, D. W., Jr. and Pardy, R. L. (1980) Localization of symbiotic dinoflagellate cells within tentacle tissue of *Aiptasia pallida* (Coelenterata, Anthozoa). *Trans. Amer. Microsc. Soc.*, 99, 426-438.

Gnaiger, E. (1977) Thermodynamic considerations of invertebrate anoxibiosis. In I. Lamprecht and B. Schaarschmidt (eds.), *Applications of Calorimetry in Life Sciences*, W. de Gruyter, Berlin, pp. 281-303.

Gnaiger, E. (1983a) Calculation of energetic and biochemical equivalents of respiratory oxygen consumption. In E. Gnaiger and H. Forstner (eds.), *Polarographic Oxygen Sensors: Aquatic and Physiological Applications*, Springer-Verlag, Berlin and Heidelberg, pp. 337-345.

Gnaiger, E. (1983b) Heat dissipation and energetic efficiency in animal anoxibiosis: economy contra power. *J. Exp. Zool.*, 228, 471-490.

Gnaiger, E. and Bitterlich, G. (1984) Proximate biochemical composition and caloric content calculated from elemental CHN analysis: a stoichiometric concept. *Oecologia*, 62, 289-298.

Gnaiger, E., Shick, J. M. and Widdows, J. (1989) Metabolic microcalorimetry and respirometry of aquatic animals. In C. R. Bridges and P. J. Butler (eds.), *Techniques in Comparative Respiratory Physiology. An Experimental Approach*, Cambridge University Press, Cambridge, UK, pp. 113-135.

Godknecht, A. and Tardent, P. (1988) Discharge and mode of action of the tentacular nematocysts of *Anemonia sulcata* (Anthozoa: Cnidaria). *Mar. Biol.*, 100, 83-92.

Gomme, J. (1982) Epidermal nutrient absorption in marine invertebrates: a comparative analysis. *Amer. Zool.*, 22, 691-708.

Gooley, P. R. and Norton, R. S. (1986) Secondary structure in sea anemone polypeptides: a proton nuclear magnetic resonance study. *Biochemistry,* 25, 2349-2356.

Goreau, T. F. (1959) The physiology of skeleton formation in corals: I. A method for measuring the rate of calcium deposition by corals under different conditions. *Biol. Bull.*, 116, 59-75.

Gosline, J. M. (1971) Connective tissue mechanics of *Metridium senile* I. Structural and compositional aspects. *J. Exp. Biol.*, 55, 763-774.

Gosline, J. M. and Lenhoff, H. M. (1968) Kinetics of incorporation of C14 proline into mesogleal protocollagen and collagen of the sea anemone *Aiptasia. Comp. Biochem. Physiol.*, 26, 1031-1039.

Gosliner, T., Williams, G.C. and D. Behrens 1996. *Coral Reef Animals of the Indo-Pacific*. Sea Challengers, Monterey, CA, USA, 314 pp.

Gosse, P. H. (1860) *Actinologia Britannica: A History of the British Sea-Anemones and Corals*, Van Voorst, London, 362 pp. + 11 plates.

Graff, D. and Grimmelikhuijzen, C. J. P. (1988) Isolation of <Glu-Ser-Leu-Arg-Trp-NH2, a novel neuropeptide from sea anemones. *Brain Res.*, 442, 354-358.

Grasshoff, M. (1981) Polypen und Kolonien der Blumentiere (Anthozoa) III: Die Hexacorallia. *Natur und Museum,* 111, 134-150.

Grasshoff, M. (1984) Cnidarian phylogeny-a biomechanical approach. In *Recent Advances in the Paleobiology and Geology of the Cnidaria, Paleontographica Americana*, No. 54, Paleontological Research Institution, Ithaca, New York, pp. 127-135.

Gravier, C. (1918). Note Preliminaire sur les Hexactiniaires etc. *Bull. Biol. Oceano.*, nr, 346.

Grebel'nyi, S. D. (1981) Symmetry of the Actiniaria and the significance of symmetry features for the classification of the Anthozoa. *Dokl. Acad. Sci. USSR, Biol. Sci.*, 253, 430-432.

Greenwood, P. G., Johnson, L. A. and Mariscal, R. N. (1989) Depletion of ATP in suspensions of isolated cnidae: a possible role of ATP in the maturation and maintenance of anthozoan cnidae. *Comp. Biochem. Physiol.*, 93A, 761-765.

Greenwood, P. G. and Mariscal, R. N. (1984a) Immature nematocyst incorporation by the aeolid nudibranch *Spurilla neapolitana*. *Mar. Biol.*, 80, 35-38.

Greenwood, P. G. and Mariscal, R. N. (1984b) The utilization of cnidarian nematocysts by aeolid nudibranchs: nematocyst maintenance and release in *Spurilla*. Tissue & Cell,16, 719-730.

Greenwood, P. G. and Mariscal, R. N. (1984c) Nematocyst maturation in vitro: the effects of ATP on isolated nematocysts. *Amer. Zool.*, 24, 31A (abstract).

Griffiths, D. (1975) Prey availability and the food of predators. *Ecology,* 56, 1209-1214.

Griffiths, R. J. (1977a) Thermal stress and the biology of *Actinia equina* L. (Anthozoa). *J. Exp. Mar. Biol. Ecol.*, 27, 141-154.

Griffiths, R. J. (1977b) Temperature acclimation in *Actinia equina* L. (Anthozoa). *J. Exp. Mar. Biol. Ecol.*, 28, 285-292.

Grimmelikhuijzen, C. J. P., Graff, D. and McFarlane, I. D., 1989 Neurones and neuropeptides in coelenterates. *Arch. Histol. Cytol., Suppl.*, 52, 265-276.

Grosberg, R. K., Rice, W. R. and Palumbi, S. R. (1985) Graft compatibility and clonal identity in invertebrates. *Science*, 229, 487-488.

Grosberg, R. K. and Quinn, J. F. (1989) The evolution of selective aggression conditioned on allorecognition specificity. *Evolution*, 43, 504-515.

Haddon, A. C. & Shackleton, A.M. (1893). Description of some new species of Actiniaria from Torres Straits. *Sc. Proc. R. Dublin Soc.*, VII P. 1. Dublin, 1893-1898.

Hall, S. J., Todd, C. D. and Gordon, A. D. (1982) The influence of ingestive conditioning on the prey species selection in *Aeolidia papillosa* (Mollusca: Nudibranchia). *J. Anim. Ecol.*, 51, 907-921.

Hall, S. J., Todd, C. D. and Gordon, A. D. (1984) Prey-species selection by the anemone predator *Aeolidia papillosa* (L.): the influence of ingestive conditioning and previous dietary history, and a test for switching behaviour. *J. Exp. Mar. Biol. Ecol.*, 82, 11-33.

Halliwell, B. and Gutteridge, J. M. C. (1985) *Free Radicals in Biology and Medicine*, Oxford University Press, Oxford, UK, 346 pp.

Hamner, W. M. and Dunn, D. F. (1980) Tropical Corallimorpharia (Coelenterata: Anthozoa) feeding by envelopment. *Micronesica*, 16, 37-41.

Hand, C. (1955a) The sea anemones of central California Part II. The endomyarian and mesomyarian anemones. *Wasmann J. Biol.*, 13, 37-99.

Hand, C. (1955b) The sea anemones of central California Part III. The acontiarian anemones. *Wasmann J. Biol.*, 13, 189-251.

Hand, C. (1959) On the origin and phylogeny of the coelenterates. *Syst. Zool.*, 8, 191-202.

Hand, C. (1966) On the evolution of the Actiniaria. In W. J. Rees (ed.), *The Cnidaria and Their Evolution*, Academic Press, London, pp. 135-146.

Hanlon, R. T. and Kaufman, L. (1976) Associations of seven West Indian reef fishes with sea anemones. *Bull. Mar. Sci.*, 26, 225-232.

Harper, J. L. (1977) *Population Biology of Plants*, Academic Press, New York, 892 pp.

Harris, L. G. (1973) Nudibranch associations. In T. C. Cheng (ed.), *Current Topics in Comparative Pathobiology*, Vol. 2, Academic Press, New York, pp. 213-315.

Harris, L. G. (1986) Size-selective predation in a sea anemone, nudibranch, and fish food chain. *The Veliger*, 29, 38-47.

Harris, L. G. (1987) Aeolid nudibranchs as predators and prey. *Amer. Malacol. Bull.*, 5, 287-292.

Harris, L. G. and Duffy, S. J. (1980) The influence of prey size on the preference hierarchy of the nudibranch *Aeolidia papillosa* (L.). *Amer. Zool.*, 20, 923 (abstract).

Harris, L. G. and Howe, N. R. (1979) An analysis of the defensive mechanisms observed in the anemone *Anthopleura elegantissima* in response to its nudibranch predator *Aeolidia papillosa. Biol. Bull.*, 157, 138-152.

Hart, C. E. and Crowe, J. H. (1977) The effect of attached gravel on survival of intertidal anemones. Trans. Amer. *Microsc. Soc.*, 96, 28-41.

Hartnoll, R. G. (1970) The relationship of an amphipod and a spider crab with the snakelocks anemone. *Ann. Rep. Mar. Biol. Sta. Port Erin*, 83, 37-42.

Hartog, J.C. DEN (1980) Caribbean Shallow Water Corallimorpharia. *Zoologische Verhandelingen*. (176): 1-83.

Harvell, C.D., Fenical, W. and C.H. Greene. 1988. Chemical and structural defenses of Caribbean gorgonians (*Pseudopterogorgia* spp.) I: Development of an *in situ* feeding assay. *Mar. Ecol. Progr. Ser. 49:287-294.*

----------------, ------------, Roussis, V., Ruesink, J.L., Griggs, C.C. and C.H. Greene. 1993. Local and geographic variation in the defensive chemistry of a West Indian gorgonian coral (*Briareum asbestinum*). *Mar. Ecol. Progr. Ser. 93:165-173.*

Haylor, G. S., Thorpe, J. P. and Carter, M. A. (1984) Genetic and ecological differentiation between sympatric colour morphs of the common intertidal sea anemone *Actinia equina. Mar. Ecol. Prog. Ser.*, 16, 281-289.

Headlee, L, L. Reed, and M. Barnes. (1996) Super Glue Use in Live Rock Culture. *SeaScope.* Volume 13, Spring 1996.

Hemmingsen, A. M. (1960) Energy metabolism as related to body size and respiratory surfaces, and its evolution. *Rep. Steno. Mem. Hosp.* (Copenhagen), 9, 1-110.

Henze, M. (1910) U ber den Einfluss des Sauerstoffdrucks auf den Gaswechse=l einiger Meerestiere. *Biochem. Z.*, 26, 255-278.

Herndl, G. J. and Velimirov, B. (1985) Bacteria in the coelenteron of Anthozoa: control of coelenteric bacterial density by the coelenteric fluid. *J. Exp. Mar. Biol. Ecol.*, 93, 115-130.

Herndl, G. J., Velimirov, B. and Krauss, R. E. (1985) Heterotrophic nutrition and control of bacterial density in the coelenteron of the giant sea anemone Stoichactis giganteum. *Mar. Ecol. Prog. Ser.*, 22, 101-105.

Herre, E. A., Leigh, E. G., Jr. and Fischer, E. A. (1987) Sex allocation in animals. In S. C. Stearns (ed.), *The Evolution of Sex and Its Consequences*, Birkhe user, Boston, pp. 219-261.

Herrera, F. C., Lopez, I., Egea, R. and Zanders, I. P. (1989) Short-term osmotic responses of cells and tissues of the sea anemone, *Condylactis gigantea. Comp. Biochem. Physiol.*, 92A, 377-384.

Herrera, F. C., Rodr=EDguez, A., Lopez, I. and Weitzmann, H. (1986) Characterization of cell ion exchange in the sea anemone Condylactis gigantea. *J. Comp. Physiol.*, B, 156, 591-597.

Hertwig, O. and Hertwig, R. (1879-80) Die Actinien anatomisch und histologisch mit besonderer Beru cksichtigung des Nervenmuskelsystems untersucht. Jena *Z. Naturw.*, 13, 14, 457-640; 39-89.

Hertzberg, S., Liaaen-Jensen, S., Enzell, C. R. and Francis, G. W. (1969) Animal carotenoids 3. The carotenoids of *Actinia equina*-structure determination of actinioerythrin and violerythrin. *Acta Chem. Scand.*, 23, 3290-3312.

Hessinger, D. A. and Lenhoff, H. M. (1976) Mechanism of hemolysis induced by nematocyst venom: roles of phospholipase A and direct lytic factor. *Arch. Biochem. Biophys.*, 173, 603-613.

Hessinger, D. A. and Lenhoff, H. M. (eds.) (1988) *The Biology of Nematocysts*, Academic Press, San Diego, California, 600 pp.

Hessinger, D. A., Lenhoff, H. M. and Kahan, L. B. (1973) Haemolytic, phospholipase A and nerve-affecting activities of sea anemone nematocyst venom. *Nature New Biol.*, 241, 125-127.

Hidaka, M. and Mariscal, R. N. (1988) Effects of ions on nematocysts isolated from acontia of the sea anemone *Calliactis tricolor* by different methods. *J. Exp. Biol.*, 136, 23-34.

Hildemann, W. H., Bigger, C. H. and Johnston, I. S. (1979) Histoincompatibility reactions and allogeneic polymorphism among invertebrates. *Transplant. Proc.*, 11, 1136-1141.

Hill, D. (1956) Rugosa. In R. C. Moore (ed.), *Treatise on Invertebrate Paleontology. Part F, Coelenterata*, University of Kansas, Lawrence, pp. F233-F324.

Hill-Manning, D. N. and Blanquet, R. S. (1979) Seasonal changes in the lipids of the sea anemone, *Metridium senile* (L.). *J. Exp. Mar. Biol. Ecol.*, 36, 249-257.

Hochachka, P. W. (1980) *Living without Oxygen: Closed and Open Systems in Hypoxia Tolerance*, Harvard University Press, Cambridge, Massachusetts,181 pp.

Hochachka, P. W. and Somero, G. N. (1984) *Biochemical Adaptation,* Princeton University Press, Princeton, New Jersey, 537 pp.

Hoffmann, R. J. (1976) Genetics and asexual reproduction on the sea anemone *Metridium senile. Biol. Bull.,* 151, 478-488.

Hoffmann, R. J. (1981) Evolutionary genetics of *Metridium senile.* I. Kinetic differences in phosphoglucose isomerase allozymes. *Biochem. Genet.,* 19, 129-144.Hoffmann, R. J. (1983) Temperature modulation of the kinetics of phosphoglucose isomerase genetic variants from the sea anemone *Metridium senile. J. Exp. Zool.,* 227, 361-370.

Hoffmann, R. J. (1985) Thermal adaptation and the properties of phosphoglucose isomerase allozymes from a sea anemone. In P. E. Gibbs (ed.), *Proceedings of the Nineteenth European Marine Biology Symposium,* Cambridge University Press, Cambridge, UK, pp. 505-514.

Hoffmann, R. J. (1986) Variation in contributions of asexual reproduction to the genetic structure of populations of the sea anemone *Metridium senile.* Evolution, 40, 357-365.

Hoffmann, R. J. (1987) Short-term stability of genetic structure in populations of the sea anemone *Metridium senile. Mar. Biol.,* 93, 499-507.

Holley, M. C. (1984) The ciliary basal apparatus is adapted to the structure and mechanics of the epithelium. *Tissue & Cell,* 16, 287-310.

Holley, M. C. (1985) Adaptation of a ciliary basal apparatus to cell shape changes in a contractile epithelium. *Tissue & Cell,* 17, 321-334.

Holley, M. C. and Shelton, G.A.B. (1984) Reversal of the direction of mucus-flow on the ciliated pharynx of a sea anemone. *J. Exp. Biol.,* 108, 151-161.

Holts, L.J. and K.A. Beauchamp 1993. Sexual reproduction in the corallimorpharian sea anemone *Corynactis californica* in a central California kelp forest. *Mar. Biol. 116:129-136.*

Hooper, S. N. and Ackman, R. G. (1971) Trans-6-hexadecenoic acid and the corresponding alcohol in lipids of the sea anemone *Metridium dianthus.* Lipids, 6, 341-346.

Hopkins, C. C. E., Seiring, J. V., Nyholmen, O. and Hermannsen, A. (1984) Ecological energetics from total lipid and total protein: fact and artifact using a gravimetric method for lipid and a biuret method for protein. *Oceanogr. Mar. Biol. Ann. Rev.,* 22, 211-261.

Horridge, G. A. (1957) The co-ordination of the protective retraction of coral polyps. *Phil. Trans. Royal Soc. Lond.,* B, 240, 495-528.

Hovland, M. and Thomsen, E. (1989) Hydrocarbon-based communities in the North Sea? *Sarsia,* 74, 29-42.

Howe, N. R. (1976a) Proline inhibition of a sea anemone alarm pheromone response. *J. Exp. Biol.,* 65, 147-156.

Howe, N. R. (1976b) Behavior of sea anemones evoked by the alarm pheromone anthopleurine. *J. Comp. Physiol.*, 107, 67-76.

Howe, N. R. and Harris, L. G. (1978) Transfer of the sea anemone pheromone, anthopleurine, by the nudibranch *Aeolidia papillosa*. *J. Chem. Ecol.*, 5, 551-561.

Howe, N. R. and Sheikh, Y. M. (1975) Anthopleurine: a sea anemone alarm pheromone. *Science*, 189, 386-388.

Hughes, R. N. (1987) The functional ecology of clonal animals. *Functional Ecol.*, 1, 63-69.

Hughes, R. N. (1989) *A Functional Biology of Clonal Animals*, Chapman and Hall, London, 331 pp.

Hunt, A. and Ayre, D. J. (1989) Population structure in the sexually reproducing sea anemone *Oulactis muscosa*. *Mar. Biol.*, 102, 537-544.

Hunter, T. (1984) The energetics of asexual reproduction: pedal laceration in the symbiotic sea anemone *Aiptasia pulchella* (Carlgren, 1943). *J. Exp. Mar. Biol. Ecol.*, 83, 127-147.

Hyman, L.H. 1940. *The Invertebrates: Protozoa through Ctenophora*. McGraw-Hill Book Co. Inc., New York, London, 726 pp.

Hyman, L. H. (1940) Chapter VII. Metazoa of the tissue grade of construction- the radiate phyla-Phylum Cnidaria. In *The Invertebrates: Protozoa through Ctenophora*, McGraw-Hill, New York, pp. 365-661.

Isay, S. V. and Busarova, N. G. (1984) Study on fatty acid composition of marine organisms-I. Unsaturated fatty acids of Japan Sea invertebrates. *Comp. Biochem. Physiol.*, 77B, 803-810.

Ishida, J. (1936) Digestive enzymes of *Actinia mesembryanthemum*. *Annot. Zool. Japon.*, 15, 285-305.

Ivleva, I. V. (1964) Elements of energetic balance in sea anemones. *Trans. Sevastopol Biol. Sta., Acad. Sci. USSR*, 25, 410-428 (in Russian).

Jackson, J. B. C. (1977) Competition on marine hard substrata: the adaptive significance of solitary and colonial strategies. *Amer. Nat.*, 111, 743-767.

Jackson, J. B. C. (1979) Morphological strategies of sessile animals. In G. Larwood and B. R. Rosen (eds.), *Biology and Systematics of Colonial Organisms. Systematics Association Special* Vol. No. 11, Academic Press, London, pp. 499-555.

Jackson, J. B. C. (1985) Distribution and ecology of clonal and aclonal benthic invertebrates. In J. B. C. Jackson, L. W. Buss and R. E. Cook (eds.), *Population Biology and Evolution of Clonal Organisms*, Yale University Press, New Haven, pp. 297-355.

Jackson, J. B. C., Buss, L. W. and Cook, R. E. (eds.) (1985) *Population Biology and Evolution of Clonal Organisms*, Yale University Press, New Haven, 530 pp.

Janssen, H. H. and Mi ller, H. (1981) Effects of various feeding conditions on *Anemonia sulcata*. Zool. Anz., 206, 161-170.

Jennison, B. L. (1979a) Annual fluctuations of lipid levels in the sea anemone *Anthopleura elegantissima* (Brandt, 1835). *J. Exp. Mar. Biol. Ecol.*, 39, 211-221.

Jennison, B. L. (1979b) Gametogenesis and reproductive cycles in the sea anemone *Anthopleura elegantissima* (Brandt, 1835). *Can. J. Zool.*, 57, 403-411.

Jennison, B. L. (1981) Reproduction in three species of sea anemones from Key West, Florida. *Can. J. Zool.*, 59, 1708-1719.

Jeuniaux, C. (1962) Digestion de la chitine chez les actiniaires (Coelenteres Anthozoaires). *Cah. Biol. Mar.*, 3, 391-400.

Johnson, L. L. and Shick, J. M. (1977) Effects of fluctuating temperature and immersion on asexual reproduction in the intertidal sea anemone *Haliplanella luciae* (Verrill) in laboratory culture. *J. Exp. Mar. Biol. Ecol.*, 28, 141-149.

Johnston, G. (1847) *A History of the British Zoophytes*, Vol. II, 2nd ed., Van Voorst, London, 74 plates.

Jones, W. C., Pickthall, V. J. and Nesbitt, S. P. (1977) A respiratory rhythm in sea anemones. *J. Exp. Biol.*, 68, 187-198.

Jeergensen, B. B. (1980) Seasonal oxygen depletion in the bottom waters of a Danish fjord and its effect on the benthic community. *Oikos*, 34, 68-76.

Josephson, R. K. (1966) Neuromuscular transmission in a sea anemone. *J. Exp. Biol.*, 45, 305-319.

Josephson, R. K. and March, S. C. (1966) The swimming performance of the sea-anemone Boloceroides. *J. Exp. Biol.*, 44, 493-506.

Kaplan, S. W. (1983) Intrasexual aggression in *Metridium senile. Biol. Bull.*, 165, 416-418.

Kaplan, S. W. (1984) The association between the sea anemone *Metridium senile* (L.) and the mussel *Mytilus edulis* (L.) reduces predation by the starfish *Asterias forbesi* (Desor). *J. Exp. Mar. Biol. Ecol.*, 79, 155-157.

Karnaukhov, V. N. (1990) Carotenoids: recent progress, problems and prospects. *Comp. Biochem. Physiol.*, 95B, 1-20.

Karlson, R.H. 1981. Reproductive patterns in *Zoanthgus* spp. from Discovery Bay, Jamaica. *Proc. 4th Int. Coral Reef Symp. Vol.2:699-704.*

Kasschau, M. R. and McCommas, S. A. (1982) Glycine concentration as a biochemical indicator of sex and maturation in the sea anemone *Bunodosoma cavernata. Comp. Biochem. Physiol.,* 72A, 595-597.

Kasschau, M. R., Ragland, J. B., Pinkerton, S. O. and Chen, E. C. M. (1984a) Time related changes in the free amino acid pool of the sea anemone, *Bunodosoma cavernata*, during salinity stress. *Comp. Biochem. Physiol.*, 79A, 155-159.

Kasschau, M. R., Skaggs, M. M. and Chen, E. C. M. (1980) Accumulation of glutamate in sea anemones exposed to heavy metals and organic amines. *Bull. Envir. Contam. Toxicol.*, 25, 873-878.

Kasschau, M. R., Skisak, C. M., Cook, J. P. and Mills, W. R. (1984b) b-alanine metabolism and high salinity stress in the sea anemone, *Bunodosoma cavernata. J. Comp. Physiol.*, B, 154, 181-186.

Kellogg, R. B. and Patton, J. S. (1983) Lipid droplets, medium of energy exchange in the symbiotic anemone *Condylactis gigantea*: a model coral polyp. *Mar. Biol.*, 75, 137-149.

Kem, W. R. (1988a) Peptide chain toxins of marine animals. In D. G. Fautin (ed.), *Biomedical Importance of Marine Organisms. Memoirs of the California Academy of Sciences,* No. 13, California Academy of Sciences, San Francisco, pp. 69-83.

Kem, W. R. (1988b) Sea anemone toxins: structure and action. In D. A. Hessinger and H. M. Lenhoff (eds.), *The Biology of Nematocysts,* Academic Press, San Diego, California, pp. 375-406.

Kiener, A. (1971) Contribution a l'ecologie, la physiologie et l'ethologie de l'actinie Diadumene luciae (Verrill). *Bull. Soc. Zool. Fr.*, seance du 14 Decembre 1971, 581-603.

Kimura, S., Hashimoto, Y. and K. Yamazato. 1971. Toxicity of the zoanthid *Palythoa tuberculosa. Toxicon 10:611-617.*

Kinzie, R. A., III (1974) Experimental infection of aposymbiotic gorgonian polyps with zooxanthellae. *J. Exp. Mar. Biol. Ecol.*, 15, 335-345.

Kinzie, R. A., III and Chee, G. S. (1979) The effect of different zooxanthellae on the growth of experimentally reinfected hosts. *Biol. Bull.*, 156, 315-327.

Kirkpatrick, D. S. and Bishop, S. H. (1973) Phosphonoprotein. Characterization of aminophosphonic acid-rich glycoproteins from sea anemones. *Biochemistry*, 12, 2829-2840.

Kittredge, J. S. and Roberts, E. (1969) A carbon-phosphorus bond in nature. *Science*, 164, 37-42.

Kleiber, M. (1961) *The Fire of Life. An Introduction to Animal Energetics,* John Wiley & Sons, New York, 454 pp.

Knop, D. (1996) Giant Clams. Dähne Verlag, Ettlingen Germany. 255pp.

Knop, D. (1997) Vegetative Vermehrung durch Fragmentation, *DATZ* (*Deutsche Aquarien- und Terrarien-Zeitschrift*), 4, 231-235.

Knowlton, N. and Keller, B. D. (1986) Larvae which fall far short of their potential: highly localized recruitment in an alpheid shrimp with extended larval development. *Bull. Mar. Sci.*, 39, 213-223.

Koehl, M. A. R. (1977a) Effects of sea anemones on the flow forces they encounter. *J. Exp. Biol.*, 69, 87-105.

Koehl, M. A. R. (1977b) Mechanical diversity of connective tissue of the body wall of sea anemones. *J. Exp. Biol.*, 69, 107-125.

Koehl, M. A. R. (1977c) Mechanical organization of cantilever-like organisms: sea anemones. *J. Exp. Biol.*, 69, 127-142.

Koehl, M. A. R. (1977d) Water flow and the morphology of zoanthid colonies. In D. L. Taylor (ed.), *Proceedings of the Third International Coral Reef Symposium, Vol. 1, Biology,* Rosenstiel School of Marine and Atmospheric Science, University of Miami, Miami, Florida, pp. 438-444.

Koehn, R. K. and Shumway, S. E. (1982) A genetic/physiological explanation for differential growth rate among individuals of the American oyster, Crassostrea virginica (Gmelin). *Mar. Biol. Lett.*, 3, 35-42.

Krijgsman, B. J. and Talbot, F. H. (1953) Experiments on digestion in sea-anemones. *Arch. Int. Physiol.*, 61, 277-291.

Krinsky, N. I. (1978) Non-photosynthetic functions of carotenoids. *Phil. Trans. R. Soc. Lond.*, B, 284, 581-590.

Krinsky, N. I. (1982) Photobiology of carotenoid protection. In J. D. Regan and

J. A. Parrish (eds.), *The Science of Photomedicine*, Plenum, New York, pp. 397-407.

Krukenberg, C. F. W. (1880) Über den Verdauungsmodus der Aktinien. *Vergl. physiol. Studien an den Küste der Adria*, 1, 33-56.

LaBarre, S.C. and J.C. Coll. 1986. Movement in soft corals: An interaction between *Nephthea brassica* (Coelenerata: Octocorallia) and *Acropora hyaccinthus* (Coelenerata: Scleractinia). *Mar. Biol. 72:119-124.*

------------------, Coll, J.C. and P.W. Sammarco. 1986. Defensive strategies of soft corals (Coelenterata: Octocorallia) of the Great Barrier Reef. II. The relationship between toxicity and feeding deterrence. *Biol. Bull. 171-565-576.*

Leone, P.A., Bowden, B.F., Caroll, A.R. and J.C. Coll. 1995. Chemical consequences of relocation of the soft coral *Lobophytum compactum* and its placement in contact with the red alga *Plocamium hamatum*. *Mar. Biol. 122:675-679.*

Larkman, A. U. (1980) Ultrastructural aspects of gametogenesis in Actinia equina L. In P. Tardent and R. Tardent (eds.), *Developmental and Cellular Biology of Coelenterates*, Elsevier/North-Holland Biomedical Press, Amsterdam, pp. 61-66.

Larkman, A. U. (1981) An ultrastructural investigation of the early stages of oocyte differentiation in *Actinia fragacea* (Cnidaria; Anthozoa). *Int. J. Invert. Reprod.*, 4, 147-167.

Larkman, A. U. and Carter, M. A. (1982) Preliminary ultrastructural and autoradiographic evidence that the trophonema of the sea anemone *Actinia fragacea* has a nutritive function. Int. *J. Invert. Reprod.*, 4, 375-379.

Lasker, H.R. 1990. Clonal propagation and population dynamics of a gorgonian coral. *Ecology 71:1578-1589.*

--------------- and K. Kim. 1996. Larval development and settlement behaviour of the gorgonian coral *Plexaura kuna* (Lasker, Kim and Coffroth). *J. Exp. Mar. Biol. Ecol. 207:161-175.*

Lawn, I. D. (1975) An electrophysiological analysis of chemoreception in the sea anemone *Tealia felina. J. Exp. Biol.*, 63, 525-536.

Lawn, I. D. (1976) Swimming in the sea anemone *Stomphia coccinea* triggered by a slow conduction system. *Nature,* 262, 708-709.

Lawn, I. D. (1980) A transmesogloeal conduction system in the swimming sea anemone *Stomphia. J. Exp. Biol.*, 83, 45-52.

Lawn, I. D. and Ross, D. M. (1982a) The behavioural physiology of the swimming sea anemone *Boloceroides mcmurrichi. Proc. R. Soc. Lond.*, B, 216, 315-334.

Lawn, I. D. and Ross, D. M. (1982b) The release of the pedal disk in an undescribed species of *Tealia* (Anthozoa: Actiniaria). *Biol. Bull.*, 163, 188-196.

Lawrence, J. M. (1987) *A Functional Biology of Echinoderms,* Croom Helm, London, 340 pp.

LeBoeuf, R. D., McCommas, S. A., Howe, N. R. and Tauber, J. D. (1981) The role of carotenoids in the color polymorphism of the sea anemone, *Bunodosoma granulifera* (Anthozoa: Actiniaria). *Comp. Biochem. Physiol.*, 68B, 25-29.

Lee, R. F., Hirota, J. and Barnett, A. M. (1971) Distribution and importance of wax esters in marine copepods and other zooplankton. *Deep-Sea Res.*, 18, 1147-1165.

Leghissa, S. (1965) Nervous organization and the problem of the synapse in *Actinia equina. Amer. Zool.*, 5, 411-424.

Lehninger, A. L. (1973) *Bioenergetics,* 2nd ed., W.A. Benjamin, Menlo Park, California, 245 pp.

Lenhoff, H. M., Heagy, W. and Danner, J. (1976) A view of the evolution of chemoreceptors based on research with cnidarians. In G. O. Mackie (ed.), *Coelenterate Ecology and Behavior,* Plenum, New York, pp. 571-579.

Lesser, M. P. (1989) Photobiology of natural populations of zooxanthellae from the sea anemone *Aiptasia pallida:* assessment of the host's role in protection against ultraviolet radiation. *Cytometry,* 10, 653-658.

Lesser, M. P. and Shick, J. M. (1989a) Effects of irradiance and ultraviolet radiation on photoadaptation in the zooxanthellae of *Aiptasia pallida:* primary production, photoinhibition, and enzymic defenses against oxygen toxicity. *Mar. Biol.*, 102, 243-255.

Lesser, M. P. and Shick, J. M. (1989b) Photoadaptation and defenses against oxygen toxicity in zooxanthellae from natural populations of symbiotic cnidarians. *J. Exp. Mar. Biol. Ecol.*, 134, 129-141.

Lesser, M. P., Stochaj, W. R., Tapley, D. W. and Shick, J. M. (1990) Physiological mechanisms of bleaching in coral reef anthozoans: effects of irradiance, ultraviolet radiation, and temperature on the activities of protective enzymes against active oxygen. *Coral Reefs,* 8, 225-232.

Levine, D. M. and Blanchard, O. J., Jr. (1980) Acclimation of two shrimps of the genus Periclimenes to sea anemones. *Bull. Mar. Sci.*, 30, 460-466.

Lewis, J.B. 1982. Feeding behaviour and feeding ecology of Octocorallia (Coelenterata: Anthozoa). *J. Zool. Lond. 196:371-384.*

Lewis, J. B. (1984) Photosynthetic production by the coral reef anemone, *Lebrunea coralligens* Wilson, and behavioral correlates of two nutritional strategies. *Biol. Bull.*, 167, 601-612.

Limbaugh, C., Pederson, H. and Chace, F. A., Jr. (1961) Shrimps that clean fishes. *Bull. Mar. Sci.*, 11, 237-257.

Lindstedt, K. J. (1971a) Biphasic feeding response in a sea anemone: control by asparagine and glutathione. *Science*, 173, 333-334.

Lindstedt, K. J. (1971b) Chemical control of feeding behavior. *Comp. Biochem. Physiol.*, 39A, 553-581.

Lindstedt, K. J., Muscatine, L. and Lenhoff, H. M. (1968) Valine activation of feeding in the sea anemone *Boloceroides*. *Comp. Biochem. Physiol.*, 26, 567-572.

Livingstone, D. R. (1983) Invertebrate and vertebrate pathways of anaerobic metabolism: evolutionary considerations. *J. Geol. Soc. London*,140, 27-37.

Livingstone, D. R., Zwaan, A. de, Leopold, M. and Marteijn, E. (1983) Studies on the phylogenetic distribution of pyruvate oxidoreductases. *Biochem. Syst. Ecol.*, 11, 415-425.

Logan, C. A. (1975) Topographic changes in responding during habituation to waterstream stimulation in sea anemones (*Anthopleura elegantissima*). *J. Comp. Physiol. Psychol.*, 89, 105-117.

Logan, C. A. and Beck, H. P. (1978) Long-term retention of habituation in the sea anemone (*Anthopleura elegantissima*). *J. Comp. Physiol. Psychol.*, 92, 928-936.

Loseva, L. M. (1971) Observations on oogenesis of actinians. II. Oogenesis in *Tealia crassicornis* (Muell), *Metridium senile* (L.) and *Protanthea simplex* (Carlg.). *Vestn. Leningr. Univ. Biol.*, 9, 22-29 (in Russian).

Losey, G. S., Jr. (1978) The symbiotic behavior of fishes. In D. I. Mostofsky (ed.), *The Behavior of Fish and Other Aquatic Animals*, Academic Press, New York, pp. 1-31.

Louis, C. (1960) Modalites et determinisme experimental de la scissip=arite chez l'Actinie *Anemonia sulcata* Pennant. *C.R. Acad. Sci. Paris*, 251, 134-136.

Lubbock, R. (1979) Chemical recognition and nematocyte excitation in a sea anemone. *J. Exp. Biol.*, 83, 283-292.

Lubbock, R. (1980a) Clone-specific cellular recognition in a sea anemone. *Proc. Nat. Acad. Sci. USA*, 77, 6667-6669.

Lubbock, R. (1980b) Why are clownfishes not stung by sea anemones? *Proc. R. Soc. Lond.*, B, 207, 35-61.

Lubbock, R. (1981) The clownfish/anemone symbiosis: a problem of cellular recognition. *Parasitology*, 82, 159-173.

Lubbock, R. and Allbut, C. (1981) The sea anemone *Actinia equina* tolerates allogeneic juveniles but alters their phenotype. *Nature,* 293, 474-475.

Lubbock, R., Gupta, B. L. and Hall, T. A. (1981) Novel role of calcium in exocytosis: mechanism of nematocyst discharge as shown by X-ray microanalysis. *Proc. Nat. Acad. Sci. USA*, 78, 3624-3628.

Lubbock, R. and Shelton, G. A. B. (1981) Electrical activity following cellular recognition of self and non-self in a sea anemone. *Nature*, 289, 59-60.

Mackie, G. O., Anderson, P. A. V. and Singla, C. L. (1984) Apparent absence of gap junctions in two classes of Cnidaria. *Biol. Bull.*, 167, 120-123.

MacMunn, C. A. (1885) Observations on the chromatology of Actini=E6. *Phil. Trans. Royal Soc. London*, Ser. II, 176, 641-663.

Maida, M, Sammarco, P.W. and J.C. Coll. 1995. Effects of soft corals on scleractinian coral recruitment. I: Directional allelopathy and inhibition of settlement. *Mar. Ecol. Progr. Ser. 121:191-202.*

Male, K. B. and Storey, K. B. (1983) Kinetic characterization of NADP-specific glutamate dehydrogenase from the sea anemone, Anthopleura xanthogrammica: control of amino acid biosynthesis during osmotic stress. *Comp. Biochem. Physiol.*, 76B, 823-829.

Manchenko, G. P. (1985) New data on high level of allozymic variation in marine invertebrates. *Genetika*, 21, 936-944 (in Russian).

Manchenko, G. P. and Balakirev, E. S. (1984) Allozymic variation in actinia *Anthopleura orientalis* from Peter the Great Bay of the Sea of Japan. *Genetika,* 20, 2072-2074 (in Russian).

Manchenko, G. P. and Shed'ko, S. V. (1987) Comparative genetic study of red and white actinians *Metridium senile fimbriatum* from Peter the Great Bay, Sea of Japan. *Soviet J. Mar. Biol.*, 13, 99-104.

Mangum, C. P. (1976) Primitive respiratory adaptations. In R. C. Newell (ed.), *Adaptation to Environment: Essays on the Physiology of Marine Animals,* Butterworth's, London, pp. 191-278.

Mangum, C. P. and Johansen, K. (1975) The colloid osmotic pressures of invertebrate body fluids. *J. Exp. Biol.*, 63, 661-671.

Mangum, C. and Van Winkle, W. (1973) Responses of aquatic invertebrates to declining oxygen conditions. *Amer. Zool.*, 13, 529-541.

Mangum, D. C. (1980) Sea anemone neuromuscular responses in anaerobic conditions. *Science*, 208, 1177-1178.

Manuel, R. L. (1988) British Anthozoa. Synopses of the British Fauna No.18 (revised), E. *J. Brill, Leiden,* 241 pp.

Mariscal, R. N. (1966) The symbiosis between tropical sea anemones and fishes: a review. In R. I. Bowman (ed.), The Galapagos. *Proceedings of the Symposia of the Galapagos International Scientific Project,* University of California Press, Berkeley, pp. 157-171.

Mariscal, R. N. (1969) The protection of the anemone fish, *Amphiprion xanthurus,* from the sea anemone, *Stoichactis kenti. Experientia*, 25, 1114.

Mariscal, R. N. (1970a) The nature of the symbiosis between Indo-Pacific anemone fishes and sea anemones. *Mar. Biol.*, 6, 58-65.

Mariscal, R. N. (1970b) *A field and laboratory study of the symbiotic behavior of fishes and sea anemones from the tropical Indo-Pacific.* Univ. of California Publ. in Zoology, 91, 1-33 + 4 plates.

Mariscal, R. N. (1970c) An experimental analysis of the protection of *Amphiprion xanthurus* Cuvier & Valenciennes and some other anemone fishes from sea anemones. *J. Exp. Mar. Biol. Ecol.*, 4, 134-149.

Mariscal, R. N. (1971) Experimental studies on the protection of anemone fishes from sea anemones. In T. C. Cheng (ed.), *Aspects of the Biology of Symbiosis*, University Park Press, Baltimore, Maryland, pp. 283-315.

Mariscal, R. N. (1972) Behavior of symbiotic fishes and sea anemones. In H. E. Winn and B. L. Olla (eds.), *Behavior of Marine Animals, Vol. 2*, Plenum, New York, pp. 327-360.

Mariscal, R. N. (1973) The control of nematocyst discharge during feeding by sea anemones. *Publ. Seto Mar. Biol. Lab.* (Proc. Second Int. Symp. on Cnidaria), 20, 695-702.

Mariscal, R. N. (1974a) Scanning electron microscopy of the sensory epithelia and nematocysts of corals and a corallimorpharian sea anemone. In *Proceedings of the Second International Coral Reef Symposium, Vol. 1*, Great Barrier Reef Committee, Brisbane, pp. 519-532.

Mariscal, R. N. (1974b) Scanning electron microscopy of the sensory surface of the tentacles of sea anemones and corals. Z. Zellforsch., 147, 149-156.

Mariscal, R. N. (1974c) Nematocysts. In L. Muscatine and H. M. Lenhoff (eds.), *Coelenterate Biology: Reviews and New Perspectives*, Academic Press, New York, pp. 129-178.

Mariscal, R. N. (1984) Cnidaria: cnidae. In J. Bereiter-Hahn, A. G. Matoltsy and K. S. Richards (eds.), *Biology of the Integument. Vol. 1. Invertebrates*, Springer-Verlag, Berlin, pp. 57-58.

Mariscal, R. N. (1988) X-ray microanalysis and perspectives on the role of calcium and other elements in cnidae. In D. A. Hessinger and H. M. Lenhoff (eds.), *The Biology of Nematocysts*, Academic Press, San Diego, California, pp. 95-114.

Mariscal, R. N., Bigger, C. H. and McLean, R. B. (1976) The form and function of cnidarian spirocysts 1. Ultrastructure of the capsule exterior and relationship to the tentacle sensory surface. *Cell Tiss. Res.,* 168, 465-474.

Mariscal, R. N., Conklin, E. J. and Bigger, C. H. (1977) The ptychocyst, a major new category of cnida used in tube construction by a cerianthid anemone. *Biol. Bull.*, 152, 392-405.

Mariscal, R. N., Conklin, E. J. and Bigger, C. H. (1978) The putative sensory receptors associated with the cnidae of cnidarians. In *Scanning Electron Microscopy, Vol. II,* SEM, Inc., O'Hare, Illinois, pp. 959-966.

Marks, P. S. (1976) Nervous control of light responses in the sea anemone, *Calamactis praelongus. J. Exp. Biol.*, 65, 85-96.

Martin, E. J. (1968) Specific antigens released into sea water by contracting anemones (Coelenterata). Comp. Biochem. Physiol., 25, 169-176.

Mason, W. T. (1972) Isolation and characterization of the lipids of the sea anemone *Metridium senile. Biochim. Biophys. Acta*, 280, 538-544.

Mathias, A. P., Ross, D. M. and Schachter, M. (1960) The distribution of 5-hydroxytryptamine, tetramethylammonium, homarine, and other substances in sea anemones. *J. Physiol.*, 151, 296-311.

Matther, P. and I. Bennett. 1993. *A Coral Reef Handbook.* 3rd ed. Surrey Beatty and Sons PTY Ltd., Chipping Norton, NSW, Australia.

Mauzey, K. P., Birkeland, C. and Dayton, P. K. (1968) Feeding behavior of asteroids and escape responses of their prey in the Puget Sound region. *Ecology*, 49, 603-619.

Maynard Smith, J. (1978) *The Evolution of Sex*, Cambridge University Press, Cambridge, UK, 222 pp.

McClendon, J. F. (1906) On the locomotion of a sea anemone (*Metridium marginatum*). *Biol. Bull.*, 10, 66-67.

McClendon, J. F. (1911) On adaptations in structure and habits of some marine animals of Tortugas, Florida. *Pap. Tortugas Lab.*, Carnegie Inst. Washington, 3, 57-62 + 2 plates.

McCloskey, L. R., Wethey, D. S. and Porter, J. W. (1978) Measurement and interpretation of photosynthesis and respiration in reef corals. Monogr. *Oceanogr. Methodol.* (UNESCO), 5, 379-396.

McCommas, S. A. and LeBoeuf, R. D. (1981) Reduced color polymorphism in a population of *Bunodosoma granulifera*. *Biochem. Syst. Ecol.*, 9, 329-332.

McCommas, S. A. and Lester, L. J. (1980) Electrophoretic evaluation of the taxonomic status of two species of sea anemone. *Biochem. Syst. Ecol.*, 8, 289-292.

McFarlane, I. D. (1969) Co-ordination of pedal-disc detachment in the sea anemone *Calliactis parasitica*. *J. Exp. Biol.*, 51, 387-396.

McFarlane, I. D. (1970) Control of preparatory feeding behaviour in the sea anemone *Tealia felina*. *J. Exp. Biol.*, 53, 211-220.

McFarlane, I. D. (1973) Spontaneous contractions and nerve net activity in the sea anemone *Calliactis parasitica*. *Mar. Behav. Physiol.*, 2, 97-113.

McFarlane, I. D. (1974) Excitatory and inhibitory control of inherent contractions in the sea anemone *Calliactis parasitica*. *J. Exp. Biol.*, 60: 397-422.

McFarlane, I. D. (1975) Control of mouth opening and pharynx protrusion during feeding in the sea anemone *Calliactis parasitica*. *J. Exp. Biol.*, 63, 615-626.

McFarlane, I. D. (1976) Two slow conduction systems coordinate shell-climbing behaviour in the sea anemone *Calliactis parasitica*. *J. Exp. Biol.*, 64, 431-446.

McFarlane, I. D. (1982) *Calliactis parasitica*. In G. A. B. Shelton (ed.), *Electrical Conduction and Behaviour in 'Simple' Invertebrates*, Oxford University Press, New York, pp. 243-265.

McFarlane, I.D. (1983) Nerve net pacemakers and phases of behaviour in the sea anemone *Calliactis parasitica*. *J. Exp. Biol.*, 104, 231-246.

McFarlane, I.D. (1984a) Nerve nets and conducting systems in sea anemones: two pathways excite tentacle contractions in *Calliactis parasitica*. *J. Exp. Biol.*, 108, 137-149.

McFarlane, I. D. (1984b) Nerve nets and conducting systems in sea anemones: coordination of ipsilateral and contralateral contractions in *Protanthea simplex*. *Mar. Behav. Physiol.*, 11, 219-228.

McFarlane, I. D., Graff, D. and Grimmelikhuijzen, C. J. P. (1987) Excitatory actions of Antho-RFamide, an anthozoan neuropeptide, on muscles and conducting systems in the sea anemone *Calliactis parasitica*. *J. Exp. Biol.*, 133, 157-168.

McFarlane, I. D. and Lawn, I. D. (1972) Expansion and contraction of the oral disc in the sea anemone *Tealia felina. J. Exp. Biol.*, 57, 633-649.

McFarlane, I. D. and Lawn, I. D. (1990) The senses of sea anemones: responses of the SS1 nerve net to chemical and mechanical stimuli. Hydrobiologia/Developments in *Hydrobiology*, (in press).

McFarlane, I. D. and Shelton, G. A. B. (1975) The nature of adhesion of tentacles to shells during shell-climbing behaviour in the sea anemone *Calliactis parasitica* (Couch). *J. Exp. Mar. Biol. Ecol.*, 19, 177-186.

McKay, M. C. and Anderson, P. A. V. (1988a) Preparation and properties of cnidocytes from the sea anemone *Anthopleura elegantissima. Biol. Bull.*, 174, 47-53.

McKay, M. C. and Anderson, P. A. V. (1988b) On the preparation and properties of isolated cnidocytes and cnidae. In H. M. Lenhoff and D. A. Hessinger (eds.), *The Biology of Nematocysts,* Academic Press, San Diego, California, pp. 273-294.

McLean, R. B. and Mariscal, R. N. (1973) Protection of a hermit crab by its symbiotic sea anemone *Calliactis tricolor. Experientia*, 29, 128-130.

Mereish, K.A., Morris, S., Cullers, G.M., Taylor, T.J. and D.L. Brunner. (1991) Analysis of palytoxin by liquid chromatography and capillary electrophoresis. *J Liq. Chrom. 14(5):1025-1032.*

Mesnil, F. (1901) Recherches sur la digestion intracellulaire et les diastases des actinies. *Ann. Inst. Pasteur*, 15, 352-397.

Metschnikoff, E. (1880) U ber die intracellule re Verdauung bei *Coelenteraten. Zool. Anz.*, 3, 261-263.

Miles, J.S. 1991. Inducible agonistic structures in the tropical corallimorpharian, *Discosoma sanctithomae. Biol. Bull. 180:406-415.*

Minasian, L. L., Jr. (1979) The effect of exogenous factors on morphology and asexual reproduction in laboratory cultures of the intertidal sea anemone, *Haliplanella luciae* (Verrill) (Anthozoa: Actiniaria) from Delaware. *J. Exp. Mar. Biol. Ecol.*, 40, 235-246.

Minasian, L. L., Jr. (1982) The relationship of size and biomass to fission rate in a clone of the sea anemone, *Haliplanella luciae* (Verrill). *J. Exp. Mar. Biol. Ecol.*, 58, 151-162.

Minasian, L. L., Jr. and Mariscal, R. N. (1979) Characteristics and regulation of fission activity in clonal cultures of the cosmopolitan sea anemone, *Haliplanella luciae* (Verrill). *Biol. Bull.*, 157, 478-493.

Miyagawa, K. (1989) Experimental analysis of the symbiosis between anemonefish and sea anemones. *Ethology*, 80, 19-46.

Miyagawa, K. and Hidaka, T. (1980) *Amphiprion clarkii* juvenile: innate protection against and chemical attraction by symbiotic sea anemones. Proc. *Japan Acad.*, B, 56, 356-361.

Miyamoto, T., Tamada, K., Ikeda, N., Komori, T. and R. Higuchi. (1994) Bioactive diter-penoids from Octocorallia: 1. Bioactive diterpenoids: *Litophynols* A and B from the mucus of the soft coral *Litophyton* sp. *J. Nat. Prod. 57:1212-1219.*

------------------, Takenaka, Y., Yamada, K. and R. Higuchi. (1995) Bioactive diter-penoids from Octocorallia: 2. Deoxyxeniolde B, a novel ichthyotoxic diterpenoid from the soft coral *Xenia elongata. J. Nat. Prod. 58:924-928.*

Miyawaki, M. (1951) Notes on the effect of low salinity on an actinian, *Diadumene luciae. J. Fac. Sci.* Hokkaido Univ., Ser. VI, Zool., 10, 123-126.

Miller, H. (1978) Nahrungsi kologische Untersuchungen an Anemonia sulcata Investi-gations of the feeding ecology of *Anemonia sulcata. Zool. Anz.,* 200, 369-373.

Moe, M. A. Jr. (1992) *The Marine Aquarium Handbook 2nd Edition Revised.* Green Turtle Publications. 318 pp.

Molodtsov, N. V. and Vafina, M. G. (1972) The distribution of b-N-acetylglu-cosaminidase in marine invertebrates. Comp. Biochem. Physiol., 41B, 113-120.

Moore, R. E. and Scheuer, P. J. (1971) Palytoxin: a new marine toxin from a coelen-terate. *Science,* 172, 495-498.

Mouchet, S. (1929) Presence de xanthine chez les actinies. *Soc. Zool. Fr. Bull.,* 54, 345-350.

Mouchet, S. (1930) L'excretion chez les actinies. Sta. Oceanogr. Salammb==F4 Notes, 15, 1-14.

Muirhead, A. and J.S. Ryland. 1985. A review of the genus *Isaurus* Gray, 1828 (Zoanthidae), including new records from Fiji. *J. Nat. History 19:323-335.*

Muirhead, A., Tyler, P.A. and M.H. Thurston. 1986. Reproductive biology and growth of the genus *Epizoanthus* (Zoanthidea) from the north east Atlantic. *J. Mar. Biol. Ass. U.K. 66:131-143.*

Muller-Parker, G. (1984a) Dispersal of zooxanthellae on coral reefs by predators on cnidarians. *Biol. Bull.,* 167, 159-167.

Muller-Parker, G. (1984b) Photosynthesis-irradiance responses and photosynthetic periodicity in the sea anemone *Aiptasia pulchella* and its zooxanthellae. *Mar. Biol.,* 82, 225-232.

Muller-Parker, G. (1985) Effect of feeding regime and irradiance on the photophysiology of the symbiotic sea anemone *Aiptasia pulchella. Mar. Biol.,* 90, 65-74.

Muller-Parker, G. (1987) Seasonal variation in light-shade adaptation of natural popu-lations of the symbiotic sea anemone *Aiptasia pulchella* (Carlgren, 1943) in Hawaii. *J. Exp. Mar. Biol. Ecol.,* 112, 165-183.

Muller-Parker, G., Cook, C. B. and D'Elia, C. F. (1990) Feeding affects phosphate fluxes in the symbiotic sea anemone *Aiptasia pallida. Mar. Ecol. Prog. Ser.,* 60, 283-290.

Muller-Parker, G., D'Elia, C. F. and Cook, C. B. (1988) Nutrient limitation of zooxan-thellae: effects of host feeding history on nutrient uptake by isolated algae. In J. H. Choat et al. (eds.), *Proceedings of the 6th International Coral Reef Symposium,* Townsville, Australia, Vol. 3, pp. 15-19.

Murata, M., Miyagawa-Kohshima, K., Nakanishi, K. and Naya, Y. (1986) Characterization of compounds that induce symbiosis between sea anemone and anemone fish. *Science*, 234: 585-587.

Muscatine, L. (1961) Symbiosis in marine and freshwater coelenterates. In H. Lenhoff and W. F. Loomis (eds.), *The Biology of Hydra*, University of Miami Press, Miami, Florida, pp. 255-268.

Muscatine, L. (1971) Experiments on green algae coexistent with zooxanthellae in sea anemones. *Pacific Sci.,* 25, 13-21.

Muscatine, L., Falkowski, P. G. and Dubinsky, Z. (1983) Carbon budgets in symbiotic associations. In E. A. Schenk and W. Schwemmler (eds.), *Endocytobiology, Vol. 2*, Walter de Gruyter, Berlin, pp. 649-658.

Muscatine, L. and Hand, C. (1958) Direct evidence for the transfer of materials from symbiotic algae to the tissues of a coelenterate. *Proc. Nat. Acad. Sci. USA*, 44, 1259-12632.

Muscatine, L. and Lenhoff, H. M. (eds.) (1974) *Coelenterate Biology. Reviews and New Perspectives*, Academic Press, New York, 501 pp.

Muscatine, L., McCloskey, L. R. and Marian, R. E. (1981) Estimating the daily contribution of carbon from zooxanthellae to coral animal respiration. *Limnol. Oceanogr.*, 26, 601-611.

Muscatine, L. and Porter, J. W. (1977) Reef corals: mutualistic symbioses adapted to nutrient-poor environments. *BioScience*, 27, 454-460.

Muscatine, L., Weissman, D. and Doino, J. (1989) By what mechanism does low temperature shock evoke exocytosis of symbiotic algae in the sea anemone *Aiptasia pulchella*? In R.B. Williams (ed.), *5th International Conference on Coelenterate Biology. Programame and Abstracts*, University of Southampton, Southampton, UK, p. 69.

Nagai, Y. and Nagai, S. (1973) Feeding factors for the sea anemone *Anthopleura midorii*. *Mar. Biol.*, 18, 55-60.

Navarro, E. and Ortega, M. M. (1984) Amino acid accumulation from glucose during air exposure and anoxia in the sea anemone *Actinia equina* (L.). *Comp. Biochem. Physiol.*, 78B, 199-202.

Navarro, E. and Ortega, M. M. (1985) Efectos metabolicos de la exposicion al aire y repuesta postaerea en el antozoo intermareal Actinia equina L. Rev. Espa=F1. Fisiol., 41, 471-478.

Navarro, E., Ortega, M. M. and Iglesias, J. I. P. (1987) Ananalysis of variables affecting oxygen consumption in *Actinia equina* L. (Anthozoa) from two shore positions. *Comp. Biochem. Physiol.*, 86A, 233-240.

Navarro, E., Ortega, M. M. and Madariaga, J. M. (1981) Effect of body size, temperature and shore level on aquatic and aerial respiration of *Actinia equina* (L.) (Anthozoa). *J. Exp. Mar. Biol. Ecol.*, 53, 153-162.

Needler, M. and Ross, D. M. (1958) Neuromuscular activity in the sea anemone *Calliactis parasitica* (Couch). *J. Mar. Biol. Ass. UK*, 37, 789-805.

Neigel, J. E. and Avise, J. C. (1985) The precision of histocompatibility response in clonal recognition in tropical marine sponges. *Evolution, 39*, 724-732.

Newell, R. C. (1979) *Biology of Intertidal Animals, Marine Ecological Surveys*, Ltd., Faversham, Kent, UK, 781 pp.

Nicol, J. A. C. (1959) Digestion in sea anemones. *J. Mar. Biol. Ass. UK*, 38, 469-476.

Nicol, J. A. C. (1967) *The Biology of Marine Animals,* 2nd ed., John Wiley & Sons, New York, 699 pp.

North, W. J. (1957) Sensitivity to light in the sea anemone *Metridium senile* (L.) II. Studies of reaction time variability and the effects of changes in light intensity and temperature. *J. Gen Physiol.*, 40, 715-733.

North, W. J. and Pantin, C. F. A. (1958) Sensitivity to light in the sea-anemone *Metridium senile* (L.): adaptation and action spectra. *Proc. R. Soc. London* B., 148, 385-396.

Nosratpour, F (1997) Is The White-Bonnet Anemonefish (*Amphiprion leucokranos*) A Hybrid ? *Aquarium Frontiers.*, March/April, 14-20.

Nyholm, K.-G. (1943) Zur Entwicklung und Entwicklungsbiologie der Ceriantharien und Aktinien. *Zool. Bidr. Uppsala*, 22, 87-248.

Nyholm, K.-G. (1949) On the development and dispersal of *Athenaria actinia* with special reference to *Halcampa duodecimcirrata, M. Sars. Zool. Bidr. Uppsala*, 27, 466-505.

Nyholm, K.-G. (1959) On the development of the primitive actinian Protanthea simplex, Carlgren. *Zool. Bidr. Uppsala*, 33, 69-78.

O'Brien, T. L. (1978) An ultrastructural study of zoochlorellae in a marine coelenterate. *Trans. Amer. Microsc. Soc.*, 97, 320-329.

O'Brien, T. L. (1980) The symbiotic association between intracellular zoochlorellae (Chlorophyceae) and the coelenterate *Anthopleura xanthogrammica. J. Exp. Zool.*, 211, 343-355.

O'Brien, T. L. and Wyttenbach, C. R. (1980) Some effects of temperature on the symbiotic association between zoochlorellae (Chlorophyceae) and the sea anemone *Anthopleura xanthogrammica. Trans. Amer. Microsc. Soc.*, 99, 221-225.

Oglesby, L. C. (1975) *An analysis of water-content regulation in selected worms. In F. J. Vernberg (ed.), Physiological Ecology of Estuarine Organisms,* University of South Carolina Press, Columbia, pp. 181-204.

Okada, Y. K. and Komori, S. (1932) Reproduction asexuelle d'une actinie (Boloceroides) et sa regeneration aux depens d'un tentacule. *Bull. Biol. Fr. Belg,* 66, 164-199.

Oliver, W. A., Jr. (1980) The relationship of the scleractinian corals to the rugose corals. *Paleobiology,* 6, 146-160.

Orlando Munoz, M., Atkinson, B. and Idler, D. R. (1976) Sterol and lipid composition of Phymactis clematis (Drayton). *Comp. Biochem. Physiol.*, 54B, 231-232.

Orr, J., Thorpe, J. P. and Carter, M. A. (1982) Biochemical genetic confirmation of the asexual reproduction of brooded offspring in the sea anemone *Actinia equina. Mar. Ecol. Prog. Ser.*, 7, 227-229.

Ortega, M. M., Iglesias, J. I. P. and Navarro, E. (1984) Acclimation to temperature in *Actinia equina* L.: effects of season and shore level on aquatic oxygen consumption. *J. Exp. Mar. Biol. Ecol.*, 76, 79-87.

Ortega, M. M., Lopez de Pariza, J. M. and Navarro, E. (1988) Seasonal changes in the biochemical composition and oxygen consumption of the sea anemone *Actinia equina* (L.) as related to body size and shore level. *Mar. Biol.*, 97, 137-143.

Ortega, M. M. and Navarro, E. (1988) Seasonal changes of the major lipid classes in *Actinia equina* L. (Anthozoa) in relation to body size and tidal position. *Comp. Biochem. Physiol.*, 89A, 699-704.

Ottaway, J. R. (1973) Some effects of temperature, desiccation, and light on the intertidal anemone *Actinia tenebrosa* Farquhar (Cnidaria: Anthozoa). *Aust. J. Mar. Freshw. Res.*, 24, 103-126.

Ottaway, J. R. (1974) Resistance of juvenile *Actinia tenebrosa* (Cnidaria: Anthozoa) to digestive enzymes. Mauri Ora, 2, 73-83.

Ottaway, J. R. (1977a) Predators of sea anemones. *Tuatara*, 22, 213-221.

Ottaway, J. R. (1977b) Pleurobranchaea novazelandiae preying on *Actinia tenebrosa*. *N.Z. J. Mar. Freshw. Res.*, 11, 125-130.

Ottaway, J. R. (1978) Population ecology of the intertidal anemone *Actinia tenebrosa* I. Pedal locomotion and intraspecific aggression. *Aust. J. Mar. Freshw. Res.*, 29, 787-802.

Ottaway, J. R. (1979a) Population ecology of the intertidal anemone *Actinia tenebrosa* II. Geographical distribution, synonymy, reproductive cycle and fecundity. *Aust. J. Zool.*, 27, 273-290.

Ottaway, J. R. (1979b) Population ecology of the intertidal anemone *Actinia tenebrosa* III. Dynamics and environmental factors. *Aust. J. Mar. Freshw. Res.*, 30, 41-62.

Ottaway, J. R. (1980) Population ecology of the intertidal anemone *Actinia tenebrosa* IV. Growth rates and longevities. *Aust. J. Mar. Freshw. Res.*, 31, 385-395.

Ottaway, J. R. and Kirby, G. C. (1975) Genetic relationships between brooding and brooded *Actinia tenebrosa*. *Nature*, 255, 221-223.

Ottaway, J. R. and Thomas, I. M. (1971) Movement and zonation of the intertidal anemone *Actinia tenebrosa* Farqu. (Cnidaria: Anthozoa) under experimental conditions. *Aust. J. Mar. Freshw. Res.*, 22, 63-78.

Paffenhi fer, G.-A. (1968) Nahrungsaufnahme, Stoffumsatz und Energiehaushalt des marinen Hydroidenpolypen *Clava multicornis*. Helgole nder wiss. *Meeresunters.*, 18, 1-44.

Paletta, M. (1996) Bleaching of Small Polyp Stony Corals in Aquaria. *SeaScope*. Fall 1996.

Palincsar, E. E., Jones, W. R., Palincsar, J. S., Glogowski, M. A. and Mastro, J. L. (1989) Bacterial aggregates within the epidermis of the sea anemone *Aiptasia pallida*. *Biol. Bull.*, 177, 130-140.

Palincsar, J. S., Jones, W. R. and Palincsar, E. E. (1988) Effects of isolation of the endosymbiont *Symbiodinium microadriaticum* (Dinophyceae) from its host *Aiptasia pallida* (Anthozoa) on cell wall ultrastructure and mitotic rate. *Trans. Amer. Microsc. Soc.*, 107, 53-66.

Pantin, C. F. A. (1935a) The nerve net of the Actinozoa I. Facilitation. *J. Exp. Biol.*, 12, 119-138.

Pantin, C. F. A. (1935b) The nerve net of the Actinozoa II. Plan of the nerve net. *J. Exp. Biol.*, 12, 139-155.

Pantin, C. F. A. (1942) The excitation of nematocysts. *J. Exp. Biol.*, 19, 294-310.

Pantin, C. F. A. (1952) The elementary nervous system. *Proc. R. Soc. Lond.*, B, 140, 147-168.

Pantin, C. F. A. (1960) Diploblastic animals. *Proc. Linn. Soc. Lond.*, 171, 1-14 + 4 plates.

Pantin, C. F. A. (1965) Capabilities of the coelenterate behavior machine. *Amer. Zool.*, 5, 581-589.

Pantin, C. F. A. and Pantin, A. M. P. (1943) The stimulus to feeding in *Anemonia sulcata*. *J. Exp. Biol.*, 20, 6-13.

Parker, G. H. (1905) The reversal of ciliary movements in metazoans. *Amer. J. Physiol.*, 13, 1-16.

Parker, G. H. (1916) The effector systems of actinians. *J. Exp. Zool.*, 21, 461-484.

Parker, G. H. (1917) Pedal locomotion in actinians. *J.Exp. Zool.*, 22, 111-124.

Parker, G. H. (1919) *The Elementary Nervous System*, Lippincott, Philadelphia, 229 pp.

Parker, G. H. (1922) The excretion of carbon dioxide by relaxed and contracted sea anemones. *J. Gen. Physiol.*, 5, 45-64.

Parry, G. D. (1983) The influence of the cost of growth on ectotherm metabolism. *J. Theor. Biol.*, 101, 453-477.

Passano, L. M. and Pantin, C. F. A. (1955) Mechanical stimulation in the sea-anemone *Calliactis parasitica*. *Proc. R. Soc. Lond.*, B, 143, 226-238.

Pathirana, C. and Andersen, R. J. (1986) Imbricatine, an unusual benzyltetrahydroiso-quinoline alkaloid isolated from the starfish *Dermasterias imbricata*. *J. Amer. Chem. Soc.*, 108, 8288-8289.

Patronelli, D. L., Zamponi, M., Bustos, A. and Vega, F. V. (1987) Morphological and physiological adaptations in the marginal sphincter of anemone *Phymactis clematis*, Dana 1849 from different environments. *Comp. Biochem. Physiol.*, 88A, 337-340.

Patterson, M. R. (1984) Patterns of whole colony prey capture in the octocoral, *Alcyonium siderium*. *Biol. Bull.*, 167, 613-629.

Patterson, M. R. (1985) *The Effects of Flow on the Biology of Passive Suspension Feeders: Prey Capture, Feeding Rate, and Gas Exchange in Selected Cnidarians*. Ph.D. dissertation, Harvard University, Cambridge, Massachusetts, 342 pp.

Patterson, M. R. and Sebens, K. P. (1989) Forced convection modulates gas exchange in cnidarians. *Proc. Nat. Acad. Sci.* USA, 86, 8833-8836.

Patterson, M.R. 1991. The effects of flow on polyp-level prey capture in an octocoral, *Alcyonium siderium. Biol. Bull. 180:93-102.*

Patton, M.L., Brown, S.T., Harman, R.F. and R.S. Grove. 1991. Effect of the anemone *Corynactis californica* on subtidal predation by sea stars in the southern Californian Bight (USA). *Bull. Mar. Sci. 48(3): 623-634.*

Pearse, J. S., Pearse, V. B. and Newberry, A. T. (1989) Telling sex from growth: dissolving Maynard Smith's paradox. *Bull. Mar. Sci.,* 45, 433-446.

Pearse, V. B. (1974a) Modification of sea anemone behavior by symbiotic zooxanthellae: phototaxis. *Biol. Bull.,* 147, 630-640.

Pearse, V. B. (1974b) Modification of sea anemone behavior by symbiotic zooxanthellae: expansion and contraction. *Biol. Bull.,* 147, 641-651.

Penry, D. L. and Jumars, P. A. (1987) Modeling animal guts as chemical reactors. *Amer. Nat.,* 129, 69-96.

Percival, E. (1968) Marine algal carbohydrates. Oceanogr. *Mar. Biol. Ann. Rev.,* 6, 137-161.

Percival, E. and McDowell, R. H. (1967) *Chemistry and Enzymology of Marine Algal Polysaccharides,* Academic Press, New York, 219 pp.

Peterson, C. H. and Black, R. (1986) Abundance patterns of infaunal sea anemones and their potential benthic prey in and outside seagrass patches on a Western Australian sand shelf. *Bull. Mar. Sci.,* 38, 498-511.

Peteya, D. J. (1973) A possible proprioreceptor in *Ceriantheopsis americanus* (Cnidaria, Ceriantharia). *Z. Zellforsch.,* 144, 1-10.

Peteya, D. J. (1975) The ciliary-cone sensory cell of anemones and cerianthids. *Tissue & Cell,* 7, 243-252.

Piavaux, A. (1977) Distribution and localization of the digestive laminarinases in animals. *Biochem. Syst. Ecol.,* 5, 231-239.

Picken, L. E. R. and Skaer, R. J. (1966) *A review of researches on nematocysts. In W. J. Rees (ed.), The Cnidaria and Their Evolution,* Academic Press, London, pp. 19-50.

Pierce, S. K., Jr. and Minasian, L. L., Jr. (1974) Water balance of a euryhaline sea anemone, *Diadumene leucolena. Comp. Biochem. Physiol.,* 49A, 159-167.

Pierce, S. K. and Greenberg, M. J. (1973) The initiation and control of free amino acid regulation of cell volume in salinity stressed marine bivalves. *J. Exp. Biol.,* 59, 435-446.

Pineda, J. and Escofet, A. (1989) Selective effects of disturbance on populations of sea anemones from northern Baja California, Mexico. *Mar. Ecol. Prog. Ser.,* 55, 55-62.

Pollero, R. J. (1983) Lipid and fatty acid characterization and metabolism in the sea anemone *Phymactis clematis* (Dana). *Lipids,* 18, 12-17.

Polteva, D. G. (1963) Regeneration and somatic embryogenesis of *Actinia equina* in different stages of ontogenetic development. *Acta Biol. Hung.*,14, 199-208.

Pond, C. M. (1981) Storage. In C. R. Townsend and P. Calow (eds.), *Physiological Ecology. An Evolutionary Approach to Resource Use*, Sinauer Associates, Sunderland, Massachusetts, pp. 190-219.

Powers, D. A., Lenhoff, H. M. and Leone, C. A. (1968) Glucose-6-phosphate dehydrogenase and 6-phosphogluconate dehydrogenase activities in coelenterates. *Comp. Biochem. Physiol.*, 27, 139-144.

Prezelin, B. B. (1987) Photosynthetic physiology of dinoflagellates. In F. J. R. Taylor (ed.), *The Biology of Dinoflagellates, Botanical Monographs*, No. 21, Blackwell Scientific Publications, Oxford, UK, pp. 174-223.

Purcell, J. E. (1977a) The diet of large and small individuals of the sea anemone *Metridium senile. Bull. S. Cal. Acad. Sci.*, 76, 168-172.

Purcell, J. E. (1977b) Aggressive function and induced development of catch tentacles in the sea anemone *Metridium senile* (Coelenterata, Actiniaria). *Biol. Bull.*, 153, 355-368.

Purcell, J. E. and Kitting, C. L. (1982) Intraspecific aggression and population distributions of the sea anemone *Metridium senile. Biol. Bull.*, 162, 345-359.

Quaglia, A. and Grasso, M. (1986) Ultrastructural evidence for a peptidergic-like neurosecretory cell in a sea anemone. *Oebalia*, 13 (n.s.), 147-156.

Quicke, D. L. J. and Brace, R. C. (1983) Phenotypic and genotypic spacing within an aggregation of the anemone, *Actinia equina. J. Mar. Biol. Ass. UK*, 63, 493-515.

Quicke, D. L. J. and Brace, R. C. (1984) Evidence for the existence of a third, ecologically distinct morph of the anemone, *Actinia equina. J. Mar. Biol. Ass. UK*, 64, 531-534.

Quicke, D. L. J., Donoghue, A. M. and Brace, R. C. (1983) Biochemical-genetic and ecological evidence that red/brown individuals of the anemone *Actinia equina* comprise two morphs in *Britain. Mar. Biol.*, 77, 29-37.

Quicke, D. L. J., Donoghue, A. M., Keeling, T. F. and Brace, R. C. (1985) Littoral distributions and evidence for differential post-settlement selection on the morphs of *Actinia equina. J. Mar. Biol. Ass. UK,* 65, 1-20.

Quin, L. D. (1965) The presence of compounds with a carbon-phosphorus bond in some marine invertebrates. *Biochemistry*, 4, 324-330.

Rahav, O., Dubinsky, Z., Achituv, Y. and Falkowski, P. G. (1989) Ammonium metabolism in the zooxanthellate coral, *Stylophora pistillata. Proc. R. Soc. Lond.*, B, 236, 325-337.

Rajagopal, M. V. and Sohonie, K. (1957) Studies on the sea anemone Gyrostoma sp. Lipids of *Gyrostoma* sp. *Biochem. J.*, 65, 34-36.

Reimer, A.A. 1971. Feeding behavior in the Hawaiian zoanthids *Palythoa* and *Zoanthus. Pac. Sci. 25:512-520.*

Reimer, A. A. (1973) Feeding behavior in the sea anemone *Calliactis polypus* (Forskål, 1775). *Comp. Biochem. Physiol.*, 44A, 1289-1301.

Richardson, K., Beardall, J. and Raven, J. A. (1983) Adaptation of unicellular algae to irradiance: an analysis of strategies. *New Phytol.*, 93, 157-191.

Riemann-Zu rneck, K. (1969) *Sagartia troglodytes* (Anthozoa). Biologie und Morphologie einer schlickbewohnenden Aktinie. *Veri ff. Inst. Meeresforsch. Bremerhaven*, 12, 169-230.

Riemann-Zu rneck, K. (1976) Reproductive biology, oogenesis and early development in the brood-caring sea anemone *Actinostola spetsbergensis* (Anthozoa: Actiniaria). *Helgole nder wiss. Meeresunters.*, 28, 239-249.

Robbins, R. E. (1980) *The Importance of Water Flow in the Biology of the Sea Anemone Metridium senile* (L.). M. Sc. thesis, University of Maine, Orono, Maine, 54 pp.

Robbins, R. E. and Shick, J. M. (1980) Expansion-contraction behavior in the sea anemone *Metridium senile*: environmental cues and energetic consequences. In D. C. Smith and Y. Tiffon (eds.), *Nutrition in the Lower Metazoa*, Pergamon Press, Oxford, UK, pp. 101-116.

Robson, E. A. (1957) The structure and hydromechanics of the musculo-epithelium in *Metridium. Quart. J. Microsc. Sci.*, 98, 265-278.

Robson, E. A. (1961a) A comparison of the nervous systems of two sea-anemones, *Calliactis parasitica* and *Metridium senile*. Quart. J. Microsc. Sci., 102, 319-326.

Robson, E. A. (1961b) The swimming response and its pacemaker system in the anemone *Stomphia coccinea. J. Exp. Zool.*, 38, 685-694.

Robson, E. A. (1961c) Some observations on the swimming behaviour of the anemone *Stomphia coccinea. J. Exp.* Biol., 38, 343-363.

Robson, E. A. (1963) The nerve-net of a swimming anemone, *Stomphia coccinea. Quart. J. Microsc. Sci.*, 104, 535-549.

Robson, E. A. (1965) Some aspects of the structure of the nervous system in the anemone *Calliactis. Amer. Zool.*, 5, 403-410.

Robson, E. A. (1966) Swimming in Actiniaria. In W. J. Rees (ed.), *The Cnidaria and Their Evolution*, Academic Press, London, pp. 333-360.

Robson, E. A. (1971) The behaviour and neuromuscular system of *Gonactinia prolifera*, a swimming sea-anemone. *J. Exp. Biol.,* 55, 611-640.

Robson, E. A. (1976) Locomotion in sea anemones: the pedal disk. In G. O. Mackie (ed.), *Coelenterate Ecology and Behavior*, Plenum, New York, pp. 479-490.

Robson, E. A. (1985) Speculations on coelenterates. In S. C. Morris, J. D. George, R. Gibson and H. M. Platt (eds.), *The Origins and Relationships of Lower Invertebrates, Systematics Association Special Vol. No. 28*, Clarendon Press, Oxford, UK, pp. 60-77.

Robson, E. A. (1988) Problems of supply and demand for cnidae in Anthozoa. In D. A. Hessinger and H. M. Lenhoff (eds.), *The Biology of Nematocysts*, Academic Press, San Diego, California, pp. 179-207.

Roche, J. (1932) Actiniohematine et cytochrome. *C. R. Hebd. Soc. Biol.*, 111, 904-906.

512

Roche, J. (1936) Les pigments hematiniques des actinies (actiniohematin=e) et le cytochrome b. *C. R. Hebd. Soc. Biol.*, 121, 69-71.

Rodriguez, A.D. 1995. The natural products chemistry of West Indian Gorgonian octocorals. *Tetrahedron 51:4571-4618.*

--------------------, Cobar, O.M. and N. Martinez. 1994. Isolation and structures of sixteen new asbestinin diterpenes from the Caribbean gorgonian *Briareum asbestinum. J. Nat. Prod. 57:1638-1655.*

Romey, G., Abita, J. P., Schweitz, H., Wunderer, G. and Lazdunski, M. (1976) Sea anemone toxin: a tool to study molecular mechanisms of nerve conduction and excitation-secretion coupling. *Proc. Nat. Acad. Sci. USA*, 73, 4055-4059.

Rosin, R. (1969) Escape response of the sea-anemone *Anthopleura nigrescens* (Verrill) to its predatory eolid nudibranch *Herviella Baba* spec. nov. *The Veliger,* 12, 74-77.

Ross, D. M. (1960a) The effects of ions and drugs on neuromuscular preparations of sea anemones. I. On preparations of the column of *Calliactis and Metridium. J. Exp. Biol.*, 37, 732-752.

Ross, D. M. (1960b) The effects of ions and drugs on neuromuscular preparations of sea anemones. II. On sphincter preparations of *Calliactis and Metridium. J. Exp. Biol.*, 37, 753-773.

Ross, D. M. (1960c) The association between the hermit crab *Eupagurus bernhardus* (L.) and the sea anemone *Calliactis parasitica* (Couch). *Proc. Zool. Soc. Lond.*, 134, 43-57.

Ross, D. M. (1965) Some problems of neuromuscular activity and behaviour in the 'elementary nervous system'. In J. W. S. Pringle (ed.), *Essays of Physiological Evolution*, Pergamon Press, New York, pp. 253-261.

Ross, D. M. (1967) Behavioural and ecological relationships between sea anemones and other invertebrates. *Oceanogr. Mar. Biol. Ann. Rev.*, 5, 291-316.

Ross, D. M. (1971) Protection of hermit crabs (*Dardanus* spp.) from octopus by commensal sea anemones (*Calliactis* spp.). *Nature*, 230, 401-402.

Ross, D. M. (1974a) Behavior patterns in associations and interactions with other animals. In L. Muscatine and H. Lenhoff (eds.), *Coelenterate Biology: Reviews and New Perspectives,* Academic Press, New York, pp. 281-312.

Ross, D. M. (1974b) Evolutionary aspects of associations between crabs and sea anemones. In W. B. Vernberg (ed.), *Symbiosis in the Sea*, University of South Carolina Press, Columbia, pp. 111-125.

Ross, D. M. (1979a) A behaviour pattern in *Pagurus bernhardus* L. towards its symbiotic actinian *Calliactis parasitica* (Couch). J. Mar. Biol. Ass. UK, 59, 623-630.

Ross, D. M. (1979b) 'Stealing' of the symbiotic anemone, *Calliactis parasitica*, in intraspecific and interspecific encounters of three species of Mediterranean pagurids. *Can. J. Zool.*, 57, 1181-1189.

Ross, D. M. (1979c) A third species of swimming actinostolid (Anthozoa: Actiniaria) on the Pacific Coast of North *America.Can. J. Zool.*, 57, 943-945.

Ross, D. M. (1983) Symbiotic relations. In F. J. Vernberg and W. B. Vernberg (eds.), *The Biology of Crustacea, Vol. 7, Behavior and Ecology,* Academic Press, New York, pp. 163-212.

Ross, D. M. and Boletzky, S. von (1979) The association between the pagurid *Dardanus arrosor* and the actinian *Calliactis parasitica*. Recovery of activity in 'inactive' *D. arrosor* in the presence of cephalopods. *Mar. Behav. Physiol.*, 6, 175-184.

Ross, D. M. and Sutton, L. (1961) The response of the sea anemone *Calliactis parasitica* to shells of the hermit crab *Pagurus bernhardus*. *Proc. R. Soc. Lond.*, B, 155, 266-281.

Ross, D. M. and Sutton, L. (1967) Swimming sea anemones of Puget Sound: swimming of *Actinostola* new species in response to *Stomphia coccinea*. *Science*, 155, 1419-1421.

Ross, D. M. and Sutton, L. (1968) Detachment of sea anemones by commensal hermit crabs and by mechanical and electrical stimuli. *Nature*, 217, 380-381.

Rossi, L. (1971) Thelytochous parthenogenesis in *Cereus pedunculatus* (Actiniaria). *Experientia,* 27, 349-351.

Rossi, L. (1975) Sexual races in *Cereus pedunculatus* (Boad.). Pubbl. Staz. Zool. Napoli (Suppl., VIII Eur. Mar. Biol. Symp.), 39, 462-470.

Roughgarden, J. (1975) Evolution of marine symbiosis-a simple cost-benefit model. *Ecology*, 56, 1201-1208.

Rubenstein, D. I. and Koehl, M. A. R. (1977) The mechanisms of filter feeding: some theoretical considerations. *Amer. Nat.*, 111, 981-994.

Rudi, A., Ketzinel, S., Goldberg, I., Stein, Z., Kashman, Y., Benayahu, Y. and M. Schleyer. 1995. Antheliatin and zahavins A and B, three new cytotoxic xenicane diterpenes from two soft corals. *J. Nat. Prod. 58:1581-1586.*

Ruesink, J.L. and C.D. Harvell. 1990. Specialist predation on the Caribbean gorgonian *Plexaurella* spp. by *Cyphoma signatum* (Gastropoda). *Mar. Ecol. Progr. Ser.* 65:265-272.

Runnegar, B. (1982) Oxygen requirements, biology and phylogenetic significance of the late Precambrian worm *Dickinsonia*, and the evolution of the burrowing habit. *Alcheringa*, 6, 223-239.

Ryland, J.S. 1995. Budding in *Acrozoanthus* Saville-Kent, 1893 (Anthozoa: Zoanthidea). *Proc. 6th Int. Conf. Coel. Biol. 1995: (in press).*

Ryland, J.S. and R.C. Babcock. 1991. Annual cycle of gametogenesis and spawning in a tropical zoanthids, *Protopalythoa* sp. *Hydrobiologia 216/217:117-123.*

Salleo, A., La Spada, G. and Denaro, M. G. (1988) Release of free Ca2+ from the nematocysts of *Aiptasia mutabilis* during discharge. Physiol. Zool., 61, 272-279.

Sammarco, P.W. (1982) Polyp bail-out: an escape response to environmental stress and a new means of reproduction in corals. *Mar. Ecol. Prog. Ser.*, 10, 57-65.

Sammarco, P.W. Coll, J.C., La Barre, S. and B. Willis. 1983. Competitive strategies of soft corals (Coelenterata: Octocorallia): allelopathic effects on selected scleractinian corals. *Coral Reefs 2:173-178.*

Sammarco, P.W. 1996. Comments on coral reef regeneration, bioerosion, biogeography, and chemical ecology: future directions. *J. Exp. Mar. Biol. Ecol. 200:135-168.*

---------------------- and J.C. Coll. 1988. The chemical ecology of alcyonarian corals (Coelenterata: Octocorallia). In: Scheuer, P.J. (ed) *Bio-organic marine chemistry.* Vol. 2. Springer-Verlag, Berin, Heidelberg, pp. 87-116.

----------------------, Coll, J.C., La Barre, S. and B. Willis. 1983. Competitive strategies of soft corals (Coelenterata: Octocorallia): allelopathic effects on selected scleractinian corals. *Coral Reefs 2:173-178.*

Sandberg, D. M. (1972) The influence of feeding on behavior and nematocyst discharge of the sea anemone *Calliactis tricolor. Mar. Behav. Physiol.,* 1, 219-238.

Sargent, J. R. (1976) The structure, metabolism and function of lipids in marine organisms. In D. C. Malins and J. R. Sargent (eds.), *Biochemical and Biophysical Perspectives in Marine Biology, Vol. 3,* Academic Press, London, pp. 149-212.

Sargent, J. R. (1978) Marine wax esters. *Sci. Prog.,* 65, 437-458.

Sargent, J. R. and McIntosh, R. (1974) Studies on the mechanism of biosynthesis of wax esters in *Euchaeta norvegica. Mar. Biol.,* 25, 271-277.

Sassaman, C. and Mangum, C. P. (1970) Patterns of temperature adaptation in North American Atlantic coastal actinians. *Mar. Biol.,* 7, 123-130.

Sassaman, C. and Mangum, C. P. (1972) Adaptations to environmental oxygen levels in infaunal and epifaunal sea anemones. *Biol. Bull.,* 143, 657-678.

Sassaman, C. and Mangum, C. P. (1973) Relationship between aerobic and anaerobic metabolism in estuarine anemones. *Comp. Biochem. Physiol.,* 44A, 1313-1319.

Sassaman, C. and Mangum, C. P. (1974) Gas exchange in a cerianthid. *J. Exp. Zool.,* 188, 297-306.

Sauer, K. P. (1989) Aggression and competition for space in sea-anemones. In R. B. Williams (ed.), *5th International Conference on Coelenterate Biology, Programme and Abstracts,* University of Southampton, Southampton, UK, pp. 82-83.

Sauer, K. P., Mu ller, M. and Weber, M. (1986) Alloimmune memory for glycoproteid recognition molecules in sea anemones competing for space. *Mar. Biol.,* 92, 73-79.

Saville-Kent, W. (1893) *The Great Barrier Reef of Australia; Its Products and Potentialities,* Allen, London, 387 pp. + 16 colour plates.

Saz, H. J. (1981) Energy metabolism of parasitic helminths. *Ann. Rev. Physiol.,* 43, 323-341.

Scelfo, G. M. (1986) Relationship between solar radiation and pigmentation of the coral *Montipora verrucosa* and its zooxanthellae. In P. L. Jokiel, R. H. Richmond and R.A. Rogers (eds.), *Coral Reef Population Biology, Hawaii Inst. Mar. Biol. Tech. Rept. No. 37,* pp. 440-451.

Scelfo, G. M. (1988) Ultraviolet-B absorbing compounds in *Anthopleura elegantissima. Amer. Zool.*, 28, 105A (abstract).

Sche fer, W. (1981) Fortpflanzung und Sexualite t von Cereus pedunculatus und *Actinia equina* (Anthozoa, Actiniaria). *Helgole nder Meeresunters.*, 34, 451-461.

Sche fer, W. G. and Schmidt, H. (1980) The anthozoan egg: differentiation of internal oocyte structure. In P. Tardent and R. Tardent (eds.), *Developmental and Cellular Biology of Coelenterates*, Elsevier/North-Holland Biomedical Press, Amsterdam, pp. 47-52.

Schlichter, D. (1968) Das Zusammenleben von Riffanemonen und Anemonefischen. Z. Tierpsychol., 25, 933-954.

Schlichter, D. (1972) Chemische Tarnung. Die stoffliche Grundlage der Anpassung von Anemonefischen an Riffanemonen. *Mar. Biol.*, 12, 137-150.

Schlichter, D. (1973) Erne hrungsphysiologische und e kologische Aspekte =derAufnahme in Meerwasser gele ster Aminose uren durch *Anemonia sulcata* (Coelenterata, Anthozoa). *Oecologia*, 11, 315-350.

Schlichter, D. (1974) Der Einfluss physikalischer und chemischer Faktoren auf die Aufnahme in Meerwasser gel e ster Aminose uren durch Aktinien. *Mar. Biol.*, 25, 279-290.

Schlichter, D. (1975a) Die Bedeutung in Meerwasser gel e ster Glucose fu r die Erne hrung von *Anemonia sulcata* (Coelenterata: Anthozoa). *Mar. Biol.*, 29, 283-293.

Schlichter, D. (1975b) Produktion oder U bernahame von Schutzstoffen als Ursache des Nesselschutzes von Anemonefischen? *J. Exp. Mar. Biol. Ecol.*, 20, 49-61.

Schlichter, D. (1976) Macromolecular mimicry: substances released by sea anemones and their role in the protection of anemone fishes. In G. O. Mackie (ed.), *Coelenterate Ecology and Behavior*, Plenum, New York, pp. 433-441.

Schlichter, D. (1978a) On the ability of Anemonia sulcata (Coelenterata: Anthozoa) to absorb charged and neutral amino acids simultaneously. *Mar. Biol.*, 45, 97-104.

Schlichter, D. (1978b) The extraction of specific proteins for the simultaneous ectodermal absorption of charged and neutral amino acids by Anemonia sulcata (Coelenterata: Anthozoa). In D. S. McLusky and A. J. Berry (eds.), *Physiology and Behavior of Marine Organisms. Proc. 12th Eur. Symp. Mar. Biol.*, Pergamon Press, Oxford, UK, pp. 155-163.

Schlichter, D. (1980) Adaptations of cnidarians for integumentary absorption of dissolved organic matter. *Rev. Can. Biol.*, 39, 259-282.

Schlichter, D. 1982. Nutritional strategies of cnidarians: the absorption, translocation and utilization of dissolved nutrients by *Heteroxenia fuscescens. Amer. Zool.* 22: 659-669.

Schlichter, D., Bajorat, K. H., Buck, M., Eckes, P., Gutknecht, D., Kraus, P., Krisch, H., and Schmitz, B. (1987) Epidermal nutrition of sea anemones by absorption of organic compounds dissolved in the oceans. *Zool. Beitr. N.F.*, 30, 29-47.

Schlichter, D. 1982a. Nutritional strategies of cnidarians: the absorption, translocation and utilization of dissolved nutrients by *Heteroxenia fuscescens. Amer. Zool. 22: 659-669.*

--------------. 1982b. Epidermal nutrition of the alcyonarian *Heteroxenia fuscescens* (Ehrb.): Absorption of dissolved organic material and lost endogenous photosynthates. *Oecologia 53:40-49.*

-------------- and G. Liebezeit. 1991. The natural release of amino acids from the symbiotic coral *Heteroxenia fuscescens* (Ehrb.) as a function of photosynthesis. *J. Exp. Mar. Biol. Ecol. 150:83-90.*

Schmidt, H. 1974. On evolution in the Anthozoa. In: *Proc. 2nd Int. Coral Reef Symp.*, Vol. 1, Great Barrier Reef Committee, Brisbane, Pp. 533-560.

Schmidt, G. H. (1982) Replacement of discharged cnidae in the tentacles of *Anemonia sulcata. J. Mar. Biol. Ass. UK*, 62, 685-691.

Schmidt, H. (1969) Die Nesselkapseln der Aktinien und ihre differentialdiagnostische Bedeutung. *Helgolender wiss. Meeresunters.*, 19, 284-317.

Schmidt, H. (1970) *Anthopleura stellula* (Actiniaria, Actiniidae) and its reproduction by transverse fission. *Mar. Biol.*, 5, 245-255.

Schmidt, H. (1971) Taxonomie, Verbreitung und Variabet von *Actinia equina* Linne 1766 (Actiniaria; Anthozoa). *Z. f. zool. Syst. Evolutionsforsch.*, 9, 161-169.

Schmidt, H. (1972a) Die Nesselkapseln der Anthozoen und ihre Bedeutung fur die phylogenetische Systematik. *Helgolender wiss. Meeresunters.*, 23, 422-458.

Schmidt, H. (1972b) Prodromus zu einer Monographie der mediterranen *Aktinien*. *Zoologica*, 42: 1-120 + 37 figures.

Schmidt, H. (1974) On evolution in the Anthozoa. In *Proceedings of the Second International Coral Reef Symposium, Vol. 1*, Great Barrier Reef Committee, Brisbane, Pp. 533-560.

Schmidt, H. and Beress, L. (1971) Phylogenetische Betrachtungen zur Toxizite t und Nesselwirkung einiger Actiniaria (Anthozoa) im Vergleich zur Morphologie ihrer Nesselkapseln. *Kieler Meeresforsch.*, 27, 166-170.

Schmidt, H. and H e ltken, B. (1980) Peculiarities of spermatogenesis and sperm in Anthozoa. In P. Tardent and R. Tardent (eds.), *Developmental and Cellular Biology of Coelenterates*, Elsevier/ North-Holland Biomedical Press, Amsterdam, pp. 53-59.

Schmidt, H. and Schefer, W. G. (1980) The anthozoan egg: trophic mechanisms and oocyte surfaces. In P. Tardent and R. Tardent (eds.), *Developmental and Cellular Biology of Coelenterates*, Elsevier/ North-Holland Biomedical Press, Amsterdam, pp. 41-46.

Schmidt, H. and Zissler, D. (1979) Die Spermien der Anthozoen und ihre phylogenetische Bedeutung. *Zoologica*, 44, 1-46 + 25 plates.

Schmidt-Nielsen, K. (1984) *Scaling: Why Is Animal Size So Important*, Cambridge University Press, Cambridge, UK, 241 pp.

Schoenberg, D. A. and Trench, R. K. (1980a) Genetic variation in *Symbiodinium* (=*Gymnodinium*) *microadriaticum* Freudenthal, and specificity in its symbiosis with marine invertebrates. I. Isoenzyme and soluble protein patterns of axenic cultures of Symbiodinium microadriaticum. *Proc. R. Soc. Lond.*, B, 207, 405-427.

Schoenberg, D. A. and Trench, R. K. (1980b) Genetic variation in *Symbiodinium* (=*Gymnodinium*) *microadriaticum* Freudenthal, and specificity in its symbiosis with marine invertebrates. II. Morphological variation in *Symbiodinium microadriaticum*. *Proc. R. Soc. Lond.*, B, 207, 429-444.

Schoenberg, D. A. and Trench, R. K. (1980c) Genetic variation in *Symbiodinium* (=*Gymnodinium*) *microadriaticum* Freudenthal, and specificity in its symbiosis with marine invertebrates. III. Specificity and infectivity of *Symbiodinium microadriaticum*. *Proc. R. Soc. Lond.*, B, 207, 445-460.

Schroeder, L. A. (1981) Consumer growth efficiencies: their limits and relationships to ecological energetics. *J. Theor. Biol.*, 93, 805-828.

Schroeder, T. E. (1982) Novel surface specialization on a sea anemone egg: 'spires' of actin-filled microvilli. *J. Morphol.*, 174, 207-216.

Schweitz, H., Bidard, J.-N., Frelin, C., Pauron, D., Vijverberg, H. P. M., Mahasneh, D. M. and Lazdunski, M. (1985) Purification, sequence, and pharmacological properties of sea anemone toxins from *Radianthus paumotensis*. A new class of sea anemone toxins acting on the sodium channel. Biochemistry, 24, 3554-3561.

Schweitz, H., Vincent, J.-P., Barhanin, J., Frelin, C., Linden, G., Hugues, M. and Lazdunski, M. (1981) Purification and pharmacological properties of eight sea anemone toxins from *Anemonia sulcata, Anthopleura xanthogrammica, Stoichactis giganteus, and Actinodendron plumosum*. Biochemistry, 20, 5245-5252.

Scrutton, C. T. (1979) Early fossil cnidarians. In M. R. House (ed.), *The Origin of Major Invertebrate Groups. Systematics Association Special Vol. No. 12*, Academic Press, London, pp. 161-207.

Sebens, K. P. (in press) Anthozoa: Actiniaria, Zoanthidea, Corallimorpharia and Ceriantharia. *Marine Flora and Fauna of the Northeastern United States*. NOAA Tech. Rept., *??:*

Sebens, K. P. (1976) The ecology of Caribbean sea anemones in Panama: utilization of space on a coral reef. In G. O. Mackie (ed.), *Coelenterate Ecology and Behavior*, Plenum, New York, pp. 67-77.

Sebens, K.P. 1977. Autotrophic and heterotrophic nutrition of coral reef zoanthids. In: *Proc. 3rd Int. Coral Reef Symp. 397-404.*

--------------- and M.A.R. Koehl. 1984. Predation on zooplankton by the benthic anthozoans *Alcyonium siderium* (Alcyonacea) and *Metridium senile* (Actiniaria) in the New England subtidal. *Mar. Biol. 81:255-271.*

-------------- and J.S. Miles. 1988. Sweeper tentacles in a gorgonian octocoral: morphological modifications for interference competition. *Biol. Bull. 175:378-387.*

Sebens, K. P. (1979) The energetics of asexual reproduction and colony formation in benthic marine invertebrates. *Amer. Zool.*, 19, 683-697.

Sebens, K. P. (1980) The regulation of asexual reproduction and indeterminate body size in the sea anemone *Anthopleura elegantissima* (Brandt). *Biol. Bull.*, 158, 370-382.

Sebens, K. P. (1981a) The allometry of feeding, energetics, and body size in three sea anemone species. *Biol. Bull.*, 161, 152-171.

Sebens, K. P. (1981b) Reproductive ecology of the intertidal sea anemones *Antho-pleura xanthogrammica* (Brandt) and *A. elegantissima* (Brandt): body size, habitat, and sexual reproduction. *J. Exp. Mar. Biol. Ecol.*, 54, 225-250.

Sebens, K. P. (1982a) The limits to indeterminate growth: an optimal size model applied to passive suspension feeders. *Ecology*, 63, 209-222.

Sebens, K. P. (1982b) Asexual reproduction in *Anthopleura elegantissima* (Anthozoa: Actiniaria): seasonality and spatial extent of clones. *Ecology*, 63, 434-444.

Sebens, K. P. (1982c) Recruitment and habitat selection in the intertidal sea anemones, *Anthopleura elegantissima* (Brandt) and *A. xanthogrammica* (Brandt). *J. Exp. Mar. Biol. Ecol.*, 59, 103-124.

Sebens, K. P. (1983a) Population dynamics and habitat suitability of the intertidal sea anemones *Anthopleura elegantissima* and *A. xanthogrammica*. *Ecol. Monogr.*, 53, 405-433.

Sebens, K. P. (1983b) Morphological variability during longitudinal fission of the intertidal sea anemone, *Anthopleura elegantissima* (Brandt). *Pacific Sci.*, 37, 121-132.

Sebens, K. P. (1984a) Agonistic behavior in the intertidal sea anemone *Anthopleura xanthogrammica*. *Biol. Bull.*, 166, 457-472.

Sebens, K. P. (1984b) Water flow and coral colony size: interhabitat comparisons of the octocoral *Alcyonium siderium*. *Proc. Nat. Acad. Sci. USA,* 81, 5473-5477.

Sebens, K. P. (1986) Community ecology of vertical rock walls in the Gulf of Maine, USA: small-scale processes and alternative community states. In P. G. Moore and R. Seed (eds.), *The Ecology of Rocky Coasts: Essays Presented to J. R. Lewis*, Columbia University Press, New York, pp. 346-371.

Sebens, K. P. (1987a) Coelenterata. In T. J. Pandian and F. J. Vernberg (eds.), *Animal Energetics, Vol. 1, Protozoa through Insecta*, Academic Press, New York, pp. 55-120.

Sebens, K. P. (1987b) The ecology of indeterminate growth in animals. *Ann. Rev. Ecol. Syst.*, 18, 371-407.

Sebens, K.P. 1988. Sweeper Tentacles in a Gorgonian Octocoral: Morphological Modifications for Interference Competition. *Biol. Bull. 175: 378-387.*

Sebens, K. P. and DeRiemer, K. (1977) Diel cycles of expansion and contraction in coral reef anthozoans. *Mar. Biol.*, 43, 247-256.

Sebens, K. P. and Koehl, M. A. R. (1984) Predation on zooplankton by two benthic anthozoans, *Alcyonium siderium* (Alcyonacea) and *Metridium senile* (Actiniaria), in the New England subtidal. *Mar. Biol.*, 81, 255-271.

Sebens, K. P. and Laakso, G. (1978) The genus Tealia (Anthozoa: Actiniaria) in the waters of the San Juan Archipelago and the Olympic Peninsula. *Wasmann J. Biol.*, 35, 152-168.

Sebens, K. P. and Paine, R. T. (1978) Biogeography of anthozoans along the west coast of South America: habitat, disturbance, and prey availability. In *Proceedings of the International Symposium on Marine Biogeography and Evolution in the Southern Hemisphere*, Auckland, New Zealand, N.Z. DSIR Inf. Ser. 137, Vol. 1, pp. 219-237.

Sebens, K. P. and Thorne, B. L. (1985) Coexistence of clones, clonal diversity, and the effects of disturbance. In J. B. C. Jackson, L. W. Buss and R. E. Cook (eds.), *Population Biology and Evolution of Clonal Organisms*, Yale University Press, New Haven, pp. 357-398.

Seilacher, A. (1983) Paleozoic sandstones in southern Jordan: trace fossils, depositional environments and biogeography. In A. M. Abed and H. M. Khaled (eds.), *Geology of Jordan. Proc. First Jordanian Geol. Conf.*, Jordan Geologists Association, Amman, pp. 209-222.

Seilacher, A. (1989) Vendozoa: organismic construction in the Proterozoic biosphere. *Lethaia*, 22, 229-239.

Severin, S. E., Boldyrev, A. A. and Lebedev, A. V. (1972) Nitrogenous extractive compounds of muscle tissue of invertebrates. *Comp. Biochem. Physiol.*, 43B, 369-381.

Shaw, P. W. (1989) Seasonal patterns and possible long-term effectiveness of sexual reproduction in three species of sagartiid sea anemones. In J. S. Ryland and P. A. Tyler (eds.), *Reproduction, Genetics and Distributions of Marine Organisms,* Olsen & Olsen, Fredensborg, Denmark, pp. 189-199.

Shaw, P. W., Beardmore, J. A. and Ryland, J. S. (1987) Sagartia troglodytes (Anthozoa: Actiniaria) consists of two species. *Mar. Ecol. Prog. Ser.*, 41, 21-28.

Shelton, G. A. B. (1982) Anthozoa. In G. A. B. Shelton (ed.), *Electrical Conduction and Behaviour in 'Simple' Invertebrates,* Oxford University Press, New York, pp. 203-242.

Shelton, G. A. B. and Holley, M. C. (1984) The role of a 'local electrical conduction system' during feeding in the Devonshire cup coral *Caryophyllia smithii* Stokes and Broderip. *Proc. R. Soc. Lond.*, B, 220, 489-500.

Sheppard, C.R.C. 1979. Interspecific aggression between reef corals with reference to their distribution. *Mar. Ecol. Prog. Ser. 1:237-247.*

Shick, J. M. (1973) Effects of salinity and starvation on the uptake and utilization of dissolved glycine by *Aurelia aurita* polyps. *Biol. Bull.*,144, 172-179.

Shick, J. M. (1975) Uptake and utilization of dissolved glycine by *Aurelia aurita* scyphistomae: Temperature effects on the uptake process; nutritional role of dissolved amino acids. *Biol. Bull.*, 148, 117-140.

Shick, J. M. (1976) Ecological physiology and genetics of the colonizing actinian *Haliplanella luciae.* In G. O. Mackie (ed.), *Coelenterate Ecology and Behavior,* Plenum, New York, pp. 137-146.

Shick, J. M. (1981) Heat production and oxygen uptake in intertidal sea anemones from different shore heights during exposure to air. *Mar. Biol. Lett.*, 2, 225-236.

Shick, J. M. (1983) Respiratory gas exchange in echinoderms. In M. Jangoux and J. M. Lawrence (eds.), *Echinoderm Studies, Vol. 1*, Balkema Publishers, Rotterdam, pp. 67-110.

Shick, J. M. (1990) Diffusion limitation and hyperoxic enhancement of oxygen consumption in zooxanthellate sea anemones, zoanthids, and corals. *Biol. Bull.*, 179, 148-158.

Shick, J. M. and Brown, W. I. (1977) Zooxanthellae-produced O_2 promotes sea anemone expansion and eliminates oxygen debt under environmental hypoxia. *J. Exp. Zool.*, 201, 149-155.

Shick, J. M., Brown, W. I., Dolliver, E. G. and Kayar, S. R. (1979a) Oxygen uptake in sea anemones: effects of expansion, contraction, and exposure to air, and the limitations of diffusion. *Physiol. Zool.*, 52, 50-62.

Shick, J. M. and Dowse, H. B. (1985) Genetic basis of physiological variation in natural populations of sea anemones: intra- and interclonal analyses of variance. In P. E. Gibbs (ed.), *Proceedings of the Nineteenth European Marine Biology Symposium*, Cambridge University Press, Cambridge, UK, pp. 465-479.

Shick, J. M. and Dykens, J. A. (1984) Photobiology of the symbiotic sea anemone, *Anthopleura elegantissima*: photosynthesis, respiration, and behavior under intertidal conditions. *Biol. Bull.*, 166, 608-619.

Shick, J. M., Gnaiger, E., Widdows, J., Bayne, B. L. and de Zwaan, A. (1986) Activity and metabolism in the mussel *Mytilus edulis* L. during intertidal hypoxia and aerobic recovery. *Physiol. Zool.*, 59, 627-642.

Shick, J. M. and Hoffmann, R. J. (1980) Effects of the trophic and physical environments on asexual reproduction and body size in the sea anemone *Metridium senile*. In P. Tardent and R. Tardent (ed.), *Developmental and Cellular Biology of Coelenterates*, Elsevier/North Holland Biomedical Press, Amsterdam, pp. 211-216.

Shick, J. M., Hoffmann, R. J. and Lamb, A. N. (1979b) Asexual reproduction, population structure, and genotype-environment interactions in sea anemones. *Amer. Zool.*, 19, 699-713.

Shick, J. M. and Lamb, A. N. (1977) Asexual reproduction and genetic population structure in the colonizing sea anemone *Haliplanella luciae. Biol. Bull.*, 153, 604-617.

Shick, J. M., Lesser, M. P. and Stochaj, W. R. (1990) Ultraviolet radiation and photooxidative stress in zooxanthellate Anthozoa: the sea anemone *Phyllodiscus semoni* and the octocoral *Clavularia* sp. Symbiosis, 8,

Shick, J. M., Widdows, J. and Gnaiger, E. (1988) Calorimetric studies of behavior, metabolism and energetics of sessile intertidal animals. *Amer. Zool.*, 28, 161-181.

Shick, J. M., Zwaan, A. de and Bont, A. M. T. de (1983) Anoxic metabolic rate in the mussel *Mytilus edulis* L. estimated by simultantous direct calorimetry and biochemical analysis. *Physiol. Zool.*, 56, 56-63.

Shimek, R. L. (1981) Neptunea pribiloffensis (Dall, 1919) and Tealia crassicornis (Muller, 1776): on a snail's use of babysitters. *The Veliger*, 24, 62-66.

Shoup, C. S. (1932) Salinity of the medium and its effect on respiration in the sea-anemone. *Ecology*, 13, 81-85.

Shumway, S. E. (1978) Activity and respiration in the anemone, *Metridium senile* (L.) exposed to salinity fluctuations. *J. Exp. Mar. Biol. Ecol.*, 33, 85-92.

Sibly, R. and Calow, P. (1982) Asexual reproduction in Protozoa and invertebrates. *J. Theor. Biol.*, 96, 401-424.

Sidell, B. D. (1983) Cellular acclimatisation to environmental change by quantitative alterations in enzymes and organelles. In A. R. Cossins and P. Sheterline (eds.), *Cellular Acclimatization to Environmental Change. Society for Experimental Biology Seminar Series No. 17,* Cambridge University Press, Cambridge, UK, pp. 103-120.

Siebert, A. E., Jr. (1973) A description of the sea anemone *Stomphia didemon* sp. nov. and its development. Pacific Sci., 27, 363-376.

Siebert, A. E., Jr. (1974) A description of the embryology, larval development, and feeding of the sea anemones Anthopleura elegantissima and *A. xanthogrammica. Can. J. Zool.*, 52, 1383-1388.

Siebert, A. E. and Spaulding, J. G. (1976) The taxonomy, development and brooding behavior of the anemone, *Cribrinopsis fernaldi* sp. nov. *Biol. Bull.*, 150, 128-138.

Simon, G. and Rouser, G. (1967) Phospholipids of the sea anemone: quantitative distribution; absence of carbon-phosphorus linkages in glycerol phospholipids; structural elucidation of ceramide aminoethylphosphonate. *Lipids,* 2, 55-59.

Simpson, J. W. and Awapara, J. (1966) The pathway of glucose degradation in some invertebrates. *Comp. Biochem. Physiol.*, 18, 537-548.

Singer, I. I. (1971) Tentacular and oral-disc regeneration in the sea anemone, *Aiptasia diaphana.* III. Autoradiographic analysis of patterns of tritiated thymidine uptake. *J. Embryol. Exp. Morph.*, 26, 253-270.

Singer, I. I. and Palmer, J. D. (1969) Tentacular and oral-disc regeneration in the sea anemone *Aiptasia diaphana.* II. Oxidative metabolism during wound healing and tentacular differentiation. *Naturwissenschaften,* 56, 574-575.

Slattery, M. and J.B. McClintock. 1995. Population structure and feeding deterence in three shallow-water antarctic soft corals. *Mar. Biol. 122:461-470.*

Sleigh, M.A. (1989) Adaptations of ciliary systems for the propulsion of water and mucus. *Comp. Biochem. Physiol.*, 94A, 359-364.

Smith, B. L. and Potts, D. C. (1987) Clonal and solitary anemones (*Anthopleura*) of western North America: population genetics and systematics. Mar. *Biol.*, 94, 537-546.

Smith, G. J. (1984) *Ontogenetic variation in the symbiotic variations between zooxanthellae* (*Symbiodinium microadriaticum* Freudenthal) *and sea anemone* (Anthozoa: Actiniaria) hosts. Ph.D. dissertation, University of Georgia, Athens, 225 pp.

Smith, G. J. (1986) Ontogenetic influences on carbon flux in *Aulactinia stelloides* polyps (Anthozoa: Actiniaria) and their endosymbiotic algae. *Mar. Biol.*, 92, 361-369.

Smith, H. G. (1939) The significance of the relationship between actinians and zooxanthellae. *J. Exp. Biol.*, 16, 334-345.

Smith, N., III and Lenhoff, H. M. (1976) Regulation of frequency of pedal laceration in a sea anemone. In G. O. Mackie (ed.), *Coelenterate Ecology and Behavior,* Plenum, New York, pp. 117-125.

Sole-Cava, A. M. and Thorpe, J. P. (1987) Further genetic evidence for the reproductive isolation of green sea anemone *Actinia prasina* Gosse from common intertidal beadlet anemone *Actinia equina* (L.). *Mar. Ecol. Prog. Ser.*, 38, 225-229.

Sole-Cava, A. M., Thorpe, J. P. and Kaye, J. G. (1985) Reproductive isolation with little genetic divergence between *Urticina* (=*Tealia*) *felina* and *U. eques* (Anthozoa: Actiniaria). *Mar. Biol.*, 85, 279-284.

Somero, G. N., Siebenaller, J. F. and Hochachka, P. W. (1983) Biochemical and physiological adaptations of deep-sea animals. In G. T. Rowe (ed.), *The Sea, Vol. 8, Deep-Sea Biology*, Wiley-Interscience, New York, pp. 261-330.

Spaulding, J. G. (1974) Embryonic and larval development in sea anemones (Anthozoa: Actiniaria). *Amer. Zool.*, 14, 511-520.

Sponaugle, S. 1991. Flow patterns and velocities around a suspension-feeding gorgonian polyp: Evidence from physical models. *J. Exp. Mar. Biol. Ecol. 148:135-145.*

---------------- and M. LaBarbera. 1991. Drag-induced deformation: a functional feeding strategy in two species of gorgonians. *J. Exp. Mar. Biol. Ecol. 148:121-134.*Sprung, J. (1989) Reef Notes. *Freshwater and Marine Aquarium Magazine* 12:11

Sprung, J. (1995) *Reef Notes* 1 (1988-1990). Ricordea Publishing. Coconut Grove, Florida. USA.

Stambler, N. and Dubinsky, Z. (1987) Energy relationships between *Anemonia sulcata* and its endosymbiotic zooxanthellae. *Symbiosis*, 3, 233-248.

Stearns, S. C. (1977) The evolution of life history traits: a critique of the theory and a review of the data. *Ann. Rev. Ecol. Syst.*, 8, 145-171.

Steele, R. D. (1976) Light intensity as a factor in the regulation of the density of symbiotic zooxanthellae in *Aiptasia tagetes* (Coelenterata, Anthozoa). *J. Zool., Lond.*, 179, 387-405.

Steele, R. D. (1977) The significance of zooxanthella-containing pellets extruded by sea anemones. *Bull. Mar. Sci.*, 27, 591-594.

Steele, R. D. and Goreau, N. I. (1977) The breakdown of symbiotic zooxanthellae in the sea anemone *Phyllactis* (=*Oulactis*) *flosculifera* (Actiniaria). *J. Zool., London*, 181, 421-437.

Steen, R. G. (1986) Evidence for heterotrophy by zooxanthellae in symbiosis with *Aiptasia pulchella. Biol. Bull.*, 170, 267-278.

Steen, R. G. (1987) Evidence for facultative heterotrophy in cultured zooxanthellae. *Mar. Biol.*, 95, 15-23.

Steen, R. G. (1988) The bioenergetics of symbiotic sea anemones (Anthozoa: Actiniaria). *Symbiosis*, 5, 103-142.

Steen, R.G. and L. Muscatine. 1984. Daily budgets of photosynthetically fixed carbon in symbiotic zoanthids. *Biol. Bull. 167:477-487.*

Steen, R. G. and Muscatine, L. (1987) Low temperature evokes rapid exocytosis of symbiotic algae by a sea anemone. *Biol. Bull.*, 172, 246-263.

Stehouwer, H. (1952) The preference of the slug *Aeolidia papillosa* (L.) for the sea anemone *Metridium senile* (L.). *Arch. Neerland. de Zoologie*, 10, 161-170.

Steiner, G. (1957) Cber die chemische Nahrungswahl von *Actinia equina* L. *Naturwissenschaften*, 44, 70-71.

Stephenson, T. A. (1928) *The British Sea Anemones, Vol. I*, The Ray Society, London, 148 pp. + 14 plates.

Stephenson, T. A. (1929) On methods of reproduction as specific characters. *J. Mar. Biol. Ass. UK*, 16, 131-172.

Stephenson, T. A. (1935) *The British Sea Anemones, Vol. II*, The Ray Society, London, 426 pp. + 19 plates.

Stevenson, K. J., Gibson, D. and Dixon, G. H. (1974) Amino acid analyses of chymotrypsin-like proteases from the sea anemone (Metridium senile). *Can. J. Biochem.*, 52, 93-100.

Stiven, A. E. (1965) The relationship between size, budding rate, and growth efficiency in three species of hydra. *Res. Pop. Ecol.*, 7, 1-15.

Stochaj, W. R. (1988) The effects of ultraviolet and visible radiation on UV absorbing compounds in cnidarians. *Amer. Zool.*, 28, 192A (abstract).

Stochaj, W. R. (1989) *Photoprotective Mechanisms in Cnidarians: UV-Absorbing Compounds and Behavior.* M. Sc. thesis, University of Maine, Orono, Maine. 67 pp.

Stoddart, J. A. (1983) *A genotypic diversity measure.* J. Hered., 74, 489.

Stoddart, J. A., Ayre, D. J., Willis, B. and Heyward, A. J. (1985) Self-recognition in sponges and corals? *Evolution,* 39, 461-463.

Storer, T. I., Usinger, R. L., Stebbins, R. C. and Nybakken, J. W. (1979) General Zoology, 6th ed., McGraw-Hill, New York, 902 pp.

Storey, K. B. and Dando, P. R. (1982) Substrate specificities of octopine dehydrogenases from marine invertebrates. *Comp. Biochem. Physiol.*, 73B, 521-528.

Stotz, W. B. (1979) Functional morphology and zonation of three species of sea anemones from rocky shores in southern Chile. *Mar. Biol.*, 50, 181-188.

Strathmann, R. R. and Strathmann, M. F. (1982) The relationship between adult size and brooding in marine invertebrates. *Amer. Nat.*, 119, 91-101.

Stricker, S. A. (1985) An ultrastructural study of larval settlement in the sea anemone *Urticina crassicornis* (Cnidaria, Actiniaria). *J. Morphol.*, 186, 237-253.

Sund, P. N. (1958) A study of the muscular anatomy and swimming behaviour of the sea anemone, *Stomphia coccinea. Quart. J. Microsc. Sci.*, 99, 401-420.

Svoboda, A. and Porrmann, T. (1980) Oxygen production and uptake by symbiotic *Aiptasia diaphana* (Rapp), (Anthozoa, Coelenterata) adapted to different light intensities. In D. C. Smith and Y. Tiffon (eds.), *Nutrition in the Lower Metazoa*, Pergamon, Oxford, UK, pp. 87-99.

Szmant-Froelich, A. (1981) Coral nutrition: comparison of the fate of 14C from ingested labelled brine shrimp and from the uptake of $NaH_{14}CO_3$ by its zooxanthellae. *J. Exp. Mar. Biol. Ecol.*, 55, 133-144.

Tapley, D. W. (1989) Photoinactivation of catalase but not superoxide dismutase in the symbiotic sea anemone *Aiptasia pallida*. *Amer. Zool.*, 29, 53A (abstract).

Tapley, D. W., Shick, J. M. and Smith, J. P. S., III (1988) Defenses against oxidative stress in the sea anemones *Aiptasia pallida* and *Aiptasia pulchella*. *Amer. Zool.*, 28, 105A (abstract).

Tardent, P. (1975) Sex and sex determination in coelenterates. In R. Reinboth (ed.), *Intersexuality in the Animal Kingdom*, Springer-Verlag, Berlin, Heidelberg, New York, pp. 1-13.

Tardy, J. (1964) Comportement predateur de *Eolidiella alderi* (Mollusque, Nudibranche). C. R. Acad. Sci. Paris, 258, 2190-2192.

Targett, N. M., Bishop, S. S., McConnell, O. J. and Yoder, J. A. (1983) Antifouling agents against the benthic marine diatom Navicula salinicola: homarine from the gorgonian *Leptogorgia virgulata* and *L. setacea* and analogs. *J. Chem. Ecol.*, 9, 817-829

Taylor, D. L. (1969a) On the regulation and maintenance of algal numbers in zoox-anthellae-coelenterate symbiosis, with a note on the nutritional relationship in *Anemonia sulcata*. *J. Mar. Biol. Ass. UK*, 49, 1057-1065.

Taylor, D. L. (1969b) The nutritional relationship of *Anemonia sulcata* (Pennant) and its dinoflagellate symbiont. *J. Cell Sci.*, 4, 751-762.

Taylor, P. R. and Littler, M. M. (1982) The roles of compensatory mortality, physical disturbance, and substrate retention in the development and organization of a sand-influenced, rocky-intertidal community. *Ecology*, 63, 135-146.

Thorington, G. U. and Hessinger, D. A. (1988) Control of cnida discharge: I. Evidence for two classes of chemoreceptor. *Biol. Bull.*, 174, 163-171.

Thorson, G. (1936) The larval development, growth, and metabolism of arctic marine bottom invertebrates compared with those of other seas. *Meddelelser om Greenland*, 100, 1-155.

Tiffon, Y. (1973) Latency and sedimentability of acid hydrolases in sterile septa homogenates of *Cerianthus lloydi* G. *Comp. Biochem. Physiol.*, 45B, 731-740.

Tiffon, Y. (1975) Hydrolases dans l'ectoderme de *Cerianthus lloydi* Gosse, *Cerianthus membranaceus* Spallanzani et *Metridium senile* (L.): mise enevidence d'une digestion extracellulaire et extracorporelle. *J. Exp. Mar. Biol. Ecol.*, 18, 243-254.

Tiffon, Y. (1987) Ordre des cerianthaires (Ceriantharia Perrier, 1883). In P.-P. Grasse (ed.), *Traite de Zoologie. Anatomie, Systematique, Biologie. Tome III. Cnidaires Anthozoaires*, Masson, Paris, pp. 211-256.

Tiffon, Y. and Bouillon, J. (1975) Digestion extracellulaire dans la cavite gastrique de *Cerianthus lloydi* Gosse. Structure du gastroderme, localisation et proprietes des enzymes proteolytiques. *J. Exp. Mar. Biol. Ecol.*, 18, 255-269.

Tiffon, Y. and Daireaux, M. (1974) Phagocytose et pinocytose par l'ectoderme et l'en-doderme de *Cerianthus lloydi* Gosse. *J. Exp. Mar. Biol. Ecol.*, 16, 155-165.

Tiffon, Y. and Franc, S. (1982) Crystal-bearing vesicles and 3 b-hydroxysterols in non calcifying Anthozoa. *J. Submicrosc. Cytol.*, 14, 141-148.

Tiffon, Y. and Hugon, J. S. (1977) Localisation ultrastructurale de la phosphatase acide et de la phosphatase alcaline dans les cloisons septales steriles de l'anthozoaire *Pachycerianthus fimbriatus*. *Histochemistry*, 54, 289-297.

Tiffon, Y., Rasmont, R., Vos, L. de and Bouillon, J. (1973) Digestion in lower Metazoa. In J. T. Dingle (ed.), *Lysosomes in Biology and Pathology, Vol. 3,* North-Holland/American Elsevier, New York, pp. 49-68.

Townsend, C. R. and Hughes, R. N. (1981) Maximizing net energy returns from foraging. In C. R. Townsend and P. Calow (eds.), *Physiological Ecology. An Evolutionary Approach to Resource Use*, Sinauer Associates, Sunderland, Massachusetts, pp. 86-108.

Trench, R. K. (1971a) The physiology and biochemistry of zooxanthellae symbiotic with marine coelenterates I. The assimilation of photosynthetic products of zooxanthellae by two marine coelenterates. *Proc. R. Soc. Lond., B,* 177, 225-235.

Trench, R. K. (1971b) The physiology and biochemistry of zooxanthellae symbiotic with marine coelenterates II. Liberation of fixed 14C by zooxanthellae in vitro. *Proc. R. Soc. Lond.*, B, 177, 237-250.

Trench, R. K. (1971c) The physiology and biochemistry of zooxanthellae symbiotic with marine coelenterates III. The effect of homogenates of host tissues on the excretion of photosynthetic products in vitro by zooxanthellae from two marine coelenterates. *Proc. R. Soc. Lond.*, B, 177, 251-264.

Trench, R.K. 1974. Nutritional potentials in *Zoanthus sociatus* (Coelenterata, Anthozoa). *Helg. Wiss Meers. 26:174-216.*

Trench, R. K. (1979) The cell biology of plant-animal symbiosis. *Ann. Rev. Plant Physiol.,* 30, 485-531.

Trench, R. K. (1987) Dinoflagellates in non-parasitic symbioses. In F. J. R. Taylor (ed.), *The Biology of Dinoflagellates. Botanical Monographs*, No. 21, Blackwell Scientific Publications, Oxford, UK, pp. 530-570.

Trench, R. K. and Blank, R. J. (1987) *Symbiodinium microadriaticum* Freudenthal, *S. goreauii* sp. nov., *S. kawagutii* sp. nov. and *S. pilosum* sp. nov.: gymnodinioid dinoflagellate symbionts of marine invertebrates. *J. Phycol.*, 23, 469-481.

Turner, J. R. (1989) Host reproduction and algal symbiont acquisition in temperate Anthozoa. In R. B. Williams (ed.), *5th International Conference on Coelenterate Biology. Programme and Abstracts* (unpaginated supplement), University of Southampton, Southampton, UK.

Tytler, E. M. and Davies, P. S. (1984) Photosynthetic production and respiratory energy expenditure in the anemone *Anemonia sulcata* (Pennant). *J. Exp. Mar. Biol. Ecol.*, 81, 73-86.

Tytler, E. M. and Davies, P. S. (1986) The budget of photosynthetically derived energy in the *Anemonia sulcata* (Pennant) symbiosis. *J. Exp. Mar. Biol. Ecol.*, 99, 257-269.

Tytler, E. M. and Trench, R. K. (1986) Activities of enzymes in b-carboxylation reactions and of catalase in cell-free preparations from the symbiotic dinoflagellates *Symbiodinium* spp. from a coral, a clam, a zoanthid and two sea anemones. *Proc. R. Soc. Lond.,* B, 228, 483-492.

Tytler, E. M. and Trench, R. K. (1988) Catalase activity in cell-free preparations of some symbiotic and nonsymbiotic marine invertebrates. *Symbiosis,* 5, 247-254.

Tixier-Durivault, A. 1964. Stolonifera et Alcyonacea. *Galathea Reports* 7:43-58.
Uchida, T. (1936) Influence of the currents upon the distribution of races and frequency of asexual reproduction in the actinian, Diadumene luciae. *Zool. Mag., Tokyo,* 48, 895-906 (in Japanese, with English summary).

Vacelet, E. and B.A. Thomassin. 1991. Microbial utilization of coral mucus in long term in situ incubation over a coral reef. *Hydrobiologia 211:19-32.*

Valentine, J. W. (1976) Genetic strategies of adaptation. In F. J. Ayala (ed.),*Molecular Evolution,* Sinauer Associates, Sunderland, Massachusetts, pp. 78-94.

Van Alstyne, K.L. and V.J. Paul. 1992. Chemical and structural defenses in the sea fan *Gorgonia ventalina*: effects against generalist and specialist predators. *Coral Reefs 11:155-159.*

----------------------, Wylie, C.R., Paul, V.J. and K. Meyer. 1992. Antipredator defenses in tropical Pacific soft corals (Coelenterata: Alcyonacea). I. Sclerites as defenses against generalist carnivorous fishes. *Biol. Bull. 182:231-240.*

Van Marle, J. (1977) Contribution to the knowledge of the nervous system in the tentacles of some coelenterates. *Bijdr. Dierkunde,* 46, 220-260.

Van-Praet, M. (1976) Les activites phosphatasiques acides chez *Actinia equina* L. et *Cereus pedunculatus P. Bull. Soc. Zool. France,* 101, 367-376.

Van-Praet, M. (1977) Les cellules econcretions d'*Actinia equina* L. C. R. Acad. Sci. Paris, 285, 45-48.

Van-Praet, M. (1978) etude histochimique et ultrastructurale des zones digestives d'*Actinia equina* L. (Cnidaria, Actiniaria). *Cah. Biol. Mar.,* 19, 415-432

Van-Praet, M. (1980) Absorption des substances dissoutes dans le milieu, des particules et des produits de la digestion extracellulaire chez *Actinia equina* (Cnidaria, Actiniaria). *Reprod. Nutr. Devel.,* 20, 1393-1399.

Van-Praet, M. (1981) Comparaison des taux d'activite amylasique, trypsique et chymotrypsique, ainsi que des types cellulaires intervenant dans la digestion chez les Actinies littorales et abyssales. *Oceanis,* 7, 687-703.

Van-Praet, M. (1982a) Absorption et Digestion chez *Actinia equina* L., Nutrition des Actiniaires. These de Doctorat d'etat es Sciences Naturelles, Museum National d'Histoire Naturelle et Universite Pierre et Marie Curie, Paris, 218 pp.

Van-Praet, M. (1982b) Amylase and trypsin- and chymotrypsin-like proteases from *Actinia equina* L.; their role in the nutrition of this sea anemone. *Comp. Biochem. Physiol.,* 72A, 523-528.

Van-Praet, M. (1983a) Regime alimentaire des Actinies. *Bull. Soc. Zool.* France, 108, 403-407.

Van-Praet, M. (1983b) Fluctuations d'activites enzymatiques digestives chez les actinies abyssales: indices d'une nutrition particulaire. *Oceanol. Acta*, 1983, 197-200.

Van-Praet, M. (1985) Nutrition of sea anemones. *Adv. Mar. Biol.*, 22, 65-99.

Van-Praet, M. and Duchateau, G. (1984) Mise en evidence chez une Actinie abyssale (*Paracalliactis stephensoni*) d'un cycle saisonnier de reproduction. *C.R. Acad. Sci. Paris*, 299, 687-690.

Verseveldt, J. 1977. Australian octocorallia (Coelenterata). *Aust. J. Mar. Freshwater Res.* 28:171-240.

----------------. 1980. A revision of the genus *Sinularia* May (Octocorallia, Alcyonacea). *Zoologische Verhandelingen 179:1-128.*

Verseveldt, J. 1977. Octocorallia from various localities in the Pacific Ocean. *Zoologische Verhandelingen* 150: 1-42

Verseveldt, J. (1983) The Octocrallian Genera *Spongodes* Lesson, *Neospongodes* Kükenthal and *Stereonephthya* Kükenthal. *Beaufortia*, 33:1. 1-13.

Verwey, J. (1930) Coral reef studies. I. The symbiosis between damselfishes and sea anemones in Batavia Bay. *Treubia*, 12, 305-366.

Voogt, P. A., Ruit, J. M. van de and Rheenen, J. W. A. van (1974) On the biosynthesis and composition of sterols and sterolesters in some sea anemones (Anthozoa). *Comp. Biochem. Physiol.*, 48B, 47-57.

Wacasey, J. W. and Atkinson, E. G. (1987) Energy values of marine benthic invertebrates from the Canadian Arctic. *Mar. Ecol. Prog. Ser.*, 39, 243-250.

Wahl, M. (1984) The fluffy sea anemone *Metridium senile* in periodically oxygen depleted surroundings. *Mar. Biol.*, 81, 81-86.

Wahl, M. (1985) The recolonization potential of *Metridium senile* in an area previously depopulated by oxygen deficiency. *Oecologia*, 67, 255-259.

Walsh, G.E. and R.L. Bowers. 1971. A review of Hawaiian zoanthids with descriptions of three new species. *Zool. J. Linn. Soc. 50:161-180.*

Walsh, P. J. (1981a) Purification and characterization of two allozymic forms of octopine dehydrogenase from California populations of *Metridium senile*. The role of octopine dehydrogenase in the anaerobic metabolism of sea anemones. *J. Comp. Physiol.*, B, 143, 213-222.

Walsh, P. J. (1981b) Purification and characterization of glutamate dehydrogenases from three species of sea anemones: adaptation to temperature within and among species from different thermal environments. *Mar. Biol. Lett.*, 2, 289-299.

Walsh, P. J. and Somero, G. N. (1981) Temperature adaptation in sea anemones: physiological and biochemical variability in geographically separate populations of *Metridium senile*. *Mar. Biol.*, 62, 25-34.

Ward, J. A. (1965a) An investigation on the swimming reaction of the anemone *Stomphia coccinea*. II. Histological location of a reacting substance in the asteroid *Dermasterias imbricata*. *J. Exp. Zool.*, 158, 365-372.

Ward, J. A. (1965b) An investigation on the swimming reaction of the anemone *Stomphia coccinea*. I. Partial isolation of a reacting substance from the asteroid *Dermasterias imbricata*. *J. Exp. Zool.*, 158, 357-364.

Waters, V. L. (1973) Food-preference of the nudibranch *Aeolidia papillosa*, and the effect of the defenses of the prey on predation. *The Veliger*, 15, 174-192.

Watson, G. M. and Hessinger, D. A. (1987) Receptor-mediated endocytosis of a chemoreceptor involved in triggering the discharge of cnidae in a sea anemone tentacle. *Tissue & Cell*, 19, 747-755.

Watson, G. M. and Hessinger, D. A. (1988) Localization of a purported chemoreceptor involved in triggering cnida discharge in sea anemones. In D. A. Hessinger and H. M. Lenhoff (eds.), *The Biology of Nematocysts*, Academic Press, San Diego, California, pp. 255-274.

Watson, G. M. and Hessinger, D. A. (1989) Cnidocyte mechanoreceptors are tuned to the movements of swimming prey by chemoreceptors. *Science,* 243,1589-1591.

Watson, G. M. and Mariscal, R. N. (1983a) Comparative ultrastructure of catch tentacles and feeding tentacles in the sea anemone *Haliplanella*. *Tissue & Cell*, 15, 939-953.

Watson, G. M. and Mariscal, R. N. (1983b) The development of a sea anemone tentacle specialized for aggression: morphogenesis and regression of the catch tentacle of *Haliplanella luciae* (Cnidaria, Anthozoa). *Biol. Bull.*,164, 506-517.

Watson, G. M. and Mariscal, R. N. (1984a) Calcium cytochemistry of nematocyst development in catch tentacles of the sea anemone *Haliplanella luciae* (Cnidaria: Anthozoa) and the molecular basis for tube inversion into the capsule. *J. Ultrastruct. Res.*, 86, 202-214.

Watson, G. M. and Mariscal, R. N. (1984b) Ultrastructure and sulphur cytochemistry of nematocyst development in catch tentacles of the sea anemone *Haliplanella luciae* (Cnidaria: Anthozoa). *J. Ultrastruct. Res.*, 87, 159-171.

Weber, R. E. (1980) Functions of invertebrate hemoglobins with special reference to adaptations to environmental hypoxia. *Amer. Zool.*, 20, 79-101.

Wedi, S. E. and Dunn, D. F. (1983) Gametogenesis and reproductive periodicity of the subtidal sea anemone *Urticina lofotensis* (Coelenterata: Actiniaria) in California. *Biol. Bull.*, 165, 458-472.

Weill, R. (1934) Contribution e l'etude des cnidaires et de leurs nematocystes. *Trav. Sta. Zool. Wimereux,* 10-11, 1-701.

Weinbauer, G., Nussbaumer, V. and Patzner, R. A. (1982) Studies on the relationship between *Inachus phalangium* Fabricius (Maiidae) and *Anemonia sulcata* Pennant in their natural environment. P.S.Z.N.I.: *Mar. Ecol.*, 3,143-150.

Weinberg, S. 1986. Mediterranean Octocorallia: description of *Clavularia carpediem* n. sp. and synonymy of *Clavularia crassa* and *C. ochracea* on ethoecological grounds. *Bijdragen tot de Dierkunde* 56(2): 232-246.

Weis, V. M. (1989) Induction of carbonic anhydrase activity in symbiotic cnidarians. In R. B. Williams (ed.), *5th International Conference on Coelenterate Biology*. Programme and Abstracts, University of Southampton, Southampton, UK, p. 97.

Weis, V. M., Smith, G. J. and Muscatine, L. (1989) A 'CO$_2$ supply' mechanism in zoox-anthellate cnidarians: role of carbonic anhydrase. *Mar. Biol.*, 100, 195-202.

Welch, H. E. (1968) Relationships between assimilation efficiencies and growth efficiencies for aquatic consumers. *Ecology*, 49, 755-759.

Wells, J. W. (1956) Scleractinia. In R. C. Moore (ed.), *Treatise on Invertebrate Paleontology. Part F, Coelenterata*, University of Kansas, Lawrence, pp. F328-F444.

Werner, B. (1973) New investigations on systematics and evolution of the class Scyphozoa and the phylum Cnidaria. *Publ. Seto Mar. Biol. Lab.*, 20, 35-61.

West, J. M., Harvell, C. D., and A.-M. Walls (1993) Morphological plasticity in a gorgonian coral (*Briareum asbestinum*) over a depth cline. *Mar. Ecol. Prog. Ser.* 94, 61-69.

Westfall, J. A. (1970) Synapses in a sea anemone, *Metridium* (Anthozoa). *Proc. 7th Int. Congr. Electron Microscopy; Soc. Fr. Microsc. Elect.*, 3, 717-718.

Widersten, B. (1968) On the morphology and development in some cnidarian larvae. *Zool. Bidr. Uppsala*, 37, 139-179 + 3 plates.

Widdows, J. and Hawkins, A. J. S. (1989) Partitioning of rate of heat dissipation by *Mytilus edulis* into maintenance, feeding, and growth components. *Physiol. Zool.*, 62, 764-784.

Wilkens, P. 1990. *Invertebrates: Stone and False Corals, Colonial Anemones.* Engelbert Pfriem Verlag, Wuppertal, germany, 134 pp.

Wilkerson, F. P., Muller-Parker, G. and Muscatine, L. (1983) Temporal patterns of cell division in natural populations of endosymbiotic algae. *Limnol. Oceanogr.*, 28, 1009-1014.

Wilkerson, F. P. and Muscatine, L. (1984) Uptake and assimilation of dissolved inorganic nitrogen by a symbiotic sea anemone. *Proc. R. Soc. Lond.*, B, 221, 71-86.

Wilkerson, F. P. and Trench, R. K. (1985) Nitrate assimilation by zooxanthellae maintained in laboratory culture. *Mar. Chem.*, 16, 385-393.

Williams, G. C. (1975) *Sex and Evolution,* Princeton University Press, Princeton, New Jersey, 200 pp.

Williams, G.C. 1992. The Alcyonacea of southern Africa. Stoloniferous octocorals and soft corals (Coelenterata, Anthozoa). *Annals of the South African Museum* 100(3): 249-358.

Williams, Gary C. (1993) *Coral Reef Octocorals. An Illustrated Guide to the Soft Corals, Sea Fans and Sea Pens inhabiting the Coral Reefs of Northern Natal.* Durban Natural Science Museum, Durban, South Africa, 64 Pp.

Williams, R. B. (1968) Control of the discharge of cnidae in *Diadumene luciae* (Verrill). *Nature*, 219, 959.

Williams, R. B. (1972a) Chemical control of feeding behaviour in the sea anemone *Diadumene luciae* (Verrill). *Comp. Biochem. Physiol.*, 41A, 361-371.

Williams, R. B. (1972b) Notes on the history and invertebrate fauna of a poikilohaline lagoon in Norfolk. *J. Mar. Biol. Ass. UK*, 52, 945-963.

Williams, R. B. (1973) Are there physiological races of the sea anemone *Diadumene luciae*? *Mar. Biol.*, 21, 327-330.

Williams, R. B. (1975) Catch-tentacles in sea anemones: occurrence in *Haliplanella luciae* (Verrill) and a review of current knowledge. *J. Nat. Hist.*, 9, 241-248.

Wilson, D. M. (1959) Long-term facilitation in a swimming sea anemone. *J. Exp. Biol.*, 36, 526-532.

Windt-Preuss, H. (1959) Beobachtungen u ber die Nahrungsaufnahme und das Verhalten der Seenelke *Metridium senile* L. *Kieler Meeresforsch.*, 15, 84-88.

Winsor, L. 1990. Marine Turbellaria (Acoela) from North Queensland. *Memoirs of the Queensland Museum* 28(2):785-800.

Woolmington, A. D. and Davenport, J. (1983) pH and PO_2 levels beneath marine macro-fouling organisms. *J. Exp. Mar. Biol. Ecol.*, 66, 113-124.

Wylie, C.R. and V.J. Paul. 1989. Chemical defenses on three species of *Sinularia* (Coelenterata: Alcyonacea): effects against generalist predators and the butterflyfish *Chaetodon unimaculatus* Bloch. *J. Exp. Mar. Biol. Ecol. 129:141-160.*

Yamazato, K., Yoshimoto, F. and N. Yoshihara. 1973. Reproductive cycle in a zoanthid *Palythoa tuberculosa* Esper. (*Proc. 2nd Int. Symp. on Cnidaria) Publ. Seto Mar. Biol. Lab 20:275-283.*

----------------, Sato, M. and H. Yamashiro. 1981. Reproductive biology of an alcyonacean coral, *Lobophytum crassum* Marenzeller. *Proc. 4th Int. Coral Reef Symp., Manila, vol2.*

Yentsch, C. S. and Pierce, D. C. (1955) 'Swimming' anemone from Puget Sound. *Science,* 122, 1231-1233.

Yonge, C. M. (1930) *A Year on the Great Barrier Reef,* Putnam, London, 246 pp.

Yoshioka, P.M. and B. Buchanan-Yoshioka. 1991. A comparison of the survivorship and growth of shallow-water gorgonian species of Puerto Rico (West Indies). *Mar. Ecol. Progr. Ser. 69:253-260.*

Zahl, P. A. and McLaughlin, J. J. A. (1959) Studies in marine biology. IV. On the role of algal cells in the tissues of marine invertebrates. *J. Protozool.*, 6, 344-352.

Zamer, W. E. (1986) Physiological energetics of the intertidal sea anemone *Anthopleura elegantissima* I. Prey capture, absorption efficiency and growth. *Mar. Biol.*, 92, 299-314.

Zamer, W. E. and Hoffmann, R. J. (1989) Allozymes of glucose-6-phosphate isomerase differentially modulate pentose-shunt metabolism in the sea anemone *Metridium senile. Proc. Nat. Acad. Sci. USA*, 86, 2737-2741.

Zamer, W. E. and Mangum, C. P. (1979) Irreversible nongenetic temperature adaptation of oxygen uptake in clones of the sea anemone *Haliplanella luciae* (Verrill). *Biol. Bull.*, 157, 536-547.

Zamer, W. E., Robbins, R. E. and Shick, J. M. (1987) b-glucuronidase activity and detritus utilization in the sea anemones *Metridium senile* and *Anthopleura elegantissima. Comp. Biochem. Physiol.*, 87B, 303-308.

Zamer, W. E. and Shick, J. M. (1987) Physiological energetics of the intertidal sea anemone *Anthopleura elegantissima* II. Energy balance. *Mar. Biol.*, 93, 481-491.

Zamer, W. E. and Shick, J. M. (1989) Physiological energetics of the intertidal sea anemone *Anthopleura elegantissima* III. Biochemical composition of body tissues, substrate-specific absorption, and carbon and nitrogen budgets. *Oecologia*, 79, 117-127.

Zamer, W. E., Shick, J. M. and Tapley, D. W. (1989) Protein measurement and energetic considerations: Comparisons of biochemical and stoichiometric methods using bovine serum albumin and protein isolated from sea anemones. *Limnol. Oceanogr.*, 34, 256-263.

Zammit, V. A. and Newsholme, E. A. (1976) The maximum activities of hexokinase, phosphorylase, phosphofructokinase, glycerol phosphate dehydrogenases, lactate dehydrogenase, octopine dehydrogenase, phosphoenolpyruvate carboxykinase, nucleoside diphosphatekinase, glutamate-oxaloacetate transaminase and arginine kinase in relation to carbohydrate utilization in muscles from marine invertebrates. *Biochem. J.*, 160, 447-462.

Zammit, V. A. and Newsholme, E. A. (1978) Properties of pyruvate kinase and phosphoenolpyruvate carboxykinase in relation to the direction and regulation of phosphoenolpyruvate metabolism in muscles of the frog and marine invertebrates. *Biochem. J.*, 174, 979-987.

Zamponi, M. O. (1981) Estructuras anatomicas adaptativas en anemonas (Coelenterata Actiniaria). *Neotropica*, 27, 165-169.

Zaslow, R.B. and Y. Benayahu. 1996. Longevity, competence and energetic content in planulae of the soft coral *Heteroxenia fuscescens. J. Exp. Mar. Biol. Ecol. 206:55-68.*

Zwaan, A. de (1977) Anaerobic energy metabolism in bivalve molluscs. *Oceanogr. Mar. Biol. Ann. Rev.*, 15, 103-187.

Zwaan, A. de (1983) Carbohydrate catabolism in bivalves. In P. W. Hochachka (ed.), *The Mollusca.* Vol. 1. Metabolic Biochemistry and Molecular Biomechanics, Academic Press, New York, pp. 137-175.

Zwaan, A. de and Putzer, V. (1985) Metabolic adaptations of intertidal invertebrates to environmental hypoxia (a comparison of environmental anoxia to exercise anoxia). In M. S. Laverack (ed.), *Physiological Adaptations of Marine Animals*, Cambridge University Press, Cambridge, UK, pp. 33-62.

Index